2nd Edition

Principles of Business Management

Principles of Business Management

2nd Edition

Edited by

JOHAN STRYDOM

Contributors

Marolee Beaumont Smith
Andreas de Beer
Maggie Holtzhausen
Jerome Kiley
Danie Nel
Cecile Nieuwenhuizen
Theuns Oosthuizen
Sharon Rudansky-Kloppers
Rigard Steenkamp

OXFORD

UNIVERSITY PRESS

SOUTHERN AFRICA

OXFORD
UNIVERSITY PRESS

SOUTHERN AFRICA

Oxford University Press Southern Africa (Pty) Ltd

Vasco Boulevard, Goodwood, Cape Town, Republic of South Africa
P O Box 12119, N1 City, 7463, Cape Town, Republic of South Africa

Oxford University Press Southern Africa (Pty) Ltd is a wholly-owned subsidiary of
Oxford University Press, Great Clarendon Street, Oxford OX2 6DP.

The Press, a department of the University of Oxford, furthers the University's objective of
excellence in research, scholarship, and education by publishing worldwide in

Oxford New York

Auckland Dar es Salaam Hong Kong Karachi
Kuala Lumpur Madrid Melbourne Mexico City Nairobi
New Delhi Shanghai Taipei Toronto

With offices in

Argentina Austria Brazil Chile Czech Republic France Greece
Guatemala Hungary Italy Japan Poland Portugal Singapore South Korea
Switzerland Turkey Ukraine Vietnam

Oxford is a registered trade mark of Oxford University Press
in the UK and in certain other countries

Published in South Africa
by Oxford University Press Southern Africa (Pty) Ltd, Cape Town

Principles of Business Management 2e

ISBN 978 0 19 599599 2

© Oxford University Press Southern Africa (Pty) Ltd 2011

The moral rights of the author have been asserted
Database right Oxford University Press Southern Africa (Pty) Ltd (maker)

First published 2008
Second edition published 2011
Fifth impression 2014

Publishing Manager: Alida Terblanche
Commissioning Editor: Astrid Meyer
Development Editor: Ilka Lane
Project Manager: Nicola van Rhyn
Editor: Patricia Myers Smith
Proofreader: Allison Lamb
Designer: Oswald Kurten
Cover design: Samantha Rowles and Oswald Kurten
Cover image: Great Stock
Indexer: Ethné Clarke

Set in Bembo Std 11 pt on 13.5 pt by Elbert Visser
Printed and bound by Castle Graphics South (Pty) Ltd.

Contents in brief

Table of contents

Preface

Business management is a dynamic field with various changes occurring at any given point in time. South Africa is seen as the gateway into southern Africa and, as such, forms the bridge between the rest of the world and southern Africa, and Africa in general. In South Africa we have seen dramatic changes that have influenced the business environment, and South African businesses have been quite adept at adapting to these changes. In keeping with the changes a team of authors from South African academic institutions decided to develop a new introductory textbook to describe these dynamic changes to this field of study.

In tertiary academic institutions various textbooks are used to teach first-year students. In most cases these textbooks are of American origin. However, in the last ten years a few South African textbooks have seen the light. Joining this line of South African textbooks, *Principles of Business Management* first edition was published in 2008. What makes this book unique is that it is aimed specifically at the first-level business management student and especially the University of Technology market.

The authors were pleasantly surprised at the uptake of the book in various markets in the South African tertiary environment. We are especially thankful for the positive criticism and recommendations that were made by various lecturers using this book. We incorporated most of these comments in this second edition of *Principles of Business Management*.

The book is divided into four parts. In the first part the general background to the field of business management is given. In the second part attention is given to the management tasks that cover the traditional fields of planning, organising, leading, motivating and controlling. In the third part of the book the functional areas are discussed, referring to operations management, logistics management, financial management, human-resources management and marketing management. The fourth part looks at entrepreneurship and the business plan.

Some of the outstanding features of this book are the following:
- Critical-thinking boxes to encourage independent thought regarding the issues under discussion. This nurtures critical evaluation and the questioning of academic content.
- Practical information boxes provide real-life examples of how the theory is applied in practice.
- Key terminology is explained throughout the textbook to unlock the world of business management, and to give students ownership of the special words that are used in this subject area.

- Case studies are provided to further embed the practical application of the theoretical discussion.
- Multiple-choice questions at the end of each chapter allow students to test their knowledge and understanding of the subject material.

Accompanying this book is excellent ancillary material, which includes PowerPoint® slides, an instructor's manual, case studies with suggested answers, a question bank and solutions to these questions. We thank Mr Theuns Oosthuizen for his hard work in this regard.

We trust that the book will be enjoyed and used by academics and business practitioners alike. Please feel free to send Prof. Johan Strydom (strydjw@unisa.ac.za) useful suggestions on how we can improve the book.

Sincerely,
The authors

PART ONE

Introduction to business management

This part explains the concept of business and the business environment.

The first chapter explains the philosophy of business, and elaborates on profit-seeking and non-profit organisations. It also touches on the corporate (group) social responsibility of the organisation.

The second chapter deals with the business environment in which the organisation operates. The business environment is dynamic, and South African businesses must be aware of how changes in the environment will influence the day-to-day operations of the business.

1

Business and its challenges

Johan Strydom

PURPOSE OF THIS CHAPTER

This chapter explains the basic concepts (ideas) on which a business is built, such as profit, the economic principle, and the factors of production. It also explains the basic economic systems in which businesses operate, and describes the importance of corporate social responsibility in the running of a business. This chapter provides a key to unlock the fascinating subject of business management at an introductory level.

LEARNING OUTCOMES

This chapter should enable you to:
- understand what the concept of business involves
- understand the concepts of profit-seeking and non–profit-seeking organisations
- show how business uses the factors of production in trying to make a profit
- distinguish between the different economic systems in which a business may operate
- describe the different stakeholders that influence South African businesses
- discuss the concept of corporate social responsibility
- explain the principles of the social contract under which South African businesses operate
- understand the model used to explain the layout of this book.

1.1 **Introduction**

Business management is a dynamic field of study that focuses on institutions that satisfy customers' needs.[1] But what is a business and why do people start businesses? The answers to these questions involve the concepts of profit, the economic principle, and the factors of production. It is also useful to look at the different economic systems in which a business could operate, and how these systems can influence the operations of that business.

One factor that is of the utmost importance for any organisation is the stakeholders with whom it interacts on a day-to-day basis. There is growing pressure on businesses to accommodate these stakeholders. This has resulted in the development of the concept of corporate social responsibility, and in the making of a social contract between businesses and South African society as a whole.

In the last section of this chapter there is a model that will make it easier to understand the logical flow of this book. This model consists of three broad sections, namely: the business environment in which a business operates; the task of the manager, and the different areas for which the manager is responsible.

1.2 **What is a business?**

The term **business** has many meanings, but the main one is an organisation that provides goods and services to its customers in the economic system in which they operate. **Goods** are all those things that we can feel and touch, such as fridges, clothing, shoes and cars. We say that these are tangible goods. **Services** are usually intangible; in

> ### CRITICAL THINKING
> Which of the following activities are a business?
> - The service provided by an auditor
> - South African Airways
> - The Spaza shop which is run by Ms Khumalo

other words, we cannot feel or touch them. Services include those provided by a doctor and a lawyer. For the purpose of this book, the term **products** includes both tangible goods and intangible services.

Most businesses deliver both goods and services to their customers – for instance the delivery of fast food to your doorstep. The Domino's pizza that is delivered is a tangible good, but the activity of delivering it to your home is a service. In this book we will concentrate more on the side of tangible goods, but will from time to time provide examples of the service industry in South Africa. (In this book the terms 'business', 'organisation', 'firm' and 'enterprise' are used to mean the same thing.)

1.2.1 Business and profits

One of the questions people ask is why would anyone want to operate or own a business? One of the answers is that people operate a business to make a profit. **Profit** is the amount of money that remains in the business after the business has paid all its costs. One could put it like this:

$$\text{profit} = \text{total revenue} - \text{total costs}$$

For instance – the business realised a R1 million profit for the year. The total revenue was R2 million and the total cost was R1 million.
(See also Chapter 15 where the concepts of profit, revenue and cost are further explained.)

A business produces a certain amount of revenue by selling its goods and services (for example, by selling and delivering pizzas). To produce this income, the business must spend money on equipment and on basic ingredients (such as flour and yeast), and must pay its employees. The money that is left after all these costs have been subtracted is the profit. Businesses must also pay tax on profits. Once this is done, the remaining profit can be distributed to the owners or can be kept within the business to re-invest and, hopefully, to expand the business. Businesses are found in both the public and private sectors.

There are also businesses that do not only look for profit, but try to get just enough income to cover costs. They are called Not-for-Profit Organisations (NPOs). Sports clubs, welfare organisations and religious organisations form part of this private sector, while political parties and labour unions are examples of public sector not-for-profit-seeking business. However, both types follow the same business principles. NPOs are established for a public purpose, and there are no financial benefits for the members except for reasonable compensation for expenses incurred.

South African business is waiting for the new Companies Act of 2008 to be introduced. The following new categories of companies will be registered when the Act is applied.

Categories of companies under the Companies Act 2008[2]

The Companies Act 2008 gives a new classification of companies which differs drastically from the old company act of 1973. The new classes of companies are as follows:

- non-profit companies (NPCs) were registered as section 21 companies under the old 1973 companies act. Under the new Companies Act of 2008 they can register as non-profit companies. The Companies Act 2008 has a special schedule devoted to non-profit companies, and it regulates such companies more tightly than the 1973 companies act regulated section 21 companies
- profit companies (PCs) are companies whose aim is to make money for their shareholders, and they are divided into the following types of profit companies:
  - » a state-owned company (SOC);
  - » a private company;
  - » personal liability companies which are the same as section 53(b) companies of the 1973 companies act. Most of the professions such as doctors, accountants and attorneys, currently use section 53(b) companies, where the directors of the company are personally liable for the company's debts; private companies, and
  - » public companies; (this is a residual category which will cover any company other than the above).

1.3 **The economic principle**

South African consumers have a varied and unlimited need for goods and services. There are, however, a finite (definite, complete) number of resources available to satisfy these needs. Most of us would like to live in a millionaire's mansion, drive a fleet of luxury cars, have a vacation home in Plettenberg Bay, go on overseas trips on a regular basis, and wear the latest designer clothing – but few of us have enough money to do this. Instead, we try to use our limited funds to get the greatest satisfaction possible. The whole matter of obtaining the greatest possible benefit with the limited resources available is the **economic principle**. Businesses also follow the economic principle. They must ensure that the profits made by the organisation must at least cover the cost of capital and leave enough profit for the business. This can, for instance, be reached if the business has a unique (the only one) product, or else by careful spending.

I.4 The factors of production

There are four basic resources available that can be used by a business to manufacture (make) and deliver goods and services. These four basic resources are known as the **factors of production** and consist of:

- natural resources
- human resources (labour)
- capital
- entrepreneurship.

Some people also consider information as a separate factor of production.

I.4.I Natural resources

Natural resources are things in nature that are regarded as valuable in their untouched form, such as a piece of land that can be used for farming, or a forest, or mineral deposits. For the farmer, land is essential to produce crops such as grain and maize. In other instances mineral deposits such as gold, coal or crude oil are factors of production that can be used in the manufacturing process.

Some of these resources can be sustained (kept going) but in most cases we are working with resources that are not sustainable. For example, we are aware that there is a finite amount of crude oil available, and the price of crude oil has increased dramatically over the past decades. Another example of a natural resource under threat is water.

Water on tap – but it could be running dry[3]

Water is seen by most people as a useful thing that appears when you open a tap. The problem is that South Africa is in fact classified as a 'semi-arid country' with a limited supply of water. With a growing population and finite water resources, there has been growing concern about the long-term supply of potable (drinkable) water for South Africans. The supply of potable water is a concern not only for South Africa. The World Health Organisation has reported that in Africa about 2.9 million people die annually of HIV/Aids. Comparing this with the water problem, in 2002 an estimated 3.4 million people died from using unsafe water and from sanitary problems related to a lack of water.

There is already speculation that South Africa may run out of water for its population by 2025. The water problem is made worse by widespread pollution by industries and mines. The acid water that is accumulating under Johannesburg in the old mining shafts is threatening the groundwater supply, leaving the authorities with about 18 months to sort out this problem. Currently only 8% of South African municipalities meet the Blue Drop safety standards. Another concerning factor is that, of the 449 municipal waste-water-treatment works assessed in a recent survey, 'skills shortages' resulted in many not being operated correctly, and water quality no longer met standards. Only 7.9% of works achieved 'green drop certification' (which is a category below the best, namely Blue Drop). It has further been reported that the quality of South African river water has dropped by 20% in the past five years.

1.4.2 Human resources

Human resources (traditionally called 'labour') are the employees who perform specific activities for an organisation. Human resources are needed to produce agricultural products such as wheat and maize, to manufacture industrial products such as cars, or to deliver medical services such as open-heart surgery.

While human resources are seen as one of the untapped sources of the South African economy, unemployment remains very high. Unemployment is seen as one of the most pressing socio-economic problems in this country, and in order to reduce the number of unemployed people, the economy must grow at 7% per year. If South African workers had higher levels of skills, this would help in achieving this growth figure.

The South African unemployment rate – reason for concern

The total South African labour force can be defined as the number of people currently employed, plus the number unemployed but actively seeking work. The non-labour force includes those who are not looking for work – this category includes the people who are discouraged, pensioners, mothers with small children, those who are institutionalised (this category includes people in jail) and those serving in the Defence Force. In the second quarter of 2010, the South African unemployment rate was reported as 25.3%, which is better than the all-time high unemployment rate of 31.2% reported in March 2003. The lowest unemployment rate was recorded in September 2003. Although the rate has stabilised and South Africa is slowly emerging from a world recession, it still raises concern that one in four South Africans is unemployed. This high unemployment rate is seen as one of the reasons for South Africa's unacceptably high crime rate and periodic flare-ups of social unrest.

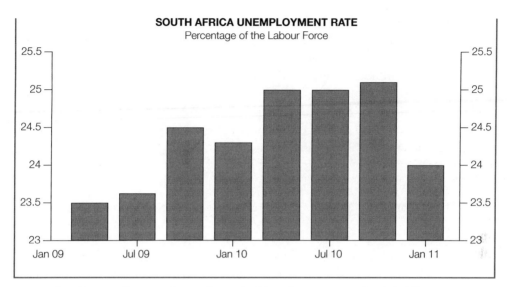

SOUTH AFRICA UNEMPLOYMENT RATE
Percentage of the Labour Force

SOURCE: http://www.tradingeconomics.com/Economics/Unemployment-rate.aspx?symbol=ZAR

1.4.3 Capital

Capital is the money or the assets (such as equipment and buildings) used to deliver something of value to customers. The capital that is provided by the owners, banks or shareholders of a business, is invested in the business. In most cases the capital is used to build the factories and buy the machinery needed to manufacture a product. In the service industry, capital could be needed to buy a franchise from an owner, so as to deliver a service.

The franchising route is seen as one of the best ways to ensure empowerment of the previously disadvantaged communities. The number of black–economic–empowerment (BEE) franchises has been growing, but is hampered by the potential franchisees' lack of capital and the problems in getting new sources of capital.

Is there a lack of capital in South Africa?[4]

One of the most mentioned problems for any entrepreneur has always been the difficulty of getting capital. It is not true that there is less capital available in South Africa than in the rest of the world. Money is available, but there are problems that must be sorted out from both the entrepreneur and the supplier regarding access to capital. The suppliers of capital (mostly the private banks) must become more transparent in what they expect and want from the possible borrower, and their criteria (standards of judgement) must also be known. Banks still use a broad one-size-fits-all communication approach, and need to focus their communication message at specific target groups.

Borrowers also need to adapt and make sure that they know what the funding institution requires in the form of information, and then provide it. There is also a 'culture of entitlement' (a general feeling among people that they have a right to be given things) which must change. Budding (starting) entrepreneurs must realise that their need for funding is not enough reason for the banks to give it to them.

1.4.4 Entrepreneurship

An entrepreneur is a person who takes the risk of starting and operating a business. **Entrepreneurship** is the process in which natural resources, human resources and capital are put together so as to manufacture a good, or offer a service, in order to make a profit.

SMEs and entrepreneurship

In South Africa, small and medium enterprises (SMEs) are one of the ways in which budding entrepreneurs can fulfil their dreams to be independent and to create wealth. There is no exact figure available on how many SMEs there are in South Africa. Estimates range from one to three million, with about half a million being formally (correctly, officially) registered.

Most of the informal SMEs are owned and operated by black South Africans. These black informal-businesspeople are often called survivalists, but are not necessarily entrepreneurs, as most of them would prefer to have a secure job in the formal sector. Entrepreneurs are those who choose to run enterprises despite personal risks, because of the larger potential profits.

One of the best South African examples of an entrepreneur is Mark Shuttleworth. In 1995 Shuttleworth was a final-year Business Science student at the University of Cape Town. He started Thawte, which is an Internet security company that helps facilitate safe payment for electronic commercial transactions. Shuttleworth sold Thawte in 1999 to Veri Sign, and then founded HBD Venture Capital and the Shuttleworth foundation.[5]

CRITICAL THINKING

Why is entrepreneurship so important for a developing country such as South Africa? Can we all be entrepreneurs?

Are South Africans becoming a nation of entrepreneurs?[6]

The FinScope SA's Small Business Survey for 2010 found that one in six adults in South Africa is a small business owner. Two-thirds of those entrepreneurs do not employ anyone else, categorising them in most cases as survivalists. Females are more likely to be involved with small businesses but are mostly involved in selling products. Males are more likely to be selling services and more likely to employ other people as workers. The study also found that there was a major gap in the market for banking services aimed at the small business owners.

1.5 The economic systems in which businesses operate

The business world is divided into four basic economic systems, namely:
- the free-market economy
- socialism
- the command economy
- the mixed economy.

FIGURE 1.1 The four economic systems

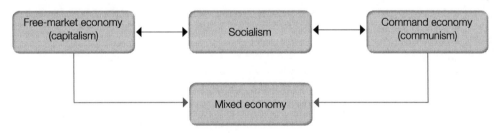

These four economic systems are depicted in Figure 1.1. On the left side we have the **free-market economy**, which is better known as 'capitalism'. The basic theory of capitalism is that each individual in society is free to choose his or her own economic activity. There is usually very little government interference and, because private individuals own most of the society's resources, they can freely use those resources in any way they wish. Every citizen of the country is free to work where they like, providing whatever service they like, or manufacturing whatever they want to.

On the other side of the picture we have the **command economy,** which is better known as 'communism'. This system uses the theory that the government owns almost all of the country's resources and that government officials can decide what goods and services should be delivered, who should be employed, where, what each person should earn, and so on.

Between these two systems we find the system of **socialism.** The theory of socialism is that individuals may own private property and choose their own form of economic activity, but the government also owns many of the country's resources, and plays a far greater role in the economy than in capitalism. With socialism, many of the large corporations (combined businesses) are owned by government and are therefore managed by government employees.

There are no clear boundaries in most countries regarding the economic system that is being followed. We find traces of socialism in the United States of America, which is regarded as the purest example of a capitalist economic system, and we find elements of capitalism in Cuba, which is one of the last examples of communism. When an economy is a mix of private enterprise, government ownership of resources, and government planning of the economy, then we call this economy a **mixed economy**.

> ### CRITICAL THINKING
> How would you classify the South African economy? Is it a mixed economy or a free-market economy?

The kind of economy in which a business functions influences the social contract that a business will have with its stakeholders.

1.6 **South African businesses and the changing social contract**

South African businesses and their managers have a social contract (understanding) with the society in which they operate. The question arises: exactly who is part of that social contract with the organisation? The assumption is that it is all the role-players in the business environment who are influenced by what the organisation does. These people or institutions in the business environment are called stakeholders, meaning that they have a stake in the performance of the organisation. We first distinguish between primary and secondary stakeholders. The **primary stakeholders** are the customers, the employees, the suppliers and the shareholders of the organisation. As we can see, these are the stakeholders nearest to the organisation. When the primary stakeholders get angry with the business, this could create a threat for the organisation – for instance, the customers can stop buying from the organisation. **Secondary stakeholders** such as the government and the broader community at large, must also be considered by the organisation. They can also exert a radical influence on the long-term existence of the organisation.

An organisation that is socially responsible will consider all the effects of the organisation's actions and the effect on all stakeholder groups. Today we find various special interest groups that can be called stakeholders of an organisation in a country such as South Africa. One example of a special-interest group is the environmentalists and their concern for the protection of the environment. Issues such as global warming, reducing greenhouse gas emissions, and preserving water resources, are at the forefront of the discussions in management meetings of corporations worldwide.

The social contract between the organisation and its stakeholders has changed over the years. There has always been a contract between top management of big businesses and the South African government, which at times is hostile and at other times co-operative. There is also a contract with employees, consumers, and shareholders. Nowadays there is an even broader set of **stakeholders** that management must consider, such as the communities in which businesses operate, the media and the non-governmental organisations (NGOs). (See Figure 1.2 for a picture of some of the stakeholders that a business must consider.)

As can be seen from Figure 1.2, there are three broad stakeholder groups that management must be aware of. **Business-related stakeholders** are the owners, investors, bankers, and the personnel of the organisation. **Opinion-related stakeholders** are

FIGURE 1.2 Stakeholders of South African businesses

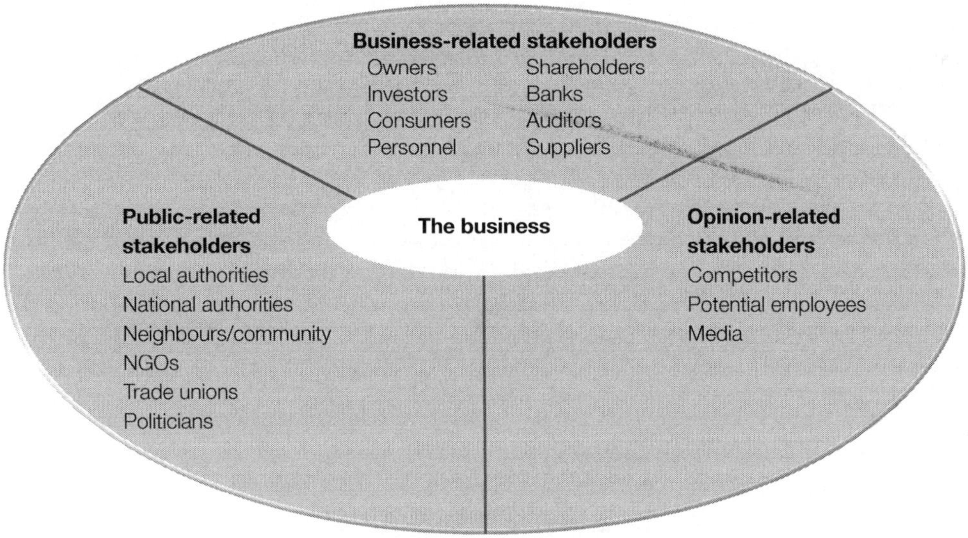

SOURCE: Adapted from Noren, G., Bendrot, I., Laurent, B., Nyberg, C., Stršmdahl, I. and Thorsenherd, M.L. 2004. *The role of business in society.* Confederations of Swedish Enterprise. p.8.

the media, potential employees, customers, and suppliers. **Public-related stakeholders** are the politicians, local and national authorities, and the NGOs. All these stakeholders have expectations regarding businesses, and these expectations will now be discussed in more detail.[7]

1.6.1 The expectations of business-related stakeholders

Each kind of business-related stakeholder will have certain expectations of a South African business:

- **Owners, shareholders and investors** expect the business to produce a profit so that they earn a return on the capital that they invested in the business.
- **Banks** expect the business to pay its interest on loans and overdrafts, to reduce the size of the loans over time, and to continue doing business with the bank.
- **Insurance companies** expect the business to be responsible in managing business risks, and they will calculate the insurance premiums accordingly.
- **Consumers** expect the business to follow acceptable commercial, marketing, and advertising principles, and to ensure that the goods and services supplied are of good quality. They also expect the right product delivered at the right time and at the right price. Increasingly, consumers are demanding that a business respects human rights. For example, they often stop buying products from businesses that manufacture articles under poor working conditions, such as the sports clothing and shoe manufacturer Nike did in the past.

Poor working conditions in Nike factories and what Nike is doing about it[8]

Nike has for many years been the *target* of labour-rights organisations who reported on the poor working conditions in Asian contract manufacturing plants, where most of the Nike products are manufactured. At the start of the labour-rights complaints which forms part of the broader stakeholders group, Nike tried to ignore these protests, claiming that they were providing new jobs in developing countries, albeit at a lower wage level so that these countries could prosper. The continued pressure on Nike paid off and today they are trying to monitor working and living conditions of workers at contract manufacturing plants in countries such as Malaysia and Vietnam. In Honduras, for instance, Nike is supplying training and vocational programmes to workers of two contract manufacturing factories that went insolvent.

Auditors expect, and ensure, that businesses obey legislation regarding accounting and other financial standards.

- **The personnel** of a business expects that business will comply with labour legislation regarding issues such as gender and race equity and non-discrimination. They also expect the business to provide an environment conducive to work.
- **Suppliers** expect to have consistent relationships with the business, and to be paid on time.

1.6.2 The expectations of opinion-related stakeholders

Each kind of opinion-related stakeholder will have certain expectations of a South African business:

- **Competitors** expect to be able to compete on equal business terms, with no threat of bribery and cartels (groups designed to limit competition or fix prices).
- **Potential employees** expect to be able to read the business's human-resources policy and employment conditions.
- **The media** expect that the business will give open, 'transparent' information on products and developments inside the business.

1.6.3 The expectations of public-related stakeholders

Each kind of public-related stakeholder will have certain expectations of a South African business:

- **The national authorities** expect the business to obey the laws of the country and pay its taxes on time. The national authorities further expect businesses to contribute to sustainable development in the country.
- **Local authorities** (such as municipalities and the metros) expect business to contribute to the social progress of society.
- **Neighbours** and the business's close **community** expect the business to comply with all the regulations about noise and pollution, and not to make trouble in its business undertakings.
- **NGOs** (non-government organisations) expect openness and progressive thinking from business leaders. These NGOs mostly focus on single issues such as human rights, protecting the environment, or employee safety.
- **Trade unions** expect a business to comply with labour laws and create a good working environment for the employees or members of the union.
- **Politicians** expect a business to fit their understanding of how organisations should be run, and be a responsible citizen.

1.6.4 Corporate social responsibility

South African businesses are always in contact with their stakeholders. In the past this contact mostly took place in the local environment of the businesses, but it has now expanded to include interaction across the nation, across many nations, and across the globe. This continuous social interaction started out as an idea called 'corporate sustainability' more than 30 years ago, and was then described as 'ecological and environmentally friendly business practices'. **Sustainability** meant the following when it was first used:

- Not only making the business look good in the eyes of the public, but having a clear understanding of the effect that the business processes and products had on the physical environment and finding ways that businesses could improve the physical environment.
- Sustainable practices could be used by employees of the business and were understandable to customers.
- Sustainability was measurable, so that progress could be reported.
- Sustainable policies were based on reality, not on spur-of-the-moment ideas. [9]

From corporate sustainability as described above has developed 'Corporate Social Responsibility', which is a wider concept that includes ethics, diversity, healthy communities, and long-term corporate governance. **Corporate social responsibility (CSR)** is the concept that organisations, especially corporations, have an obligation to consider the interests of customers, employees, shareholders, communities, and ecological (connections between organisms and their environment) environments, in all aspects of their operations. [10] CSR means different things in different countries. In countries such as South Africa, Turkey and South Korea, CSR is seen as the responsibility of large businesses to give back to the community. In countries such as the USA, Brazil and Chile, CSR is seen as the duty to treat employees fairly. In countries such as China, India and Russia, CSR is seen mainly as the delivery of safe, good-quality products.

> **CRITICAL THINKING**
> Why are South African businesses so worried about environmental pollution? Is there a link between pollution and business profits?

In South Africa the King I, King II and King III Reports have provided guidelines for responsible corporate management. Some of these guidelines are connected to sustainable environmental development. The sustainability commitments of Pick n Pay regarding climate change, as stated in its financial year report, illustrate this point.

The reaction of Pick n Pay to climate change[11]

Most of Pick n Pay's carbon emissions are generated through electricity usage from the national electricity grid. Pick n Pay believes in proactive energy management by means of measurement of their carbon footprint. They are also committed to continue to extend the measurement and accuracy of their carbon footprint calculation. They are promising to keep on disclosing their carbon usage performance in their annual financial year reports. The following table from the 2009/2010 Annual Report of Pick n Pay reflects their carbon footprint:

Source of operational carbon emissions	Carbon equivalent metric tonnes used 2009/2010	Carbon equivalent metric tonnes used 2008/2009
Energy usage at stores, distribution centres and offices	586 268 26	584 530
Diesel usage from commercial fleet, company cars and generators	28 275	24 582
Petrol usage from commercial fleet and company vehicles	7 620	7 487
Business air travel	851	914

In most of the categories Pick n Pay's carbon footprint increased. It will be interesting to see how they are going to reduce their carbon footprint in South Africa in future.

1.6.5 The current social contract of a South African business

Society's understanding of a business's responsibilities can be divided into three aspects,[12] namely:

- the **formal contract**, which refers to society's unspoken expectations from business, such as keeping global laws and environmental standards, and following the country's industry codes and norms. (A business must fulfil these expectations at all times.)
- the **semi-formal contract**, which refers to new spoken expectations that some people have about the responsibilities of a business, and which may affect formal contracts in the future. (For example, some people have criticised the products sold by global fast-food businesses such as McDonald's and Kentucky Fried Chicken, saying they lead to poor health.)

- **frontier (future) expectations**, which refer to issues that will have an impact on business in the future, such as the health effects of obesity (being overweight). (As some of these expectations change, issues may shift towards a semi-formal or formal contract. Some of the frontier issues that are shaping the social contract between businesses and their stakeholders are listed in Table 1.1.)

TABLE 1.1 Shifting expectations in the social contract of businesses[13]

Trends	Implications for the social contract of businesses
Rising inequality between countries and continents	An uneven distribution of wealth and power puts pressure on international businesses such as pharmaceutical companies to provide products to poorer countries at discounted prices (for example, HIV/Aids medicines to African countries).
Changes in population patterns	Major shifts are occurring in the population figures of many countries (for example, there is a smaller percentage of prime-of-life adults in countries suffering from the HIV/Aids pandemic).
Changes in availability of resources	As certain natural resources (for example, oil) become less, there is increasing pressure on businesses to manufacture cars that consume less fuel and are more environmentally friendly.
Changes in climate	Changing climates are resulting in pressure to reform manufacturing practices and reduce harmful emissions into the atmosphere.
Blurring boundaries between private responsibilities and laws	Responsibility regarding issues such as obesity, medical provisions and pensions is shifting away from individuals onto companies.

The social contract between the South African long-term life-insurance industry and its stakeholders

The South African life-insurance industry has been criticised for its policies regarding the surrender value of retirement annuities (RAs). This has forced this industry to rethink its policy according to implicit expectations from government and society in general regarding this issue. This has led to a statement of intent (SOI) on 1 December 2006, limiting the reduction in the final value of an RA when policy holders make contractual changes to their RAs.

The SOI[14] set minimum standards for surrenders and early terminations across a range of life savings products, including retirement annuities. Future premium cessation (stopping payments) would require the industry to credit the affected policy as follows:

- 'Each RA fund member policy with the value of at least 70% of the investment account of the policy at the date immediately preceding the premium cessation.'

The SOI called on life companies to view the above as the minimum standard to apply to early termination values. It also set out appropriate compensation for early termination and surrenders before the SOI effective date. These were seen as minimum standards binding on all members of the long-term insurance industry over time.

1.7 **The parts of this book**

This book is organised into four parts.

Part 1 is made up of this introductory chapter and a chapter on the business environment. Every business must scan its environment all the time, and use this information when managing its activities. (See Chapter 2.)

Part 2 covers the tasks of management, starting with an introductory chapter. (See Chapter 3.) The management process is then broken down into planning, organising, leading, motivating, and controlling.

- **Planning** is the process of determining objectives and finding methods to reach these objectives. (See Chapter 4.)
- **Organising** is the process of creating a structure for the business that will help the employees to attain the set objectives of the business. It decides what jobs need to be done, who will do them, and how they will be managed and co-ordinated. (See Chapter 5.)
- **Leading** is the process of influencing employees to reach the business objectives. (See Chapter 6.)
- **Motivating** employees to perform well is one of the manager's tasks. (See Chapter 7.)
- **Controlling** is the task of checking whether the set objectives were achieved, and if they were not, finding out why not. Control is therefore the start of a new planning process. (See Chapter 8.)

Part 3 starts by discussing the functional areas to be found in any business:
- **Operations management** deals with the activities that transform resources into goods or services while fulfilling the objectives of the business. (See Chapter 9.)
- **Logistics management** is the planning, implementation, and control of the flow of goods and services, from the point of production to the point of consumption. (See Chapter 10.)
- **Financial management** is the planning, processing, and management of the business's funds to accomplish the set objectives of the business. (See Chapter 11.)
- **Human–resources management** deals with the function of attracting, developing and retaining enough capable employees to attain the objectives of the business. (See Chapter 12.)
- **Marketing management** includes identifying a target market, as well as the process of developing, pricing, promoting and distributing products to this target market. (See Chapter 13.)

Part 4 discusses the unique aspects that make a person an entrepreneur (see Chapter 14), as well as business plans (see Chapter 15).

The above discussion is represented by Figure 1.3.

FIGURE 1.3 The topics covered in the chapters that follow

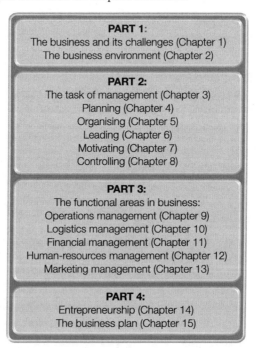

PART 1:
The business and its challenges (Chapter 1)
The business environment (Chapter 2)

PART 2:
The task of management (Chapter 3)
Planning (Chapter 4)
Organising (Chapter 5)
Leading (Chapter 6)
Motivating (Chapter 7)
Controlling (Chapter 8)

PART 3:
The functional areas in business:
Operations management (Chapter 9)
Logistics management (Chapter 10)
Financial management (Chapter 11)
Human-resources management (Chapter 12)
Marketing management (Chapter 13)

PART 4:
Entrepreneurship (Chapter 14)
The business plan (Chapter 15)

CASE STUDY: Shoprite 2010 annual report – how the Shoprite group is interacting with its stakeholders[15]

The following are extracts taken from the 2010 Shoprite Annual Report. Shoprite has a clearly defined programme in respect of the codes of the Broad-based Black Economic Empowerment Act (Act 53 of 2003). The programme is discussed below in terms of those codes.

Preferential procurement

Ongoing updating of the procurement database which has grown by 10% over the reporting period based on the value of goods bought from BEE-compliant businesses. This was done by assisting black suppliers to establish and develop their businesses. It was also done by encouraging existing suppliers to improve their BEE status.

Enterprise development

Two forms of enterprise development were used by Shoprite, namely the Greenfields project and the Nyama Nyama Emnandi project.

Greenfields project

This project aims to enable emerging BEE suppliers to compete on an equivalent playing field with established suppliers. Small BEE suppliers who are on par with established suppliers are assisted by the structuring of deliveries and payments to Shoprite. Freshmark, Shoprite's fruit and vegetable procuring arm, supports 358 small farmers in the countries in which it does business, to produce fruit and vegetables that fulfil the required quality standards.

Nyama Nyama Emnandi

This project assists emerging farmers in South Africa to be sustainable. Shoprite works closely with the Department of Agriculture, the various provincial governments, and local government structures. Shoprite's aim is to provide the BEE farmers who have achieved the required quality standards, with a consistent demand for products from its Shoprite and Checkers chains. A consistent supply of quality meat is being distributed to the markets of the Western Cape and Gauteng. The project is being broadened to include the Eastern Cape and the Karoo areas of South Africa.

Shoprite's programme on sustainability

The Shoprite group has the following policies in place to improve sustainability:

Property development

The Shoprite group respects the physical environment in which it operates. When Shoprite rents space in a shopping centre, it insists that such a centre be run in an environmentally sensitive manner. When it develops its own shopping facilities, it tries not to infringe on the physical surroundings. Shoprite will not buy or develop an environmentally sensitive site such as a wetlands area, and it will not undertake a development that is harmful to the bio-physical or built surroundings.

Packaging and waste management

Most packaging material, for instance that used for fruit and vegetables, is manufactured from oil derivatives. Shoprite has an ongoing commitment to reduce the use of these types of packaging material. Freshmark has for several years now been using recyclable plastic crates instead of wooden ones as well as cardboard cartons for packing and transporting most of its produce.

Distribution strategy

Shoprite has been very successful in its centralised distribution facilities, with its warehouses being spread out over Southern Africa. This has led to significant environmental and economic advantages such as lower transport carbon emissions, reduced waste production, and the ability to recycle waste effectively. It also results in smaller store land-use area, reduced retail store energy use, and less water consumption.

Worm-farming/vermiculture

Freshmark acquired a Vermi (Earthworm) Compositing system, which is a fresh, simple and environmentally friendly way to recycle waste into organic compost and 'vermi tea'. The vermi tea, which is a liquid fertiliser, and vermi compost, are some of the best fertilisers available to improve soil conditions and the health of plants.

Energy management

Energy is a scarce resource which is strictly managed by Shoprite management and has a direct impact on the profitability and environmental sustainability of the Shoprite Group. Shoprite has a policy to select energy-efficient equipment. It also tries to keep ahead of technological advances. In the 2010 financial year more than 30 energy-efficient technologies were investigated. These technologies focus on improving the energy efficiency of the refrigeration, lighting, heating, ventilation, and air-conditioning equipment of the Shoprite group.

QUESTIONS

1. Name the stakeholders that are being addressed by Shoprite in this extract from the 2010 Annual Report.
2. Is the Shoprite group fulfilling its Corporate Social Responsibility through the above-mentioned activities?
3. It is stated that the South African economy is a free-market economy. Are the activities of the Shoprite Group discussed above in line with the principles of the capitalist system? Explain your answer.
4. Is there a social contract between Shoprite and its stakeholders? Explain your answer.

SUMMARY

The factors of production are the key resources used by a business to start and to grow, and consist of land, labour, capital, and entrepreneurship. The four economic systems in which a business may operate are capitalism, socialism, communism, and the mixed economy. Currently there is a big debate in South Africa about the way forward and the economic system that South Africa should follow. All businesses are involved with key stakeholders; some have more stakeholders than others. The different kinds of stakeholders in a business are business-related stakeholders, opinion-related stakeholders, and public-related stakeholders. All South African businesses are also involved through a social contract with their stakeholders, which can be broken down into explicit expectations, implicit expectations, and frontier issues.

GLOSSARY

business: an organisation that provides goods and services to its customers in the economic system in which they operate

business management: the study of those organisations that satisfy the needs of their consumers

business–related stakeholders: people closely involved in the business, who will influence the direction in which the business is moving

capital: the money or assets (such as equipment or buildings) that are used to produce or deliver something of value to the customer

command economy (communism): a system where the means of production are owned by the community and controlled by the government

controlling: the process of regulating and achieving an organisation's goals

corporate social responsibility (CSR): the idea that organisations must consider the interests of customers, employees, shareholders, local communities, and ecological environments in all aspects of their operations

economic principle: the idea that people try to get the greatest possible benefit with the available resources

entrepreneurship: the practice of creating a new organisation in response to an identified opportunity

factors of production: resources used for the production of goods and services, such as natural resources (land), human resources (labour), capital, and entrepreneurship

financial management: the management of money to reach the goals of the business

free–market economy (capitalism): an economic system in which trade and industry are mostly controlled by private owners and operated for profit, and in which investments, income, and pricing of goods and services are determined by a free market

goods: tangible products (such as gold rings)

human–resources management: the strategic and logical approach to the management of an organisation's employees so that they contribute to the goals of the business

human resources (labour): people who perform specific activities for an organisation

leading: the process of directing employees to contribute to the success of an organisation

logistics management: the control of the flow of goods and services, as well as other resources, from the source of production to the marketplace

marketing management: the development of products aimed at a target market and the progress in selling these products to the target market

mixed economy: a mixture of private enterprise, government ownership of resources, and government involvement in running the economy

motivating: the process of getting employees to want to achieve the goals of a business

natural resources (land): naturally occurring resources that are regarded as valuable in their untouched form, such as gold or coal

non-profit-seeking businesses: businesses that try to use the funding received from donors to provide a service to customers (for example, an Article-21 company)

operations management: the area of management that focuses on the physical production of goods or services, and uses specialised techniques for solving manufacturing problems

opinion-related stakeholders: stakeholders outside the business that can influence the running of the business (for example, the media)

organising: the act of assigning and grouping tasks into departments, as well as giving out authority and resources across the organisation

planning: the process of thinking about the activities that must be performed in order to reach organisational goals

private sector: the part of the economy that is run by private citizens or groups of private citizens that form organisations such as companies, generally with the aim of making a profit. These businesses are not controlled by government.

profit: the positive difference between sales and the costs of running a business, that results in an increase in wealth

profit-seeking businesses: businesses that try to make a profit

products: tangible (physical) goods or intangible (non-physical) services that can be offered to a market in order to satisfy a need or a want

public-related stakeholders: stakeholders, such as government, that influence the running of a business, such as Eskom

public sector: the public sector, also called the government sector, is the part of government that deals with the production, delivery, and allocation of goods and services to government institutions, as well as the people at national, provincial, and municipal level.

service: a non-material product that is intangible in nature (such as a bus trip)

socialism: a range of socio-economic systems where the distribution of wealth is controlled by the community or government

stakeholders: individuals or groups within or outside an organisation that have a stake in the organisation's performance, and affect or can be affected by the actions of the organisation

MULTIPLE-CHOICE QUESTIONS

XYZee is a manufacturing company residing in an industrial area in Johannesburg. The company is involved in the manufacturing of car batteries and related products and is responsible for a lot of smoke pollution in the mostly sub-economic housing areas surrounding it. There have been numerous complaints from residents regarding respiratory ailments which they ascribed to the mercury being used in the manufacturing processes of the company. The CEO published a press release making the following statements:

1. 'XYZee's main objective is to provide the greatest possible need-satisfaction with the limited resources it has.'
2. 'XYZee is working in a business environment where socialism is the political/economic system of the day.'
3. 'XYZee propose that the social political/economic system be replaced with a free-market system which would have a positive effect on government interference in the economy.'
4. 'XYZee is influenced by stakeholders and would love a competitive environment which is free of the threat of cartels and allegations of bribery.'
5. 'XYZee is a corporate socially responsible organisation.'

You are a new reporter for the 'Daily Indigestion', a newspaper that provides political and economic analysis on a daily basis. You are preparing an analysis on the statements by the CEO of XYZee. You must obtain background information regarding the statements raised. Here are some of the issues that you must understand (identify the most correct answer):

Statement 1: XYZee's main objective is known as:
1. Need satisfaction
2. Productivity
3. Rate of return on capital
4. The economic principle

Statement 2: Socialism has some disadvantages that must be included in the article. One disadvantage is that:
1. Socialism creates cyclical fluctuations in the economy.
2 Socialism usually results in a lower standard of living.
3. Socialism can result in state organisations run in an unproductive manner.
4. Socialism creates an unstable business environment.

Statement 3: The effect of the free-market system on government interference is limited to:

1. A minimum
2. A maximum
3. Within reason
4. No influence at all

Statement 4: The influence of stakeholders and a competitive environment which is free of the threat of cartels and bribery is found in:

1. The domain of business-related stakeholders
2. The domain of public-related stakeholders
3. The domain of opinion-related stakeholders
4. No domain of the business

Statement 5: The statement of XYZee being a good corporate socially responsible organisation as stated by the CEO is made to:

1. Make the organisation looks good in the eyes of the stakeholders.
2. Make stakeholders understand that the company has a positive effect on the physical environment.
3. Impress the stakeholders that XYZee is busy with environmentally friendly practices.
4. Temper the pressure on XYZee and can be seen as part of a cover-up.

REFERENCES AND END-NOTES

1. Du Toit, G.S., Erasmus, B.J. & Strydom, J.W. 2010. *Introduction to business management*. 8th ed. Cape Town: Oxford University Press, p. 29.
2. *The new Companies Act 2008 Categories of companies*. [Online]. Available: http://www.roodtinc.com/newsletter29.asp [30 September 2010].
3. *Govt, labour to address water crisis*. [Online]. Available: http://www.news24.com/SouthAfrica/News/Govt-labour-to-address-water-crisis-20100928 [30 September 2010].
   And [Online]. Available: http://www.eia.doc.gov/emeu/eabs/AOMC/overview.html [22 May 2007].
4. Pitman, J. 2010. *Struggling to access capital?* [Online]. Available: http://www.entrepreneurmag.co. za [1 October 2010].
5. Shuttleworth, M. 2007. *Biography*. [Online]. Available: http://www.markshuttleworth.com/biography [23 May 2007].
6. [Online]. Available: http://www.fin24.com/Entrepreneurship/1-in-6-adults-owns-a-small-business-20100917 [30 September 2010].
7. *One in six adults owns a small firm* [Online]. Available: http://www:iblf.org./docs/CGIRoleofBusiness.pdf [14 May 2007] p. 12.
8. Read, R. 2008. *Nike's focus on keeping costs low causes poor working conditions, critics say*. [Online]. Available: http://www.oregononlive.com/business/Oregonian/index/news/1217908505503.

[25 January 2011]; & Nikebiz. 2010. *Vision Tex and Hugger.* [Online]. Available: http://www.nikebiz.com/media/pr/2010/04/20_VisionTexandHuggerHonduras.html [27 January 2011].

9. FLOWER, J. 2009. Knowledge Review: Sustainable goes strategic. *Strategy + Business,* 54:1-10.

10. DU TOIT, G.S., ERASMUS, B.J. & STRYDOM, J.W. 2007. *Introduction to business management.* 7th ed. Cape Town: Oxford University Press, p. 8.

11. Pick n Pay. 2010. *Annual Report 2010.* p. 18.

12. BONINI, S.M., MENDONCA, L.T. & OPPENHEIM, J.M. 2006. The social issues become strategic. *The McKinsey Quarterly,* 2:20–32.

13. NOREN, G., BENDROT, I., LAURENT, B., NYBERG, C., STRÖMDAHL, I. & THORSENHERD, M.L. 2004. *The role of business in society.* Confederations of Swedish Enterprise.

14. STOKES, G. 2010. *Is the retirement annuity back in vogue?* [Online]. Available: http://www.fanews.co.za/article.asp?Life_Insurance;9,Retirement;1175,Is_the_retirement_annuity_back_in_vogue 8114 [10 October 2010].

15. Shoprite, 2010. *Annual Report 2010.*

ANSWERS TO MULTIPLE-CHOICE QUESTIONS

1. Correct answer is 4, the economic principle. See Section 1.3 where it is expressly stated that obtaining the greatest possible benefit with the limited resources available can be described as the economic principle.

2. Correct answer is 3. Socialism cannot be held responsible for an unstable, cyclic and lower standard of living as this also occurs in a free-market system. There is however evidence that government-led private institutions are run in an unproductive manner.

3. Correct answer is 1. The whole aim of the free-market system is minimum government intervention.

4. Correct answer is 3. Competitors form part of the domain of the opinion-related stakeholders.

5. Correct answer is 4. It is clear with the information provided that XYZee have no concern for the physical environment. It is done to make the organisation look good in the eyes of the stakeholders but even more strongly is a cover-up to try and deny the impact of the company on the residents and the environment.

2

The business environment

Jerome Kiley

PURPOSE OF THIS CHAPTER

This chapter discusses the concept of systems thinking, because all aspects of a business, both internal and external, are interconnected. This chapter examines how the micro-environment, the market environment, and the macro-environment affect the success of a business, and it explains how to perform a SWOT analysis.

LEARNING OUTCOMES

This chapter should enable you to:
- understand the concept of systems thinking
- explain the level of control that management has over the different organisational environments
- describe the micro-environment and how the various management functions affect the success of the business
- explain how the different role-players in the market environment affect the success of the business
- understand how the sub-environments in the macro-environment affect the business and its continued existence
- analyse the impact of the environment on an organisation, using a SWOT analysis.

2.1 Introduction

Because a business is an open system, it is affected both by the forces within it and those outside of it. The manager needs to understand how these forces affect the business in order to manage the consequences (results) of these for the business.

2.2 **The systems approach**

The **systems approach** is based on the idea that organisations are made up of inter-dependent parts that can only be understood by looking at the whole.[1] Any system consists of three components, namely inputs, processes and outputs.

FIGURE 2.1 The organisation as a system

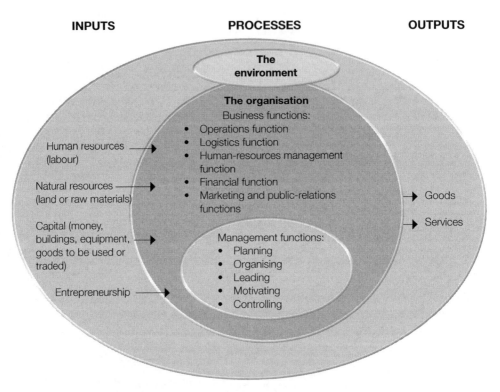

The **inputs** are all the things that are brought together in an organisation (human resources, natural resources, capital and entrepreneurship). The inputs are then processed by carrying out the different management functions (operations management, logistics management, financial management, human-resources management, and marketing and public-relations management), with the end result being outputs in the form of goods or services.

A business does not exist in a vacuum. Everything that happens, both within and outside the organisation, affects the organisation. The easiest way to understand this is to think of the human body with its different parts and organs. If any one of the organs does not function properly, it affects the functioning of the entire body. For example, if a person stubs her or his big toe, this affects the body's functioning by causing that person to limp and be distracted by the pain.

A business organisation is governed by the same principles, namely: if any part of the system is not functioning properly, it will affect the functioning of the whole organisation. For example, if there is a problem in the human–resources department, this can affect all the other departments by demotivating (making less enthusiastic) the employees and causing an overall drop in their performance, and therefore in the overall performance of the business.

2.3 **The organisational environment**

A business's **organisational environment** is the world outside the business as well as what goes on inside the business.[2] These work together in affecting the success of the business.

FIGURE 2.2 The business environment

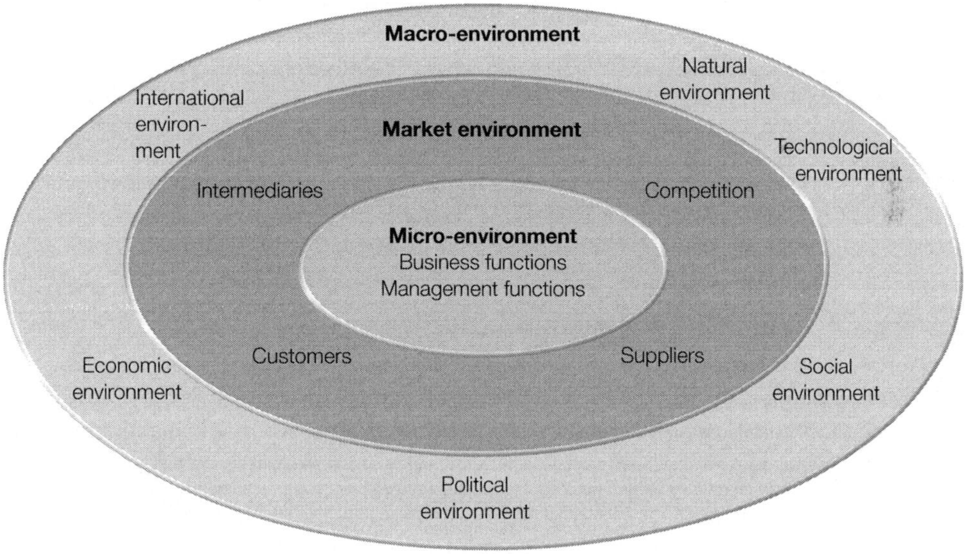

The organisational environment has three parts:
- The micro-environment is the environment inside the business that consists of the different business functions and the way they are managed.
- The market environment is the environment outside the business, where the business gets its resources and trades its products. It comprises the suppliers, intermediaries, customers, and competition of the business.

- The macro-environment includes all those factors that affect the business, including the natural, technological, social, political, economic, and international environments.

An important point about these three parts of the organisational environment is the degree of control that the manager has over each one.

FIGURE 2.3 Levels of management control over the three components of the organisational environment

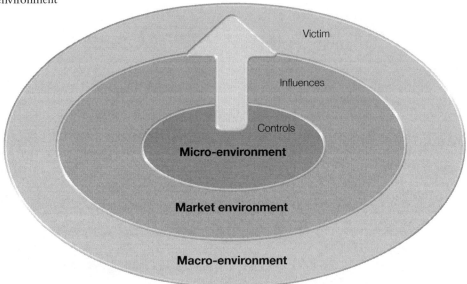

The manager has direct control over the micro-environment. This is the environment inside the business that the manager makes decisions about on a daily basis. These decisions have a direct effect on the micro-environment.

The market environment, which is the environment immediately outside the business, is influenced by management. For example, the decisions of management on advertising and pricing may attract customers to the business. However, there are many things that management has little or no control over, such as the availability of goods and skilled labour.

The organisation can be seen as a victim of the macro-environment, in that management has very little or no control over events on the national and international levels. These are often the events that we hear about on the news. Management has to deal with the effects of these events on the organisational environment. This is why the SWOT analysis forms such an important part of the manager's job description. (See Section 2.4.)

It is management's responsibility to form strategies (plans) for the business to achieve a competitive advantage that will eventually make the business a success.[3] Rather than being passive victims of fate, managers must be proactive (respond quickly) in managing the organisational environment. However, one of the major challenges for management is dealing with the huge amount of information that is available, and making accurate predictions based on this.[4]

2.3.1 The micro-environment

The **micro-environment** (also known as the 'internal environment') is the environment inside the business. It includes the business functions (operations, logistics, finance, human-resources management, marketing and public-relations) and the management tasks (planning, organising, motivating, leading, and controlling) that are involved in running the organisation.

FIGURE 2.4 Relationships between the functions in the micro-environment

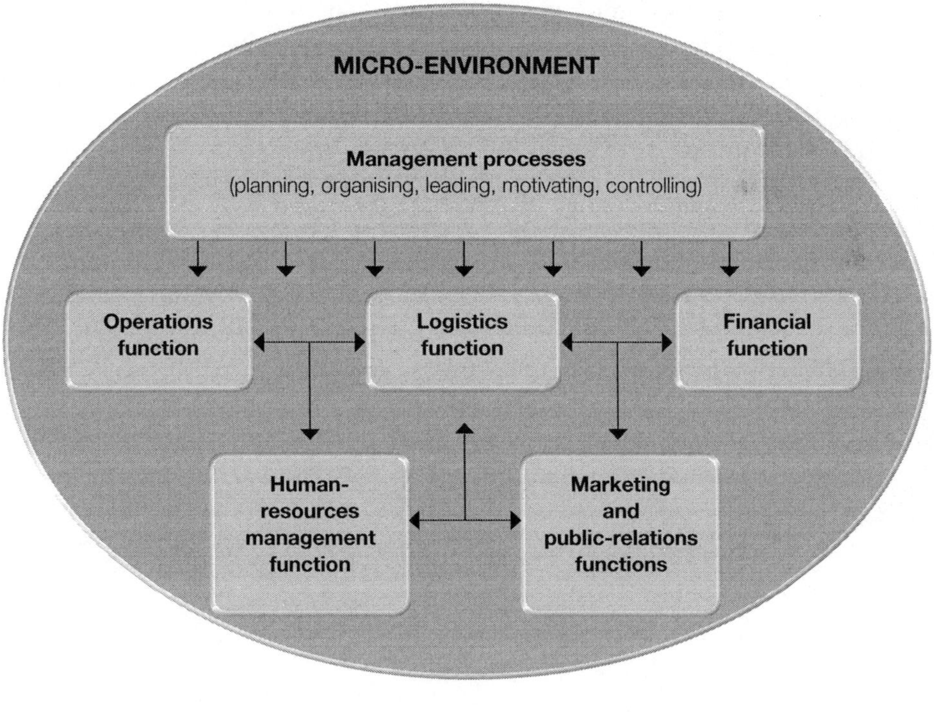

The effectiveness of managers in carrying out the various management has a direct effect on the functioning of a business. To see this in action, think of two branches of a supermarket chain. The one store functions well. The staff members are friendly and

helpful, the shelves are full, the floors are clean, and the food is fresh. The other store has unfriendly and unhelpful staff, they are continually out of stock of many items, the food is stale, and the floors are often dirty. You will probably notice that in the first store, the manager is present and actively involved with the staff, while in the second the manager is often absent, or if present, she or he has very little to do with the other staff members and how they are performing. The success of a business depends on how well the manager does his job.

The **operations function** is responsible for getting the products that the business sells. If the operations function does not perform effectively, the business will not be able to supply its customers with the required quantity and quality of products.

The **logistics function** is responsible for getting the right quality products, in the right quantity, at the right time, and at the right price (**purchasing**), as well as for distributing the products of the business, either within the organisation or by delivering them to the customer. If the function is not working well, the products of the business will not be in the right place at the right time, at the right price, and the business will lose customers.

The **financial function** must operate effectively to ensure that the business has enough capital to run the business in both the short and the long term. It must collect debts and pay the creditors of the business. If this does not work properly, the business will definitely fail.

The **human–resources management** (HRM) **function** must get the right quality of employees for the business and then look after them in the business, so that they stay, and help the business to achieve its goals.

The **marketing function** is there to tell potential (likely) customers about the products sold by the business, and to persuade them to buy these goods and services. A business can have the best goods or services in the world, at the best possible price, but if customers do not know about them, they will not buy them. The business must also have a 'positive image' (attractive mental picture). If it does not, customers may not buy its goods and services. The **public-relations function** is there to make sure that the business keeps a positive image among its customers, as well as in the broader society. (Although the public-relations function is a separate function, for the purposes of this book, it is dealt with together with the marketing function in Chapter 13.)

2.3.2 The market environment

The **market environment** (also known as the 'task environment') is where the organisation conducts its business. It is here that the organisation gets the inputs into the business from its suppliers and their intermediaries, sells its goods and services to the customers, and competes for these customers with competitors who sell the same or similar products.

The **suppliers** are other businesses that give the business its raw materials, if it is a manufacturer, and its goods, if it is a retailer. It is essential that businesses have suppliers that can provide raw materials or goods of the right quality, in the right quantity, at the right price, at the right time. If any of these requirements are absent, it will affect the functioning of the business, and eventually its profits. Some of the consequences of the absence of these requirements are illustrated in the table below.

TABLE 2.1 Consequences of ineffective suppliers

Product-requirement problem	Consequences
Poor quality	• Customers will be dissatisfied. • Manufacturing failures will result. • Customers will buy elsewhere, and the business's profits will decrease.
Not the right quantity	• If too little is delivered, customers will be disappointed. • If too much is delivered, stock will spoil in the store. • Customers will buy elsewhere, and the business's profits will decrease.
Not at the right place	• If the product is not delivered where the manufacturing process requires it to be, work will be interrupted. • If the product is not delivered to the retail stores where it is required, customers will not get what they need.
Too expensive	• If the raw materials or processed ingredients are too expensive, the manufactured products will be too expensive. • Customers will buy somewhere else, and the business's profits will decrease.

Intermediaries are the wholesalers and other businesses that act as 'middlemen' between the manufacturer and the consumer. Each of these intermediaries adds their **mark-up** to the product. This is the percentage that each adds to the price that they pay for the product, which is passed on to the next person in the supply chain. The more people in the supply chain, the more expensive the end product becomes. If any of the intermediaries are not functioning effectively, there will be a ripple effect, with the same consequences being experienced as set out in Table 2.1.

FIGURE 2.5 An example of how intermediaries affect the end-cost of a product

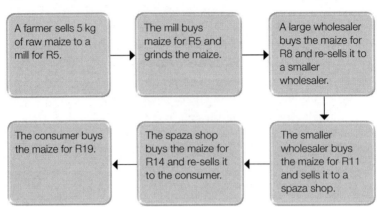

Competitors are other businesses that sell the same or similar products or services. They create competition for a business because they are rivals for the same customers; they may attract potential customers or tempt existing customers away. The result could be lost profits for the business owing to:

• reduced sales
• reduced prices (to stay competitive)
• possible increases in advertising costs (both to keep existing customers and to attract new customers).

Finally, the **customers** of a business are the patrons who buy the business's goods or services. These can be members of the public, other businesses, non-governmental organisations, or government departments. The bottom line is that if a business does not have customers, it will have no-one to buy its products. Then it will not make a profit, which is the very reason why the business exists.

2.3.3 The macro-environment

The **macro-environment** is all the factors on the national and international levels that affect the success of the business. These are the factors over which the management of the organisation has very little or no control. These are events and circumstances to which the business is a 'victim'. The best that management can do is to try to predict these factors and deal with their consequences, which can be either positive or negative for the business.

The macro-environment consists of a number of 'sub-environments', including the natural, technological, social, political, economic, and international environments, which have a wide-ranging impact on business activities.

FIGURE 2.6 Factors in the macro-environment

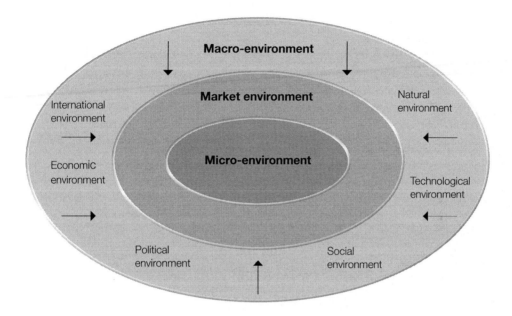

2.3.3.1 **The natural environment**

The **natural environment** includes the availability of natural resources, which are the raw materials that the manufacturing industry uses, as well as matters such as the climate, weather patterns, and natural disasters.

Global warming affects South Africa

Global (all over the earth or 'globe') warming will have extreme and frightening effects on South Africa over the next 40 to 100 years, which include higher temperatures and extreme weather changes. Some climate experts estimate that by 2100 a third of the earth will be ruined by hunger, thirst, war, migration, and death, as a direct result of global warming.[5] One example where this is having an effect on business in South Africa relates to water, which is critical to agriculture (farming) as well as many manufacturing processes.

Global warming will be particularly severe in South Africa, which will suffer lower rainfall and rising temperatures. Such weather changes will reduce water supply, and will cause major difficulties in areas of the country which already are relatively arid (dry). The agricultural industry will be affected particularly badly by these conditions. One of the alarming expert opinions in the second edition of 'The Environmental Handbook: A Guide to Green Business in South Africa' of August 2010, was that 'If urgent steps are not taken, South Africa will run out of water for future economic growth within the next five years.'[6]

However, the pressures of the natural environment are not all bad news. Some businesses have actually profited by 'going green'. An example of this is the Bembani Group, who provide sustainability strategies for companies in South Africa, and a number of other southern African countries. They are involved in a number of environmentally sustainable businesses, such as their EnviroChoice, a system which municipalities can use to switch off home geysers from a distance. They are also involved in a project to recycle old tyres and turn them into shoes and conveyor belts.

2.3.3.2 **The technological environment**

Technology is the processes by which people make tools and machines to influence and understand the physical world. In 1970 Alvin Toffler wrote the book *Future Shock*,[7] where he stated that the only thing we can be sure of is change, and that this change is exponential (tremendously fast) as opposed to additive.

Nowhere can this be seen more clearly than in the changes in the **technological environment**. Technology has enabled computers and machinery to become smaller, faster, and cheaper, and this is happening at an ever-increasing rate. Think of the changes that have occurred in computing. The Sony Playstation 2, which is already outdated, has more computing power than the computer that was used to put the first man on the moon. Goods at till points are now scanned, when previously they were entered by hand. Production lines that had dozens of employees are now mechanised and controlled by computers.

The key concepts here are **invention**, which is the discovery or creation of a new product or process, and **innovation**, the process through which new ideas and inventions become a reality.[8]

A business that fails to keep up with the developments in the technological environment cannot remain competitive, and will be overtaken by its competitors.

The broadband revolution

In the modern business–place, communication is essential to success. Critical to this is effective and fast Internet access. Both South Africa and Africa in general have been lagging behind many other nations with poor Internet speeds and expensive telecommunications. Much of this is changing with the new Seacom and Sat3 undersea fiber optic cables that have been laid from Europe to Africa, with more to follow.

This will have the effect that the prices of telecommunications and data transfers will fall, at the same time becoming faster. This will make teleconferencing and video conferencing cheaper and more efficient, which reduces the need to travel for meetings.[9] Dan Engel, the regional sales manager for communications vendor Polycom, notes: 'Such technologies have the ability to offer consumers and businesses communication possibilities beyond imagination – all of which will allow for smoother, more effective and efficient communication to take place that can be considered key to remaining afloat in what's currently a very volatile market.'[10]

2.3.3.3 **The social environment**

The **social environment** is comprised of the characteristics of the society in which the business is located. The statistical characteristics are referred to as the society's **demographics**. These may include such details as the average age, religion, culture, language, educational levels, degree of urbanisation, or any other relevant characteristic. These are all issues that you will examine when defining your target market in Chapter 13.

CRITICAL THINKING

How important is public sentiment to a company? Woolworths decided to stop selling five Christian magazines with fairly small circulations, but the backlash was huge. Can you think of other examples of businesses that have been seriously affected by social pressures? What should businesses do to manage such incidents?

Woolworths faces boycott

Woolworths recently reversed a decision to stop stocking five Christian magazines. It is not clear what caused the decision, but it resulted in a number of Christian organisations calling for a boycott of the retailer. The strong feelings that this caused are clear from the amount of comment made both on Facebook and the News24 article that reported this.[11] Faced with the whiplash of public sentiment, Woolworths felt that they had little option but to reverse their decision.

2.3.3.4 **The political environment**

Politics can be defined as the competition for power within a society. The **political environment** is the environment in which this competition takes place. A stable democratic environment where political parties compete for power peacefully is helpful to conducting business. The political environment influences how society functions in general.

An example of the impact of the political environment

During the 1980s, South Africa was in political and social upheaval. Industry was in turmoil, with strikes and marches almost daily events. Violence was everywhere in the country. The National Party's army and police suppressed opposition by force, and the armed struggle hit back with regular bombings and attacks on government targets. The United Nations had imposed sanctions on South Africa, which meant that many goods could not be imported or exported. This had a dramatic impact on South African manufacturers. Their markets were limited, and they could not get many types of raw materials and spare parts. When they did get them, they cost much more than in other countries.

Another issue of particular concern in the political environment is the laws made by the government, and whether they make business easier or harder. Laws are made by the ruling party and are based on their policies. Some examples of **legislation** include:
- laws giving the tax rate for businesses
- laws that allow subsidies and tax breaks for new businesses
- labour laws to protect employees, but which can also cost money and trouble for the businesses
- Black-economic-empowerment (BEE) policies that require businesses trading with the government to have a percentage of black owners.

2.3.3.5 **The economic environment**

The **economic environment** is a complex sub-environment with many factors that affect a business in different ways. Economics is the science that describes and analyses the producing, distributing and using of goods and services,[12] and the role played by money or the lack of money. The economic environment is one of the most important environments that a manager needs to be able to predict and deal with, as it is directly linked to the profit and survival of the business.

The **economy** of a country refers to all the ways goods and services are produced, distributed and consumed (used) by people and businesses. A **healthy economy** is one where new businesses are starting and job creation is growing, which leads to more spending, and in turn leads to more businesses and jobs.

Many businesses rely on a customer's **disposable income**, which is the bit of a person's income over which she or he has complete control.[13] This is the income that the person has left after all the essentials (such as housing, electricity, water, transport, and food) have been paid for.

The **average income** of individuals in a community, province or country determines the **spending power** of a business's potential customers. The higher the average income, the more money people will be able to spend on goods and services. However, higher salaries push up the cost of goods, which results in more products becoming less affordable.

The **interest rate** is the cost of borrowing money, which is calculated as a percentage of the amount borrowed.[14] Interest rates vary from time to time. This affects a business because it affects how much it costs for that business to borrow money, and therefore affects how much profit the business makes. For example, if a business took out a R100 000 loan, at an interest rate of 10% the business would have to repay R10 000 interest per year, while at an interest rate of 25% the business would have to pay R25 000 interest per year.

Productivity is the ratio between work-hours and the number of goods produced. Combined with the cost of labour, this has a major impact on the cost price of goods in the production process. Poor levels of productivity, accompanied by high labour costs, are one of the main concerns to South African industry. Productivity levels and labour costs influence the ability of South African businesses to compete both nationally and internationally.

Inflation is the term used to describe the decrease in the value of money in relation to the goods it can buy over time.[15] The lower the rate of inflation, the more money people have to buy goods and services. When inflation increases, people have less money to buy goods and services because their money is being spent on **servicing debt**. The South African Reserve Bank aims to keep South African inflation at 6% per annum. Compare this with Zimbabwe's inflation rate, which is more than 10 000%. This means that in one year the price of a loaf of bread increased from R5 to R5,30 in South Africa, but it increased 100 times in Zimbabwe.

The **business cycle** refers to increases and decreases in the levels of production and employment in a country over time.[16] This means that at times business is good in a country, while at other times things are a lot tougher. This is similar to the changing of the seasons, in that it cannot be summer all the time.

The **exchange rate** is the principal rate at which two currencies can be traded.[17] Businesses are increasingly trading across international boundaries. This can be seen, for example, in all the Chinese goods we can now get in South African shops. As with interest rates, the exchange rates also change over time and are very difficult to predict (foretell). The effects are illustrated in the figure below.

TABLE 2.2 The effect of exchange rates[18]

	26 October 2008 $1 = R11,17	1 November 2010 $1 = R6,98
South African business imports spare parts for $100	Cost: R1 117	Cost: R698
South African business exports products priced at R1 000	Cost to foreign buyer: $89	Cost to foreign buyer: $143

Cheap rand will hit the poor: Gareth Ackerman, the chairman of Pick n Pay, has warned that any move by government to devalue the rand will hit the poor in South Africa the hardest. 'South Africa is a net importer of food, and food commodity products are dollar-denominated. A wide range of foodstuffs including bread, rice, coffee, tea and other staples are all based on the dollar,' he said. This may very well cause food costs to rise quickly again, hurting the poorest in our country, who are already suffering from lower disposable incomes, rising costs, and the threat of unemployment. Poor people spend much more of their income on food compared with richer ones. Official figures show that the richest fifth of the population spend 9.2% of household income on food, while the poorest fifth spend 37.5% of their much smaller income.[19]

The majority of international trade takes place in United States dollars ($). If the exchange rate increases (if United States dollars become more expensive) prices of imported products increase, while if the rate decreases then imported goods become cheaper.

2.3.3.6 **The international environment**

The **international environment** refers to the events that happen in other countries that affect the business. **Globalisation** is the development of business activities on an international level, which includes competition, markets, and the increasing interdependence (they keep getting more dependent on each other) of global economies.[20]

Factors in the international environment can range from policy decisions in other countries, to natural disasters, wars, and terrorist attacks. Examples of events at the international level that have had an impact on business in South Africa include the following:

- The 9/11 terrorist attacks on the Twin Towers in New York negatively affected the South African travel industry because of the increased fear of flying, although firms making security equipment had increased sales.
- The war in Iraq led to increases in the crude oil price, which in turn has led to the increased price of petrol and diesel in South Africa. This in turn has resulted in increased prices for everything from food to transport.
- The collapse of the American home-loan market has led to increased South African interest rates.
- The increased levels of cheap products from Eastern countries have hurt the South African manufacturing industry, in particular the clothing sector, where many jobs have been lost.

Importing Zakumi – The SA clothing industry struggles to compete with cheap Chinese imports

The FIFA World Cup, which was marketed (advertised) as bringing major development to South Africa, was criticised (found fault with) when it was discovered that the mascot Zakumi was being produced in China.[21] This was in spite of the fact that the SA clothing industry was struggling to compete with cheap imports, and had huge job losses over the last number of years.

2.4 Conducting a SWOT analysis (study of the parts) of a business's environment

In order to stay competitive and manage the impact of the factors in the environment, a business needs to analyse both the internal environment (the micro-environment) and the external environment (the market- and macro-environments). This is done through a process known as a **SWOT analysis** ('SWOT' stands for strengths, weaknesses, opportunities, and threats.) The process involves analysing the internal environment's strengths (what the business is good at) and its weaknesses (what needs to be improved in the business). Then the external environment is analysed by identifying its opportunities (prospects that the business could use to grow and make more profits) and its threats (factors that could stop the business from growing and making profits).

TABLE 2.3 Example of a SWOT analysis for Thabo's Fish and Chips

Internal	External
Strengths: • skilled and motivated employees • well-run purchasing function • effective marketing strategies	Opportunities: • customers loyal to the brand • new technology that can lower production costs • new markets
Weaknesses: • high number of rejects during production • senior manager is approaching retirement • shortage of funds to finance expansion	Threats: • shortage of raw materials • increasing interest rates • increased competition

The table above is a summary of the SWOT analysis that Thabo carried out on his business, Thabo's Fish and Chips. In the internal environment of the business (the micro-environment) the strengths were: the skilled and motivated employees Thandi and Joe; the good-quality raw fish and potatoes used; and the fact that the business was well-known because of their big signs and the advertisements put in the local paper. But there were a number of weaknesses that needed to be fixed. Several pieces of fish got burnt during frying; Thabo was 60 years old and would like to retire; and the business could not open a second branch because of a lack of capital. In the external environment (the market- and macro-environment) there were a number of opportunities: the loyal group of customers who regularly bought the fish and ships; the new chip fryers that used less electricity; and the fact that shortly a new shopping centre was opening close by, which would be an ideal place to open a second branch. The main threats were that: at times there was a shortage of fish because of over-fishing in the past; interest rates were increasing; and a number of other fast-food businesses had opened in the neighbourhood.

Thabo needs to take steps to fix the weaknesses in his business. For example, he needs to find someone to lend him capital at a reasonable interest rate, so that he can use the opportunity of opening a second branch and buying more economical equipment.

CASE STUDY: Pick n Pay

Pick n Pay is a supermarket chain that most people in South Africa have used at some or other time. Listed below are some direct quotes from the address by the chairman Mr Gareth Ackerman at the annual general meeting that took place on 18 June 2010.[22]

'What I wish to do this morning is to talk about the significance of the very major restructuring which the company has undergone in the past three to four years and how this strategic reorientation has prepared us for the challenges that are presented by the state of the economy, the aspirations of our customers, and the changing nature of the business environment.

The last few years have seen us dedicate considerable resources to prepare for an uncertain future. The past decade has seen unprecedented changes in South Africa's retail sector.

At the same time, the very nature of competition in South Africa's retail environment will be changed by the possible entry into the local market of leading international retailers such as Wal-Mart.

When we launched our strategy four years ago, we were clear that this ambitious and visionary project would be costly in terms of both money and energy – and so it has proved. We have invested heavily in such components of the strategy as SAP, centralising distribution, capacity, rebranding, the Score conversions and a number of other key capital-intensive undertakings.

From the very outset of our Australian venture, we have encountered spirited opposition. In retrospect, it is clear that we should have concentrated more on the larger and more promising African market. For that reason, we are stepping up our operations in the SADC region, where our first store is about to open in Zambia and where we have signed up franchise partners in Mozambique, while identifying sites for expansion into Mauritius. Other developments on the continent are underway.

Within South Africa, I would like to emphasise that our focus will be on profitable market share and not merely on market share for its own sake.

As never before, our customers expect to receive sales and service support, and are generally better informed, more demanding and savvier than any previous generation. That mastery of information – combined with the rise of consumer activism and the exponential growth of the Internet

– has enabled them to exercise choice with a power and freedom that was totally foreign to their forebears.

And it is our primary duty to adapt to that new generation of shoppers, ensuring that the right product is available at the right price at the right time.

Secondly, we will absolutely adhere to the maxim that doing good is good business. Pick n Pay was one of the first companies in South Africa to make a strong commitment to corporate social responsibility and it will remain as one of the pillars on which the company philosophy is founded.

Thirdly, our commitment to business efficiency and decentralization will remain undiluted. While we have already made major progress through the Group's restructuring project, the quest for efficiency can never be said to be complete. This will be achieved through measures such as augmenting the way we use SAP to improve process efficiency, and reducing the cost of doing business through goods not for resale enhancements and further cuts in overheads.

The Pick n Pay brand remains a strong and envied one. Our reputation for maintaining low prices during periods of high food inflation and our long history of championing the consumer have not been developed over-night or won easily. Our identity has been designed both to meet the demands of changing financial norms and to match the aspirations of our customers. We continue to project the image of a modern, vibrant and dynamic organisation which conducts itself ethically and responsibly.

As we confront the challenges of a struggling world economy and as we share the financial difficulties that face our loyal customers, we will not abandon the business model or ethical foundations that have served us so well for almost half a century.'

You have all shopped in one or other of Pick n Pay's stores, so consider both your experiences while shopping there as well as any other relevant information about the market- and macro-environment in South Africa that you may be aware of when answering the questions that follow.

QUESTIONS

1. What are the key factors in the micro-environment that impact on the success of different Pick n Pay stores? Here you could refer to one or more specific stores that you are familiar with.
2. What are the different factors in the market-environment that have an effect on Pick n Pay?
3. Identify different factors in the macro-environment that impact on Pick n Pay.
4. Draw up a basic SWOT analysis for Pick n Pay. Make some suggestions on how Pick n Pay could build on the strengths that you have identified in the SWOT analysis.
5. What could Pick n Pay do to address the weaknesses and threats that you identified in the SWOT analysis?
6. Provide some suggestions as to how Pick n Pay could make use of the opportunities that you identified in the SWOT analysis.

SUMMARY

In understanding how the business environment affects a business, it is vital to understand the concept of systems thinking. This states that everything is interconnected, therefore if something occurs in one part of the system it affects all the other parts of the system. While the business affects the environment in which it exists, this environment also has a major impact on the business's success.

The micro-environment is the context within the organisation, and over which the management has almost complete control. It comprises the business functions of operations, logistics, finance, human-resource management, marketing, and public relations. These are interdependent. Their effective functioning, and the functioning of the business as a whole, depends on the ability of management to plan, organise, motivate, lead, and control effectively.

The market environment is immediately outside the organisation. This is where the organisation conducts its business, and over which the management has some influence. It includes the organisation's suppliers and their intermediaries, the potential customers, and the competitors who compete for their customers.

Finally the macro-environment comprises the events that take place on the national and international level, over which management has almost no control. The macro-environment can be divided into the natural, technological, social, political, economic, and international sub-environments.

Because the business environment determines the success of a business, it is essential that management analyses and checks it. This is done by means of a SWOT analysis, where the internal strengths and weaknesses, as well as the external opportunities and threats, are noted and analysed.

GLOSSARY

average income: the total of all the income for a group of persons divided by the number of persons in that group

business cycle: a periodic increase and decrease in the levels of production and employment in a country over time

business functions: a series of related activities or tasks that are performed together to produce the products of the business

competitors: other businesses that sell the same or similar products as one's own business

customers: the people who buy the products of a business

demographics: the statistical details of a group or society

disposable income: the portion of an individual's income left over after the essentials such as food, accommodation and transport have been paid for

economic environment: the events that affect the availability of money in a country

economics: the study of the production, distribution and consumption of goods and services, and the role played by money

exchange rate: the principal rate at which two currencies can be traded

financial function: the business function that manages the flow of money, including getting, using, administering and reporting on financial matters

globalisation: the development of business activities on an international level, which includes competition, markets, and the increasing interdependence of global economies

healthy economy: an economy where new businesses are opening with an accompanying growth in job creation, which leads to more spending, and in turn leads to the creation of more businesses and jobs

human–resources management (HRM): the function that finds, keeps and develops qualified workers for the organisation

inflation: the term used to describe the decrease in the value of money in relation to the goods it can buy over time

inputs: those things put into a system that enable the system to function, such as human resources, raw materials, or entrepreneurship

innovation: the process through which new ideas and inventions become an operational or business reality

international environment: the events that take place in other countries that affect the business

invention: the discovery or creation of a new product or process

interest rate: the cost of borrowing money, which is normally calculated as a percentage of the amount loaned

intermediaries: the wholesalers and other businesses that act as 'middlemen' between the manufacturer and the consumer

legislation: rules created by government, also known as 'laws'

logistics function: the business function responsible for getting the materials, goods and services in a supply chain where they are needed at the precise time that they are needed (This includes purchasing and distribution.)

macro-environment: the factors on the national and international level that affect the success of the business

management tasks: the broad tasks that the management process can be divided into, namely planning, organising, leading, motivating, and controlling

market environment: the environment immediately outside the business, where the business gets its resources and trades its products

marketing function: the business function that is responsible for making the target market aware of the business's products, as well as persuading people to buy these products

mark-up: the difference between the cost price of an item and its sale price

micro-environment: the environment inside the business comprising the various business functions and the way in which they are managed

natural environment: the availability of natural resources, which are the raw materials that the manufacturing industry uses, as well as matters such as the climate, weather patterns and natural disasters

operations function: the business function that is responsible for the manufacture of the goods or services supplied by the business

organisational environment: the context in which the business operates, which consists of the world outside the business and also the functioning of the firm inside

outputs: the goods or services that the business produces

political environment: the context created by political organisations and their competition for power

productivity: the ratio between work-hours and number of goods produced

public-relations function: the business function that is responsible for creating and maintaining a positive public opinion of the business

purchasing: the part of the logistics function that is responsible for obtaining materials, goods or services, and arranging how these will get from the suppliers to the business

social environment: the demographics of the society in which the business is located

spending power: the amount of money that an individual or group has available to spend

suppliers: the businesses in society that provide other businesses with the goods and services that they require to produce their goods and services in turn

systems approach: the idea that organisations are made up of interdependent parts that can only be understood by looking at the whole

SWOT analysis: an analysis of a business's internal strengths and weaknesses, and external opportunities and threats

technological environment: the technological state of the society in which the business operates (its tools, machinery and computers)

technology: the processes by which human beings fashion tools and machines to increase their control and understanding of the physical environment

MULTIPLE-CHOICE QUESTIONS

1. In the systems model products or services are part of the _____.
    a) processes
    b) inputs
    c) outputs
    d) environment

2. The business functions form part of the _____ environment.
    a) micro–
    b) macro–
    c) market–
    d) political

3. The fact that the price of oil increased due to the overthrow of the Egyptian president is an example of a factor in the _____ environment.
    a) market–
    b) micro–
    c) social–
    d) macro–

4. What degree of control does a manager in a business have over the macro–environment?
    a) no control at all
    b) complete control
    c) some control some of the time
    d) some influence over it

5. The function in the market environment responsible for procuring the raw materials required to produce the goods or services that the business sells is the _____ function.
   a) logistics
   b) operations
   c) purchasing
   d) marketing

REFERENCES AND END-NOTES

1. NEEDLE, D. 2004. *Business in context: An introduction to business and its environment.* 4th ed. London: Thompson.
2. FITZROY, P. & HULBERT, J. 2005. *Strategic management: Creating value in turbulent times.* London: John Wiley & Sons.
3. NEEDLE, D. 2004. *Business in context: An introduction to business and its environment.* 4th ed. London: Thompson.
4. CONNOR, P.E., LAKE, L.K. & STACKMAN, R.W. 2003. *Managing organizational change.* 3rd ed. Portsmouth: Greenwood.
5. GORDIN, J. 2006. *Weather wise: SA's in for a rough ride.* [Online]. Available: http://www.iol.co.za/index.php?from=rss_South%20Africa&set_id=1&click_id=&art_id=vn20061008083921736C491277 [14 November 2007].
6. iafrica.com. 2010. *SA flirts with water crisis.* [Online]. Available: http://business.iafrica.com/news/653833.html [27 October 2010].
7. TOFFLER, A. 1970. *Future shock.* New York: Random House.
8. NEEDLE, D. 2004. *Business in context: An introduction to business and its environment.* 4th ed. London: Thompson.
9. DINGLE, S. 2009. *Telkom prices will come down.* [Online]. Available: http://www.fin24.com/Companies/Telkom-Prices-will-come-down-20090728 [27 October 2010].
10. FIN24. 2009. *Broadband revolution.* [Online]. Available: http://www.fin24.com/Finweek/This-weeks-survey/Information-and-Communication-Technology-2009-20091106 [27 October 2010].
11. ESTERHUYSE, S. 2010. *Woolworths bans Christian mags.* [Online]. Available: http://www.news24.com/SouthAfrica/News/Woolies-bans-Christian-mags-20101020 [1 October 2010].
12. ENCYCLOPDIA BRITANNICA. 2006. *Ultimate Reference Suite DVD.*
13. Ibid.
14. Ibid.
15. JONES, S.L. 2005. *Inflation and deflation.* Microsoft Encarta 2006 [DVD]. Redmond: Microsoft.
16. BONELLO, F.J. 2005. *Business cycle.* Microsoft Encarta 2006 [DVD]. Redmond: Microsoft.
17. ENCYCLOPÆDIA BRITANNICA. 2006. *Ultimate Reference Suite DVD.*
18. ABSA. 2007. ABSA exchange rate history. [Online]. Available: http://www.absa.co.za/absacoza/content.jsp?VGN_C_ID=c2fcac45985bc010VgnVCM1000003511060aRCRD&VGN_CI_ID=03ce ef21f24cc010VgnVCM1000003511060aRCRD [10 November 2007].
19. These figures are hypothetical.
20. STONEHOUSE, G., CAMPBELL, D., HAMILL, J. & PURDIE, T. 2004. *Global transitional business: Strategy and management.* 2nd ed. Chichester: John Wiley & Sons.
21. KING, J. 2010. *Zakumi and cup apparel letting down SA industry.* [Online]. Available: http://www.timeslive.co.za/opinion/letters/article299738.ece [1 November 2010].

22. [Online]. Available: http://www.picknpay-ir.co.za/downloads/minutes_of_agm_picknpay_stores_limited_18_june_2010_website.pdf

ANSWERS TO MULTIPLE-CHOICE QUESTIONS

1. Answer = c) (p. 22)
2. Answer = a)
3. Answer = d)
4. Answer = a) (p. 23)
5. Answer = c)

PART TWO

Management tasks

Management is a vital part of the running of a business, whether it is a profit or non-profit organisation. This part looks at the various tasks of management.

Chapter 3 introduces all of the management tasks, then each of the five chapters that follows it explores a particular management task.

Chapter 4 explains the task of planning, which is the start of the management process, where business objectives are developed and methods are considered on how to obtain these objectives.

Chapter 5 concentrates on the task of organising, dealing with the organisational structure and the jobs that need to be done to fulfil the objectives of the organisation.

Chapter 6 covers the task of leading, which refers to the task of guiding the employees in an organisation.

Chapter 7 focuses on the task of motivating employees to commit to an organisation's objectives.

Chapter 8 describes the task of controlling, which is the last step in the management process, and which is where performance is judged to determine if the set objectives were reached.

These five tasks of management form a continuous cycle, and are also interactive processes. While separating each of these tasks allows each one to be carefully studied, a manager will carry out each task better if she or he understands what the other tasks involve.

The task of management

Theuns FJ Oosthuizen

PURPOSE OF THIS CHAPTER

This chapter explains the basic concepts of management, and it identifies the different organisations in which managers work. It explains the levels at which managers fulfil their tasks, the tasks that they perform, and the areas of an organisation in which they work. This chapter also examines the skills and competencies (abilities) that managers need to have, and the roles that they need to perform.

LEARNING OUTCOMES

This chapter should enable you to:
- understand what being a manager involves
- distinguish between the different types of organisations in which managers work
- identify the different levels of managers
- explain the various tasks performed by managers
- distinguish between the different areas of management
- describe the various management skills
- list a number of important management competencies
- explain the various management roles and sub-roles.

3.1 Introduction

The role of management increasingly includes all levels of employees in the organisation. Managers must act as leaders, but employees should also now take responsibility for managing themselves. This chapter analyses the meaning of management and examines what a manager needs in order to succeed in the 'global village'(the world that seems as small as a village because of modern communication).

3.2 **What is management?**[1]

Management can be defined as the process of **co-ordinating** work-related activities so that the people performing them complete these activities effectively and efficiently. In each management function, the specialised manager needs to apply all the management tasks (planning, organising, leading, motivating, and controlling). However, while 'management' can refer to a combination of managerial tasks, it can also be seen as a specific function (for example, marketing or finance) in an organisation. 'Management' can also be the term used to refer to the people with formal power in an organisation.

3.3 **What is a manager?**[2]

A manager is a person who has been appointed in a managerial position in an organisation, and who has certain responsibilities to carry out management tasks. Managers have power, and should provide leadership to the employees reporting to them.

Management is a continuous and active process that gets and organises resources, in order to reach certain goals.

Managers and other employees need to work together to:
- develop plans and objectives
- structure tasks in a sensible way
- act in organised structures while considering authority
- motivate each other
- communicate clearly, and
- develop and act according to set performance standards.

The effectiveness of a manager lies in her or his ability to:
- maintain a favourable work environment
- create opportunities for all employees to perform at their best
- act as a leader (and a follower, depending on the situation)
- communicate continuously with other employees and motivate them, and
- acknowledge and reward good performance considering the limited resources.[3]

South Africa National Boss of the year 2010

Celebrating 21 years of South Africa's National Boss of the year award in 2010 is an example of how successful managers in a leading capacity, irrelevant of management level or organisational size, are recognised in South Africa. Previous title bearers include the likes of Edward Kieswetter and Brand Pretorius. In 2010 this prestigious title was awarded to Lerato Mosiah, a general manager at Afrox.

The organisers of this event and brand owner of this award, Dictum Publishers, passionately believe in South African managers: 'We're looking to identify and recognise bosses throughout South Africa who make people look forward to go to work! ... We need great business leaders with vision, who can articulate that vision, passionately own it and drive it to completion. Without passion, the position of leadership is meaningless. And passionate leaders inspire others to strive for more and achieve more; they inspire confidence and success in their peers and colleagues. Good leaders make people feel that they are at the very heart of the success of the organisation; that they make an essential difference. When that happens, people grow and deliver and go on to inspire others.'[4]

3.4 Organisations in which managers work

Managers work in a variety of organisations, which can be classified as commercial, governmental, or voluntary. Table 3.1 is a summary of these types of organisations.[5]

TABLE 3.1 Organisations in which managers work

Type of organisation	Possible forms	Specific examples
Commercial organisation (an organisation that manufactures goods, provides services, or retails (sells directly to consumers) products)	Sole (single) proprietors, partnerships, close corporations, public and private companies, franchises, holding companies, conglomerates, multi-national corporations, virtual companies, and co-operatives	Volkswagen, Checkers, Spur, Woolworths, McDonald's, Protea hotels, Virgin Active, Kalahari.net, BHP Billiton, Makro

Type of organisation	Possible forms	Specific examples
Governmental organisation (a tax-funded department, or unit that is formalised by the government, to ensure a framework of support and the application of legislation according to the country's bill of rights)	Government departments and public enterprises	Department of Trade and Industry, South African Revenue Services, Department of Transport, Department of Arts and Culture, Statistics South Africa, Eskom, SAA, Transnet
Voluntary organisation (an organisation that focuses on a specific agenda and creates income not for profit but to ensure funding of this agenda)	Political parties, pressure groups, charities, clubs, associations, professional bodies and trade associations	African National Congress, Democratic Alliance, Freedom Front Plus, Johannesburg Country Club, SAICA, Starfish Foundation, ASATA

3.5 **Levels of management**[6]

When structuring an organisation, the various management levels are identified, and the authority, responsibility, duties and tasks for each management level and each specific manager, are made clear. A small organisation may have only one layer of management, while a large organisation may have many levels.[7] In general, the three main levels of management are top management, middle management, and first–level management. (See Figure 3.1.)

FIGURE 3.1 Management levels

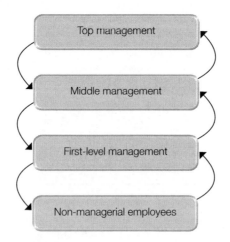

3.5.1 Top management

Top management is responsible for the overall direction of an organisation. Top managers have to develop and communicate the organisation's vision, its mission statement, and its long-term goals, plans, and strategies. Top managers also establish overall organisational policies. Typical examples of top managers are presidents, directors, and chief executive officers (CEOs), or managing directors. For instance, Maria Ramos is the CEO of Absa, and she oversees all the strategic activities in the group.

3.5.2 Middle management

Middle management is made up of department heads, functional managers (such as marketing or human-resources managers), branch managers, or project managers. These middle managers must have a good understanding of the overall organisational strategy. Middle managers create the link between top management and first-level management. They receive broad, general strategies and policies from top managers, and they change them into specific goals and action plans to be implemented (put into practice) by first-level managers. Middle managers are usually responsible for ensuring that all organising tasks are conducted, and they take care of operational (practical) planning.

3.5.3 First-level management

First-level managers implement all the strategic plans sent through to them via middle managers from top managers. **First-level management** takes responsibility for operational planning, which means that these mangers are responsible for the production of goods or the provision of services. First-level managers are also responsible for controlling activities.

In most organisations, first-level managers do not spend much time with higher management or with people from other organisations. Their focus and responsibility are on specific operational issues only. Typical examples of first-level managers are supervisors, crew leaders, and section heads. At a large wholesaler such as Makro, the floor manager will be classified as a first-level manager.

Non-managerial employees report to first-level managers, and are responsible for the basic process of production or service provision.[8]

Managing operations at different levels

Top management of a vehicle manufacturer will decide on their organisation's overall goals and strategies such as the establishing of export contracts and the developing of new assembly facilities globally.

On middle management level, a functional manager such as the operational manager will develop an operations plan and strategy to design and assemble a new model which will satisfy the needs of existing and potential new customers. This manager will liaise with various operations experts such as engineers, designers, and floor managers to plan for a new assembly line. As a middle manager, this person will consider the strategic goals and vision statements of the organisation and align her or his functional strategies and goals with these. During the liaison process this middle manager will then communicate these strategies to the operational managers on the first level of management, to ensure that the implementation of these strategies is effective and efficient.

Then, at first-level management, the manager in charge of design will take on the responsibility to design the new vehicles, engineers will assist with developing and upgrading equipment for the assembly plant, and assembly-plant floor managers will train plant personnel with the necessary skills to use new technology and implement the new assembly processes.

A non-managerial employee such as an electrical technician will acquire the skills to assemble the electrical components for the new vehicle, and when the plant is up and running, she or he will be responsible for installing all electronic wiring and equipment into the vehicle.

3.6 **Management tasks**

The primary management tasks are planning, organising, leading, motivating, and controlling.[9] For each of these tasks to succeed, effective **communication** is important.[10]

3.6.1 Planning

Planning is an essential process for almost every business activity. **Planning** is deciding in advance what to do, how to do it, when to do it, and who is supposed to do it. Planning involves choosing different strategies and actions for every individual, team, and department in an organisation, and for the organisation as a whole. Planning allows the business to define its overall objectives, together with the goals for each part of the business. Planning allows members of an organisation to achieve their vision, mission, and purpose, as stated in their objectives.

During the process of planning, managers must make various decisions. Different types of decisions are made at different levels of management. **Decision-making** focuses on the identification of possible alternatives and the selection of the most appropriate one as the solution to address an opportunity or problem. Decision-making does not only happen during the planning process, but also when any of the management tasks are conducted. (Planning is discussed in more detail in Chapter 4.)

Successful management and growth

Cellphone companies are going ga-ga, as the reality of their dreams are going far beyond their vision. According to a World Wide Worx 2010 report, the use of mobile Internet services has exploded in South Africa. The report confirmed that usage of specific applications like Mxit and Facebook Mobile far outpace Internet browsing on the phone, even though both are available on almost two-thirds of the phones used by South Africa's urban cellular users. The implications are significant for cellular providers, as the South African Internet user base increased in less than a year from the 5.3 million reported by World Wide Worx at the end of 2009 to 9.6 million in 2010. By adding instant messaging users to the number, the total becomes 10.56 million. This is double that of the Internet user base at the end of 2009.[11]

3.6.2 Organising

Organising is the structuring (arranging), co-ordinating and directing of an organisation's resources in order to achieve its objectives. When involved in the task of organising, managers structure and oversee resources such as people, materials, equipment, money, and time. This task involves delegating (passing on) work to other employees so that they can carry out the necessary activities effectively, and act according to their set authority and responsibilities. (Organising is discussed in more detail in Chapter 5.)

3.6.3 Leading

Leading is directing, guiding, and motivating other employees. Leaders play an important role in organisations, and are not only assistants to CEOs. Leadership in today's organisation is needed on all levels in the organisation. Managers need to act as leaders in order to influence other employees to achieve set objectives.[12] (Leading is discussed in more detail in Chapter 6.)

Leadership at McCarthy

McCarthy started as a bicycle shop family business in Durban in 1910. Justin McCarthy, the 'founder' of McCarthy, started his career in the motor trade, which he saw as the business of the future. McCarthy has remained a family business despite having grown under the leadership of the current CEO, Brand Pretorius, into an R18-billion-turnover industry leader which sells 85 000 vehicles per year across 32 brands out of a network of 120 dealerships, and which conducts 750 000 services and repairs. McCarthy has been a pioneer since its earliest days and, to this day, remains an industry leader in various fields, but, most of all, the McCarthy team remains true to the vision of its founders.[13]

3.6.4 Motivating

Motivating people is the act of influencing them so as to cause, channel and sustain certain goal-directed behaviours. While managers need to lead their employees, they also need to motivate them to perform in such a way as to maximise (enlarge to its biggest) their objectives, as well as the objectives of their team and the whole organisation. However, motivation is not only the duty of a manager; every employee should ensure self-motivation. (Motivating is discussed in more detail in Chapter 7.)

3.6.5 Controlling

Control makes a link between the other management tasks. Controlling is the process of developing performance standards according to the set objectives developed during the planning process. This is followed by measuring the actual performance of employees and teams, in order to know if they are performing according to the set standards. The outcome shows whether employees perform acceptably or whether they do not, and if corrective action is needed.[14] (Controlling is discussed in more detail in Chapter 8.)

> **CRITICAL THINKING**
>
> Why is management development so important for a country such as South Africa? Why can't we all be employees and have no managers? Why do we need to develop business leaders? Answer these questions and give reasons for your answers.

> ## Leadership at SAP[15]
>
> SAP's R3 software package, which aims to make businesses more efficient, is used on more than 22 000 companies, including Lufthansa, Unilever and BMW. Much of SAP's success has been a result of Hugo Plattner's drive, vision and leadership. Plattner is joint chairman and CEO of SAP, and operates the company's research and development centre in California.

3.7 **Areas of management**[16]

The five main business functions (which are discussed in detail in Part 3) are operations, logistics, finance, human-resources management, and marketing. These different functions are usually performed by different managers who implement all the management tasks in relation to their departments.

3.7.1 Production and operations managers

Production and operations managers develop and administer (supervise) all activities in transforming the organisation's resources into final goods or services. (Management of the operations function is discussed in more detail in Chapter 9.)

3.7.2 Logistics managers

A logistics manager is responsible for the management tasks connected with incoming logistics (purchasing) and outgoing logistics. This includes the collection of resources as well as the packing, storage, transportation, and sales of completed goods. (Management of the logistics function is discussed in more detail in Chapter 10.)

3.7.3 Information-technology managers

An information-technology manager is responsible for implementing, maintaining, and controlling technology (systematic application of knowledge) in the organisation. Information-technology managers ensure the effective flow of information for effective management decision-making.

3.7.4 Financial managers

Financial managers focus on getting the money needed to operate the organisation, as well as managing these funds in the best interests of the organisation. These funds are used to achieve the organisational goals. (Management of the financial function is discussed in more detail in Chapter 11.)

3.7.5 Human-resources managers

The human-resources managers handle all the staffing needs. They work out the human-resources needs of the organisation, and manage the finding and hiring of new employees, their training and development, and also their performance judging and all other relevant (connected) administrative applications. (Human-resources management is discussed in more detail in Chapter 12.)

3.7.6 Marketing managers

Marketing managers are responsible for the establishment of need-satisfying goods or services for the organisation's customers. They must then consider pricing, marketing communications, and how to make the products available. (Marketing management is discussed in more detail in Chapter 13.)

3.7.7 Public-relations managers

Public-relations managers are involved in communicating and keeping in touch with internal and external groups in order to start or maintain a good relationship with all stakeholders.[17] These stakeholders include: employees, suppliers, government, communities, customers, and others.

> **CRITICAL THINKING**
>
> How would the roles, tasks and responsibilities of a logistics manager differ from those of a logistics employee? Consider a large manufacturer of products such as Tiger Brands that needs to purchase resources as well as distribute final products to retailers and wholesalers such as Pick n Pay and Makro. Firstly identify the tasks of the logistics department – then work out how the responsibilities and roles for these tasks will be divided between management and other employees in the logistics department.

3.7.8 Administrative managers

Administrative managers are responsible for an entire business or a major division in the organisation. They are not specialists in the way that the other types of managers are; instead they co-ordinate the activities of the specialised managers.

3.8 **Management skills**

For managers to fulfil their planning, organising, leading, motivating and controlling roles, they need to use three groups of **management skills**, namely: conceptual skills, human skills, and technical skills. Each of these groups of skills will now be discussed in more detail.

3.8.1 Conceptual skills

Managers use conceptual skills to understand abstract (cannot be seen or touched etc.) ideas, so that they can consider various possible solutions to a problem, and can then select the best solution. Having the appropriate (suitable) conceptual skills means that a manager can understand the entire organisation, department or range of products, as well as the interrelationship among the various parts.

Planning and organising require a great level of conceptual skill. Because top managers mostly perform planning and organising tasks, they require particularly good conceptual skills. All managers should develop their conceptual skills, because these allow them to see beyond the immediate situation, and to consider alternatives while still keeping in mind the long-term goals of the organisation.

Because businesses are competing in a continually changing global environment, conceptual skills are increasingly required. Managers need this skill in order to see the bigger picture, in order to handle the constant changes in the internal and external business environment.

3.8.2 Human skills

Managers use **human skills** to understand and change the attitudes and behaviour of individuals and groups. Human skills are needed to manage change and conflict among employees, as well as workforce diversity (differences). Current (present) management trends include participative management, where non-management-level employees participate (share) in managing resources. Participative management can be implemented more effectively if managers have strong human skills.

Communication skills are essential human skills without which no-one can be an effective manager (or team member). The ability to communicate, lead, co-ordinate and motivate people, and to mould individuals into a cohesive (sticking together) team, distinguishes effective from ineffective managers.

While good human skills allow managers at all levels to motivate and interact with the employees for whom they are responsible, it is probably middle managers who have the greatest need for human skills.

3.8.3 Technical skills

Managers use **technical skills** when they use job-specific knowledge and techniques to perform an organisational role. These skills reflect a manager's understanding of the business's methods.

The specific technical skills that a manager needs depend on that manager's position and job description. For example, one manager may need to draw up a budget, another may need to present a marketing campaign, and another may need to train a production team. (However, every manager needs to be able to plan, organise, lead, motivate, and control, as all of these are essential for effective management.)

> ### CRITICAL THINKING
> Access the website of any of your favourite retailers, for example, for food go to Checkers, for clothes go to Edgars, for communication go to MTN, and so on. Identify a specific management job title at each of these organisations. Compare the job requirements in terms of management skills required for each of these managers. See also if you can classify these management skills as technical, human, and conceptual.

First-level managers and middle managers are the most likely to need specific technical skills.

3.9 **Management competencies**[18]

Management competencies can be described as sets of skills, knowledge, attitudes and behaviour that a manager needs to be effective in a variety of organisational settings and managerial jobs.

Research has been done regarding the competencies that managers need be successful. Michael Bristow analysed research on 60 different organisations. The top five competencies identified were:[19]
- communication (written and oral [spoken] communication)
- self-management (personal effectiveness, self-control, self-discipline, self-confidence and resilience [easy recovery from something unpleasant])
- organisational ability (organisational awareness, delegation, control and structure)
- influence (impact on others, motivation, leadership, networking [contacting people], and negotiation)
- teamwork (team membership and team leadership).

Some of the other important competencies that were identified were: interpersonal skills, analytical ability, results orientation, customer focus, developing people's potential, strategic ability, commercial awareness, decision-making, planning, leadership, self-motivation, specialist knowledge, flexibility, creativity, initiative, change orientation, dealing with information, concern for quality, reliability, an ethical approach and financial awareness. These results indicate that interpersonal skills are an essential requirement for today's manager.

3.10 **Management roles**

A **management role** is a set of specific tasks that a person is expected to perform because of the position she or he holds in an organisation.[20] In the 1970s Henry Mintzberg identified ten roles indicating the specific tasks that managers need to perform. These managerial roles can be grouped into three categories, namely:[21]

- decisional roles
- interpersonal roles
- informational roles.

Managers take on each of these roles in order to influence the behaviour of individuals and groups, either inside or outside the organisation. Managers often perform several of these roles simultaneously (at the same time).[22]

3.10.1 Decisional roles

Managers are exposed to a variety of problems and opportunities, and they need to make decisions about them. The types of decisions that managers need to make, as well as the conditions under which they are made, vary.

The **decisional role** includes four sub-roles:

- entrepreneur
- disturbance handler
- negotiator
- resources allocator (giver).

These sub-roles are described in Table 3.2.

The decisional role can be connected with the methods used by managers to plan strategies and use resources.

TABLE 3.2 Decisional sub-roles identified by Mintzberg [23]

Type of decisional sub-role	Description	Example
Entrepreneur	In this role the manager must make decisions involving the creative use of organisational resources, and think of alternative (other) possibilities.	A manager decides to solve an energy-crisis problem at a manufacturing plant by introducing alternative energy sources, such as wind energy and sun energy.
Disturbance handler	In this role the manager must deal with conflict situations quickly. These situations could be expected or unexpected, and internal or external.	After the organisation has caused an oil spillage in a coastal town, a manager consults with the angry community in finding an acceptable solution to deal with the pollution.
Negotiator	In this role the manager must create an acceptable solution in a negotiating situation.	During a relocation (moving) of offices, a manager negotiates with employees to ensure an acceptable solution to ensure that all employees are satisfied with their new offices.
Resource allocator	In this role the manager must establish the best possible ways to allocate and use resources.	If a retailer has an annual sale, a manager could decide to move the majority or all regional staff to the three biggest retail outlets where the sale will be held.

3.10.2 Interpersonal roles

Managers take up the **interpersonal role** in order to interact with people, to co-ordinate and supervise organisational employees, and to give direction to all organisational members.

The interpersonal role includes three sub-roles, namely:
- figurehead
- leader
- liaison person.

All these sub-roles are essential at all levels of management, although the importance of each role might vary depending on the management level or situation. These roles are described in Table 3.3.

TABLE 3.3 Interpersonal sub-roles identified by Mintzberg [24]

Type of interpersonal sub-role	Description	Example
Figurehead	In this role the manager must act as a representative of the organisation, team, or division.	The CEO of an organisation represents the organisation and delivers a speech at the annual South African Productivity Prizegiving Ceremony.
Leader	In this role the manager must give direction, and motivate employees.	The Gauteng regional manager of a car dealership motivates the staff to increase their annual sales, in order to qualify for an international European holiday as the top sales team.
Liaison person	In this role the manager must establish a working agreement between two business units, or co-ordinate tasks or link resources between different parts of a business.	A financial manager acts as a liaison officer with media during a conference, while presenting an organisation's annual financial statements.

3.10.3 Informational roles

In today's global business environment, the role of information and the associated technology is very important. Successful managers access, interpret, and provide information to all relevant parties at the exact moment when this information is needed to maximise an opportunity.

The **informational role** of managers includes three sub-roles, namely:

- monitor
- disseminator
- spokesperson.

These roles are described in Table 3.4.

TABLE 3.4 Informational sub-roles identified by Mintzberg[25]

Type of interpersonal sub-role	Description	Example
Monitor	In this role the manager must collect useful information.	The sales manager evaluates annual data on industry sales and trends presented by a leading market-research organisation.
Disseminator	In this role the manager must focus on distribut-ing useful information inside or outside the organisation.	The human-resources manager informs employees on the outcome of the annual negotia-tions about salary increases.
Spokesperson	In this role the manager must communicate on behalf of the organisa-tion, division, or team.	The public-relations officer of an accounting firm makes a public announcement at the launch of a new tax service for businesses.

CASE STUDY: Toys for Africa

Themba is the CEO of an organisation that manufactures and distributes toys in southern Africa. Their products are sold at Game and Toys-R-Us in South Africa, Botswana and Namibia. Apart from toys, a variety of computer games are also manufactured in large quantities. Their product range includes:
- Toys: toy dolls, doll clothing, and jewellery
- Games: computer games.

They have received a large order for 5 000 toy dolls from Game and 7 000 electronic games from Toys-R-Us. They have three months to manufacture and deliver the ordered goods.

Busi is responsible for sales and marketing, and she has 14 employees in her department. Mpho is the sales team manager, and she reports to Busi. The sales team consists of four people: Marcus, Mavis, Marie, and Mpho – better known as the four Ms. Themba has newly appointed Joe, who is in charge of produc-tion and operations of all toys and games. He has 40 employees reporting to two factory managers: Paul is handling toys and Pumba is in charge of games. The financial manager, Suzie, is responsible for the acquisition of capital, investment decisions, creditors and debtors. She has four people receiving orders from her, and they all report to her.

QUESTIONS

1. What type of organisation is Toys for Africa?
2. Identify the different management levels and relevant people at Toys for Africa.
3. Who in the operations department is responsible for implementing the Toys for Africa strategy and operational planning?
4. What management levels are they on?
5. What different managerial roles do you think should be predominantly fulfilled by Themba?
6. Which managerial skills do you suggest should be developed by Suzie, the financial manager, so that Toys for Africa can develop into a global business?

SUMMARY

A manager can work in commercial organisations, governmental organisations, or voluntary organisations. In an organisation a manager can be part of top-level management, middle management or first-level management. Each manager is involved in five main management tasks: planning, organising, leading, motivating, and controlling. But each manager will also have a special focus, depending on which area of the organisation she or he is working in (for example, finance). All managers need conceptual skills, human skills, and technical skills, and managers also benefit from having a specific range of competencies. In each position that they hold, managers must play a variety of roles, which can be divided into decisional roles, interpersonal roles, and informational roles.

GLOSSARY

communication: a process in which one person or a group creates a meaning that is shared by another person or group by means of various channels

conceptual skills: understanding abstract ideas in order to select the best solution to a problem

controlling: the process of establishing and implementing ways to ensure that objectives are achieved

co-ordinating: integrating organisational or departmental tasks and resources to meet objectives

decisional role: according to Mintzberg, the managerial role in which a manager must plan strategies and choose how to use resources (incorporating the sub-roles of entrepreneur, disturbance handler, negotiator, and resource allocator)

decision-making: the identification of possible alternatives and the selection of the best one as the solution to an opportunity or problem

disseminator: according to Mintzberg, the informational sub-role in which a manager gives other employees or people outside of the organisation relevant information

disturbance handler: according to Mintzberg, the decisional sub-role in which a manager must quickly address problems facing the organisation

entrepreneur: according to Mintzberg, the decisional sub-role in which a manager decides how to use organisational resources in creative ways

figurehead: according to Mintzberg, the interpersonal sub-role in which a manager represents the organisation, team, or division

first-level management: the managers responsible for implementing all the organisation's strategic and tactical plans, and who are responsible for operational planning and overseeing the production of goods or provision of services

human skills: the ability of an individual to understand, alter, lead, and control the attitudes and behaviour of individuals or groups

informational role: according to Mintzberg, the managerial role in which a manager focuses on collecting, disseminating and communicating information (incorporating the three sub-roles of monitor, disseminator and spokesperson)

interpersonal role: according to Mintzberg, the managerial role where a manager interacts with people, co-ordinates and supervises organisational employees, and gives direction to all organisational members (incorporating the three sub-roles of figurehead, leader and liaison person)

leader: according to Mintzberg, the interpersonal sub-role in which a manager gives direction and motivates employees

leading: the process of directing, guiding and motivating employees towards accomplishing goals

liaison person: according to Mintzberg, the interpersonal sub-role in which a manager establishes a working agreement between two business units, or co-ordinates tasks or links resources between different parts of a business

management: the process of co-ordinating work-related activities in order to complete management tasks and activities effectively and efficiently, to achieve the set objectives with and through other people

management competencies: sets of skills, knowledge, attitudes and behaviour that a manager needs to be effective in a variety of organisational settings and managerial roles

management role: a set of specific tasks that a person is expected to perform because of the position she or he holds in an organisation

management skills: the conceptual, human and technical skills that allow managers to fulfil their management tasks

manager: a person who has been appointed in a position of leadership and power in an organisation, and who is responsible for achieving specified work-related activities through effective and efficient use of human and other resources

middle management: the managers that form the interactive link between top management and first-level management, often heading up departments, divisions or particular projects

mission statement: the stated reason why the organisation exists

monitor: according to Mintzberg, the informational sub-role in which a manager collects useful information

motivating: encouraging people's desire, direction and willingness to achieve the goals of an organisation

negotiator: according to Mintzberg, the decisional sub-role in which a manager reaches agreements with external parties

non-managerial employees: employees who do not have management responsibilities

organising: the act of assigning and grouping tasks into departments, as well as the assignment of authority and the allocation of resources across the organisation

planning: the process of thinking about the activities that must be performed in order to reach organisational goals

resource allocator: according to Mintzberg, the decisional sub-role in which a manager allocates resources to different departments, functions or projects

spokesperson: according to Mintzberg, the informational sub-role in which a manager communicates on behalf of the organisation, division or team

technical skills: job-specific knowledge and techniques that allow the manager to perform an organisational role

top management: the managers who are responsible for the overall direction of an organisation as presented in its vision and mission statements, and who have to develop goals, policies and strategies for the entire organisation

vision: dream

MULTIPLE-CHOICE QUESTIONS

1. The determination of deviations by comparing actual results with planned results in order to take corrective steps refers to which one of the following?
   a) leading
   b) organising
   c) controlling
   d) disciplining

2. First-level management is responsible for _____ planning.
   a) operational
   b) long-term
   c) functional
   d) strategic

3. _____ are typical organisations that manufacture goods, retail goods, and/or provide services.
   a) Government organisations
   b) Commercial organisations
   c) Voluntary organisations
   d) Community organisations

4. Technical skills include _____.
   a) communication and negotiation skills
   b) administrative and computer skills
   c) conceptual skills
   d) engineering skills

5. The _____ function manages the recruitment and hiring of new employees, as well as the training and development of staff.
   a) marketing
   b) human-resources
   c) operations
   d) sales

REFERENCES AND END-NOTES

1. OOSTHUIZEN, T.FJ. 2007. *Management tasks for managerial success.* 3rd ed. Johannesburg: FVBC.
2. Ibid.
3. LUSSIER, R.N. 2009. *Management fundamentals: Concepts, applications, skill development.* 4th ed. Cincinnati: South Western Cengage learning.
4. DICTUM PUBLISHERS. 9 April 2010. www.simplylinks.co.za. [Online]. Available: http://www. simplylinks.co.za/article830_bossoftheyearawardcallfornominations.htm [13 October 2010]. And interview Trinco O. South African national boss of the year 2010 award. Sandton. [15 October 2010].

5. LEWIS, P.S., GOODMAN, S.H. & FANDT, P.M. 2001. *Management: Challenges in the 21st century.* 3rd ed. Cincinnati: South Western; And Smith, M. 2007. *Fundamentals of management.* London: McGraw-Hill.

6. OOSTHUIZEN, T.F.J. 2007. *Management tasks for managerial success.* 3rd ed. Johannesburg: FVBC.

7. KROON, J. (ed.) 1995. *General management.* Pretoria: Kagiso.

8. ROBBINS, S.P. & COULTER, M. 1999. *Management.* (6th international ed.) London: Prentice Hall.

9. DIXON, R. 1994. *The management task.* Oxford: Butterworth Heinemann.

10. LUSSIER, R.N. 2009. *Management fundamentals: Concepts, applications, skill development.* 4th ed. Cincinnati: South Western Cengage learning; And HELLRIEGEL, D., JACKSON, S.E., SLOCUM, J., STAUDE, G., AMOS, T., KLOPPER, H.B., LOUW, L. & OOSTHUIZEN, T.F.J. 2008. *Management.* (3rd SA ed.) Cape Town: Oxford University Press.

11. MAIL AND GUARDIAN. 2010 May 27. www.mg.co.za [Online]. Available: http://www.mg.co.za/article/2010-05-27-mobile-internet-booms-in-south-africa [13 October 2010].

12. LUSSIER, R.N. & ACHUA, C.F. 2006. *Leadership – Theory, application, skill development.* Cincinnati: South Western.

13. McCARTHY. 2010. www.mccarthy.co.za [Online]. Available: http://www.mccarthy.co.za/asp/articles.asp?parentID=55&ipkArticleID=33 [13 October 2010].

14. JONES, G.R. 1998. *Contemporary management.* Boston: Irwin McGraw-Hill.

15. HAMM, S. 2008. SAP: Less ego more success. *Business Week.* July 23.

16. BENNETT, J.A. & NIEMAN, G. (eds.) 2006. *Business management: A value chain approach.* Pretoria: Van Schaik.

17. KATZ, R. 1974. Skills of an effective administrator. *Harvard Business Review.* September/October 1974. pp. 90–102.

18. HELLRIEGEL, D., JACKSON, S.E., SLOCUM, J., Staude, G., AMOS, T., KLOPPER, H.B., LOUW, L. & OOSTHUIZEN, T.F.J. 2008. *Management.* 3rd SA ed. Cape Town: Oxford University Press.

19. BRISTOW, M. 2001. *Management competencies.* Manchester: University of Manchester Institute of Science and Technology.

20. ROBBINS, S.P. & COULTER, M. 1999. *Management.* 6th international ed. London: Prentice Hall.

21. MINTZBERG, H. 1990. The manager's job: Folklore and fact. In: *Harvard Business Review.* pp. 49–61.

22. OOSTHUIZEN, T.F.J. 2007. *Management tasks for managerial success.* 3rd ed. Johannesburg: FVBC.

23. MINTZBERG, H. 1990. The manager's job: Folklore and fact. In: *Harvard Business Review.* pp. 49–61.

24. Ibid.

25. Ibid.

ANSWERS TO MULTIPLE-CHOICE QUESTIONS

1. Answer = c)
2. Answer = a)
3. Answer = b)
4. Answer = b)
5. Answer = b)

CHAPTER 4

Planning

Sharon Rudansky-Kloppers

PURPOSE OF THIS CHAPTER

This chapter explores the planning task of the management process. First the necessity and importance of planning are explained. Then the chapter looks at the three steps that must be executed in the planning process, namely: the setting of goals, the development of action plans, and the implementation of these action plans.

LEARNING OUTCOMES

This chapter should enable you to:
- explain why planning is needed in an organisation
- explain what a goal is
- discuss the steps in the planning process
- compare the different organisational goals used by top, middle, and lower management
- discuss the requirements that must be met when setting goals
- compare the different plans that can be used by the organisation
- differentiate between strategic, tactical, and operational planning.

4.1 Introduction

One of the major tasks of a manager is to plan where the organisation should go in the future, and how to get there. Planning is also the starting point of the management process. It entails a systematic and intelligent description of the direction a business organisation must follow to accomplish its goals.

The first section of the chapter deals with the need to plan in an organisation, and gives specific reasons why planning is so important. The rest of the chapter covers the three steps of planning, namely: goal formulation, the development of action plans to accomplish these goals, and the implementation of these plans.

4.2 Why planning is necessary

Tariq Siddique wrote: 'If you are failing to plan, you are planning to fail.'[1] This neatly sums up the importance of planning.

There are many reasons why planning is important as part of the management process.[2]

- Firstly, planning helps the organisation to discover new opportunities and to anticipate and avoid future problems. Each organisation must look to the future, anticipate (foresee) changes and reflect on how these changes will influence the organisation.
- Secondly, planning provides direction to the organisation. It provides the road map that tells the organisation where to go and how to get there.
- Thirdly, planning helps the different functional areas of a business to work together. Through planning, the different areas of a business can be co-ordinated and stable (steady).
- Fourthly, by creating desirable changes, improving productivity and maintaining organisational stability, planning improves the chances of achieving the organisation's goals.
- Lastly, through the realisation of the organisation's goals, planning enables the organisation to achieve long-term growth, maintain profitability, and survive.

4.3 The planning process

In some organisations, especially smaller ones, planning is informal (casual). In others, managers follow a well-defined planning framework. However, planning is always considered the foundation on which the other management tasks are based. If planning is not done properly, it will have a detrimental (harmful) effect on how the tasks of organising, leading, motivating and controlling are performed. It is important to understand how planning is linked with the other management tasks, as depicted in Figure 4.1.

FIGURE 4.1 The management process

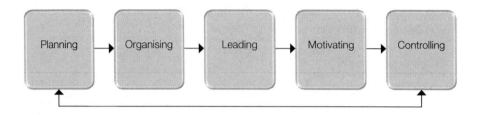

Planning should not happen in isolation (by itself), nor as a once-off activity. It is an ongoing process, as indicated in Figure 4.2.

FIGURE 4.2 The planning process

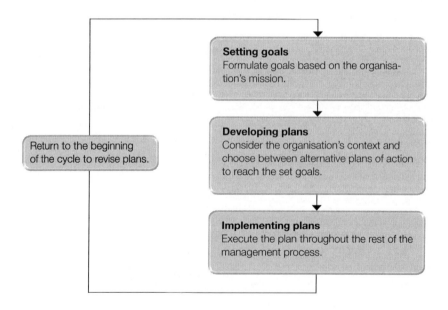

SOURCE: Based on the diagram in Du Toit, G.S., Erasmus, BJ & Strydom, J.W. 2010. *Introduction to business management.* (8th ed.) Cape Town: Oxford University Press. p. 183.

The planning process consists of three steps. The first step is goal-setting, which includes the mission of the organisation. The second step is the development of plans based on the information obtained from an environmental scan. The third step is the implementation of the plans by means of the other management functions (organising, leading, motivating, and controlling). Then there is the feedback loop, which starts the whole process again. This is called the **reactive planning stage**, but is also called 'learning from your mistakes'.

> **CRITICAL THINKING**
>
> Why is it so important for a business to follow the three steps in the planning process? Why can plans not just be developed and implemented?

4.3.1 Setting goals

Top management selects **organisational goals** for the long-term survival and growth of the business.[3] These goals fulfil a number of purposes in an organisation:[4]

- Goals provide a sense of direction by directing and guiding employees' efforts towards specific targets and important outcomes.
- Goals give a reason for decisions made in the organisation.
- Goals serve as performance criteria (standards) since they define desired outcomes for the organisation.
- Goals provide a source of motivation and commitment (agreement) for employees.
- Goals help managers decide where to allocate resources.
- Goals are influenced by the mission statement of the organisation, the business environment in which the organisation operates, the values held by management, and the experience gained by management.[5]

4.3.1.1 **The mission statement of the organisation**

The mission statement of the organisation is a definition of the organisation's basic business scope (extent) and operations that distinguishes it from similar types of organisations.[6] It is the organisation's purpose, as set out by the management.

For example, in the mission statement of Pick n Pay on the next page,[7] the first part, 'We serve', refers to the organisation's focus on the customers. The second part of the statement refers to the dream of the organisation that it will create a wonderful place for its employees to work. The last part refers to the fact that the organisation wants to create a wonderful place for its customers to shop. The mission statements of other organisations are not always so brief. Telkom's vision, mission and values are indicated in the block below.

The mission statement appears at the top of the goal hierarchy of an organisation. It forms the basis for the development of all goals and plans.

Pick n Pay's mission and values

Mission
- We serve
- With our hearts we create a great place to be
- With our minds we create an excellent place to shop

Values
- We are passionate about our customers and will fight for their rights
- We care for, and respect each other
- We foster personal growth and opportunity
- We nurture leadership and vision, and reward innovation
- We live by honesty and integrity
- We support and participate in our communities
- We take individual responsibility
- We are all accountable

Telkom's vision, mission and values[8]

Vision
Being Africa's preferred ICT service provider by:
- Customers recognising Telkom as their first choice when deciding on ICT communication solutions
- Employees viewing Telkom as the preferred employer in the ICT industry
- Shareholders regarding Telkom as a company that offers competitive returns
- Government and the Regulator considering Telkom as a trustworthy and respectful enabler of the economy
- Suppliers recognising Telkom as a valued partner in delivering world-class ICT services
- The community distinguishing Telkom as a responsible, caring and trust-worthy South African corporation

Mission

Telkom SA Limited is a leading South African-based international ICT services group focused on long-term profitability through growth in existing and new markets by:

- Providing differentiated high quality fixed, wireless and converged products and services directly or through our subsidiaries and partners
- Striving for excellence in serving our valued domestic retail and wholesale, as well as international customers
- Achieving unprecedented organic growth of existing assets
- Targeting acquisitions and new partnerships to achieve core strategies
- Acting as a responsible and caring corporate citizen

Core values

- **Providing performance improvement**
  We seek continuous improvement and do things quickly, effectively and innovatively. We learn from our mistakes to enhance our performance and become more responsive to customer needs.
- **Honesty**
  We keep our promises and commitments. We always tell the truth and are open and transparent in all our dealings with each other, our customers, our stakeholders and the broader community.
- **Accountability**
  We take full ownership of our actions and deliverables. We do not blame others and always give our best. We are passionate and walk the extra mile for our customers.
- **Respect**
  We treat everyone with courtesy, politeness and kindness, and actively listen to others. We value diversity and always seek to first understand.
- **Teamwork**
  We are team players with a common goal and shared vision. We deliver business results through cooperation and share our knowledge and resources to the benefit of the business.

4.3.1.2 **The environment of the organisation**

As discussed in Chapter 2, when determining the goals of an organisation, management must consider the environment in which it operates. But it is difficult for management to keep track of all the changes in the business environment, let alone predict how it will change in the future. Peter Drucker, the world-famous management thinker, said: 'Trying to predict the future is like trying to drive down a country road at night with no lights, while looking out the back window.'[9]

4.3.1.3 **The values of management**

Management's values also influence the goals of an organisation. For example, in an annual report Pick n Pay stated the values given in the block on page 80.[10]

Similarly, the values of Telkom's management are given in the box on page 81.

4.3.1.4 **The experience of management**

The experience of management also plays a role in determining organisational goals. In 1986 Sean Summers, the current CEO of Pick n Pay, was involved in opening the first Pick n Pay Hypermarket outside South Africa, in Brisbane, Australia. This was later sold off because of South Africa's despised political position at the time. He said that this was a tough time, and that he had learned from it.[11]

4.3.2 A hierarchy of goals

In each organisation there is a **hierarchy of goals**, with each level being subservient to the levels above.

4.3.2.1 **The mission statement**

In the area of goal-setting, the mission statement is a guide for the organisation. Therefore in Figure 4.3 the mission statement appears at the top of the hierarchy of goals.

FIGURE 4.3 The hierarchy of organisational goals

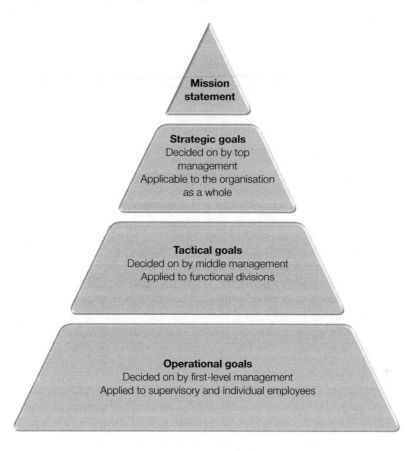

SOURCE: Daft, R.L., Kendrick, M & Vershinina, N. 2010. *Management*. Mason: South-Western. p. 247.

4.3.2.2 **The strategic goals**

Strategic goals (long-term goals) are set by top management. They look towards the future, and use a time frame of three to ten years. The plans to achieve these goals focus on the organisation as a whole. An example of a strategic goal set by Telkom is the goal of giving thousands of people access to telephones in rural communities across South Africa. The South African Revenue Service's (SARS's) strategic goals are given in the box on page 84.[12]

> ### SARS'S 3-year strategic goals (2010/11–2012/13)
>
> - Drive revenue realisation to deliver now and ensure sustainability
> - Drive productivity, service quality and cost efficiency
> - Fully deliver on our Customs mandate in a way that is aligned with government's stated intentions
> - Clarify the SARS operating model, streamline governance and strengthen leadership
> - Implement segmentation to strengthen our business model
> - Enable our people to perform at their peak
> - Deepen key external relationships to enhance reputation and results

4.3.2.3 The tactical goals

Tactical goals (functional goals) are determined by middle management. They cover a period ranging from one to three years. For example, Telkom is promoting ADSL Internet connections by means of an intensive (powerful) marketing campaign over a period of more than one year.

4.3.2.4 The operational goals

Operational goals (short-term goals) are set by first-level management. They cover a maximum period of one year. As an example, Telkom is sending out promotional (advertising) leaflets about the ADSL service together with monthly telephone bills. This is an example of a short-term plan to increase the uptake (number of people taking part) of this service.

4.3.3 Criteria for setting effective goals

In order to set effective goals, management should consider the following requirements:
- Goals should be specific and measurable. For example, a goal to increase profits by 4% states exactly what is wanted. If goals are not quantifiable (able to be measured), they cannot be controlled.
- Goals should be set for a specific time period. For example, a goal to increase

profits by 4% within the next 12 months clearly states when reaching the goal should be measured.

- Goals must be consistent (the parts agreeing). For example, if different functional areas have conflicting (different) goals, they will not be able to work together.
- Goals must be challenging but realistic. For example, if employees must work 150 hours per week to accomplish a goal, it will be impossible to reach the goal.[13]
- Particular employees must be made responsible for particular goals. For example, a goal to launch a six-month advertising campaign should be the job of a particular manager.
- Goals must be linked to rewards. For example, as an incentive (encouragement), employees who reach goals could be rewarded with salary increases, promotions or awards.

There are two basic ways to set goals in an organisation. First there is a **top–down approach**, where top management decides the goals. One of the risks of following this approach is that top management does not always know enough about what is going on at the grassroots level when setting goals. Second there is the **bottom–up approach** where the subordinates (the less powerful ones) also have a say in setting goals. This second approach is also called **management by objectives** (MBO). The most obvious advantage of this approach is that employees feel more motivated (encouraged) as they have been part of the goal-setting process.

Targets at General Electric[14]

General Electric (GE) has existed for 120 years, and its management practices are widely admired. As the following extract illustrates, meeting targets is an important part of these practices:

> 'I love you, and I know you can do better. But I'm going to take you out if you can't get it fixed.' That was Jack Welch's warning to Jeff Immelt, the present CEO of GE in early 1995. when he was heading GE's plastics division. Rising costs had made Plastics miss its 1994 earnings target by $50 million. This story from Welch's memoir, *Jack: Straight from the Gut*, illustrates that at GE you don't get to be a CEO by missing your targets. Immelt got it fixed. That's how GE works. Targets are set, first of all at a three-year planning meeting every summer known as 'session one', and then improved for the

coming year at 'session two' in November or December. Some adjustments are made for economic conditions and industry-specific difficulties, but the true GE heroes are those who meet their targets even when times are tough. And if you're able to help out with something extra to let the company meet its overall goals when other divisions are struggling, well, that's even better. Like the last year when GE's 'short cycle' businesses such as appliances and light bulbs weren't going to meet their targets because of the weak economy, 'long-cycle' businesses (power systems, medical systems) were asked to 'do better'. 'Do better' meant they sold more CT scanners, they sold more turbines, they cut costs harder, and they had the opportunity to grow faster in China.

4.3.4 Developing action plans

Once the organisational goals have been set, action plans are developed in order to reach these goals. Three types of plans can be distinguished at the different levels of the organisation, namely strategic plans, tactical plans, and operational plans.

FIGURE 4.4 Different types of action plans

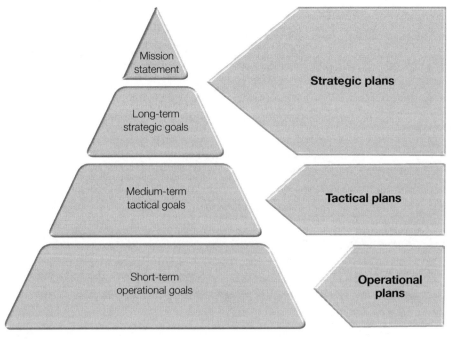

4.3.4.1 **Strategic plans**

Strategic plans (long-term plans) are developed by top management to fulfil the organisation's mission. These plans have a time frame of three to ten years, or more. A typical example would be a **concentration strategy** where the organisation directs all its efforts of the organisation on what it does best to achieve its mission. For example, the airline company 1Time concentrates 100% on being a low-cost airline company. Other examples are a **horizontal-integration strategy**, to take over similar businesses (for example, Edgars' taking over Boardmans) or a **joint-venture strategy**, where two or more businesses join in a project that is too big for one business to do on its own (for example, Vodacom's joint venture with Vodaphone for the Internet and G3).

4.3.4.2 **Tactical plans**

Tactical plans (functional plans) are usually made for a period of one to three years.[15] They are carried out by middle management and detail the actions and resources needed to reach the objectives and to support strategic plans. Each of the functional management areas sets specific tactical plans. Marketing strategies, for instance, deal with how the organisation will sell its goods and services. Finance strategies, on the other hand, work out what the best methods are to get and use the organisation's money.[16]

4.3.4.3 **Operational plans**

Operational plans (short-term plans) are developed by first-level management to achieve operational goals and to support tactical plans. These plans are made for less than a year, and they focus on the daily and weekly tasks of supervisors, department managers, and individual employees. Schedules and budgets are usually drawn up to indicate (show) the resource allocation (setting aside) and the dates when each of the required tasks must be completed.

4.4 **Implementing the selected plans**

Having goals and having plans is very important in any organisation. But if these plans are not implemented effectively, the goals will not be achieved. The implementation of these plans involves organising how they will be executed (carried out), leadership to set the plans in motion, motivation to make all employees commit to finishing the plans, and the exercising of control to determine whether the activities are going according to plan.[17] In short, it involves the other four tasks of the management process. These four elements are discussed in the four chapters that follow.

4.5 **The full circle**

Planning is only the starting point of the whole management process – the point where management has to decide what has to be done. Management must also carry out four other essential tasks in order to complete the full circle and get results. For example, without performing the task of controlling, management will not find any deviations (changes) from the plans and correct them. Controlling also forces management to reconsider (look again at) goals and set new ones, in that way completing the circle and starting all over again.

CASE STUDY: Medical scheme takes action

Many medical aid schemes have realised the benefits of health and wellness programmes. They have realised that eating right, exercising and sleeping well play a very important role in the health and wellness of their members. These medical schemes offer members the opportunity to improve their health and reward them for doing so. Discovery, for instance, encourage members to join Vitality, where they get discounts on gym membership, travel, accommodation and movies. As members accumulate points, so the benefits increase. Vitality also provides access to a network of healthcare professionals for fitness assessments and health screenings.[18]

Unisa lecturers live very sedentary (sitting down) lives with long hours in front of a computer and at a desk marking assignments and doing research. The medical scheme they belong to has done research and has found that they must become more active to live more productive lives. After all, both the government and Unisa have invested thousands of rands in training them.

The medical scheme has a mission statement in which it states that its members should be healthy and feel well in themselves. The goal that the medical scheme set in order to realise this mission statement, was that obese lecturers must lose weight, which will also be good for their blood pressure. To achieve this, the medical scheme took the following action:
- It evaluated research that was published and information from its own database.

- It sent out a questionnaire to all lecturers about their current (present) weight and physical exercise pattern.
- It compared the information from the questionnaires with their own records about the medical history of these lecturers.
- It found the high-risk cases, and invited these lecturers to join the High Performance Training Centre in Pretoria for more tests so that they could be given a personal trainer.

The medical scheme decided to measure the success of this programme after one year, hoping that at least 30% of the obese lecturers would have a normal body-fat ratio and that 40% of them would have a normal blood-pressure reading.

QUESTIONS

1. Why do medical schemes promote health and wellness programmes?
2. Does the Unisa medical scheme have a mission statement? If so, what is it?
3. Which goals have been drawn up by the Unisa medical scheme?
4. Action plans should be developed to attain the set goals. Explain the plans that have been developed by the Unisa medical scheme to achieve its goals.
5. What did the medical scheme do during the implementation phase of the planning process?

SUMMARY

Planning is defined as the first step in the management process. It involves the development of goals, the formulation of action plans to reach these goals, and the implementation of these plans. The three types of goals that are set at different levels in the organisation are strategic goals, tactical goals, and operational goals. The three types of action plans necessary to reach these three types of goals are strategic plans, tactical plans, and operational plans. Implementing them involves the other four tasks of management: organising, leading, motivating, and controlling.

GLOSSARY

bottom-up approach: the approach to goal-setting where subordinates are also involved, and which is also known as 'management by objectives' (MBO)

concentration strategy: the strategy where the organisation directs all its efforts to the profitable growth of a single product in a single market

hierarchy of goals: the sequence of goals that are set in an organisation, starting with the mission statement at the top, then the strategic goals, the tactical goals and the operational goals

horizontal-integration strategy: the strategy where an organisation takes over similar businesses

joint-venture strategy: the strategy where two or more businesses engage in a project that is too big for one business to do on its own

management by objectives: another term for the bottom-up approach to goal-setting, where subordinates are involved in the goal-setting process

mission statement: an organisation's purpose or reason for existence

operational goals: short-term goals that are formulated by first-level management

operational plans: short-term plans developed at the lower levels of the organisation in order to achieve the operational goals

organisational goals: the desired future state of affairs that the organisation sets out and would like to accomplish over a fixed period of time

planning: a management function that involves defining goals for future organisational performance and formulating action plans to attain these goals

reactive planning stage: the revision of goals and plans based on the results of the previously executed plans

strategic goals: the long-term future state of affairs as determined by top management, and which pertains to the organisation as a whole

strategic plans: long-term plans developed by top management which define the actions necessary to accomplish the strategic goals

tactical goals: goals that are set by middle management for a period of one to three years, and which pertain to the different functional areas in the organisation

tactical plans: medium-term plans developed by middle management for the functional departments in the organisation

top-down approach: the approach to goal-setting where the organisation's top management decides on the goals of the organisation

MULTIPLE-CHOICE QUESTIONS

1. Achieving unprecedented organic growth of existing assets is part of Telkom's _____.
   a) mission statement
   b) core values
   c) vision
   d) tactical goals

2. SAR's goal to deepen key external relationships to enhance reputation and results is set by _____ management.
   a) middle
   b) first
   c) lower-level
   d) top

3. When employees are part of the goal setting process, this is known as the _____ approach.
   a) top-down
   b) management by objectives
   c) authoritative
   d) strategic

4. Edgars' acquisition of Boardmans is an example of a _____ plan.
   a) tactical
   b) strategic
   c) middle management
   d) operational

5. Goals that are set for one to three years are known as _____ goals.
   a) lower-level
   b) strategic
   c) operational
   d) tactical

REFERENCES AND END-NOTES

1. Heartquotes Center. 2007. *Business Quotes and Proverbs*. [Online]. Available: http://www.heart-quotes.net/Business.html [1 April 2008].

2. Slocum, J.W., Jackson, S.E. & Hellriegel, D. 2008. *Competency-based management*. Mason: Thomson South-Western. p.215.

3. Slocum, J.W., Jackson, S.E. & Hellriegel, D. 2008. *Competency-based management*. Mason: Thomson South-Western. p.218.

4. Daft, R.L., Kendrick, M. & Vershinina, N. 2010. *Management*. Mason: South-Western. pp. 247-248.

5. Cronjé, G.J. de J., Du Toit, G.S., Marais, A. & de K. 2004. *Introduction to business management*. 6th ed. Cape Town: Oxford University Press. pp.144–145.

6. Daft, R.L., Kendrick, M. & Vershinina, N. 2010. *Management*. Mason: South-Western. p.250.

7. Pick n Pay. 2009. *Annual Report* 2009. p.3.

8. [Online]. Available: https://secure1.telkom.co.za./ir/sustainability/vision-and-missionjsp.

9. Gillooly, B. 2004. Create your own future. *Optimize magazine*. December. [Online]. Available: http//linuxriot.com/article/showArticle.jtml?.articleID=54200108 [17 July 2007].

10. Pick n Pay. 2009. *Annual Report* 2009. p.1.

11. Gilmour, C. 2005. General retailers. *Financial Mail*, 25 November, p. 27.

12. South African Revenue Service. 2007. *Mandate and vision*. [Online]. Available: http://www.sars.gov.za/brochures [17 July 2007].

13. Daft, R.L. 2005. *Management*. 7th ed. Mason: South-Western. p. 246.

14. Murali, K. 2005. *Financial Express*. 1 December.

15. Bovee, C.L. & Thill, J.V. 2005. *Business in action*. Mason: Pearson Prentice Hall. p. 145.

16. Slocum, J.W., Jackson, S.E. & Hellriegel, D. 2008. *Competency-based management*. Mason: Thomson South-Western. p. 229.

17. Du Toit, G.S., Erasmus, B.J. & Strydom, J.W. 2010. *Introduction to business management*. 8th ed. Cape Town: Oxford University Press. pp. 188–189.

18. [Online]. Available: http://www.peterpyburn.co.za/discovery_medical_aid.html [14 January 2011].

ANSWERS TO MULTIPLE-CHOICE QUESTIONS

1. Answer = a)
2. Answer = d)
3. Answer = b)
4. Answer = b)
5. Answer = d)

Organising

Andreas de Beer

PURPOSE OF THIS CHAPTER

This chapter is about organising business activities. It lists the steps in the organising process. Then it discusses the seven key concepts of organising, namely: co-ordination, authority, responsibility, accountability, delegation, specialisation and divisionalisation. Lastly, it summarises the different organisational structures available.

LEARNING OUTCOMES

This chapter should enable you to:

- define the term 'organising'
- list the steps in the organising process
- discuss the different forms of authority
- distinguish between authority, accountability, responsibility, and delegation
- explain the reason for specialisation
- discuss the different types of divisional structures, and a reason for using each one
- give your views on co-ordination
- identify the different types of organisational structures.

5.1 **Introduction**

Once planning is completed, these plans must be put into action. To do this, one must organise. **Organising** means combining activities so that goals can be reached. As a management task, organising is mainly a matter of classifying activities, putting them into divisions, creating posts in these divisions, and deciding on employees' jobs, responsibilities and authority (taking charge).[1]

Organisation is a shared function within the management process; it must go hand-in-hand with planning, leading, motivating, and controlling. It must also take note of the business environment. The environment determines the business's strategy, and this strategy determines the business's structure, therefore the way the business is organised must change with the environment.

5.2 **The organising process**

Organisation takes place when two or more people co-operate (work together) to reach a common goal. This means that the process must start with deciding how, when, by whom, and with which resources a task will be done.

The organising process is made up of six steps: gathering information, identifying and analysing activities, classifying activities, allocating staff, assigning authority and responsibility, and facilitating work.

5.2.1 Gathering information

In the planning process, managers make plans showing how they want to reach the goals. They get information about what human and other resources are available.

5.2.2 Identifying and analysing activities

Management must decide which activities need to be carried out to reach its goals. Then it can analyse which tasks will make up these activities.

5.2.3 Classifying activities

Management must group together related activities, so that the same activities are not duplicated by different people in different places.

5.2.4 Allocating staff

This step is the starting point of the job-design process. Management must decide exactly how many and what kind of people will be needed to do the work in each division.

5.2.5 Assigning authority and responsibility

Management must decide precisely what authority (power) and responsibility go with each post or position, so that whoever fills a position knows exactly what his or her duties, authority and responsibilities are. The relationship between the different posts and divisions must be clearly set out in order to encourage liaison (close connection) and co-operation.

5.2.6 Facilitating (encouraging) work

Everything should be prepared beforehand, because plans will only work if all the requirements (such as workers, equipment, procedures, and budgets) are available at the right time and place. Management must inform other staff members of the work methods, so that the plans can be carried out correctly and in good time.

5.3 Principles (basic rules) of organising

When managing the organisation of a business, certain principles are used.

5.3.1 Co-ordination

Co-ordination means putting together the parts of the business to achieve the outcome one wants, in the most efficient way. Co-ordination covers all management functions, and is one of the most important principles in the organising process.

There are three parts to co-ordination:
- the chain of command
- unity of command
- span of control.

5.3.1.1 The chain of command

The **chain of command** means the line of authority that flows from the top of the business down to any employee. This chain clarifies relations, avoids confusion and tends to improve decision-making and communication.[2]

5.3.1.2 Unity of command

This principle means that each employee should answer to only one immediate superior (person above her or him). The reasoning goes: if each employee has only one manager, this will make it easier for the employee to understand what is required of her or him. Not being clear about authority can lead to conflict, frustration and inefficiency.[3]

However, matrix organisations (see Section 5.4.5) use a dual (double) line of command because they believe that this helps in co-ordinating across functions and between different locations.

5.3.1.3 Span of control

The **span of control** refers to the number of direct subordinates (people in a lower position) reporting to any manager. The span of management may vary greatly from manager to manager, but generally about eight subordinates can be linked to a manager. Overloading a manager with too many subordinates can lead to poor performance, inefficiency and a lack of control.[4]

A manager's span of control can be influenced by:
- the manager's training, qualifications and competence (ability)
- the subordinates' training, qualifications and competence
- the physical distances between employees (the further separated employees are, the less the manager's span of control)
- the degree of unsupervised tasks included in the manager's job description
- the interaction required with the subordinates (the more interaction that is required, the less the manager's span of control)
- the similarity of the subordinates' tasks (the less similar the tasks, the less the manager's span of control)
- the level of standardisation (how defined it is) of the subordinates' work (the less standardised the work is, the less the manager's span of control)
- the frequency of new problems (the more frequent new problems are, the less the manager's span of control)
- the strictness of control required (the stricter control that is required, the less the manager's span of control).

5.3.2 Authority

Authority is the right to make decisions, issue orders and use resources. The types of authority that a business uses will depend on how it is structured (built or put together).

5.3.2.1 Line authority

Line authority refers to the direct authority that a manager has over an employee who is under her or his line of command. For example, a marketing manager can issue a direct order to an employee working in the marketing department.

5.3.2.2 Staff authority

Staff authority is more a matter of giving advice, and is most common on the middle-management level. An example of staff authority is when the legal manager advises the marketing manager about new competitive advertising laws.

5.3.2.3 Line-and-staff authority

Line-and-staff authority is when line managers and staff managers form a collaborative (combined) partnership. Line departments would not be successful without the support of staff departments.

5.3.2.4 Functional authority

Functional authority is the right that staff specialists have to give orders to line employees in an established area of responsibility. For example, employees from the safety department may instruct employees from the production department to follow the safety regulations.

5.3.2.5 Project authority

Project authority is the horizontal (sideways) authority of a project manager, which can extend over many different departments.

The difference between authority and power

Most people confuse the terms 'authority' and 'power'. But a manager's authority goes with the management level of his or her job, while power refers to an individual's ability to influence decisions. Because the formal rights that come with a managerial position are just one means by which an individual can affect the decision process, authority can be seen as part of the larger concept of power.

To illustrate the difference between authority and power, consider the example of a CEO's secretary. While the secretary may have little authority, he or she probably has a great deal of power because this secretary has a considerable say over whom the CEO sees and when. This secretary may be low in the authority hierarchy but is close to the power core.[5]

FIGURE 5.1 Authority versus power

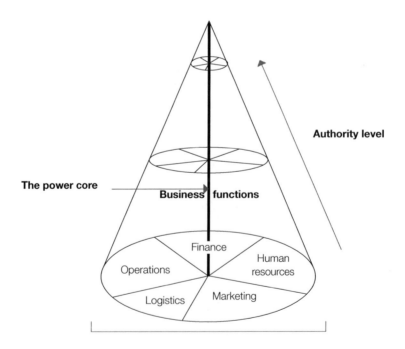

SOURCE: Adapted from Robbins, S.P. & De Cenzo, D.A., 2011. *Fundamentals of management*. 7th edition. Upper Saddle River: Prentice Hall. p. 136.

5.3.3 Responsibility

Responsibility means the duty to do certain work. In accepting a job, the employee takes responsibility for performing the activity involved in it. The employee should always know the nature, scope (range) and details of specific job responsibilities whether she or he is at a managerial level or not.[6]

5.3.4 Accountability

Accountability is any way of ensuring that the employee who is supposed to do a job in fact performs it, and does so correctly. In other words, accountability means that an employee must give an 'account' of the activities and tasks that were allocated to her or him. No organisation can function effectively without a system of accountability.[7]

5.3.5 Delegation

Delegation is the process by which managers allocate (give) to subordinates the responsibility and authority to make decisions about goals and carry them out   in certain situations.

When delegating, a manager can use the following guidelines:

- Establish measurable goals and standards to which the subordinates agree.
- Define authority and responsibility to the subordinates. Make sure that the subordinates understand the tasks that they must do, as well as the range of their authority.
- Involve the subordinates in day-to-day activities and decision-making.
- Expect the subordinates to complete their tasks on their own.
- Empower the subordinates with the necessary training for them to have the skills and knowledge to do their jobs.
- Provide timely, accurate feedback to enable each subordinate to compare her or his performance against the set standards, and correct any deficiencies (things that are lacking).

What can a manager delegate?

Although the distinction between accountability, responsibility and delegation may appear to be only a technical one, it is not. For example, a line manager might be held accountable to higher management for the way in which the operating supplies are looked after in the department. The manager has the choice to delegate this responsibility with the necessary authority to one of his employees. This employee must now take all the necessary steps to protect these supplies. If the employee was to misuse these supplies or to lose track of them, the manager might discipline the employee for failing to carry out her or his responsibility in this matter. But the manager will still be held accountable to her or his line manager for what happened, regardless of who was at fault. In other words, you can delegate responsibility, but you cannot delegate accountability.

5.3.5.1 **Centralisation and decentralisation**

The **centralisation** and **decentralisation** of authority are management philosophies of delegation. Centralisation is the degree to which the decision-making power is concentrated at a single point in the organisation. Decentralisation, on the other hand, means including lower-level management in the decision-making process.

Ideally, decision-making should take place at the level of the people who are most directly affected, and know the most about the problem. This is particularly important when the business environment is changing fast, and decisions must be made quickly. The level that deals directly with problems and opportunities has the most relevant information and can best predict the consequences of decisions.[8]

There is no absolute centralisation or decentralisation. No manager can make all the decisions by her- or himself, but also all the decisions cannot be delegated.

5.3.6 Specialisation

Specialisation refers to the division of work in order to improve how goals are achieved. Few employees have the necessary skills, knowledge and expertise to perform every task in a business, so employees with special skills are appointed to work in a division where they can apply their special skills, interests and knowledge to their jobs.

A real-life example of specialisation can be seen in the building business illustrated in Figure 5.2.

FIGURE 5.2 Example of specialisation in a building business

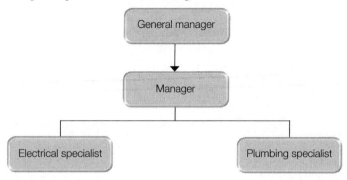

5.3.7 Divisionalisation

When a business grows, it usually gets more diversified (containing differences). Because the business's departments are likely to find it hard to manage a wide variety of products, customers and places, the business may restructure (change its structure) using divisionalisation. **Divisionalisation** means creating self-managing units within a business. Each division then has its own departments.

There are several ways to create a divisional structure.

5.3.7.1 **A divisional structure based on business functions**

Most businesses have certain basic functions that must be performed. For example, the different divisions of the business will all have logistics, operations, finance, marketing, and human-resources departments.

FIGURE 5.3 Divisionalisation according to business functions

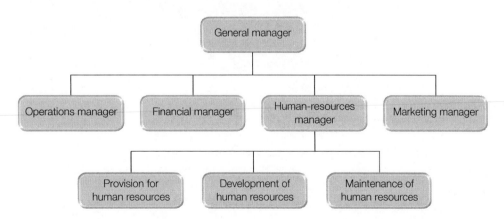

A functional structure can also be organised around a business's value chain. A value chain is a series of activities that flow from getting raw materials to the delivering of a complete product. In other words, a value chain describes the relationships among separate activities that create a good or service.[9]

FIGURE 5.4 A generic (whole group) value chain

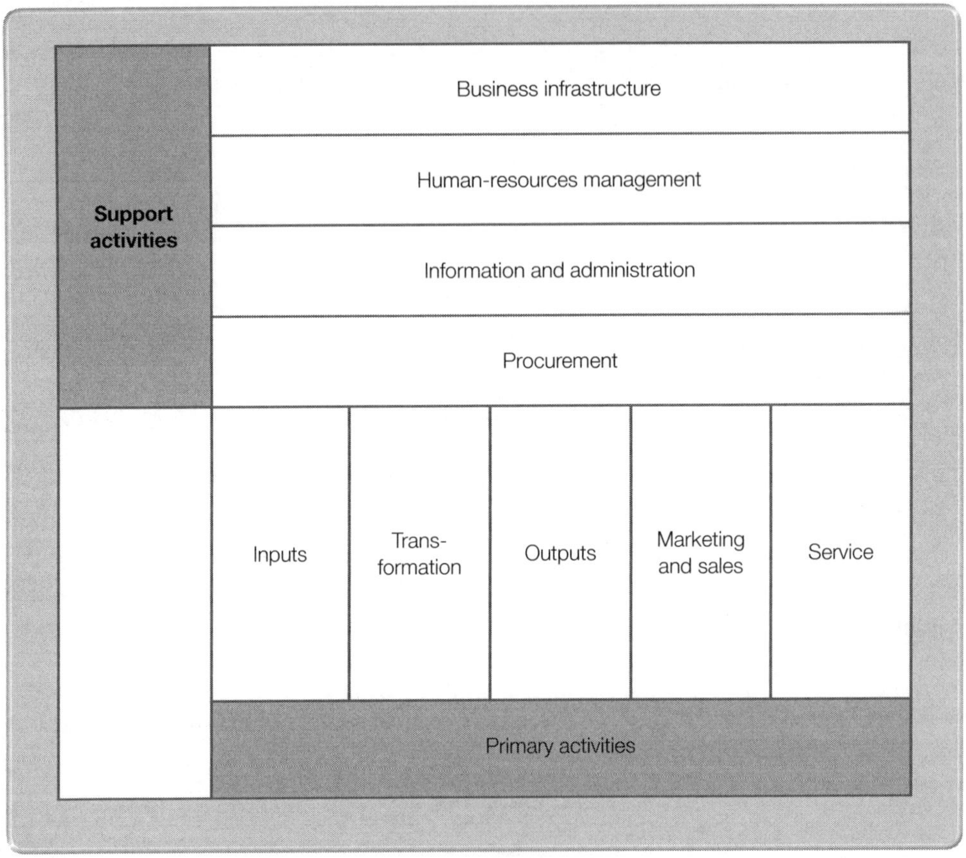

Support activities	Business infrastructure				
	Human-resources management				
	Information and administration				
	Procurement				
	Inputs	Trans-formation	Outputs	Marketing and sales	Service
	Primary activities				

5.3.7.2 **A divisional structure based on products**

In an operational business, all the functions that contribute to a given product are grouped together under one manager. Because this structure is fairly flexible (easily changed) it is suitable when the environment is unstable (not fixed) and the business must adapt quickly to changes in the environment.

FIGURE 5.5 Divisionalisation according to product

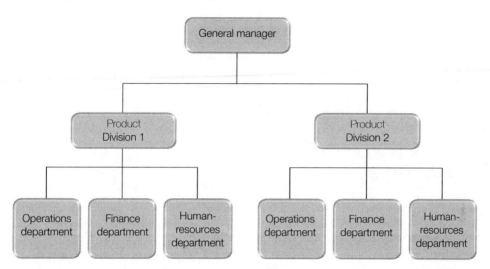

5.3.7.3 **A divisional structure based on geographic location (place on the earth)**

Businesses can build divisions in many different geographic areas. The biggest advantage for businesses with geographical divisions is that the business can focus on the customers' needs and provide faster service. Like all the other forms of divisionalisation, duplicating activities across geographic areas is expensive.

5.3.7.4 **A divisional structure based on projects**

When divisionalisation is based on projects, the organisation has functional divisions that overlap with other divisions. Therefore there are dual reporting relationships where some employees report to two managers. A structure like that can be useful with co-ordination, particularly for global businesses.

5.3.7.5 **A divisional structure based on consumer or client needs**

Divisionalisation according to consumer or client needs normally occurs (takes place) in businesses that provide services and want to meet the special needs of their consumers or clients. The divisions are based on the needs of the consumer or client.

FIGURE 5.6 Divisionalisation according to geographic location

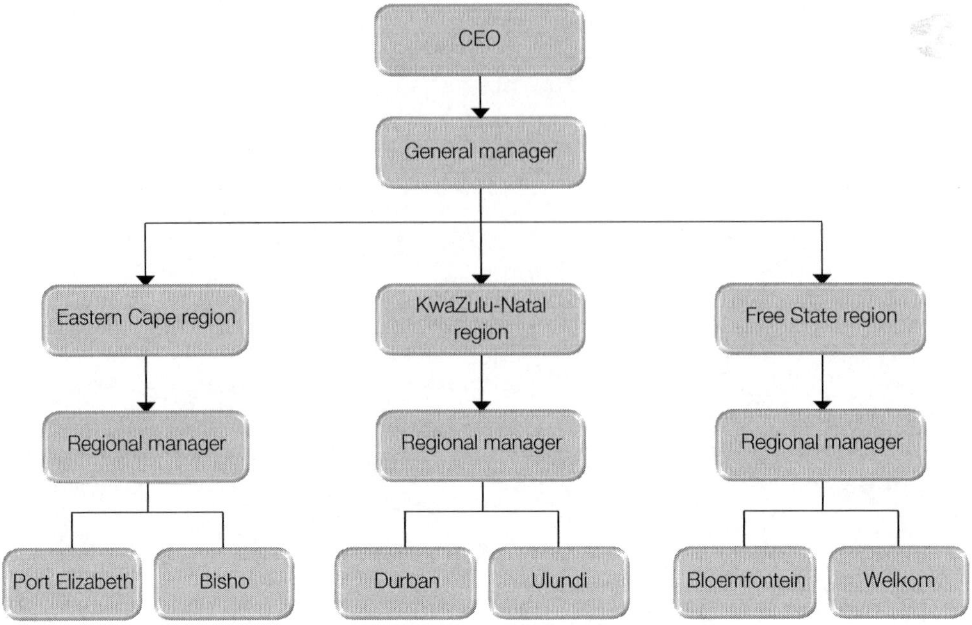

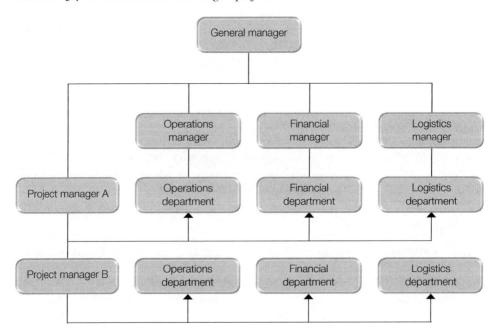

FIGURE 5.7 Divisionalisation according to projects

FIGURE 5.8 Divisionalisastion according to consumer or client needs

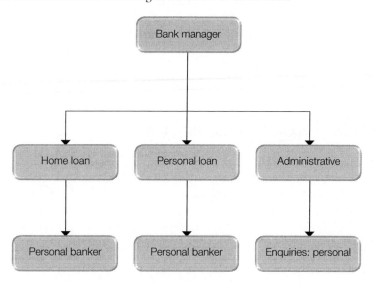

FIGURE 5.9 An example of a line organisational structure

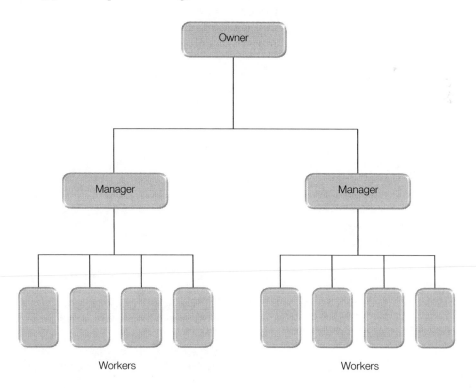

5.4 **Organisational structures**

The **organisational structure** of a business helps the business to achieve its goals by providing a framework (system or plan) for managers to divide responsibilities, allocate authority, co-ordinate activities, control performance, and hold employees accountable for their work.[10]

5.4.1 The line organisational structure

The **line organisational structure** is a simple hierarchy (system of levels from lowest to highest) where the lines of authority run vertically (straight down) from the top to the bottom of a business. Each line manager has authority (direct control) over particular subordinates.

This organisational structure is used mostly by small businesses. The most important characteristic of the line organisation is a clear vertical line of authority.

5.4.2 The line-and-staff organisational structure

A **line-and-staff organisational structure** has vertical lines of authority for its basic functions, but staff specialists are added to perform more complicated functions. Staff

FIGURE 5.10 An example of a line–and–staff organisation

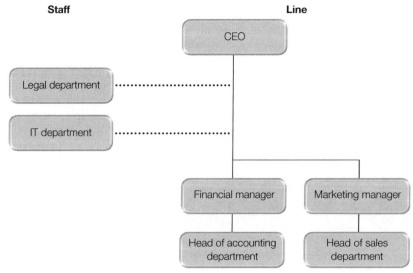

specialists cannot give orders that must be obeyed. Staff authority gives advice and support to the line–management hierarchy.

5.4.3 The functional organisational structure

In many cases the structure of a line organisation reflects the basic functions of a business. In this case the structure is often called a 'functional organisational structure'. Managers have line authority over functional activities such as marketing. 'Functional authority' is the right to control activities which are linked with specific staff responsibility and are carried out in another department. This functional authority gives the specialist the power to set goals and to see to their implementation within the clearly defined authority.

FIGURE 5.11 An example of a functional organisational structure

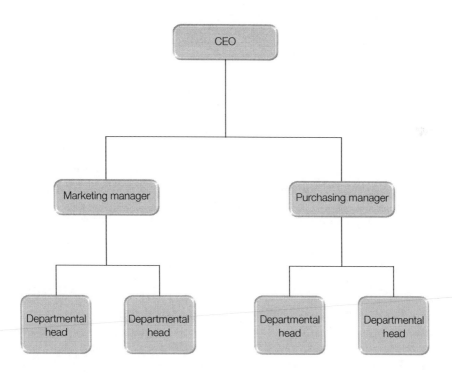

5.4.4 The divisional organisational structure

A **divisional organisational structure** aims to support self-contained divisions. These divisions are in most cases independent (work on their own), with a divisional manager responsible for the operations activities and having operational decision-making authority.

FIGURE 5.12 An example of a divisional organisational structure

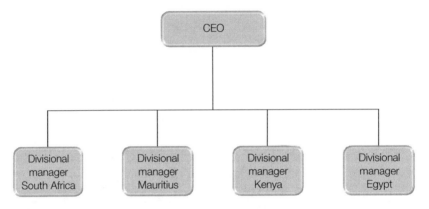

5.4.5 The matrix organisational structure

A **matrix organisational structure** uses both vertical and horizontal lines of authority. The vertical functional line of authority provides control inside functional departments, while the horizontal divisional line provides co-ordination across functional departments. The advantage of this structure is that the organisation can undertake a variety of projects at the same time, while the disadvantage of this structure is that unity of command is not always possible because a staff member can have two heads to whom feedback must be given.[11]

5.4.6 The teams organisational structure

A new trend in divisionalisation is to use a **teams organisational structure**. Two different kinds of teams can be distinguished, namely the cross-functional team and the permanent team. A **cross-functional team** is a selected group of employees from different functional departments who meet as a team to solve shared problems. A **permanent team** is a group of employees from several functions whose permanent job is to solve continuing general problems. A teams organisational structure helps a business to be more flexible in the competitive global environment.[12]

FIGURE 5.13 An example of a matrix organisational structure

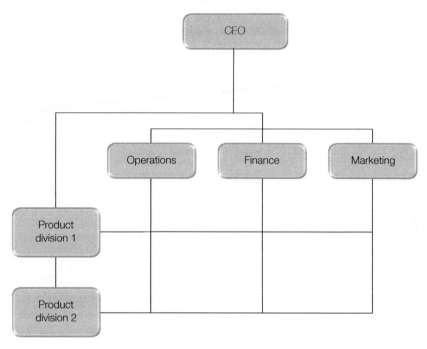

FIGURE 5.14 A teams organisation

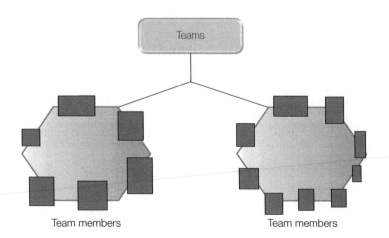

5.4.7 The network organisational structure

A **network organisational structure** has its business functions operating as separate businesses, which are run by a small headquarters business. Instead of the various business functions operating under one roof, these services come from separate businesses that are working under contract, and are connected electronically (computers, Internet, e-mail) to the central office.[13] An example of a network organisational structure is where a group of independent brokers (agents who buy and sell things) with different areas of expertise form a new firm. This new firm will act as a one-stop service for all the customers. For example, if the customer needs a person to help her or him with their short-term insurance, or with financial advice, they will refer the customer to the broker who specialises in that area. This new firm will also be responsible for all their administration activities.

FIGURE 5.15 An example of a network organisational structure

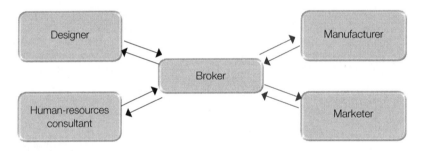

5.5 **The changing organisation**

Today's businesses function in an 'economy of ideas'. Never before in the history of business has so much change been introduced so quickly. Many of these changes are due to the changing business environment, in particular the rise of new communication technologies, multinational businesses, and globalisation.

Uncertainty occurs when the external environment is rapidly changing and complex. An uncertain environment causes:
• increased differences among divisions/departments
• an increased need for co-ordination between divisions/departments
• a need for the business to adapt to change.

In a **changing organisation** the most important energy comes from good, new ideas. Knowledge management means using the intellects of the people who work for the business. It refers to the finding, unlocking and sharing of the people's expertise, their skills, their wisdom and, lastly, their relationships. Communication among different divisions, departments or other sub-units of the business, must be of a high level.

Management changes have become a critical managerial function. For a business to be able to adjust to market needs, it will sometimes mean that the business has to change its whole organisational structure. Businesses in the past were designed to make life easier for management, rather than to please the customer. Today businesses are realising they must have an organisational structure that can respond quickly to the needs of the market.

A business's environment determines a business's strategy, and this strategy determines the business's structure; therefore the business structure must change with the environment. Only if changes in the environment are recognised will it be possible to keep developing an effective organisational structure.

CASE STUDY: Jonny Happy Feet Limited

Jonny Happy Feet Limited is a manufacturer and distributor of shoes. Jonny Happy Feet Limited was established in 2005 in Port Elizabeth. They mainly specialised in the making of formal men's and ladies' shoes, but in 2009 the shoe market for sport shoes became so profitable that they decided to enter into this market.

After a study of the sport shoes market, Jonny Happy Feet Limited decided to start producing running, tennis and squash shoes. Before they started with the production of sport shoes they spent a substantial amount on research and development.

As a result of the increasing sales of sport shoes the management considered reorganisation. The business was making use of a functional organisation structure. John Matamela, the managing director, felt that the business should be organised in product divisions. The head of the marketing section, Andy Ndala and his staff agreed. However Randy Negota, the head of the manufacturing division, thought that a functional division would be more advantageous. Shara Latola, from the financial department, was indifferent and had no preference.

John Matamela's reorganisation plan made provision for three production divisions namely, formal men's shoes, formal ladies' shoes and sport shoes. The sport shoes section was responsible for more than 65% of the business's sales, and the formal men's shoes section was showing signs of rapid growth. According to the market research department's predictions, the formal ladies' shoes sales should increase in the near future.

QUESTIONS

Develop a proposed organisation structure.

1. What recommendations would you make to John Matemela regarding the organisational structure of Jonny Happy Feet Limited? Motivate your recommendation.
2. What recommendations would you make to John Matemela regarding centralisation and decentralisation?

ANSWERS

1.

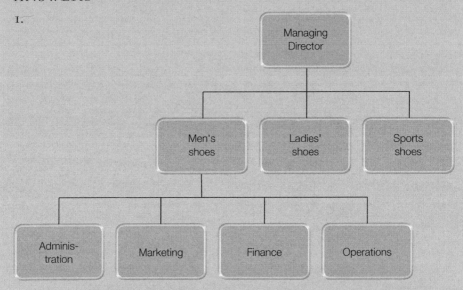

A product-divisional strategy and organisational structure are recommended. The business's strengths and weaknesses have to be determined. Training should take place in new areas. The challenges coming from Randy Negota, the head of the manufacturing division, is possibly due to a lack of talent.

2. Decentralisation. Ideally, decision-making should occur at the level of the people who are most directly affected and have the most intimate knowledge about the problems. This is particularly important when the business environment is fast-changing and decisions must be made quickly. The level that deals directly with problems and opportunities has the most relevant information and can best predict the consequences of decisions.

SUMMARY

Organising involves the use of certain principles for identifying and arranging the activities and resources of a business. This can be done by structuring the business at both horizontal and vertical levels through the allocation of duties, responsibilities and authority to members of the workforce and to divisions. Through organisation, an effective business structure can be developed that will contribute to achieving the objectives of the business in the most efficient way possible, and will encourage co-operation.

GLOSSARY

accountability: the final result which a person cannot delegate to anyone else

authority: the right to make decisions and to take action

centralisation: the decision-making power is concentrated at a single point in the organisation

chain of command: the line of authority in the organisation that runs from the top level to the lowest levels

changing organisation: an organisation that changes its structure

co-ordination: linking the various activities of the organisation

cross-functional team: members of the workforce who work together

decentralisation: lower-level management takes part and gives input into the decision-making process

delegation: the process by which managers get work done through the efforts of others

divisionalisation: departments are grouped based on similar outputs

functional authority: the right of staff specialists to give orders to line employees in an established area of responsibility

line-and-staff authority: line managers and staff managers form a group partnership

line-and-staff organisational structure: when an organisation has vertical lines of authority, but also has staff specialists

line authority: the direct authority that a manager has over an employee

line organisational structure: a hierarchy where the lines of authority run vertically from the top to the bottom of a business

matrix organisational structure: a system with both vertical and horizontal lines of authority

network organisational structure: its business functions work as separate businesses, which are run by a small headquarters business

organisational structure: a formal system of working relationships that both separate and combine the activities of the organisation

organising: co-ordinating activities and the allocation of work to certain people so that goals can be achieved

permanent team: employees from several functions who are permanently assigned to solve continuing problems of general interest

project authority: the horizontal authority of a project manager

responsibility: accepting the results of actions and duties

power: influence over others

span of control: the number of people a manager can control

specialisation: activities that are divided into smaller meaningful units

staff authority: mostly advice from the middle-management level

teams organisational structure: a new trend in divisionalisation that uses cross-functional teams or permanent teams

unity of command: an employee is answerable to only one manager

MULTIPLE-CHOICE QUESTIONS

1. A formal system of working relationships that both separates and integrates the activities of the organisation is known as:
   a) vertical structure
   b) decentralise structure
   c) centralise structure
   d) organisational structure

2. The co-ordination of activities and the allocation of work to certain people so that the goals and objectives of the organisation can be achieved is known as:
   a) organising
   b) planning
   c) leading
   d) controlling

3. When all important decisions are referred to the top, it is known as:
   a) decentralisation
   b) delegation
   c) co-ordination
   d) centralisation

4. Knowledge management refers to the _____ of the people's expertise.
   a) finding, unlocking and sharing
   b) finding, unlocking and shaping
   c) finding, locking and shaping
   d) finding, locking and sharing

5. If one looks at the interaction between the degree of complexity and the rate of change in the external environment, the degree of complexity in choosing an orgnisational structure is a:
   a) low uncertainty
   b) high uncertainty
   c) low certainty
   d) high certainty

REFERENCES AND END-NOTES

1. LE ROUX, E.E., DE BEER, A.A., FERREIRA, E.J., HÜBNER, C.P., JACOBS, H., KRITZINGER, A.A., LABUSCHAGNE, M., STAPELBERG, J.E. & VENTER, C.H. 1999. *Business management: A practical and interactive approach.* Johannesburg: Heineman.
2. HELLRIEGEL, D., JACKSON, S.E., SLOCUM, J., STAUDE, G., AMOS, T., KLOPPER, H.B., LOUW, L. & OOSTHUIZEN, T. 2001. *Management.* (SA ed.) Cape Town: Oxford University Press.
3. Ibid.
4. Ibid.
5. ROBBINS, S.P. & DECENZO, D.A. 2008. *Fundamentals of Management: Essential Concepts and Applications.* 6th ed. Upper Saddle River: New Jersey: Pearson/Prentice Hall.
6. MONDY, R.W. & PREMEAUX, S.R. 1993. *Management: Concepts, practices and skills.* 6th ed. Boston: Allyn & Bacon.
7. Ibid.
8. ROBBINS, S.P. & DECENZO, D.A. 2001. *Supervision today.* Upper Saddle River: Prentice Hall.
9. BATEMAN, T.S. & SCOTT, A.S. 2002. *Management competing in the new era.* 5th ed. New York: McGraw-Hill.
10. OOSTHUIZEN, T.F.J. 2002. *Management tasks for managerial success.* Johannesburg: Entrepro Publishers.
11. DE BEER, A.A. & ROSSOUW, D. 2005. *Focus on Operational Management: A generic approach.* Cape Town: Juta.
12. DAFT, R.L. 1995. *Understanding Management.* Forth Worth: Dryden Press.
13. Ibid.

ANSWERS TO MULTIPLE-CHOICE QUESTIONS

1. Answer = d)
2. Answer = a)
3. Answer = d)
4. Answer = a)
5. Answer = b)

CHAPTER 6

Leading

Maggie Holtzhausen

PURPOSE OF THIS CHAPTER

This chapter discusses the important function of leading in a business. It explains the difference between managing and leading. It also looks at some leadership theories and tools. Lastly, it discusses some problems and trends in leadership.

LEARNING OUTCOMES

This chapter should enable you to:

- define leadership and discuss the leadership process
- discuss the importance of leading as one of the five management functions
- explain the differences between management and leadership
- discuss some leadership theories
- identify (recognise) leadership's tools of the trade
- explain the problems of leadership and diversity
- identify some problems and trends connected with leadership.

6.1 **Introduction**

Leading an organisation is a complex process with many parts, and defining it is not easy. It will probably be defined differently in different societies.[1]

For the purposes of this book, two definitions of **leadership** are:

- the process by which a person exerts influence over other people, inspires them, and directs their activities to help them reach group goals.[2]
- the process of influencing employees to work willingly towards reaching their goals.[3]

The three components (parts) of leadership (see Figure 6.1 and the discussion in Section 6.2 below) can be seen in these definitions. They are:

- **the leader** – the one who gets the process off the ground (in other words, who makes sure that something happens as a result of the interaction between the leader and the followers)
- **the followers** – the organised group (in other words, the employees)
- **the situation** – the given set of circumstances and environment (both external and internal) in which the organisation functions.

FIGURE 6.1 The three components of leadership

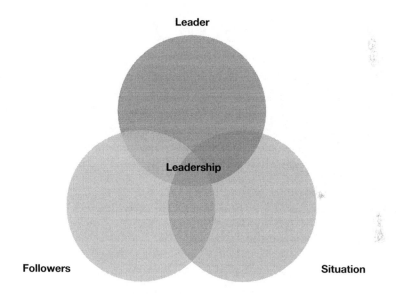

SOURCE: Adapted from Hughes, R.L., Ginnet, R.C. & Curphy, G.J. 2006. Leadership. *Enhancing the lessons of experience.* (5th ed.) Singapore: Irwin McGraw-Hill. p. 1.

Leadership aims at achieving the goals of a group or organisation. Because our focus is on management, we will focus on the goals of an organisation. Note that the second definition also points to the fact that leaders inspire people to willingly take part in this behaviour.

A business will only succeed if someone is leading the people in that business effectively. Part of the responsibility of managers in an organisation is to lead it effectively to achieve success. To do this, Charlton, in Amos *et al.*, points out that: 'it is the competence of managers and, in particular, leaders of people, that determines, in large part, the returns that organisations realise from their human capital, or human resources.'[4]

Some crucial aspects of leadership are:[5]

- The essence of leadership lies in vision, inspiration and momentum (keep moving).
- Leadership is almost always connected with change – in fact, leaders are often referred to as 'change-agents'.
- Leading is a highly creative activity.
- Leadership is basically a personal activity.
- Leaders are more effective when they get buy-in from their followers.

6.2 **The three components of leadership**

One of the most important things to keep in mind about leadership is that it is not a position, but a process. As Hughes *et al.* emphasise, 'leadership involves something happening as a result of the interaction between a leader and followers'.[6] This chapter will therefore focus on the process of leading. It will study aspects of the leaders, the followers, and the situation (or context). These three components are the cornerstones of leadership. Differently put, leadership is the outcome of a complicated set of exchanges among these three elements.

6.2.1 An interactive framework of leadership

The three elements of leadership (the leader, the followers, and the situation) can be studied separately or together to see the interaction among them. When the three elements are studied together they are referred to as an 'interactive framework'. Some of the theories in this chapter focus on just one component, while others refer to all three components.

Figure 6.1 can be adapted into Figure 6.2 by including a number of factors:

- The leader comes to the table as an individual with a unique personal history, interests and characteristics.
- The followers' expectations, maturity levels and skills will also affect leadership. There is thus movement both from the leader downwards to the followers, and also upwards from followers helping in the process of problem-solving.
- Finally, the situation is important. Hughes *et al.* put it like this: 'the right behaviour in one situation is not necessarily the right behaviour in another situation'.[7]

FIGURE 6.2 An interactive framework of leadership

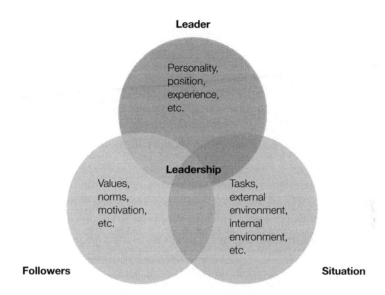

SOURCE: Hughes, R.L., Ginnet, R.C. & Curphy, G.J. 2006. *Leadership. Enhancing the lessons of experience.* (5th ed.) Singapore: Irwin McGraw-Hill. p.24.

6.3 **Leadership versus management**

Although an organisation cannot be effectively managed without strong leadership, leadership is not the same as management. Management is wider than leadership, because the manager is responsible for more tasks than leading.[8] In a way, management is involved in the everyday running of the business, while leadership bring an inspiring and emotional element into the organisation.[9]

People who are managers are not necessarily leaders, and the other way round. The leader of an informal group may have more influence on such a group than its manager.[10] Organisations may also have self-managed work teams, which will need both management and leadership. Ideally, organisations should have managers in key positions who are strong leaders at the same time. Many functions of management and leadership may actually overlap. Most importantly, both management and leadership are vital to organisational success.[11]

Figures 6.3 and 6.4 show how the elements of management and the elements of leadership differ. For example, where a leader will have more new ideas, a manager will work with existing activities.

FIGURE 6.3 Elements of management

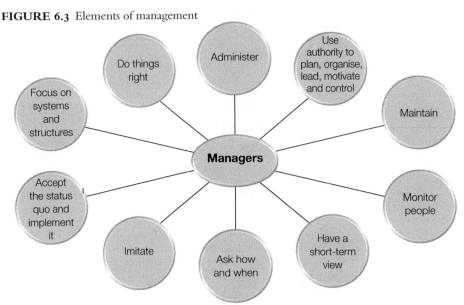

Sources: Adapted from Hughes, R.L., Ginnet, R.C. & Curphy, G.J. 2006. *Leadership. Enhancing the lessons of experience.* (5th ed.) Singapore: Irwin McGraw-Hill. pp. 9–10; & Swanepoel, B.J., Erasmus, B.J., Van Wyk, M. & Schenk, H. 2003. *South African human resource management. Theory and practice.* (3rd ed.) Cape Town: Juta & Co. pp. 356–358.

FIGURE 6.4 Elements of leadership

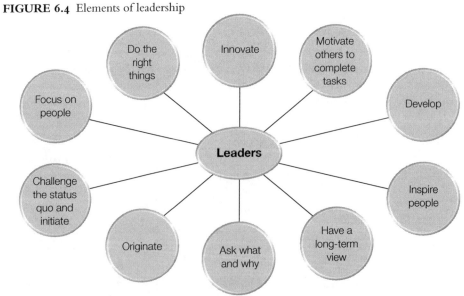

Sources: Adapted from Hughes, R.L., Ginnet, R.C. & Curphy, G.J. 2006. *Leadership. Enhancing the lessons of experience.* (5th ed.) Singapore: Irwin McGraw-Hill. pp. 6–10.; & Swanepoel, B.J., Erasmus, B.J., Van Wyk, M. & Schenk, H. 2003. *South African human resource management. Theory and practice.* (3rd ed.) Cape Town: Juta & Co. pp. 356–358.

6.4 A brief history of leadership theories

Many theories on leadership have developed over the years. These can be divided into earlier and more recent theories, although some thoughts run through both periods.

6.4.1 Earlier leadership theories

There are three main categories of earlier leadership theories. These are illustrated in Figure 6.5.

FIGURE 6.5 Earlier leadership theories

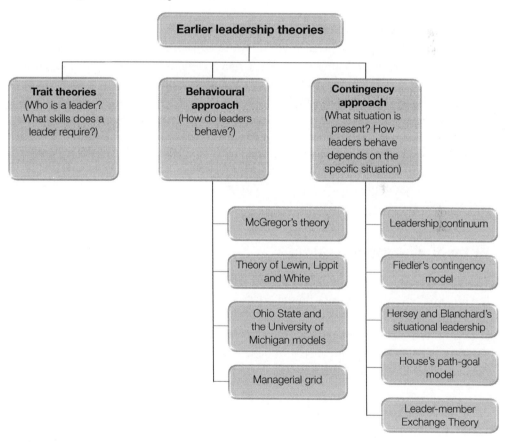

Source: Adapted from Amos, T., Ristow, A. & Ristow, L., Pearse, N.J. 2008. *Human resource management.* (3rd ed.) Lansdowne: Juta & Co. p.200.

6.4.1.1 **Trait theories**

The earliest research on leadership assumed that physical, social and personal characteristics are inborn in leaders. Traits (characteristics, qualities) like good communication skills, confidence and honesty, were thought to be part of a good leader, and distinguished leaders from non-leaders. **Trait theories** assumed that good leaders were born, not made. So research focused on deciding what traits were necessary for a good leader. However, in the late 1950s researchers decided that no single trait or group of traits exists that separates leaders from non-leaders.[12]

6.4.1.2 **Behaviour theories**

From the late 1940s to the 1960s, research focused on the behaviour patterns of leaders (in other words, how they delegated, communicated and motivated their followers).[13] Lewin, Lippit and White's theory was that there were 'three classic styles of leader behaviour'.[14] According to this theory, leaders are either authoritarian (the leader makes all the decisions), democratic (followers have a say in decision-making), or laissez-faire (the leader shares authority with the followers).

In general, **behaviour theories** distinguish between two broad groups of behaviour.[15] The first group is people-orientated (they meet the emotional/social needs of employees). The second group is task-orientated (they focus on work methods and jobs to be done). This forms the basis of the research done at the University of Michigan.[16]

6.4.1.3 **Situational approaches**

According to **situational approaches** (also called 'contingency approaches') to leadership, effective leadership depends on the situation in which it occurs. Effective leadership is therefore seen as a process of analysing the situation, and then choosing the best leadership style to suit it.[17] **Fiedler's Contingency Theory** is an example. According to this model, effective group behaviour depends on a good match between the leader's style and the situation.

6.4.2 Newer leadership approaches

From these earlier leadership theories, newer approaches have developed. Figure 6.6 shows some of these approaches and examples of each.

6.4.2.1 **A re-birth of earlier trait theories**

In the last few years trait theories have again become prominent. The interest lies in understanding leaders' performance by trying to find what characteristics people think of when they say someone is a leader.[18]

One group concentrate on competencies (abilities) instead of personality traits. Recent researchers have named eight competencies that are widely accepted as signs of leadership: drive, leadership, motivation, integrity (honour), self-confidence, intelligence, knowledge of business, and emotional intelligence (using one's emotions intelligently).[19]

Another group concentrate on principles (codes of conduct) and beliefs rather than personality traits.[20] According to this approach, leaders have and use honesty, integrity, openness, humanity, equality, recognition, participation, and empowerment. Therefore they stress values and attitudes in the behaviour and relationships of the leader.

The third group concentrates on ethics, and is closely related to the principle-centred group.[21] Ethics are standards of right and wrong, and they influence leadership behaviour. This approach examines how the actions of leaders can encourage an ethical or unethical culture in an organisation.

FIGURE 6.6 Some newer leadership approaches

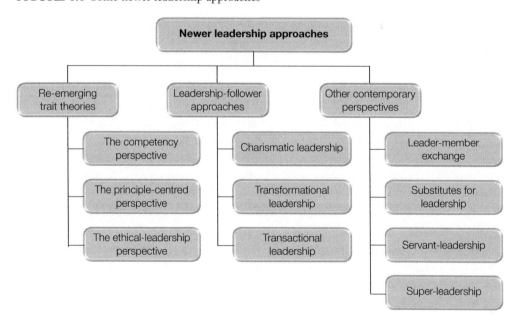

6.4.2.2 **A move towards leadership–follower approaches**

A number of new approaches move away from the earlier leadership beliefs to focus on the interaction between the leader and the follower.[22] These leadership theories now focused more on a combination of the trait, behaviour, and situational leadership styles, rather than just one of these aspects.[23]

An example of such a theory is the **Theory of Charismatic Leadership**.[24] This theory assumes that charisma (great charm) is a trait of a leader (and so this theory is also related to the earlier trait theories). This theory suggests that charismatic leaders have a special type of relationship with followers. Charismatic leaders have vision, and will establish goals and objectives to reach those goals. They will also have a strong personal commitment to those goals. They are seen as unconventional and self-confident, and as radical change-agents. In South Africa, Nelson Mandela is probably the best-known example of a charismatic leader.

Avolio and Bass's **Theory of Transformational Leadership** is closely related to the **Theory of Charismatic Leadership**. It looks at the set of abilities that allow a leader to recognise the need for change, and to create a vision of how to achieve that change.[25] The Transformational Theory of Leadership uses four 'I's to describe this style of leadership:

- *idealised influence* (Transformational leaders behave in a way that makes them role-models to their followers.)
- *inspiration* (Transformational leaders motivate and inspire their followers by giving meaning and challenge to their work.)
- *intellectual* stimulation (Transformational leaders stimulate their followers to think differently about their situations with new and creative ideas.)
- *individual* consideration (Transformational leaders pay special attention to followers' individual needs for achievement and growth by acting as mentors or coaches.)

(See also Section 6.6.2 for a discussion on *Ubuntu* – a closely related African leadership style.)

Avolio and Bass's **Theory of Transactional Leadership** suggests that all leaders use a combination of leadership styles.[26] The use of contingent (dependent) rewards is an example – employees are given compensation when they perform according to contract or what is expected. It is therefore almost like an arrangement that benefits both parties.

The management-by-exception (MBE) style is the opposite approach.[27] **Passive management by exception** is a leadership style where leaders only interfere with their followers' work if goals are not met. **Active management by exception** is a leadership style where leaders will correct followers if they are not trying their best.

According to Robbins *et al.*, the transformational leadership and transactional leadership styles are not opposites, and effective leadership can include both of them.[28]

6.4.2.3 **Other leadership perspectives (theories)**

At the moment, there are four other important leadership theories.[29]

The **Leader-member-exchange (LMX) Theory** focuses on the relationship between the leader and the followers, rather than on their qualities. A special relationship forms between the leader and each follower based on the leader's distribution of roles and responsibilities. Leaders often act differently towards different people, and often tend to have favourites.[30] This forms the basis of the LMX model. Two types of leadership-exchange relationships are formed:

- the in-group exchange – where the leader creates mutual trust, influence and attraction
- the out-group exchange – where the leader is seen as just a checker of her or his followers, without a relationship of trust and respect.

The **Substitutes-for-leadership Theory** challenges the need to have a leader – the argument being that experienced followers can follow their own minds to fulfil a task. According to this theory, certain individuals, jobs and conditions can actually act as substitutes for leadership – almost as if these conditions neutralise the leader's effect on her or his followers.[31]

The **Servant-leadership Theory** suggests that if people believe in serving others rather than themselves, followers will become wiser and more independent. Followers are therefore empowered.[32]

The **Super-leadership Theory** proposes that a leader can lead in such a way that followers learn to lead themselves. It is therefore closely related to self-management. The leader fulfils the role of coach, and followers are helped to think productively, which leads to increased feelings of self-control and personal motivation.

TABLE 6.1 The traditional versus the emerging views on leadership

Traditional views on leadership	Emerging views on leadership
Leadership is good management.	The leadership process is different from management.
Leaders have certain traits and behaviours.	Leaders and followers work together in a relationship.
Followers must conform to the leader's wishes.	Followers do what both the leaders and the followers want.
Leaders follow all organisational goals.	Leaders pursue goals influencing real change.
Leaders use any justifiable behaviours.	Leaders use influence.

SOURCE: Adapted from Swanepoel, B.J., Erasmus, B.J., Van Wyk, M. & Schenk, H. 2003. *South African human resource management. Theory and practice.* (3rd ed.) Cape Town: Juta & Co. p. 356.

Many other theories of leadership exist, and are coming out all the time.

6.5 **Leadership tools**

The structure and the authority relations created by the organisation (see Chapter 5) give managers the right to use authority, power, responsibility, accountability and delegation to persuade their employees to achieve the organisation's goals.[33] These items can be described as the apparatus used by leaders, or as the 'tools of the trade'. Du Toit *et al.* explain these concepts as follows:[34]

- authority – the right of a manager to give reasonable commands to, and expect action from her or his employees. (This includes demanding that tasks be completed and disciplining those who do not fulfil their tasks.)
- power – the ability of a manager to influence the behaviour of her or his employees (position power, or personal power)
- responsibility – the duty a manager has to achieve set organisational goals
- delegation – passing responsibility and authority for achieving goals, down the line of command, to employees
- accountability – judging how well employees meet their responsibilities.

6.6 **Leadership and diversity**

South Africa's unique diversity demands an unusual approach to leadership in South African organisations.

6.6.1 Leadership and gender

Most people agree that women change the situation in the workplace. While general ideas about men or women should not affect how individuals are seen, Werner *et al.* suggest some general differences between the leadership behaviour of men and women:[35]

- Women tend to be more relationship-orientated, while men tend to be more task-orientated.
- Women tend to be less assertive (clearly confident), and men tend to be more dominant (commanding).
- Women tend to be more adaptable (able to change) and flexible than men.
- Women tend to value themselves less than men.
- Women tend to use a more democratic and participative leadership style, while men tend to use a more autocratic (single head) and directive (commanding) leadership style.

These differences were supported by Booysen in a study of the influences on leadership among South African workers in the banking sector.[36] In that study, male managers scored higher on performance orientation, future orientation and assertiveness. Female managers valued social equality more. However, the one style is not totally different to the other – men can display more feminine styles and the other way round. Booysen concludes that a mixture of both styles can be useful to the organisation.

6.6.2 Leadership and culture

Culture (the customary beliefs, social forms, and traits of a racial, religious, or social group) is an important factor in deciding which leadership style will be most effective.[37] Robbins *et al.* give the example of the Asia Department Store in China which openly boasts about its 'heartless' management style. All their employees are sent to 2–4 weeks of military training in order to increase their obedience. In-house (belonging to the organisation) training takes place in public places where employees can be openly embarrassed by their mistakes. The authors point out that this is a clear example of leaders doing what their followers expect. More examples are cited by Robbins *et al*: Korean leaders are expected to be paternalistic (like a father) towards employees, whilst

Dutch leaders who praise an employee in public will most likely embarrass that employee. House *et al.* comment on the problems of cultural differences: 'It is clear that integrity is a universally desirable attribute. But does it mean the same thing to a Chinese as it does to an American? How do people in different cultures conceptualize, perceive and exhibit behaviour that reflects integrity? What specific behaviours comprise high integrity leadership, and do they have the same function and impact across cultures?'[38]

South African leaders need to understand diversity issues and manage these effectively. Diversity programmes, and using a diverse workforce, should be viewed as a way of improving organisational effectiveness. Robbins *et al.* refer to this as a 'culturally intelligent organisation'.[39] South African companies need to realise that an organisational culture that is closely centred around Europe may not be successful in the South African context.

For instance, African cultures do not support the idea that individual achievement is everything, but rather focus on the benefits of working together in a group. The concept of *Ubuntu*, a Southern African concept, means that 'we are what we are through our interaction with others'[40] or 'I am because of what you are'.[41] This informs African leadership styles, because it suggests that when leaders get in touch with their own humanity, they enable other people and their organisations to uncover their own authenticity (truth). *Ubuntu* suggests a concern for people, as well as being good and working for the common good.[42] African management will therefore not be founded on the singular authority of the manager, but will rather focus on building a spirit of agreement within a group. The manager values individual worth and promotes trust amongst the members. All the members of the group are consulted, and the aim is to reach consensus on matters.[43]

According to Avolio[44] *Ubuntu* is closely related to transformational leadership in the sense that it relates to transformational leaders who work towards creating a culture where each individual and group can reach their full potential (possibility). Team members are encouraged to sacrifice personal gains for the good of the group. Typical characteristics of an *Ubuntu* leadership style are open communication, creative co-operation, teamwork, and moral obligations (duties).[45]

Papi Molotsane on the need for robust and vigorous leadership in South Africa[46]

'As a business leader my experience is that the solution of a crisis happens when we are brutally honest about the nature of the problem. Only then will we ask the right questions that can produce the right answers. We can overcome the terrible burden of poverty and high unemployment and create a high-road future for this country and an African success story. To do so, we need the dedicated skills and leadership of all ... who are willing to use those skills not only for their own advantage, but particularly for the betterment of the society as a whole...

... South Africa needs competent leadership in every sphere of its national life.... What we need to make South Africa the world-class country it has all the potential to be, is world-class leadership. And leadership is in essence an ongoing learning experience ... The benchmarks I suggest we measure ourselves against as we mature in the leadership for which we have been well prepared, is to grow in emotional and spiritual intelligence as much as we have done in logical and analytical skills required by different fields of specialisation ...

There is no magic or quick-fix formula to being an effective leader ... It is no easy task. We will need to mobilise the very best of the skills, emotions, and values that we can muster, to develop the robust and vigorous leadership this country needs. To succeed, we need everyone in the leadership race to perform at the peak of their ability.'

6.6.3 Integrating diverse leadership styles

Swanepoel *et al.* highlight the importance of both gender and cultural diversity for South African organisations. They say: 'Only a diverse leadership team that includes both feminine and masculine and Eurocentric and Afrocentric strengths will be strong and flexible enough to help South African organisations to compete in today's highly competitive global marketplace'.[47] By managing diversity issues (rather than just obeying employment-equity laws, for example), an organisation may be really successful.

6.7 Worldwide leadership trends

A study by the Society for Human Resource Management (SHRM)[48] on workplace trends showed that there is a need for global leadership and a need to cultivate specific global leadership competencies. It also found a trend for employee-employer relationships to develop into partnerships. But probably the most important conclusion the SHRM reached was how important it is to build leadership capability. It stated that one of 'the key differentiators among organisations that thrive and survive in the next decade will be their ability to attract, grow and fully leverage (use) their leaders'.[49]

John Donahoe, President and CEO of the US-based global online marketplace eBay Inc, explains the future challenges of a CEO, and thus the organisation's leader, as follows:

'It is necessary to strike a balance between fighting each day to ensure your survival, while keeping a strong hand on the tiller in order to steady the ship. It's balancing the long term with the urgency of the short term and having the wisdom to discern what's what.'[50]

CASE STUDY: Me, myself as manager and leader[51]

Imagine that you are standing at your own retirement party. One of your colleagues, having worked for you for the past ten years, stands up and goes to the podium to pay tribute to you. What is said? Perhaps even more importantly, what is not said? Your job is to write the tribute that you would want to hear.

1. Your tribute should include:
   a) your main tasks and responsibilities as manager of the section
   b) your main tasks and responsibilities as leader of the section.
2. Highlight at least three specific characteristics of your leadership style and identify the effect that each may have had on your subordinates.
3. Give examples of those leaders that have inspired your own leadership style.
4. Mention some of the challenges you have faced as a manager and leader in a South African organisation, and how your leadership overcame them.
5. Finally, as an inspiration to others, describe an occasion when you felt you were a true leader. Describe your qualities as a leader, the characteristics of your followers, and the nature of the specific situation. What took place, who was involved, and what were the results?

SUMMARY

Good leadership, which is not the same thing as good management, is essential for organisational success. Good leadership is an interactive process influenced by the leader, the followers, and the situation it takes place in. There are diverse theories about what makes good leadership, but many models of leadership can be used in combination with others, as they often focus on different areas. Leadership faces many challenges today, such as globalisation and diverse workforces.

GLOSSARY

active management by exception: a leadership style where leaders will interfere with their followers' work when they are not making the effort expected of them

behaviour theories: theories that differentiate mainly between two broad groupings of behaviour, namely people-orientated leadership behaviour and task-orientated leadership behaviour

competency-based perspective: a leadership theory focusing on broader competencies, instead of personality traits

ethical-leadership perspective: a theory examining how the actions of leaders can encourage an ethical or unethical culture in an organisation

Fiedler's Contingency Theory: a theory based on the assumption that effective group behaviour depends on the appropriate match between the leader's style of relating to her or his followers, and the favourableness of the situation

Leader-member-exchange (LMX) Theory: a theory focusing on the quality of the relationship between the leader and followers

leadership: the process of influencing employees to work willingly toward the achievement of organisational objectives

leading: one of the management tasks, which involves bringing an inspirational and emotional element to the organisation through creating a shared vision and inspiring followers to achieve that vision

passive management by exception: a leadership style where leaders only interfere with their followers' work if desired goals are not met

principle-centred perspective: a leadership theory focusing on beliefs instead of personality traits

Servant-leadership Theory: a theory based on the idea that an increased service to others will empower others

situational approaches: leadership theories focusing on the process of analysing the situation, and then identifying the most effective leadership style accordingly

Super-leadership Theory: a theory based on the belief that a leader can lead in such a way that followers learn to lead themselves

Substitutes-for-leadership Theory: a theory challenging the necessity of leadership because experienced followers can follow their own minds and execute tasks

Theory of Charismatic Leadership: a leadership theory that assumes charisma to be a trait of a leader

Theory of Transactional Leadership: a theory based on the assumption that all leaders employ a combination of styles of leadership in an organisation

Theory of Transformational Leadership: a theory examining the set of abilities that allow a leader to recognise the need for change, and to create a vision of how to achieve that change effectively

trait theories: theories based on the assumption that certain physical, social and personal characteristics are inborn in leaders

MULTIPLE-CHOICE QUESTIONS

1. Which of the following statements about leading in the workplace context is incorrect?
   a) Leading refers to the process by which an individual exerts influence over other people and inspires, motivates and directs their activities to help achieve group or organisational goals.
   b) Leading involves something happening as a result of the interaction between the situation and followers.
   c) Leading refers to the process of influencing employees to work willingly toward the achievement of organisational objectives.
   d) Leading should bring an inspirational and emotional dimension to the organisation through creating a shared vision and inspiring followers to achieve that vision.

2. Read the statements below on the three elements of leadership and indicate the correct one.
   a) A good choice of appropriate behaviour for a specific situation influences the quality of leadership.
   b) The followers' expectations, maturity levels and competencies will not affect the quality of leadership, only the quality of followership.
   c) A leader's unique personal history, interests and characteristics would not influence the quality of leadership, just his behaviour.
   d) Leaders and followers only need to consider the specific situation in order to be effective.

3. Which of the following statements are incorrect?
   a) An organisation cannot be effectively managed without strong leadership.

b) Leadership and management are interdependent. People who are good managers are also good leaders, and vice versa.

c) Management is broader in scope than leadership, as leading is but one of the tasks of management.

d) Management is related to the everyday running of the business.

4. Which one of the following includes typical elements of management?
   a) do things right, develop, ask what and why
   b) do things right, maintain, ask how and when
   c) develop, ask how and when, focus on people
   d) ask how and when, focus on systems and structures, originate

5. Which one of the following includes typical elements of leadership?
   a) have a long-term view, do things right, administer
   b) administer, do the right things, have a long-term view
   c) inspire people, motivate others to complete tasks, originate (correct)
   d) focus on people, do the right things, maintain

REFERENCES AND END-NOTES

1. SWANEPOEL, B.J., ERASMUS, B.J. & SCHENK, H. 2008. *South African human resource management: Theory and practice.* 4th ed. Cape Town: Juta & Co. pp. 340-341.

2. WADDELL, D., DEVINE, J., JONES, G.R. & GEORGE, J.M. 2007. *Contemporary Managment.* North Ryde: McGraw-Hill. p. 193.

3. LUSSIER, R.N. 2006. *Management fundamentals Concepts. Applications. Skills Development.* 3rd ed. Cincinnati: South-Western. p. 11.

4. AMOS, T., RISTOW, A., RISTOW, L. & PEARSE, N.J. 2008. *Human resource management.* 3rd ed. Lansdowne: Juta & Co. pp. 193-196.

5. LANDSBERG, M. 2000. *The tools of leadership.* London: Harper Collins. p. ix.

6. HUGHES, R.L., GINNET, R.C. & CURPHY, G.J. 2006. *Leadership: Enhancing the lessons of experience.* 5th ed. Singapore: Irwin McGraw-Hill. p. 1.

7. HUGHES, R.L., GINNET, R.C. & CURPHY, G.J. 2006. *Leadership: Enhancing the lessons of experience.* 5th ed. Singapore: Irwin McGraw-Hill. p. 43.

8. LUSSIER, R.N. 2006. *Management fundamentals Concepts. Applications. Skills Development.* 3rd ed. Cincinnati: South-Western. p. 459.

9. WERNER, A. (Ed.). BAGRAIM, J., CUNNINGHAM, P., POTGIETER, T. & VIEDGE, C. 2007. *Organisational behaviour: A contemporary South African perspective.* 2nd ed. Pretoria: Van Schaik. p. 288.

10. DU TOIT, G.S., ERASMUS, B.J. & STRYDOM, J.W. (Ed.) 2010. *Introduction to business management.* 8th ed. Cape Town: Oxford University Press. p. 210.

11. HUGHES, R.L., GINNET, R.C. & CURPHY, G.J. 2006. *Leadership: Enhancing the lessons of experience.* 5th ed. Singapore: Irwin McGraw-Hill. pp. 9-10.

12. SWANEPOEL, B.J., ERASMUS, B.J., & SCHENK, H. 2008. *South African human resource management: Theory and practice.* 4th ed. Cape Town: Juta & Co. pp. 341-342; DU TOIT, G.S., ERASMUS, B.J. & STRYDOM,

J.W. (Ed.). 2010. *Introduction to business management.* 8th ed. Cape Town: Oxford University Press. pp. 214-215; AMOS, T., RISTOW, A., RISTOW, L. & PEARSE, N.J. 2008. *Human resource management.* 3rd ed. Lansdowne: Juta & Co. p. 200.

13. DU TOIT, G.S., ERASMUS, B.J. & STRYDOM, J.W. (Ed.). 2010. *Introduction to business management.* 8th ed. Cape Town: Oxford University Press. p.215; & SWANEPOEL, B.J., ERASMUS, B.J. & SCHENK, H. 2008. *South African human resource management: Theory and practice.* 4th ed. Cape Town: Juta & Co. p. 342.

14. SWANEPOEL, B.J., ERASMUS, B.J. & SCHENK, H. 2008. *South African human resource management: Theory and practice.* 4th ed. Cape Town: Juta & Co. pp. 342-343.

15. AMOS, T., RISTOW, A., RISTOW, L. & PEARSE, N.J. 2008. *Human resource management.* 3rd ed. Lansdowne: Juta & Co. p. 202.

16. DU TOIT, G.S., ERASMUS, B.J. & STRYDOM, J.W. (Ed.). 2010. *Introduction to business management.* 8th ed. Cape Town: Oxford University Press. p. 215.

17. SWANEPOEL, B.J., ERASMUS, B.J. & SCHENK, H. 2008. *South African human resource management: Theory and practice.* 4th ed. Cape Town: Juta & Co. p. 344.

18. SWANEPOEL, B.J., ERASMUS, B.J. & SCHENK, H. 2008. *South African human resource management: Theory and practice.* 4th ed. Cape Town: Juta & Co. p. 342.

19. MCSHANE S.L. & VON GLINOW, M.A. 2000. *Organisational behavior.* New York: McGraw-Hill. p. 437.

20. WERNER, A. (Ed.), BAGRAIM, J., CUNNINGHAM, P., POTGIETER, T. & VIEDGE, C. 2007. *Organisational behaviour: A contemporary South African perspective.* 2nd ed. Pretoria: Van Schaik. pp. 290-291.

21. WERNER, A. (Ed.), BAGRAIM, J., CUNNINGHAM, P., POTGIETER, T. & VIEDGE, C. 2007. *Organisational behaviour: A contemporary South African perspective.* 2nd ed. Pretoria: Van Schaik. p.291.

22. SWANEPOEL, B.J., ERASMUS, B.J. & SCHENK, H. 2008. *South African human resource management: Theory and practice.* 4th ed. Cape Town: Juta & Co. p. 349.

23. Ibid.

24. SWANEPOEL, B.J., ERASMUS, B.J. & SCHENK, H. 2008. *South African human resource management: Theory and practice.* 4th ed. Cape Town: Juta & Co. pp. 349-350.

25. SWANEPOEL, B.J., ERASMUS, B.J. & SCHENK, H. 2008. *South African human resource management: Theory and practice.* 4th ed. Cape Town: Juta & Co. pp. 350–351.

26. AMOS, T., RISTOW, A. & RISTOW, L. 2004. *Human resource management.* 2nd ed. Cape Town: Juta & Co. pp. 221–222.

27. AMOS, T., RISTOW, A., RISTOW, L. & PEARSE, N.J. 2008. *Human resource management.* 3rd ed. Lansdowne: Juta & Co. p. 214.

28. ROBBINS, S.P., ODENDAAL, A. & ROODT, G. 2003. *Organisational behaviour: Global and South African perspectives.* Cape Town: Pearson. p. 252.

29. KREITNER, R. & KINICKI, A. 2001. *Organizational behavior.* 5th ed. Boston: McGraw-Hill Irwin. pp. 571–577.

30. ROBBINS, S.P., ODENDAAL, A. & ROODT, G. 2003. *Organisational behaviour: Global and South African perspectives.* Cape Town: Pearson. p. 248.

31. ROBBINS, S.P., ODENDAAL, A. & ROODT, G. 2003. *Organisational behaviour: Global and South African perspectives.* Cape Town: Pearson. p. 250.

32. KREITNER, R. & KINICKI, A. 2001. *Organizational behavior.* 5th ed. Boston: McGraw-Hill Irwin. p.576.

33. DU TOIT, G.S., ERASMUS, B.J. & STRYDOM, J.W. (Ed.). 2010. *Introduction to business management.* 8th ed. Cape Town: Oxford University Press. p. 212.

34. Ibid.

35. WERNER, A. (Ed.), BAGRAIM, J., CUNNINGHAM, P., POTGIETER, T. & VIEDGE, C. 2007. *Organisational behaviour: A contemporary South African perspective.* 2nd ed. Pretoria: Van Schaik. p. 301.

36. WERNER, A. (Ed.), BAGRAIM, J., CUNNINGHAM, P., POTGIETER, T. & VIEDGE, C. 2007. *Organisational behaviour: A contemporary South African perspective.* 2nd ed. Pretoria: Van Schaik. pp. 301-302.

37. ROBBINS, S.P., ODENDAAL, A. & ROODT, G. 2003. *Organisational behaviour. Global and South African perspectives.* Cape Town: Pearson. pp. 256–257.
38. HOUSE, R.J., HANGES, P.J., JAVIDAN, M., DORFMAN, P.W., & GUPTA, V. (Eds.). 2004. *Culture, Leadership, and Organizations. The GLOBE Study of 62 Societies.* Sage Publications: Thousand Oaks, California. p. 727.
39. ROBBINS, S.P., ODENDAAL, A. & ROODT, G. 2003. *Organisational behaviour. Global and South African perspectives.* Cape Town: Pearson. p. 256.
40. WERNER, A. (Ed.), BAGRAIM, J., CUNNINGHAM, P., POTGIETER, T. & VIEDGE, C. & 2007. *Organisational behaviour. A contemporary South African perspective.* 2nd ed. Pretoria: Van Schaik. p. 303.
41. ROBBINS, S.P., ODENDAAL, A. & ROODT, G. 2003. *Organisational behaviour. Global and South African perspectives.* Cape Town: Pearson. p. 256.
42. KHOZA (1994) & MBIGI (1995), both in: SWANEPOEL, B.J., ERASMUS, B.J., & SCHENK, H. 2008. *South African human resource management. Theory and practice.* 4th ed. Cape Town: Juta & Co. p. 361.
43. VAN ZYL, E. (Ed.) DALGISH, C., DU PLESSIS, M., LUES, L. & PIETERSEN, E. 2009. *Leadership in the African Context.* Lansdowne: Juta & Co. pp. 33–34.
44. SWANEPOEL, B.J., ERASMUS, B.J. & SCHENK, H. 2008. *South African human resource management. Theory and practice.* 4th ed. Cape Town: Juta & Co. p. 360.
45. KHOZA (1994), MBIGI (1995) & AVOLIO (1995), all cited in: SWANEPOEL, B.J., ERASMUS, B.J. & SCHENK, H. 2008. *South African human resource management. Theory and practice.* 4th ed. Cape Town: Juta & Co. p. 361.
46. From the abstracts of a speech by Papi Molotsane, chief executive of Fedics, the food-service division of the Tsebo Outsourcing Group, at a graduation ceremony of the Technikon Witwatersrand. Management Today. 18:4, May 2002.
47. SWANEPOEL, B.J., ERASMUS, B.J. & SCHENK, H. 2008. *South African human resource management. Theory and practice.* 4th ed. Cape Town: Juta & Co. p. 363.
48. SOCIETY FOR HUMAN RESOURCE MANAGEMENT. 2008. *The 2007–2008 workplace trends list.* Alexandria: Society for Human Resource Management.
49. SOCIETY FOR HUMAN RESOURCE MANAGEMENT. 2008. *The 2007–2008 workplace trends list.* Alexandria: Society for Human Resource Management. p. 8.
50. PRICEWATERHOUSECOOPERS *12th Annual Global CEO Survey 2009.* p. 4. [Online]. Available: www.pwc.com/ceosurvey [28 October 2010].
51. Adapted from Deming, V.K. 2004. *The Big Book of Leadership Games.* McGraw-Hill: New York.

ANSWERS TO MULTIPLE-CHOICE QUESTIONS

1. Answer = b)   Leading involves something happening as a result of the interaction between the leader and followers (based on the situation), and not the situation and followers.

2. Answer = a)   It is the only correct option.

3. Answer = b)   People who are good managers are not necessarily also good leaders, and vice versa.

4. Answer = b)   To do things right, to maintain processes, procedures and so forth, and to ask how and when are typical management elements.

5. Answer = c)   To inspire people, to motivate others to complete tasks, and to originate new ideas are typical leadership elements.

7

Motivating

Jerome Kiley

PURPOSE OF THIS CHAPTER

This chapter looks at how an employee's behaviour can be influenced to achieve the goals of an organisation. It discusses what makes each person unique, and it examines what employees need and expect. It considers different things that affect employees' motivation. Lastly, the chapter shows how to check morale in a workplace, and offers practical ways to motivate people.

LEARNING OUTCOMES

This chapter should enable you to:
- understand how individual differences have an effect on motivation
- discuss the various levels of need satisfaction described by Maslow, Alderfer, and McClelland
- explain how goal-setting and changes in behaviour can affect employee behaviour
- understand how employees' expectations about their jobs and their perceptions (what they think) of their treatment, affect their motivation
- explain how the quality of work life and job design affect employee motivation
- distinguish between maintenance and motivational factors
- discuss the motivational effects of money
- list signs of poor morale in an organisation
- choose useful strategies to motivate employees in an organisation.

7.1 **Introduction**

Understanding what makes people act in a particular way in an organisation is one of the core (basic) functions of a manager. The manager needs to understand what she or he must do to motivate employees to work towards the **goals** of the organisation. However, this is a complex task as there are many factors that can affect employees' motivation.

There are also many theories about motivation. These theories do not compete with each other, they just deal with different aspects of behaviour. Figure 7.1 illustrates these theories.

FIGURE 7.1 Models of employee motivation

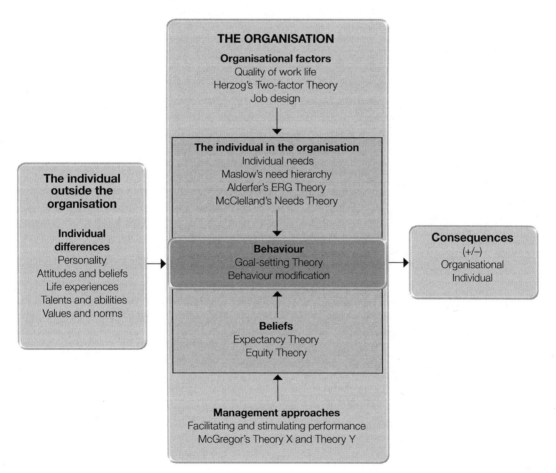

7.2 **What is motivation?**

The word **motivation** comes from the Latin word *motivus*, which means 'a moving cause' and refers to forces acting on or inside a person that create behaviour.[1] So it means actions or events that make people behave in different ways. In an organisation, motivation means the desire and willingness of employees to reach the goals of the business.

The term 'motivation' can also apply to groups, such as departments, and the organisation as a whole. An important term relating to motivation is morale. This is the general level of confidence or optimism that a group of people feel.[2]

Management aims to reach five goals in connection with motivation. The manager wants:
- to get capable people who will fit in with the organisation, to join it
- the person who has joined to stay with the organisation because lots of time, money and effort are spent on her or him
- the employees to come to work regularly
- the employees to work on or above a certain expected level
- to show good group citizenship, not just following the rules, but also accepting the culture and values of the organisation.

An employee's motivation is affected by:
- her or his personality, attitudes and beliefs, life experiences, abilities and values
- the behaviour of management, the responses to the employee's behaviour, and the way the organisation works.

7.3 **The needs and expectations of employees**

7.3.1 Individual differences

People differ from one another in a number of ways, which affect the way they behave in an organisation. In psychology one studies how people differ from one another. Some of these differences include:
- **demographic variables** (such as gender, language, culture, family background, social class and age)
- **life experiences** (such as school, suburb, socio-economic group, family background and work experience)

> **CRITICAL THINKING**
>
> A manager introduces overtime, for which employees receive 1½ times their normal salary, but this means that they have to spend more time away from home. Would this motivate or demotivate employees?

- **beliefs about reality** (which include beliefs about 'what is important' and 'how life should be')
- **competencies** (knowledge, skills and abilities) and capacities to develop other competencies
- **attitudes** (thoughts, feelings and behaviours).[3]

All of these combine to form one's **personality**, which is the unique pattern of thoughts, feelings, qualities and behaviours that make each person unique.[4]

Because people are unique, different things motivate different people. The reality is that a management action that motivates one employee may demotivate another one.

7.3.2 The needs of individuals

Various theorists have tried to explain what people need, and, in a work context, how these needs can be met.

7.3.2.1 Maslow's hierarchy of needs

Abraham Maslow's **Theory of Human Motivation**[5] was first published in 1943, and today it is still one of the best theories of motivation. The theory suggests that people are motivated by needs that are like a hierarchy (a graded or ranked series, often looking like a triangle). The needs at the bottom of the hierarchy must be satisfied before those higher up can be fulfilled. (See Figure 7.2.)

Maslow's **lower-order needs** are really the same as the needs of animals:

- **Physical needs** for staying alive (the needs for food, water and shelter) and pro-creating (the need for sex and having children). These needs are generally experienced through physical drives such as hunger and thirst.
- **Safety/security needs** relate to physical safety (for example, jumping out the way of a car) and psychological security (for example, taking a steady job).
- **Social needs** relate to interaction with others.

Maslow's **higher-order needs** are found in humans because their brains are more highly developed:

- **Ego** (self-respect) **needs** relate to humans' desire for recognition of their achievements and the fact that they are unique individuals. These needs can be met through praise, recognition and actions that improve social position.
- **Self-actualisation needs** relate to individuals' desires to achieve their full potential. (Maslow believed the average person is only 10% self-actualised.)

Higher-order needs are particularly important when motivating people in an organisation.

Although Maslow's model is still widely used today, it has been criticised as being too simple, and it is pointed out that lower-order needs do not always have to be satisfied before higher-order needs can be fulfilled.

FIGURE 7.2 Maslow's hierarchy of motivation

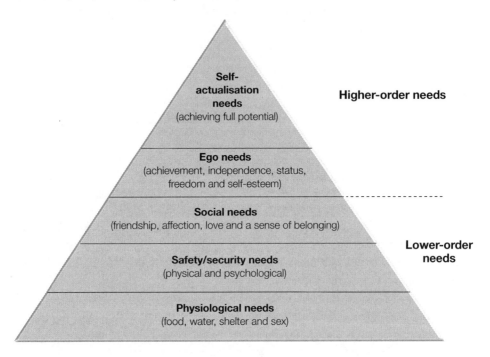

7.3.2.2 **Alderfer's ERG Theory**

Alderfer's ERG Theory[6] proposes that people have three sets of needs, namely:
- **Existence** needs (all material and physical needs for survival)
- **Relatedness** needs (the desire to have relationships in which feelings and thoughts are shared)
- **Growth** needs (the desires to develop, be productive and create change in oneself and the environment).

As opposed to supporting a hierarchy of needs, this theory proposes that a number of needs can operate at the same time. Alderfer argues that modern individuals are motivated to satisfy existence and growth needs at the same time.

7.3.2.3 **McClelland's Needs Theory**

David McClelland identified a number of basic needs that are learned by people in society, through the influence of our parents and other significant individuals.[7] These include:

- the need for affiliation (**NAff**), which is reflected in the desire to be liked and to get on with colleagues and people in general
- the need for achievement (**NAch**), which is characterised by the desire to be successful and achieve goals
- the need for power (**NPow**), which is the desire to control and influence others. (Personalised power involves exploiting and manipulating others. Socialised power is more positive as it is used to improve the organisation and larger society.)

The needs in **McClelland's Needs Theory** are not 'either/or' needs. In other words, people do not choose only one, but they have some of each, and these often change over time. The three different needs are expressed as a percentage in terms of how strong each one is for a particular individual. McClelland argued that an effective manager has strong needs for both achievement and power.

FIGURE 7.3 An example of a motivational profile for a manager

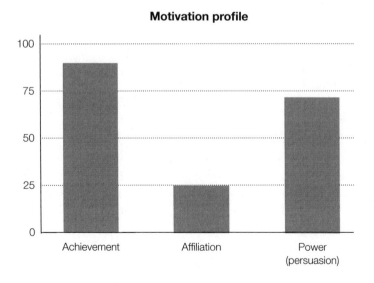

7.3.3 The expectations of employees

7.3.3.1 **Expectancy Theory**

Expectancy Theory is based on the work of Victor Vroom, who argued that people are rational (able to reason) beings who analyse the costs and benefits of possible behaviours.[8] The underlying basis of this theory is that employees are motivated by the expected results of their actions. An expected result is made up of three elements:

- **valence** (the degree of satisfaction that an employee anticipates (expects) to get from a particular outcome)
- **instrumentality** (the amount that the employee believes that her or his actions will lead to the desired outcome)
- **expectancy** (the likelihood that the outcome will be achieved).[9]

FIGURE 7.4 Motivation and expectancy

Expectancy Theory is particularly helpful in predicting whether a particular motivational strategy will work in an organisation or for a particular employee. The theory can be divided into three key questions that employees can ask themselves about their work:[10]

> **CRITICAL THINKING**
>
> Do you play the Lotto? Can you explain why you do or do not play the Lotto by using the three elements of Expectancy Theory?

- Do I value the results or the reward? (valence)
- Are personal results linked to my **performance**? In other words is the reward directly linked to my actions e.g. working hard? (instrumentality)
- What are the chances that I will actually get this reward? (expectancy).

Employees are more motivated when they value the results of their behaviour, see a direct link between their behaviour and the rewards or punishments, and believe that their efforts will affect the success or failure of a task.

7.3.3.2 **Equity Theory**

Equity Theory proposes that employees judge themselves against others, and feel that they should receive the same rewards as others for doing the same job, under the same circumstances. Equity focuses on relationships that are effort-performance-reward.[11] The question that the employee asks is: 'What are the payoffs in recognition, status, benefits, money, promotion, and allocation (being given) of tasks relative to my effort, skills, job knowledge, and work level?'

Employees also use external comparisons where they compare their effort-perfor-mance-reward ratios to other employees doing the same kind of work. These compari-sons can be made on three levels[12] namely:

- comparisons to other particular people (Employees compare themselves to a colleague [worker in the same job] or friend.)
- comparisons to groups (The employee may compare her or his department to a similar department in the organisation.)
- comparisons to general occupational classes (Employees may compare themselves to people doing the same kind of jobs in other organisations.)

7.4 **Managing employees' motivation**

Some approaches to motivation focus on directly influencing employee behaviour. Others concentrate on how to create an environment that will encourage high morale.

7.4.1 Directly influencing employee behaviour

Managers must encourage employees to work hard. The manager should inspire employ-ees to perform, reward good work, and help to improve poor work.

7.4.1.1 **Goal-setting Theory**

Goal-setting Theory is based on the idea that employees are motivated by goals they can see. Management therefore needs to set specific goals for employees. A good book on goal-setting theory is *The one minute manager*[13] by Ken Blanchard and Spencer Johnson.

A core (central) principle when setting a goal is that it should be acceptable to both the manager and employee. This means that goals should be set by consultation (discus-sion) rather than by the manager forcing goals onto the employee. The reason for this is that if employees are involved in goal-setting, they become 'our goals' and not 'management's goals'. This means that the employee is much more interested in succeeding because she or he feels that 'we succeed or fail together', rather than management succeeding or failing.

The principles involved in setting effective goals appear in the acronym (abbreviation) **SMART**. Goals should be:
- **S**pecific (They should be have one particular result.)
- **M**easurable (One should be able to measure their success or failure.)
- **A**chievable (They should not be too hard, but not too easy, as this will lead to the employee getting bored.)
- **R**ealistic (They should take account of the employee's abilities and circumstances)
- **T**ime-based (There should be a deadline for completing them).

7.4.1.2 **Behavioural modification (change)**

Behavioural modification is based on the law of effect that states that behaviours that are followed by positive outcomes will be repeated, while those followed by negative outcomes will not be repeated.[14] B.F. Skinner was a psychologist who explored this phenomenon (fact or event).

FIGURE 7.5 The consequences of behaviour

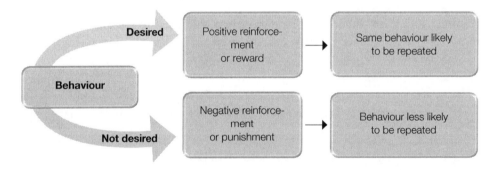

The idea is that employees will repeat behaviours that management rewards them for, while behaviours that they are punished for are less likely to be repeated, provided that the employee likes the reward and dislikes the punishment.

Rewards can be divided into two categories:[15]
- **intrinsic rewards** (These are experienced internally by the employee when she or he feels a sense of achievement, satisfaction, personal growth, and development.)
- **extrinsic rewards** (These come from an external source such as management or colleagues.)

Extrinsic rewards can be further divided into:
- **social rewards** in the form of being accepted, and being given affection and status from management, colleagues, friends, and people in general.
- **economic rewards** in the form of pay, bonuses, commissions (acting as an agent for someone) and other financial rewards (Performance at work gives the employee money, which gives her or him access to other things.)[16]

Managers can also try to change an employee's behaviour by using punishments such as disciplinary actions, reprimands (scolding), or the withholding of rewards. The effectiveness of punishment often depends on the manager being present. In any case, seeing that employees often resent (get angry with) punishment and the effects do not last long, it is much better to use positive reinforcement rather than punishment to encourage desired behaviour.

All employees will experience rewards and punishments differently. What may motivate one employee may have little or no effect on another, and could even be demotivating.

Money as a motivator

We live in a consumerist society where the increasing consumption (using up) of consumer goods is regarded as desirable.[17] Money is the thing that makes this possible, so it should make sense that money is a major source of motivation.

According to management tradition, nothing influences employees more than high wages. Pay and pay increases are seen as linked to performance.[18] However, later research has shown that while money is an important source of motivation, other factors such as social and intrinsic rewards play just as important a role in motivating employees.[19] In short, it does not matter how much someone is paid; if they are unhappy in their job and do not get intrinsic rewards from their work, they will not perform well.

The most effective methods for motivating employees do not cost much

Having an effective strategy to motivate employees gives management huge returns. One of the most widespread mistaken ideas about motivation is that it only revolves around money in the form of increased pay and bonuses. But if salaries are similar to others in the industry, they will not always have a big motivational effect.

> The really effective motivational strategies are public and private praise and recognition for a job that has been well done. A simple thing like sending a birthday card can have a huge impact on employee motivation. Similarly, sending e-cards to say thank you for performing a task well can motivate people by showing that the input and effort of the employee are appreciated. However, there are a few principles to keep in mind. A greeting should be personal, it should happen as soon as possible after the event, and the message should be genuine and meaningful.

7.4.2 Facilitating (helping to bring about) employees' good performance

Management has to give employees an environment that makes it easier to do their jobs. For example, if an employee does not have the necessary resources (like equipment), no matter how motivated she or he is to perform the job, it will not happen. Facilitating (encouraging) good performance can involve anything from providing physical resources to reducing paperwork and other office problems.

7.4.2.1 **The quality-of-work-life approach**

Some researchers have tried to find out through the **quality-of-work-life** (QWL) **approach** to motivation what makes employees happy. They have found the following factors:[21]

CRITICAL THINKING

The QWL approach focuses on practical motivation strategies in the workplace. You will notice that many of these are included in the other models of motivation covered in this chapter.

- adequate (enough) compensation (pay) that meets employees' needs and is seen by them as fair
- challenging (interesting) work that stimulates employees by using and developing their capacities (abilities)
- opportunities for personal growth through training and development
- a physical working environment that is pleasant, attractive, healthy, and safe
- regarding employee welfare as very important, so that the employees feel they are being cared for
- a general belief in personal identity, equal treatment, a sense of belonging, and the chance to move upwards
- a democratic work environment, where employees have a say about the things that affect them, and where their opinions are important and are used
- an absence of unnecessary stress in the workplace

- opportunities to move upwards (with promotions) and sideways (between different jobs and departments)
- healthy social and personal relationships, which should be encouraged and developed
- a fair amount of job security for employees
- a work environment that does not interfere too much with the personal, family, and leisure time of the employee.

7.4.2.2 **Herzberg's Two-Factor Theory**

Frederick Herzberg's **Two-factor Theory** distinguishes between 'maintenance' factors and 'motivational' factors.[22] **Maintenance** (hygiene) **factors** relate to work that results in job satisfaction if they are present, and dissatisfaction if they are absent (for example, an acceptable salary, respectable status, good working conditions, good interpersonal relationships, good supervision, efficient administration, and fair company policies). **Motivational factors** result in increased levels of performance. These motivators include a challenging job, personal growth opportunities, recognition, and feelings of achievement.

7.4.2.3 **The job characteristics model**

The way in which an employee's job is designed has a direct impact on the satisfaction that an employee gets from her or his job. According to the motivational approach to **job design**, there are four core ways to make a job interesting and stimulating, namely:
- job rotation
- job enlargement
- job enrichment
- self-managing work groups.

Job rotation means changing employees between different jobs in the organisation. This gives the chance, especially with lower-level jobs, for the employee to get experience and skills, she or he does not become bored by doing the same tasks over and over, and it increases feelings of being valued by the organisation. Because of the wide range of skills and experience that it develops in employees, job rotation also makes it easier to promote employees.

   Job enlargement means adding similar tasks at the same level of difficulty and responsibility to a job. The employee therefore performs a wider range of tasks, which can reduce boredom.

   Job enrichment means giving the employee tasks that are more complex and have more responsibility and authority. This will help to develop the employee and also to improve her or his employment prospects.

With job enlargement, and especially job enrichment, employees will often expect more money. If this does not happen, the changes may be de-motivating, rather than being motivating, as was intended.

A more modern approach to job design is creating **semi-autonomous work groups or self-managing teams,**[23] where groups of employees are given tasks and given the authority to carry them out on their own, with hardly any interference from management.

7.4.2.4 **McGregor's Theory X and Theory Y, and the self-fulfilling prophecy**

Douglas McGregor noticed that managers could have opposite ideas about employee behaviour. These ideas resulted in managers treating employees very differently.[24] McGregor labelled the philosophies (ideas) of some managers Theory X, and the ideas of other managers as Theory Y. **McGregor's Theory X and Theory Y** are summarised in Table 7.1.

TABLE 7.1 Theory X versus Theory Y

Theory X	Theory Y
Managers believe that: • Employees are lazy. • Employees avoid work and responsibility where possible. • Employees cannot be trusted. • Employees need to be closely supervised. • Employees need to be forced to work.	Managers believe that: • Employees are ambitious. • Employees enjoy work and want responsibility. • They get satisfaction from doing a good job. • Employees can be trusted to work on their own.

The beliefs that managers have are important for human behaviour, as they can become **self-fulfilling prophecies.**[25] This means that if you expect something will happen (you prophesy it) it will often happen. Although there are always exceptions, in most cases if managers believe employees are lazy and untrustworthy (as in Theory X), this is how their employees will behave. The opposite is also likely to be true. If managers believe their employees work hard, and are responsible and trustworthy, (as in Theory Y), their employees will probably be like that.

7.5 **Monitoring employee morale**

Morale is the general level of motivation among the employees of an organisation. There are a number of indicators of the level of morale in a workplace. Many of these seem obvious, yet there are many organisations that ignore these indicators.

TABLE 7.2 Indicators of the levels of employee morale in an organisation

High morale	Low morale
• High level of commitment to the organisation and the team • High levels of productivity • Good customer service • Good work attendance • Low level of employee turnover (leaving the job) • Constructive conflict between individuals and departments	• Low levels of commitment to the team and organisation • Low levels of productivity • Poor customer service • High levels of sick leave and absenteeism • High level of employee turnover • Destructive conflict between individuals and departments

An organisation should continually check the indicators of morale as they are the 'thermometer' of the organisation in terms of employee motivation. Management needs to decide what the right levels of motivation are, watch their current levels, and take corrective action where necessary.

7.6 **Practical motivational strategies**

There are many strategies that can be used to motivate employees, and these fit into the different theories of motivation in various ways. One of the key factors in deciding how to motivate employees in an organisation is the **psychological contract**, which is the unwritten agreement between the individual and the organisation, stating what the two expect from each other. This is based on **Exchange Theory**, which is the idea that one can predict (forecast) give-and-take relationships between them, by matching employee expectations (pay and working conditions) with what they are prepared to give in exchange (work performance).[26]

Some of these strategies are as follows:[27]

• having and communicating a clear vision, mission and set of values for the organisation, that inspires and directs employees
• using fair, objective methods to find and hire new employees who share the values of the organisation

- having fair organisational policies and applying these all the time
- providing two-way communication channels so that management and employees can communicate with each other to share ideas and to discuss concerns
- creating a sense of community based on participation and teamwork, that make employees feel that they belong
- providing development opportunities through challenging jobs, promotion opportunities, and training, both on and off the job
- committing to people-first values, where people are valued more than short-term profits and productivity
- hiring and developing the 'right kind' of managers who are competent, and show the right kinds of organisational values and management practices
- empowering employees, by providing working conditions that help them to feel competent and in control both in the jobs that they perform and in life in general[28]
- setting challenging goals that are specific, measurable, achievable, and realistic, and which have deadlines, as well as giving regular feedback on them[29]
- paying salaries and benefits that are fair, and are linked to performance and merit.[30]

Different combinations of the above strategies can be used. The key is to create a general feeling of creativity and open-mindedness to attract, stimulate and keep skilled and talented employees.[31] This means that management should continually look for new and active strategies to motivate the employees of the organisation.

CASE STUDY: SA's top employers as voted for by students[32]

Now in its seventh year, the South African Student Survey (SASS) is conducted by Magnet Communications (www.magnetcommunications.co.za) every year. It is an independent, numerical survey that aims to explore the career mindsets and motivations of students studying at the 23 major tertiary educational institutions across South Africa.

The survey is the largest of its kind, having reached over 26 000 South African students in 2009. The aim is to identify the employers that students think are their ideal employers. These employers are then ranked annually for each area of study, namely Commerce, Science, Engineering, and Humanities.

Here are some of the comments giving reasons why the companies were thought to be the best employers. These comments come from interviews conducted with role-players in some of the companies.

Absa: 'I am really impressed with the diverse growth opportunities and the way in which the company supports their employers' (Tiziana Burton – student). 'We make it our business to understand the needs of those entering the job market, and are committed to providing challenging work and meaningful career development opportunities for all of our employees' (Fergus Marupen – Chief Human Resource Executive). 'It's Absa's people that make it the best place to work. They are warm and sincere, and genuinely interested in seeing you grow and develop – both as a human being and as a professional' (Kgomotso Seisa, MI Analyst).

SA Reserve Bank (SARB): 'Central banks typically are inherently prestigious organisations ... the organisation is stable and secure and offers a wide range of developmental and career-growth prospects, opportunities for international travel ... I also take great pleasure in being a mentor and coach.' 'At the SARB you can be sure of two things – that the hard work you do will contribute towards the betterment of the South African people, and that the training you receive and challenges you will face will ensure you excel in your chosen field. If these excite you, this is the place for you' (Marea Sing, Assistant Economist).

SA Revenue Service (SARS): 'SARS offers organisational stability and job security for those who are fully engaged and deliver optimally' (Lindewe Sebesho, Executive Performance Management and Rewards). 'I wanted to start my career at a reputable company that would help me develop my skills and gain valuable knowledge. SARS fulfilled these criteria ... Team work is essential. Trusting and co-operating with one's colleagues can mean the difference between a success story and a failure! ... SARS has various ways of acknowledging the good performance of staff. These include: annual bonuses for employees who attain high percentages on their performance scorecards; "Amakhwezi" vouchers recognising good performance throughout the year; the "Amakhwezi Awards" at the end of the year to recognise the organisation's top performers and various promotions within the organisation.'

PriceWaterhouseCoopers (PWC): 'Our accountants and consultants play a crucial role in influencing how companies and governments are run' (Glory Koko Khumalo, PwC partner). 'PwC is a large firm with a good

reputation … They offer diverse opportunities in various lines of service'
(Ruan Greeff, Trainee Accountant). 'PwC people are encouraged and supported at all times to develop their careers and enhance their skills, and
there are numerous training courses on offer.' (Namhla Sitshinga, Trainee
Accountant).

QUESTIONS

1. Identify at least one example for each of the different levels of Maslow's
   needs hierarchy from the discussion of the different companies.
2. Which of McClelland's needs appear to figure more strongly in the case
   study? Explain why you say so.
3. Explain how SARS could use Expectancy Theory to determine how
   effective their Amakhwezi Awards are.
4. Do any of the companies appear to use Goal-setting Theory? Explain
   why you say so.
5. According to Herzberg's theory, do 'motivators' or 'hygiene factors' figure
   more strongly in the discussions of the different companies? Motivate
   (explain) your answer.
6. Identify examples of practical motivational strategies that are applied by the
   different employers discussed in the case study.

SUMMARY

'Motivation' refers to actions or events that activate, direct and maintain behaviour. The
motivation of employees is a complex issue that is influenced by many factors.
Individuals' unique characteristics affect how and by what they can be motivated.
Maslow, Alderfer and McClelland have tried to explain how individual needs and their
fulfilment affect motivation. Expectancy Theory deals with the employee's personal
understanding of whether behaviours will actually lead to getting those needs. Equity
Theory examines the employees' perceptions of how they are rewarded for their
behaviours, as compared to their peers.

Goal-setting Theory and behaviour modification are both ways of directly influencing employees' behaviour. On the organisational level, the quality-of-work-life approach,
Herzberg's Two-Factor Theory, and job design, all examine factors in an organisation
that create positive morale. McGregor's Theory X and Theory Y explore the direct
impact of management on motivation.

There are a number of indicators of poor morale and motivation in an organisation. If these are noticed, there are various practical strategies that can be used to improve the morale and motivation of employees.

GLOSSARY

assumptions: beliefs that something is true without there being proof

attitudes: beliefs about an object or person, which can be positive, negative or neutral, and which are generally accepted to have three components: cognitive components, emotional components and behavioural components

behavioural modification: the theory that behaviours that are followed by positive outcomes will be repeated, while those followed by negative outcomes will not be repeated

beliefs about reality: core ideas about how the world works

competencies: the knowledge, skills and attitudes that enable an employee to perform a job

consumerist society: a society where existing things are continually replaced by new and better things, and most things are disposable once they have been used or go out of fashion

demographic variables: the characteristics of human populations (for example, age, gender, size, education, culture and race)

economic rewards: extrinsic rewards in the form of pay, bonuses, commissions and other financial rewards

ego needs: part of Maslow's hierarchy of needs, those needs that relate to the recognition of an individual's achievements

Equity Theory: the theory that explores how employees believe that they should receive similar rewards to others doing a similar job

ERG Theory: Alderfer's theory that people have three sets of needs: existence, relatedness and growth

Exchange Theory: the theory that focuses on the relationship between employee expectations (regarding remuneration and working conditions) and what these employees are prepared to give in exchange (work performance)

existence needs: according to Alderfer's ERG Theory, the material and physical desires that are required for survival

expectancy: according to Expectancy Theory, the element of an expected result that is concerned with the probability that the outcome will be achieved

Expectancy Theory: the theory that proposes that employees are motivated by the expected results of their actions

extrinsic rewards: when motivation for a task is provided by an external source, such as management or colleagues

goals: things that a person or organisation wants to achieve

Goal-setting Theory: the theory that explores how employees are motivated by conscious goals

growth needs: according to Alderfer's ERG Theory, these are the desires for development, for productivity, and for effecting change

higher-order needs: according to Maslow, those needs higher up on his hierarchy of needs (ego needs and self-actualisation needs)

instrumentality: according to Expectancy Theory, the element of an expected result that is concerned with the firmness of an employee's belief that his or her actions will lead to the desired outcome

intrinsic rewards: when motivation for a task is derived from doing the task itself

job design: a motivational approach that focuses on three core ways to stimulate employees: job rotation, job enlargement and job enrichment

job enlargement: giving an employee more tasks that are at the same level of difficulty in order to stimulate that employee

job enrichment: giving an employee tasks that are more complex and carry a greater level of responsibility and authority so as to stimulate that employee

job rotation: changing employees between different jobs in an organisation in order to stimulate them

life experiences: what has happened to a person in his or her life so far

lower-order needs: according to Maslow, those needs lower down on his hierarchy of needs (physiological needs, safety/security needs and social needs)

maintenance factors: factors that Herzberg thought resulted in job satisfaction if they were present and dissatisfaction if they were absent

McClelland's Needs Theory: McClelland's theory that people have three learned needs: affiliation, achievement, and power

McGregor's Theory X and Theory Y: the two managerial philosophies identified by McGregor, with Theory X managers having negative expectations of employees and Theory Y managers having positive expectations of employees

morale: the general level of confidence or optimism experienced by a group of people

motivation: the desire and willingness to achieve the goals of a business/actions or events that activate, direct and maintain behaviour

motivational factors: factors that Herzberg thought resulted in increased levels of performance

need for achievement: one of the basic needs identified by McClelland, which is characterised by the desire to be successful and achieve goals

need for affiliation: one of the basic needs identified by McClelland, which is reflected in the desire to be liked and to get on with people

need for power: one of the basic needs identified by McClelland, which is the
desire to control and influence others

perception: the selective process through which information is selected and which
consequently shapes beliefs about reality (seeing; understanding)

performance: the way in which someone does a job, and how well she or he
does it

personality: the unique pattern of thoughts, feelings, qualities and behaviours that
makes an individual unique from others

physiological needs: part of Maslow's hierarchy of needs, those needs related to
staying alive and pro-creating

psychological contract: the unwritten agreement between the individual and the
organisation that specifies what the two expect from each other

quality-of-work-life (QWL) approach: an approach to motivation that focuses
on the factors that influence feelings of well-being and satisfaction among
employees

relatedness needs: according to Alderfer's ERG Theory, the desire to have relationships in which feelings and thoughts are shared

safety/security needs: part of Maslow's hierarchy of needs, those needs that relate
to physical safety and psychological security

self-actualisation needs: part of Maslow's hierarchy of needs, those needs that
relate to people's desires to achieve their full potential

self-fulfilling prophecies: predictions that directly or indirectly cause themselves
to become true

semi-autonomous work groups (self-managing teams): groups of employees
who are assigned tasks and given the autonomy and authority to accomplish these
on their own, with minimum management involvement and interference

social needs: those needs that relate to interaction with others

social rewards: extrinsic rewards in the form of acceptance, affection and status
from management, colleagues, friends, and people in general

SMART acronym: an acronym that summarises the characteristics of effective
goals (specific, measurable, achievable, realistic, time-based)

Theory of Human Motivation: Maslow's theory about the hierarchical nature of
human needs

Two-factor Theory: Herzberg's theory that distinguishes between maintenance
(hygiene) factors and motivational factors

valence: according to Expectancy Theory, the element of an expected result that is
concerned with how much the person values the outcomes

MULTIPLE-CHOICE QUESTIONS

1. According to Maslow the _____ need involves achieving your full potential and being all that you can be.
   a) social
   b) self-actualisation
   c) ego
   d) safety

2. The 'R' in the SMART acronym refers to _____.
   a) realistic
   b) reasonable
   c) rational
   d) relevant

3. According to Alderfer the _____ need includes the desire to have relationships in which feelings and thoughts are shared.
   a) affiliation
   b) relatedness
   c) growth
   d) existence

4. According to David McClelland, someone who has a strong desire to be successful has a strong need for _____.
   a) power
   b) affiliation
   c) control
   d) achievement

5. Sam comes to work early and is complimented on this by his manager. According to the Law of Effect this is _____ which will make it _____ that he will arrive early again.
   a) positive reinforcement; more likely
   b) negative reinforcement; less likely
   c) positive reinforcement; less likely
   d) negative reinforcement; more likely

REFERENCES AND END-NOTES

1. ENCYCLOPÆDIA BRITANNICA. 2006. *Encyclopædia Britannica 2006 Ultimate Reference Suite DVD.*
2. MICROSOFT ENCARTA. 2006. *Microsoft Encarta 2006 Premium Reference Suite DVD.*
3. THERON, A. *Attitudes and values.* In BERGH, Z. & THERON, A. (Eds.) 2006. *Psychology in the work context.* Cape Town: Oxford University Press.
4. Ibid.
5. MASLOW, A.H. 1943. A theory of human motivation. *Psychological Review,* July, pp. 370–396.
6. ALDERFER, C. 1972. *Existence, relatedness, and growth: Human needs in organizational settings.* Glencoe: Free Press.
7. MCCLELLAND, D. 1961. *The achieving society.* New York: Van Nostrand Reinhold.
8. KASSIN, S. 2006. *Psychology in modules.* Upper Saddle River: Prentice Hall.
9. MULLINS, L. 2005. *Management and organisational behaviour.* Edinburgh Gate: Pearson.
10. COOK, C.W. & HUNSACKER, P.L. 2001. *Management and organizational behaviour.* 3rd ed. New York: McGraw-Hill.
11. Ibid.
12. Ibid.
13. BLANCHARD, K.H. & JOHNSON, S. 1983. *The one minute manager.* New York: Berkley.
14. KASSIN, S. 2006. *Psychology in modules.* Upper Saddle River: Prentice Hall.
15. STEERS, R.M., PORTER, L.W. & BIGLEY, G.A. 1996. *Motivation and leadership at work.* 6th ed. Singapore: McGraw-Hill.
16. MULLINS, L. 2005. *Management and organisational behaviour.* Edinburgh Gate: Pearson.
17. ENCYCLOPÆDIA BRITANNICA. 2006. *Encyclopædia Britannica 2006 Ultimate Reference Suite DVD.*
18. ARNOLD, J., SILVESTER, J., PATTERSON, F., ROBERTSON, I., COOPER, C. & BURNES, B. 2005. *Work motivation.* 4th ed. Edinburgh Gate: Prentice Hall.
19. MULLINS, L. 2005. *Management and organisational behaviour.* Edinburgh Gate: Pearson.
20. KOONAR, K. 2006. The Most Effective Methods for Motivating Employees Are Low Cost. [Online]. Available: http://searchwarp.com/swa102262.htm [7 April 2008].
21. WYATT, T.A. & WAH, C.Y. 2001. Perceptions of QWL: A study of Singaporean employees development. *Research and Practice in Human Resource management,* 9(2): 59–76.
22. WILSON, F.M. 2004. *Organizational behaviour and work: A critical introduction.* New York: Oxford University Press.
23. ARNOLD, J., SILVESTER, J., PATTERSON, F., ROBERTSON, I., COOPER, C. & BURNES, B. 2005. *Work motivation.* 4th ed. Edinburgh Gate: Prentice Hall.
24. HELLRIEGEL, D., JACKSON, S.E., SLOCUM, J., STRAUDE, G., AMOS, T., KLOPPER, H.B., LOUW, L. & OOSTHUIZEN, T. 2004. *Management.* 2nd SA ed. Cape Town: Oxford University Press.
25. COOK, C.W. & HUNSACKER, P.L. *Management and organizational behaviour.* 3rd ed. New York: McGraw-Hill.
26. IVANCEVICH, J.M. & MATTESON, M.R. 2002. *Organizational behaviour and management.* 6th ed. New York: McGraw-Hill.
27. Ibid.
28. COOK, C.W. & HUNSACKER, P.L. *Management and organizational behaviour.* 3rd ed. New York: McGraw-Hill.
29. KLEIN, H.J. 1996. An integrated control theory model of work motivation. In: STEERS, R.M., PORTER, L.W., & BIGLEY, G.A. (Eds.) *Motivation and leadership at work.* Singapore: McGraw-Hill.
30. GIBSON, J.L., IVANCEVICH, J.M. & DONNELLY, J.M. 2000. *Organizations: Behavior, structure, processes.* New York: McGraw-Hill.

31. MULLINS, L. 2005. *Management and organisational behaviour.* Edinburgh Gate: Pearson.
32. MAGNET COMMUNICATIONS. 2010. *Companies of the future: Keeping you inspired and informed: 2010.* Johannesburg: Magnet Communications.

ANSWERS TO MULTIPLE-CHOICE QUESTIONS

1. Answer = b)
2. Answer = a)
3. Answer = b)
4. Answer = d)
5. Answer = a)

8

Controlling

Theuns FJ Oosthuizen

PURPOSE OF THIS CHAPTER

This chapter explains the basic concepts (ideas) about control as a management task. It explains the types of controls and when they are used in a transformation (big change) process. Then it explores how control can be implemented (put into practice) in order to make continuous improvements regarding employees and not restrain them. Contemporary (modern) approaches to control are discussed, as well as the importance of quality in organisations.

LEARNING OUTCOMES

This chapter should enable you to:
- define the term 'control'
- explain why controlling is an important management task
- identify the different types of control
- analyse the different types of control in terms of the transformation process
- describe the steps in the control process
- understand various modern approaches to control.

8.1 Introduction

Control is part of an active management process that is used to monitor (watch and check) planning and support leadership. Managers use it to check that all the organisation's activities are working well together in line with its aims. In general, 'control' can be described as the process of establishing and implementing mechanisms (working parts) to ensure that goals are reached. The focus of control as a management task is checking and improving an organisation's activities.

Controlling ensures that the performance and behaviour of individual employees, groups and teams, as well as the rules and procedures of the organisation, meet the set standards. Control therefore allows management to deal with theft, unnecessary wasting, and poor use or allocation of resources, as well as mistakes and low productivity. South African organisations can improve their performance, competitiveness and profitability by means of effective control.[1]

Control practices at McDonald's[2]

Key ingredients (inputs) for food available on the McDonald's menu are beef, chicken, bread, potatoes, and milk. The people who supply these products certainly influence the quality of burgers or chips served by McDonald's to their customers. It is therefore essential for McDonald's to have a good relationship with the suppliers to ensure quality resources and the highest customer satisfaction, health and safety at its branches all over the world. Suppliers are usually keen to ensure that they can meet McDonald's required control standards for quality inputs. McDonald's therefore emphasises that their pre-control standards for inputs are based on quality, value, and cleanliness practices. Another company with strict control practices is Woolworths.[3]

8.2 **Types of control**[4]

When resources (input factors) are transformed into final goods and services (outputs), this is called the **transformation process.** Managers can select the type of control to use according to the stage of the transformation process they are in. The three types of control are: pre-control, concurrent control, and post-control.

8.2.1 Pre-control[5]

The first type of control focuses on the inputs of the transformation process. **Pre-control** is a process that anticipates and prevents input factors from negatively influencing their transformation (see Table 8.1). Pre-control focuses on inputs such as human resources, materials for production, capital, technology, and information.

Management should try to anticipate a problem beforehand rather than solving problems only once they occur. If management and employees come up to the pre-control standards, the organisation is likely to achieve its goals.

TABLE 8.1 Pre-control of input factors

Input factors	Pre-control example
Human resources	Skilled, experienced and qualified employees who will be able to provide the required service (for example, telesales agent), manufacture the required good (for example, vehicle assembly technician), or manage a team (for example, a sales team).
Materials	Good-quality, affordable materials for manufacturing (for example, the plastic, metal, microchip and glass to assemble a cellphone) or good-quality, affordable goods required for retailing (for example, the cellphones manufactured by Nokia and retailed by Cell C).
Capital	Suitable funding (for example, money or credit at a bank) for day-to-day costs and long-term projects as well as vehicles, offices, land, equipment and buildings.
Technology	Computer software and hardware (for example, as required for online retailing by an organisation such as kalahari.net) or equipment used by robots (for example, on the assembly line of a vehicle manufacturer or mass production facility for radios).
Information	Complete information (for example, financial statements, reports and minutes of meetings, SA-census data, and research reports).

8.2.2 Concurrent control[6]

During the transformation process, inputs are transformed into outputs. This is when materials are manufactured into final goods, when an employee provides a service to a customer, or when a salesperson sells a product to a customer. During this process, managers can use concurrent control in order to monitor the transformation activities.

Concurrent control focuses on the quality control of activities in the transformation process (the production process, the service process, or the retail process). The focus of concurrent control is dealing with problems while they are developing (see Table 8.2).

TABLE 8.2 Concurrent controls of the transformation process

Transformation factors	Concurrent control example
Production / Operations process	The control of all activities relating to producing tangible products such as food, clothing, furniture and cars (for example, the assembly processes and activities in building a car or the cooking and décorating processes to arrange a banquet).
Retail process	The control of all activities relating to the selling process of tangible products such as food, clothing, furniture and cars (for example, the process of selling food and clothing to customers at Woolworths).
Service process	The control of all activities relating to the process of providing a service to clients, such as legal services, medical services, entertainment services, and banking services (for example, the process to follow in getting a home loan from a bank, or a hot-air balloon ride for a 21st birthday).

Concurrent control for the Gautrain

The operations and control centre for the Gautrain is located at the Midrand Depot. This centre controls all the train movements on the different routes. It consists of a communications control centre to monitor the bus feeder system and key stations on a concurrent basis. 'This comprises Bombardier's CITYFLO 250 system, a fixed-block signalling system based on "distance to go" principles, with major information being regularly transmitted to the onboard Automatic Train Protection (ATP) system.' The train itself has been fitted with a fully integrated audio and visual internal and external passenger information system. This system has many uses, but in terms of concurrent control, it will help train drivers and conductors to make announcements using the public address system in case of any delays.[7]

8.2.3 Post-control[8]

Post-control is the final type of control, and this focuses on output factors, such as final goods provided and services given. In the manufacturing industry, the final goods of a transformation process must be checked before they are delivered to other retailers, or used as parts or material in the next transformation process. In the service industry, it is important to check the feedback (comments from clients) on services given.

Post-control is particularly necessary in cases where pre-control and concurrent control have failed. Post-control focuses on fixing a problem that has come up. This means that the damage has already been done, but the aim is to make sure that this mistake will not happen again.

> ### CRITICAL THINKING
>
> Why are the different types of control important for a manufacturing organisation like BMW or a service organisation like Protea Hotels? Do these organisations use all these types of controls? Are all these types of control equally important? Investigate these organisations and then answer these questions, giving reasons for your answers.

TABLE 8.3 Post-control of output factors

Output factor	Post-control example
Final goods	Checking the final goods in order to establish whether the product is up to standard. (For example, at a Steers branch, a manager will taste whether a hamburger is fresh) and check whether all the items (sauce, garnish, bread) are according to the specifications for a Wacky Wednesday burger. A quality controller at BMW will assess a final vehicle ready for delivery, using a point checklist.
Final services	Measuring the final service given, in order to check whether it was up to standard. (For example, a manager at a hotel will check with a couple when they are checking out, whether the room, housekeeping and restaurant were satisfactory, or a matron at a clinic will judge nursing staff's help by asking a patient to complete a questionnaire when leaving).

8.3 Sources of control[9]

There are four main sources of control in most organisations, namely:
• individuals
• groups
• the organisation
• stakeholders.

8.3.1 Individual self-control

Individual self-control is a mix of conscious and unconscious control, as well as guiding functions that work inside people's brains. Being a professional person or an employee involves detailed knowledge, specialised skills, and suitable attitudes and ways of behaving, as minimum standards. For example, a salesperson at an insurance company will handle a rude customer according to the customer-relationship practices and professional behaviour described by the organisation's consumer-relationship policy statements.

8.3.2 Group control

Group control is based on the standards and values that group members share and keep going through rewards and punishments. A group will, for example, not accept any 'wrong' behaviour such as bribing someone to get a 'good deal' in any of the group's activities.

8.3.3 Organisational control

Organisational control is the rules and ways of preventing or correcting plans that do not work, and for reaching desired goals like standards and budgets. For example, at a bank, a policy on sexual harassment will state which behaviour is unacceptable, or at a large clothing shop, a policy on customer relations will guide salespeople on the right or wrong way to treat customers.

8.3.4 Stakeholder control

Stakeholder control is made up of pressure groups from outside, which aim to change the present behaviour of organisations. These stakeholders include worker unions, government institutions, communities, customers, shareholders and equal-rights groups. Government, for example, can develop laws like the Employment Equity Act and the Health and Safety Act, which state acceptable actions for organisations.

8.4 **The control process**[10]

Considering the 'systems approach', when inputs are being transformed into outputs, the control process consists of four major steps:
- Step 1: *developing* standards of performance that match the goals
- Step 2: *measuring* the actual performance of employees
- Step 3: *comparing* the actual performance with set standards
- Step 4: *reinforcing* good performance or correcting if necessary.[11]

FIGURE 8.1 The control process

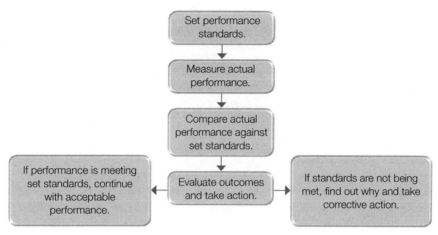

SOURCE: Oosthuizen T.F.J. 2007. *Management tasks for managerial success.* (3rd ed.) Johannesburg: FVBC.

8.4.1 Developing performance standards

The first step in the control process is to develop **performance standards**. All standards must be linked to the set objectives or goals of the organisation, department, group, or individual. Standards cannot be developed away from the planning process. **Standards** first consider objectives, and then judge performance that will produce these objectives. Standards can be described in various ways. Some standards are measurable, and others describe a corrrect level of behaviour.

TABLE 8.4 The most common ways of describing performance standards[12]

Type of standards	Description	Example
Quantity standards	Standards that are given as a number in terms of units	• Printing logos on 100 t-shirts per print-run
Cost standards	Standards that are given as a number in terms of currency	• A medical consultation fee of R400 per consultation
Time standards	Standards that are given as a number in terms of time	• Delivering one truck load of bricks per hour

Type of standards	Description	Example
Quality standards	Standards that are given as a number in terms of mistakes	• Having less than two faulty pens in a manufacture run for a 1 000 pens
Behaviour standards	Standards that are set according to correct behaviour	• Providing good and friendly customer service

Effective control standards need to be complete standards. The more detail such a standard has, the better it can be put into action. The various types of standards can also be put together to make a whole set of standards with many different categories. It is very important that standards are clear, and in order to be clear, they must state who must do what, how, and when.

8.4.2 Measuring actual performance[13]

Performance measurement is the second step in the control process. **Performance measurement** reflects whether an organisation is successful, and how successful it is, or, if it is not, at what level of performance the organisation is, and on what it must improve.

Management needs to consider what to measure and how often to measure it. It is very important that measurement is done objectively (without being emotionally involved). Subjective (with emotional involvement) measurement results in incorrect or biased (one-sided) information. Measurement must be reliable, valid (justifiable), and linked to the objectives. It must focus on the critical performance areas of the job, and it must result in the reinforcement of good performance or else the taking of corrective action.

8.4.3 Comparing actual performance with performance standards

The third step of the control process involves comparing the actual performance results (which were measured during the second step) with the standard (which was laid down in the third step). This information tells a manager if performance is up to standard, and whether the objective has been, or will be, achieved.

TABLE 8.5 Comparison of standards against actual performance at a hotel[14]

Measurable factor	Performance standards	Actual performance measurement averages or total for:		
		Week 1	**Week 2**	**Week 3**
Litres of water used per week	100 000 litres	70 000 litres	150 000 litres	100 000 litres
Rooms occupied per week	50 rooms	53	75	68
Eggs baked per breakfast session	150 eggs	158	165	140
Cleaning staff on duty per shift	12 cleaning staff members	10	10	12

8.4.4 Reinforcing good performance, and correcting if necessary

The fourth and final step in the control process can take two directions. Depending on the outcome of the third step, two possible actions can be taken. **Reinforcement** (encouragement) is needed if performance matches or exceeds (goes beyond) the set standards, and **corrective action** is needed if performance does not meet the set standards.

Corrective action must focus on defining the actual problem, based on the results in the third step. Once the reason for the problem is understood, corrective action can be taken. Where the problem is small, reinforcement can still be used to encourage improvement.[15]

8.5 **When to use a control measure**[16]

Not everything can or should be controlled. For a control measure to be useful, its advantage must be bigger than its cost.

The **cost–benefit model** is a computer tool for managers to use when they are considering whether the benefit of a control is worth more than its cost. The cost–benefit model estimates the effectiveness of an organisation's control system. Although the best amount of control is hard to decide, effective managers probably come closer to getting it right than ineffective managers do.

Managers have to consider trade-offs when choosing the amount of organisational control to use. With too little control, the cost of mistakes can exceed the benefits of having enough control measures in place. As the amount of control increases, effectiveness also increases, but only up to a point. Beyond a certain point, effectiveness declines (gets less) with further increases in the amount of control exercised.

For example, an organisation might benefit from reducing the number of people in the span of control from 20 to 14 employees. This would involve hiring more managers. However, to reduce the span further to 10 employees would require doubling the initial number of managers. The costs of the increased control (managers' salaries) might far outweigh the expected benefits.

When deciding how much control is needed, three factors should be considered:

- *Innovation and adaptability*: over-strict controls can limit entrepreneurial (creative, enthusiastic) behaviour in an organisation. Entrepreneurial spirit is valuable to ensure that employees are willing to take risks and are constantly looking for new ways to solve problems or to be creative in developing alternatives.
- *Economic factors*: the cost of applying controls should not exceed the benefit. Ideal control systems should actually save costs.
- *Behavioural factors*: if controls are applied in an autocratic ('bossy') way, they could spoil the motivation of employees. Employees should see the benefit of controls, and controls should be applied in a democratic manner.

Financial controls for the Blue Train[17]

Financial management of the Blue Train is seen as very important to ensure overall business excellence. The Blue Train's Finance Manager's role involves using a good internal control system. This will allow the management team to make the right decisions based on valid, accurate and complete financial information as well as up-to-date forecasts of expenses. Responsibilities also include complete, accurate recording and reporting of all financial events, compiling a budget, and ensuring that line manager's expenses fit the given financial performance standards, using control tools such as budgets and business plans.

8.6 **Financial controls**

Financial controls are techniques to prevent or correct a wrong allocation of resources. When implementing financial controls, managers use financial information like financial statements, financial ratios, and budgets. Various calculations, such as break–even analysis, are used to work out what will be profitable. Budgeting is used to establish standards, and income sheets and balance sheets are used to compare current performance with those of previous years.[18] (See Chapter 11 for more details on financial controls.) Internal auditing departments (such as the accounting department or the treasury department) or external auditors (such as KPMG and Ernst & Young) then monitor the effectiveness of an organisation's financial controls.[19]

8.7 **Quality controls**[20]

Quality controls are important in the continuous improvement of an organisation's performance. There are several quality-control techniques.

ISO 9000

The International Standards Organisation (ISO) aims to standardise quality in a global economy. More than 150 countries are involved, and thousands of organisations are registered with this organisation. IS 9000 is a set of international standards produced by the ISO that relate to quality management. These standards set the same guidelines for processes to ensure that products keep to customer wishes.

SOURCE: Daft, R.L., Marcic, D. 2007. *Management: The new workplace.* Australia: Thomson.

8.7.1 Total quality management

Total Quality Management (TQM) is an approach by many organisations to maintain quality in every activity in the organisation by means of continuous improvement. TQM is regarded as a pre-control, as it aims to be proactive (prevent problems rather than solve them).

8.7.2 Quality circles

Quality circles are groups of 6–12 employees who meet regularly to discuss and solve problems affecting the quality of their work. For example, at an aircraft factory, technicians and engineers will voluntarily (by their own choice) meet to resolve problems, so that they continuously improve the quality of their aircraft.

8.7.3 Six Sigma

Six Sigma is a determined approach to establishing higher quality at a lower cost. Sigma (σ) is a symbol used in statistics to measure how far away something is from perfection, and Six Sigma (6σ) stands for the goal of being free of mistakes 99.9997% of the time.

This approach is based on a five-step problem-solving method: defining, measuring, analysing, improving, and controlling problems that affect quality and cost. Many financial institutions, such as banks, practise Six Sigma to maintain their drive for profit togther with a high level of customer service.

8.7.4 Benchmarking

Benchmarking is a process where a specific good, service, practice or process is identified in an organisation and then measured against major competitors. For example, cellphone service providers will compare their latest program to cover sports or the financial markets against those of other providers.

8.7.5 Continuous improvement

Continuous improvement is based on making many small improvements in all areas of the organisation on an ongoing basis. For example, a car dealer will contact customers after a car service to ask how satisfied they are with the service. This information can then be used to update services or to deal with complaints.

8.7.6 Reduced cycle time

A cycle time indicates the number of steps taken to complete a process. By reducing the cycle time of a product, an organisation can simplify processes and ensure high quality at a lower cost.

> ## Quality controls at Mr Price
>
> The Mr Price group is committed to ensuring the highest levels of professionalism and integrity in terms of their products and services. This focus is especially true when considering their relationship with suppliers. They have established a supplier code of conduct. Mr Price uses an internationally accredited quality assurance institution to conduct regular factory audits at the time of quality control inspection. These audits cover compliance with local environmental and labour laws. During 2010, the Mr Price Apparel division has completed the roll-out of quality assurance at origin, using a third party inspection agency.[21]

8.8 The balanced scorecard[22]

The **balanced scorecard** is a strategic instrument that can be seen as a comprehensive management system that balances traditional financial measures with measures of aspects such as customer service, an organisation's capacity for learning and growth, as well as internal business processes.[23] For each of these elements the balanced scorecard considers the targets, measures the performance and interprets the outcomes, and then finally proposes an initiative for improvement. The balanced scorecard can therefore also be utilised as a strategic control tool. (See Figure 8.3.)

8.9 The benefits of controlling[24]

The aim of controlling is to give a manager information about why a certain objective, performance standard or any other indicator is not met. The manager can then do any of the following five tasks:

* *Revise and update plans.* Continuous development is required to keep a business sustainable over time. Buying behaviour, economic trends and fashion trends are examples of changing factors that should be considered by businesses. For example, new trends in cellphone use have resulted in various manufacturers adding features to their telephones, such as cameras and video-calling.
* *Standardise.* To ensure that customers are satisfied, standardisation (making things fit the same standard) of goods and services is useful. (For example, a frequent traveller has certain expectations when she or he buys a Kentucky Rounder at Kentucky Fried Chicken. By standardising recipes and ingredients as well as

processes, these expectations of that customer can be met no matter at which branch the Kentucky Rounder is bought.)

- *Judge employee performance.* With an effective control process in place, it becomes easier to judge the performance levels of employees in the organisation. (For example, a performance standard stating how many calls a telesales employee should handle in an hour, makes it possible for a manager to work out whether a consultant is performing well or poorly.)

- *Prevent problems and crises.* By having controls in place, managers and employees can be proactive (act before a problem, not after it) in their daily tasks. (For example, a financial manager will use quarterly financial statements to think about the organisation's performance in order to see if there is likely to be a cash–flow problem coming.)

- *Protect the organisation.* Controls ensure that all assets, such as equipment and buildings, are protected from malfunctioning (not working) or errors. (For example, a restaurant will install a fire alarm in its kitchen to ensure that patrons and employees get warning if there may be a fire danger.)

CASE STUDY: Environmental management controls at African giant and entertainment group – African Skies

The African Skies Group consists of hotels, resorts and entertainment facilities. The best known in South Africa is the Lion King resort with two hotels including the world-famous De Diamont Hotel, known for its French flair, as well as the Leisure Club and the popular Entertainment World. Other hotels in the group include the African Kingdom Spa and the Cape Classic Hotel as well as entertainment facilities such as the Quattro Forte Magic World, Blue Wave Fun Valley, Magic Waters, to mention a few.

The African Skies Group has been proactively involved in dealing with 'green' issues such as wastage, recycling, and alternatives for energy consumption. During 2011 the energy use for the group resulted in a small reduction compared with 2010. This was in spite of further efforts that have been made at a number of properties in 2011. Although energy management and improved technology have resulted in respectable savings of 15% at Magic Waters, a net reduction of only 2% was achieved for the whole group. Various factors such as forced load-shedding and a newly introduced environmental management programme, have contributed to lower consumption in general. Unfortunately, even these efforts for reduced energy consumption resulted in a shortfall (less than required) by the mandated performance standard of 10% expected of the hospitality sector in South Africa, and less than the 11% achieved in 2010.

Improved reporting standards and more accurate monitoring of consumption at all properties during 2011 have also contributed to the less-than-expected decrease in consumption. This is seen as a positive outcome in the sense that the new 'be green' environmental management programme is getting more effective. Even though the highest reporting accuracy has not yet been achieved, African Skies is confident that the current data is more accurate about actual consumption in general.

Continuous efforts have been made to review and manage energy consumption during 2011 as a concurrent (happening at the same time) control measure. Examples of concurrent control measures included comprehensive energy audits and improved use of energy-management systems. These were conducted at properties such as The Cape Classic Hotel and The Leisure Club. Refurbishments (new furnishings) and upgrading at a number of properties has also resulted in improved technology, resulting in improved pre-control measures being introduced. These pre-controls that were put in place are aimed at reducing and managing consumption on a concurrent basis in the future. Pre-control measures introduced were a smart-card system at the Lion King Hotel as well as the adoption of group refurbishment and energy management policies with minimum performance standards in respect of all refurbishments and developments in the future.

The use of other renewable energy systems is another example of a pre-control measure introduced to support future concurrent controls, for example, the first solar array for hot-water production at the Elephant Kingdom Hotel and Resort. The use of energy-efficient rechargeable lighting systems has also increased from the 45% reported in 2010 to an estimated 62% in 2011. This preventative control measure is being expanded wherever possible in an effort to further reduce consumption over the next three years.

Improved performance by environmental committees at each of the group's properties in 2011 has contributed to more significant environmental performance in most cases. In cases where the structures and systems were not fully operational (not yet working properly), specific attention and support were given by the Global Renewable Energy Consulting Company. This collaboration effort with the group's external environmental certification partner is to ensure that shortcomings identified in post-control assessments are addressed in the interests of improved performance.

QUESTIONS

1. What is the South African government's energy reduction minimum performance standard for the hospitality sector? Did the African Skies Group reach it in 2011?
2. Does African Skies have a partner helping them with post-control performance assessment?
3. What pre-controls were put in place for the African Skies Group to ensure overall improved environmental management performance?
4. What concurrent controls were put in place for the African Skies Group to ensure overall improved environmental management performance?
5. What post-controls were put in place for the African Skies Group to ensure overall improved environmental management performance?

SUMMARY

Control is the management task where performance is monitored to find errors, and so help the organisation achieve set goals and objectives. Three types of controls can be applied, namely pre-control, concurrent control, and post-control. The ideal is to combine the three types of control and focus on proactivity rather than reactivity.

During the control process it is essential to develop standards that are tied in with organisational objectives. These standards must be acceptable to those whose performance is measured according to them. Planning and control are interactive management tasks.

For effective control, management must work with employees and create a win–win situation for all the parties involved. Management must not focus only on financial controls to control performance. Organisations depend on their employees, and managers must remember that they are controlling employees and not finances.

GLOSSARY

balanced scorecard: a strategic instrument that can be seen as a comprehensive management system that balances traditional financial measures with measures of aspects such as customer service, an organisation's capacity for learning and growth, as well as internal business processes

behaviour standards: standards that are set according to what is seen as acceptable behaviour

benchmarking: a continuous process where a specific good, service, practice or process in an organisation is measured against that of major competitors

concurrent control: control measures that monitor activities while they are taking place in the transformation process in order to ensure that set standards and objectives are met

continuous improvement: the implementation of a large number of small improvements in all areas of the organisation on an ongoing basis

control: the systematic process through which managers regulate organisational activities in order to make them fulfil the expectations established during the planning process, and to help managers and employees reach the predetermined standards of performance

corrective action: action taken to correct mistakes and/or improve the performance of employees

cost-benefit model: a managerial tool that gauges the effectiveness of an organisation's control system

cost standards: standards that are expressed as numbers in terms of currency

financial controls: the methods, techniques and procedures intended to prevent or correct the misallocation of resources

group control: the norms and values that group members share and maintain through rewards and punishments

individual self-control: the conscious and unconscious control and guiding mechanisms that function in each person

organisational control: the formal rules and procedures for preventing or correcting shsortcomings in plans, and for achieving desired goals such as standards and budgets

performance measurement: measurement that shows whether an organisation is successful, and, if so, by how much, or, if it is not, at what level of performance the organisation is, and what it needs to improve on

performance standards: criteria that are based on organisational objectives and are used to evaluate qualitative and quantitative characteristics of performance, so as to meet the organisational objectives

post-control: a control measure after an action intended to reduce poor behaviours or undesirable results in terms of final goods or services, so as to reach set standards and achieve organisational goals

pre-control: a proactive measure before an action to anticipate and prevent input factors from negatively influencing their transformation and preventing the achievement of set objectives

quality circles: groups of 6–12 volunteer employees who meet regularly to discuss and solve problems affecting the quality of their work

quality standards: standards that are given as a number in terms of the number of errors that have been made

quantity standards: standards that are given as a number value in terms of units

reduced cycle time: when an organisation minimises the steps taken to complete an organisational process

reinforcement: positive feedback given to employees when their performance meets or exceeds set standards

Six Sigma (6σ): a determined approach to establishing higher quality at a lower cost, that is based on five steps of problem–solving: defining, measuring, analysing, improving, and controlling problems

stakeholder control: pressure groups formed by outside sources, whose aim is to change the current behaviour of organisations

standards: criteria used to evaluate the quality and quantity that is produced

time standards: standards that are given as numbers in terms of time

total quality management (TQM): an approach by many organisations to maintain quality in every activity in the organisation by means of continuous improvement

transformation process: the transformation of inputs into outputs

MULTIPLE-CHOICE QUESTIONS

1. Fresh produce sold at Fruit and Veg has a minimum standard of acceptable freshness and quality, as stated by the sell–by date. This example represents pre-control of _____.
   a) technology
   b) materials
   c) information
   d) capital

2. Which one of the following statements does not explain why control is necessary?
   a) It brings a focus to standardised quality.
   b) It minimises or even prevents crises.
   c) It prevents theft, wastage, damage, and malpractice.
   d) It allows an unstructured source for conducting performance evaluations.

3. Which one of the following is the third step of the control process?
   a) Develop performance standards.
   b) Compare performance with standards.
   c) Measure actual performance.
   d) Reinforce or correct current performance.

4. The different types of control can be connected to the various stages in the transformation process. Select the correct type of control below:
   a) Concurrent control is applied during the input process.
   b) Pre-control is applied during the transformation process.
   c) Post-control is applied during the output process.
   d) Post-control is applied during the transformation process.

5. Completing a project within two days is an example of which standard category?
   a) cost
   b) quality
   c) time
   d) behaviour

REFERENCES AND END-NOTES

1. DIXON, R. 1994. *The management task.* Oxford: Butterworth Heinemann.
2. MCDONALDS. 2010. www.bized.co.uk. [Online]. Available: http://www.bized.co.uk/compfact/mcdonalds/mc13.htm [14 October 2010].
3. WOOLWORTHS. 2007. *Our company.* [Online]. Available: http//www.woolworths.co.za [3 September 2007].
4. OOSTHUIZEN, T.F.J. 2007. *Management tasks for managerial success.* 3rd ed. Johannesburg: FVBC.
5. HELLRIEGEL, D., JACKSON, S.E., SLOCUM, J., STAUDE, G., AMOS, T., KLOPPER, H.B., LOUW, L., OOSTHUIZEN, T.F.J. 2004. *Management.* 2nd SA ed. Cape Town: Oxford University Press.
6. Ibid.
7. Gautrain. 2010. www. Railway.technology.com [Online]. Available: http://www.railway-technology.com/projects/gautrain [15 October 2010].
8. HELLRIEGEL, D., JACKSON, S.E., SLOCUM, J., STAUDE, G., AMOS, T., KLOPPER, H.B., LOUW, L., OOSTHUIZEN, T.F.J. 2004. *Management.* 2nd SA ed. Cape Town: Oxford University Press.
9. KATZ, R. Skills of an effective administrator. *Harvard Business Review.* September/October 1974:90–102; Daft, R.L., Marcic, D. 2007. *Management: The new workplace.* Australia: Thomson.
10. LUSSIER, R.N. 2006. *Management fundamentals: Concepts, applications, skill development.* 3rd ed. Cincinnati: South–Western.
11. KROON, J. (Ed.). 1995. *General management.* Pretoria: Kagiso Tertiary.
12. OOSTHUIZEN, T.F.J. 2007. *Management tasks for managerial success.* 3rd ed. Johannesburg: FVBC.
13. BENNETT, J.A., NIEMAN, G. (Ed.). 2005. *Business management: A value chain approach.* Pretoria: Van Schaik.
14. OOSTHUIZEN, T.F.J. 2007. *Management tasks for managerial success.* 3rd ed. Johannesburg: FVBC.
15. MINTZBERG, H. 1990. The Manager's Job: Folklore and Fact. *Harvard Business Review.* March/April: 49–61; Mintzberg, H. 1974. The Manager's Job: Folklore and Fact'. *Harvard Business Review.* July/August: 49–61.
16. HELLRIEGEL, D., JACKSON, S.E., SLOCUM, J., STAUDE G., AMOS, T., KLOPPER, H.B., LOUW, L., OOSTHUIZEN, T.F.J. 2004. *Management.* 2nd SA ed. Cape Town: Oxford University Press.
17. BLUE TRAIN. 2010. www.bluetrain.co.za [Online]. Available: http://www.bluetrain.co.za/management.htm [16 October 2010].

18. MR PRICE. 2010. www.mrpricegroup.com [Online]. Available: http://www.mrpricegroup.com/images/2010AnnualReport/divisional_review.pdf [15 October 2010].
19. JONES, G.R. & GEORGE, J. 1998. *Contemporary management.* Boston: Irwin McGraw-Hill.
20. DAFT, R.L., MARCIC, D. 2007. *Management: The new workplace.* Australia: Thomson; LUSSIER, R.N. 2006. *Management fundamentals: Concepts, applications, skill development.* 3rd ed. Cincinnati: South-Western; LEWIS, P.S., GOODMAN, S.H., FANDT, P.M. 2001. *Management: Challenges in the 21st century.* 3rd ed. Cincinnati: South-Western.
21. DAFT, R.L., MARCIC, D. 2007. *Management: The new workplace.* Australia: Thomson.
22. LUSSIER, R.N. 2006. *Management fundamentals: Concepts, applications, skill development.* 3rd ed. Cincinnati: South-Western.
23. LUSSIER, R.N. & ACHUA, C.F. 2006. *Leadership – Theory, application, skill development.* Cincinnati: South-Western.
24. RUE, L.W. & BYARS, L.L. 2005. *Management skills and application.* 11th ed. Boston: McGraw-Hill; Robbins, S.P. & Coulter, M. 1999. Management. 6th international ed. London: Prentice Hall.

ANSWERS TO MULTIPLE-CHOICE QUESTIONS

1. Answer = b)
2. Answer = d)
3. Answer = b)
4. Answer = d)
5. Answer = c)

PART THREE

The functional areas of management

Any business, big or small, has functional areas that are needed for the business to run smoothly. The chapters in this section are arranged according to these functional areas.

Chapter 9 deals with operations management, which is about where the goods or services are made.

Chapter 10 focuses on logistics management, which means how the flow of inputs and outputs is managed.

Chapter 11 introduces financial management, which is central to the business and influences every other area.

Chapter 12 explores human-resources management, which deals with attracting, developing, and retaining personnel, and is one of the most important ways to keep a competitive advantage for a business.

Chapter 13 deals with marketing management, and concentrates on identifying a target market and how to market an article or a service to a customer.

Operations management

Rigard Steenkamp

PURPOSE OF THIS CHAPTER

Operations management is a wide field, and this chapter introduces the basic ideas of the subject. It explains the importance of operations management as the core function. It also focuses on process management and the concepts (thoughts or ideas) involved in productivity and lean production. It examines the tasks of planning and control in this area, and briefly deals with operations improvement and quality management.

LEARNING OUTCOMES

This chapter should enable you to:
- understand how an operations plan relates to a business's plan
- understand the importance of operations management as the core function
- discuss what productivity is
- describe the characteristics of different operations systems
- understand the operations guidelines of design
- explain operations planning and control
- understand sequencing, scheduling, and bottlenecks (narrow places where flow is restricted)
- think of ways to change capacity to suit change in demand
- discuss how to manage inventory, calculate order quantities, and decide when to re-order required materials
- understand project management as an important and alternative operations system
- use basic Gantt charts and network analysis
- understand the essence of operations improvement
- discuss the principles of operations safety, quality, maintenance, and improvement.

9.1 **Introduction**

Operations management (OM) involves managing the transformation processes in a business where goods are made and/or services are provided. It is the closest that business comes to creating things. Because operations management is about being creative, productive, and value-adding, it should be at the core of any business. An **operation** is a **process** in which inputs are transformed into outputs, but the word can also refer to any new task that involves a transformation, such as a new set-up, improving facilities, maintenance, or making something unique. Operations managers can manage several operations systems like repeating a process, or managing a job operation, or they can act as project managers for tasks that have a clear beginning and end.

Today's economies depend on businesses having good operations management. The contributions of operations management to society include:[1]

- better quality goods and services
- higher standards of living
- improved working conditions
- a concern for the environment.

9.2 **A brief history of operations management**

In the past, the act of overseeing the manufacturing of products was described as production management. Today the term operations management is used instead, although this new term also covers the management process in service-delivery organisations.

Production or operations management began in the Industrial Revolution. Adam Smith, for instance, insisted that workers should specialise (concentrate on special skills). Henry Gantt, Frank and Lillian Gilbreth, and Frederick Taylor were also important people in this field. Gantt began using schedule charts, the Gilbreths (who had 12 children and used the slogan 'cheaper by the dozen') used time-and-motion studies, and Taylor used process analysis.

In the past 100 years, production or operations management has developed from a set of newly discovered ideas to a collection of developed and combined concepts. Operations management is now very important for competitive business.

9.3 **Operations management is the core function of any organisation**

Operations management is the core (central) function in all organisations, and is also important in all parts of the business, because all the activities aim to add value. Operations management is a 'make or break' activity because in most businesses it works with the bulk of its assets and resources. It is easy to understand the importance of operations management in making tangible products like furniture, paint, motor vehicles, etc. It may not be so clear in the service industries, although any business produces something, whether it is tangible or not. Even not-for-profit organisations use resources to produce something. The process of adding value (making money) is an operations function. Slack, Chambers and Johnston state: 'Operations management uses resources to appropriately create outputs that fulfil defined market requirements'. These authors also say that operations decisions are the same in commercial and not-for-profit organisations, but that a new agenda is arising because of a changing business environment and modern business pressures.[2] Some examples of the items on this new agenda are ethical sensitivity, health and safety, sound environmental management, and seeking ways to use new technologies. Operations management will continue to remain crucial, in spite of all the new challenges. It will continue to affect profitability, it will remain the way to achieve strategic performance objectives, and it will continue trying to satisfy a wide range of stakeholders.

If one needs to pick out one particular performance objective, then this would be **agility**, which in physical terms means being quick and supple. It is also therefore the ability to react quickly and flexibly. An agile operation responds to uncertainty in the market (the external customer) and also has several advantages for the internal customer. An agile operation is one where the trade-offs between performance objectives (speed, cost, quality, etc.) are limited. These abilities will benefit several other objectives, and agility should therefore be an obvious strategic business principle.

9.4 **Effectiveness, efficiency, and productivity**

Businesses come in many forms, and therefore have many operations (see Table 9.1). However, all operations should be value-adding processes in which inputs are transformed into outputs. Operations management involves making these processes effective (doing the right things to create the most value for the company) and efficient (doing something at the lowest possible cost).

TABLE 9.1 Examples of transformation processes

Business type	Inputs	Transformation	Outputs
Bakery	Ingredients (such as flour and sugar), equipment (such as ovens), training people (such as bakers, with knowledge of recipes)	Preparing food according to specifications, setting up machines, mixing, moulding, baking and packing	Cakes, pies, bread, ready for delivery
Maker of custom-made ear plugs	Trained audiom-etrists, materials and equipment to take moulds, transport to visit factories and laboratory	Calibrating filters, making acrylic ear plugs from soft moulds, assembling filters and cords, embedding names, packing ear plugs neatly, personally fitting ear plugs, doing a seal test	Workers have personalised and comfortable ear plugs that protect them from noise and prevent hearing loss from noise
Hospital	Patients, doctors, nurses, theatres, rooms, ambulances, equipment	Medical procedures, therapy, service delivery, professional handling and care of patients, application and administration of medicine	Improved quality of life, satisfied clients, recovered and healthy patients, extended life expectancies

An operations manager's key challenge is to increase the value of the business's outputs relative to the cost of its inputs. **Productivity** is a common measure of how well inputs are being used by a business (micro-productivity) or a country (macro-productivity).

Productivity is sometimes measured by means of the following formula:

CRITICAL THINKING

Think of an example to explain why outputs – inputs = productivity is a better way of describing productivity than output income – input expenses = productivity.

> **outputs ÷ inputs = productivity**

But just saying that productivity is 'output divided by input' is not the whole story.

One can be 'productive' without really producing usable output. Productivity is therefore not only efficiency, but also effectiveness. In addition, there must be a market for what is produced, in order for the process of production to be considered 'productive'. This brings us to a more accurate formula for productivity that uses output income, which is usable output quantity, and input expenses, which are the available input quantity:

> **output income ÷ input expenses = productivity**

Lead time, or throughput time refers to general time for the actual manufacturing process. The main elements of lead time are:
- queue time: the period for which a job stays in the queue at a work centre
- setup time (the time needed to prepare equipment for processing a new job)
- processing time (the actual time needed to process the job)
- waiting time (the empty time between the processing of a job and its transportation to the next work centre)
- transportation time (the time needed to move the job from one work centre to the next)
- inspection time (the time needed to check whether the job comes up to quality standards).

Operations management is concerned all the time with process management, reducing all kinds of lead-time elements to improve both effectiveness and efficiency. Process throughput time can be reduced by:
- re-engineering
- getting new equipment
- performing activities in parallel (side by side)
- changing the order of activities
- reducing interruptions.

9.5 **Operations strategies**

All business activities are aimed at achieving objectives. Business strategies are wider, large-scale plans for the future, which aim to achieve these objectives in the very best way. Significant (meaningful) decisions that have a big effect can also be called business strategies.

Pearce and Robinson identify the following core aspects of a business's strategic decisions:[3]

- Strategic decisions are future-orientated. They are made on the basis of anticipation and forecast, aiming to choose the most promising strategic position.
- Strategic decisions must involve top-level management because they affect several areas of the business. At this level, there is a need to understand and anticipate the wide effects of such decisions.
- Strategic decisions involve a lot of resources. Human and non-human resources must come from either inside or outside the business.

Slack *et al.* define **operations strategies** as the total patterns of decisions and actions that form the roles, objectives and activities of each part of the operation, so that they support the organisation's business strategies.[4] Operations strategies are designed, created, and implemented to make the business more competitive in the market.

In general, the operations-management function has three important strategic roles, namely:

- driving business strategy
- supporting business strategy
- implementing business strategy.

Performance objectives are the skills that drive business strategy. They can be referred to as 'strategic performance objectives'. Examples of these are quality, cost, service delivery, speed, reliability, consistency, responsiveness, and flexibility. Businesses try to achieve more than one of these at the same time.

However, it often happens that when one performance objective is achieved very well, another one is achieved less well. According to **Trade-off Theory**, operations managers must choose to trade-off one performance objective against another. The best example is the quality versus cost trade-off. However, the Trade-off Theory has been challenged. It has been suggested that rather than deciding which performance objectives to sacrifice in order to concentrate on others, operations managers should change whatever is causing one objective to go downhill when another improves, and create continuous improvement.

9.6 **Product design and operations design**

Product designs are plans for goods or services. Operations designs are plans for how to produce goods or services. Good things come from good product designs and good operations designs; bad things usually come from bad product designs or bad operations designs.

Examples of South African inventions[5]

1. Appletiser and Grapetiser – a pure aerated (sparkling) fruit juice recipe
2. Kreepy Krauly – the well-known automatic pool-cleaning device
3. PUDU crime-prevention project (explosive gel that freezes the cash if a robbery of cash/goods occurs)
4. Pratley's Putty – a two-part clay-like mixture which bonds into a very hard and strong compound
5. Mine-hoist cage door that reduces loading time from 72 to 42 seconds
6. Computicket – the first computerised ticket-sales system in the world
7. Noise Clipper custom-made hearing protectors with filtering devices

---

Take note of the following ten guidelines for effective product and operations designs:[6]

1. Take into account target-market expectations and target costs. (Designers should be experimental in their search for materials and methods to ensure that the new product designs are not too expensive.)
2. Simplify assemblies and reduce the number of parts or operations to bring down costs, improve quality, and make production or service easier.
3. Ensure that exact customer or client requirements are known, so that designs are based on actual needs. Designers should also be absolutely clear about the required specifications and possible variations.
4. Ensure that there is enough available process ability to carry out the design.
5. Use standard materials, parts, methods and procedures of known and proven quality. Untested materials and methods are risky.
6. Design parts and service elements that are multi-functional (have several uses) and that can be used in different circumstances or situations.
7. Design products for ease of joining, separating or rejoining, and services for ease of coupling or uncoupling.
8. Design for one-way assembly and one-way travel, by avoiding back-tracking and return visits.
9. Avoid special, complicated fasteners and connectors for products and off-line services, or elements that break and spoil the service.
10. Design for robustness (strength), and avoid designs that require a great deal of care during manufacture or delivery, or that otherwise may lead to poor or unsafe performance.

If a product is to be produced in a large quantity with very low variety, it will use a continuous method of operation. On the other hand, a unique product will need a very flexible design. Between these two extremes are **batches** of products which are not unique, but are only slightly different from each other. **Continuous operations systems**, **batch operations systems**, and **project operations systems**, will have different layouts in order to streamline work flow.

TABLE 9.2 The characteristics of the three main categories of operations systems

	Continuous/ repetitive operations system	Batch/job operations system	Project operations system
Product type	Standardised	Diversified	Unique
Layout	Product layout in which facilities are placed along flow lines according to the product's subcomponents	Process layout where similar processes, skilled labour or facilities are grouped together in one place	Fixed-position layout – where the product is kept at a fixed position and the production facilities come to it
Product flow	Standardised	According to requirements of particular product	Almost none
Materials handling	Materials flow determinable, systemised and often automated	Handling depends on the product, therefore highly variable and expensive	Special equipment often necessary; high cost
Raw materials inventory	High turnover	Low turnover	Variable because of production time
Work-in-progress	Small quantities	Large quantities	Single product
Production cost components	Relatively high fixed cost; low variable cost per unit	Relatively low fixed cost; high variable cost per unit	Relatively high fixed cost; high variable cost
Labour requirements	Highly specialised routine tasks at a specific rate	Highly skilled artisans working without supervision and with moderate adaptability	High degree of adaptability to various tasks commissioned

An operations manager can also be involved in **job design**, which is the grouping of activities that one person must perform. Designing jobs allows the operations manager to use employees' strengths effectively and to maintain employees' motivation.

9.7 Operations planning and control

Operations strategy governs the **operations-management policy**, which is a set of guidelines for carrying out and controlling specific actions to achieve continuity, consistency, and integration (putting together). This policy governs operations planning, so that the operations manager's decisions fit in with the planning done by the business.

One of the main tasks of the operations manager is **capacity planning**, which is planning for the resources needed over a certain time period. **Fixed-capacity planning** is done for a long-term period, and **variable-capacity planning** is done for a short-term or medium period.

The operations manager is also responsible for controlling the transformation processes. This function includes all the steps taken to set standards, and to evaluate (judge) the operations system against these standards. Some of the control functions carried out by the operations manager include cost control, quality control (which includes proactive and reactive methods to prevent, detect, and rectify faults) and quantity control (which is the measurement of productivity).

9.7.1 Reconciling (dealing with opposites) supply and demand (give and take)

Planning and control require handling[7] supply and demand in terms of volumes, timing, and quality. To reconcile volume and timing, four overlapping activities are performed:
- loading (allocating amounts of work to particular work centres)
- sequencing (deciding on the order in which the work will be performed)
- scheduling (making timetables showing when jobs should start and end)
- monitoring (checking that the operations are happening according to plan).

9.7.1.1 **Loading**

Loading involves allocating amounts of work to particular **work centres**. In 'finite loading', work is allocated up to a set limit, which is the estimated amount that the centre can take. In 'infinite loading', work limits are not set, and the work station tries to cope with the work that arrives.

9.7.1.2 **Sequencing**

Sequencing involves deciding on the order in which the work will be done. When priorities (being placed at the start) are given to work in an operation, some pre-defined (already decided) set of rules may apply, or the physical nature of the materials being processed may determine the order of priority.

Pre-defined sets of sequencing rules could include:
- customer or client priority sequencing (important or angry customers or clients are put first, whatever the order of arrival.)
- due-date (DD) priority sequencing (the time the work is done depends on when the order is due for delivery, whatever the size of each job or the importance of the customer or client.)
- first-in-first-out (FIFO) priority sequencing (Customers or clients are served as they arrive. This approach is also known as 'first come, first served'.)
- last-in-first-out (LIFO) priority sequencing (For practical reasons, sometimes the jobs that arrive last must move out first.)
- longest-operation-time (LOT) priority sequencing (Jobs that take the longest time go first.)
- shortest-operation-time (SOT) priority sequencing (When cash is needed, the short jobs may be done first, in order to invoice and get payment faster.)

9.7.1.3 **Scheduling**

Schedules are statements of volume (content) and timing in different types of operations systems. **Scheduling** means deciding how many jobs are to be done, and when they are to be completed. A **master production schedule** (MPS) gives the broad plan of firm orders and forecasts for similar product groups to be manufactured over the medium term (in medium time).

Schedulers must deal with different types of capacity and resources at the same time, while machines and staff have different capabilities. The number of possible schedules increase as the number of activities and processes increase.

Operations scheduling consists of four separate activities:
- First the operations must be timed and routed. **Timing** involves deciding when a particular operation will take place, and **routing** fixes the place where the operation will be performed.

- The second activity is called **dispatching**. This involves issuing a **shop order** (authorisation for a job) so that the operation can take place.
- The third activity decides the status of the shop order. This is necessary since the progress of the shop order must be known at all times.
- The fourth activity is **expediting**. This tries to get an order completed more quickly.

Push systems and **pull systems** are what trigger the work. A push system pushes out the work without noticing the exact time or use of the customer, and in a pull system the pace (speed) is determined by the customer or the next process.

Production time (P):demand time (D) ratios[8]

In the production time: demand time ratios, **demand time** (D) is the total length of time the customer must wait, and **production time** (P) is the entire throughput time, including lead-time elements such as sourcing and delivery. The higher P is, compared to D, the more thinking is taking place in the operation. Speeding up any part of P will reduce customer's waiting time, D. When capacity is high and everything is made to a firm order, the P and D are equal – this is the resource-to-order situation (for example, projects). The smaller D is, compared to P, the smaller the risk. P is slightly greater than D in a **make-to-order** operation (for example, in the production of custom-made furniture). For high volume **make-to-stock** operations, D is much smaller than P (for example, in the production of retail products).

Effective scheduling:
- is realistic
- allows for any essential changes
- allows enough time for all the operations, as well as before and after the operations
- gives employees responsibility for keeping to schedules
- does not release all available jobs by means of shop orders
- does not schedule all the available capacity of the plant.

Undercapacity scheduling means that less than the total available capacity is scheduled, in order to prevent burnout and allow maintenance and quality to be considered. For example, 95% of available capacity may be scheduled for a particular shift.

The starting point of a schedule has a big effect on the schedule. In forward scheduling, the approach is to begin at the present date, and to schedule forward according to the times needed to perform all the operations necessary to complete the order. When all the times have been added, the manufacturer can give the customer an idea when the order will be ready. In **backward scheduling**, the date a customer requires a product is used as a starting point, so that the time for each activity is subtracted from the due date.

9.7.1.4 **Monitoring**

Monitoring is a controlling activity to ensure that the planned actions are happening according to schedule. The planned output of a work centre is monitored and compared with the plan. If a deviation (change) from the plan occurs, it can be fixed by some kind of intervention.

9.7.1.5 **Addressing bottlenecks**

All operations managers are faced by **bottlenecks** and the results of poor service and higher costs. Nicholas and Steyn[9] define the **Theory of Constraints** (TOC) as a systems approach to improving business systems. A chain is as strong as its weakest link, and to improve the chain, one must find its weaknesses. The basic idea of the TOC is that only a few elements (work stations or subsystems) prevent it from achieving its goal.

Each operations manager has a set of methods to deal with each situation (for example, outsourcing during peak periods or organising employees to work overtime). The challenge is to develop schedules that focus on bottlenecks, to maximise (enlarge) the flow of value-added processes, to minimise time spent on set-ups when changing over from one product to another, to not overload processes, and to shift resources at the right time and place to minimise the idle (non-working) time lost at bottlenecks. The TOC is one method that can be applied. Also referred to as the 'drum–buffer–rope method', the basic idea of the TOC is to focus on bottlenecks to increase throughput. For example, if the welder is creating a bottleneck, she or he is identified as a system constraint.

The procedure is:
- Step 1: Identify the constraint.
- Step 2: Decide how to exploit the constraint.
- Step 3: Subordinate non-constraints to the decision(s) made in step 2.
- Step 4: Elevate the constraint(s).
- Step 5: Return to step 1 to determine if a new constraint has appeared.

This method is very effective, and is applied in project management. Methods to reduce the length of time of the project are always a priority. When the TOC method is applied to project scheduling, it is called the Critical Chain Method (CCM).

9.7.2 Demand management

Demand and capacity are interrelated, since demand for a specific range of products implies a certain level of capacity (both fixed and variable). In the medium term, **demand management** is used to determine **aggregate demand**, which is the demand for a group of products sharing the same capacity in the plant. **Aggregate planning** refers to the anticipation of aggregate demand, and includes capacity planning. It is a broad view of the market and what an operation can handle in terms of capacity.

Forecasting is the science of anticipation (using several techniques) determining the demand for a product in the light of future events. Broadly speaking, forecasting techniques are divided into three categories:

- Quantitative techniques, such as time–series analysis, which uses numerical data and mathematical calculations to make forecasts about the future.
- Qualitative techniques which use data, but the forecasts that are made are based on the forecaster's feelings about the data rather than actual calculations.
- Causal methods which determine a cause-and-effect relationship.

9.7.3 Fixed-capacity planning

The long–term objective of demand management relates to fixed–capacity planning. A business's **capacity** is the greatest workload that a business can handle. Capacity is limited by human resources, natural resources, capital, technology, and methods. The best use of capacity is important to maximise production ability. The elements of fixed–capacity planning are:

- identifying a suitable place
- deciding the size of the production unit
- designing the layout of the production unit
- the choice and design of equipment
- considering the safety of the workers.

9.7.4 Adapting capacity to a change in demand

If a production unit is working at full capacity, a change in demand could mean that the capacity has become either too small or too big. If the capacity to produce a product is smaller than the demand for the product, the production unit could:

- hire more employees or get additional machines
- introduce overtime or introduce an extra shift
- specialise in a particular type of that product

- use a temporary means of production or accept a transfer of surplus capacity from other divisions
- open a new section in the factory.

If the capacity to produce a product is greater than the demand for the product, the productive unit can:
- close a section of the factory
- scale down workers' hours or use fewer shifts
- combine products
- reduce the temporary means of production
- move surplus capacity to another division or sell excess equipment.

9.7.5 Inventory management

Materials management is a set of activities and methods used for getting, handling, storing, and controlling materials. **Inventory management** is the planning and controlling of all types of **inventory** (raw materials, sub-assemblies, consumables, finished products and so on) with the focus on cost, timing, and quantities. The central part of inventory management (planning and control) is to have just enough inventory at any given time. This involves two major areas, namely timing and quantity. The principles for good inventory management are:
- The most economical quantities should be ordered.
- Production should never be held up by a shortage of a certain item in the inventory.
- Losses should be prevented by controlling all incoming inventory as regards quality, quantity, and the requirements, as given in the purchase order.
- A great mixture of different items should be avoided. Standardisation and simplification are very useful.
- The financial investment in inventory must be controlled, to save on interest and cost.
- A scientific and factual method to simplify purchases (by using mathematical models) needs to be created.
- Dead or slow-moving stock should be identified and managed.
- There should be a reduction in possible losses as a result of obsolescence (objects getting old and out-of-date) and incorrect or excessive purchases.
- Inventory control must serve as a source of information for management decisions.

A business's capital should not be tied up in idle stock. Stock which is tied up in this way is called the **carrying cost**. The total inventory carrying cost usually includes the following elements:

- Direct inventory carrying-cost elements: the two direct-cost components (parts) are **capital cost** (interest or opportunity cost) and **holding cost** (the cost involved in renting storage facilities, warehouse equipment, electricity, insurance, security, handling, book-keeping, warehousing, labour, and damage).
- Indirect inventory carrying-cost elements: these are the costs attached to obsolescence, record-keeping, physical stocktaking, inventory planning and control, the cost of production floor space used for work-in-progress, scrap and rework, as well as the costs involved in handling and packing into containers.

The mode of operation will determine the type of timing and quantity planning and control:
- Make-to-stock operations (continuous and batch operations) will do planning and control based on forecasting, safety-stock levels, and economic order quantities.
- Make-to-order operations (smaller job operations referred to as 'job shops') will hold the minimum inventory, and will obtain inventory according to the custom order by the client.
- Resource-to-order (project operations) will keep no stock.

> ### CRITICAL THINKING
>
> The entrepreneurs of custom-made hearing protection devices in South Africa need to be flexible and adaptable to the high demand for quality acrylic custom-made ear plugs. Assume it would cost R2 750 to rearrange the NOISE CLIPPER (Pty) Ltd laboratory facilities inside one of their work centres, in order to get rid of R5 500 worth of inventory. I = the annual carrying cost rate, which is based on the direct inventory carrying cost elements. If I = 0,25 will the rearrangement be worth it?
>
> ### Answer
> This is a saving of 0,25 x R5 500 per year (in other words, R1 375 per year) which means that the R2 750 will be recovered within two years. Therefore, it would probably be worth it.

The order cost is the cost that must be paid to place an order. An item may be ordered twice, three times or more per year, and even daily in just-in-time (JIT) systems. If these orders are to be manufactured internally, the order cost will consist mainly of machinery setups.

The traditional model for deciding when to reorder inventory items involves a **re-order point** (ROP). A re-order point is the level of a stock at which it must be renewed or re-ordered. There are variations of re-order points. The periodic inventory system is used by restaurants, service stations, and other retailers where inventory is ordered daily or weekly. Some manufacturers include the ROP in the product. Examples of this are cheque books. The two-bin system is a continuous inventory system often used in small warehouses. As soon as one bin is empty, an order is placed.

Reorder points are calculated according to experience of consumer patterns, 'rule-of-thumb' (practical, on-the-job) judgement, or by applying a formula. However, the formula also demands a degree of judgement, since it includes demand patterns and sets a level for the **safety stock** (an additional but limited level of inventory that is kept in case a stock-out situation arises).

The ROP formula is:

$$\text{ROP} = \text{D(LT)} + \text{SS}$$

where ROP = reorder point
  D = average demand per time period
  LT = average lead time (how long customers have to wait to receive products)
  D(LT) = average demand during lead time
  SS = safety stock

CRITICAL THINKING

Noise Clipper's one laboratory has an average monthly demand for Mr. Clean-EAR cleaning spray (for occupational hygiene) of 105 litres. If the order lead time is one week, and a safety stock of five litres is applicable, what will the ROP be?

Answer

ROP = D(LT) + SS. In other words

$$\text{ROP} = 105\frac{7}{30} + \frac{105}{30}5$$

= _____ + _____

= _____ litres of Mr. Clean-EAR cleaning spray

9.7.6 Material-requirements planning

Material–requirements planning (MRP) is a 'push system', and helps operations managers decide when to issue orders for materials and how much to order.

A simplified example of MRP for screwdriver handle

A company that makes tools uses screwdriver handles made by a certain supplier. All three screwdrivers that the company makes (2 mm, 7 mm and Star 5) use the same type of handle. The item master file shows the following planning factors:
- Batches are set at quantities of 20.
- Safety stock is set at two handles.
- The available inventory is 70.
- The lead time for orders is two weeks.

Question

When will orders be issued, and what size will these orders be? (Refer to Tables 9.3 and 9.4 below.)

TABLE 9.3

Item	Week				
	1	2	3	4	5
2 mm	10			10	
7 mm	8		18		18
Star 5	18	8	8	8	8

TABLE 9.4

Item	Week				
	1	2	3	4	5
Gross requirements	36	8	26	18	26
Scheduled receipts					
Available inventory = 70	34	26	20	2	16
Planned orders	20		40		

Answer

The order in week 1 must be for 20 handles. The order in week 3 must be for 40 handles.

Ordering small quantities more frequently will result in higher order costs. When orders are large and not placed often, too much inventory will be tied up in capital. In 1915, F.W. Harris developed the concept of the **economic order quantity** (EOQ), which is the quantity ordered in each order cycle, that keeps total inventory costs minimal. Harris designed formulas to determine the correct order quantities. Although Harris's assumptions do not always apply in practice, they are still usually close enough to make the model useful (see Chapter 10).

9.7.7 Make-or-buy decisions

Break-even analysis is often used for determining the volume at which total earnings are equal to total cost. The same technique can be used to determine when the cost to make a component equals the total cost to buy it. One can use this to decide whether to make or buy something, or when two production methods are compared. It can also be used to find the profit potential of a new product.

9.7.8 Operations improvement

The basic performance objectives of any operation include improvement. Speediness, cost-effectiveness, and flexibility are a few examples of such improvements. To get and keep these things demands a constant process of improvement and seeking ways to improve the entire operational system. Agility, as mentioned earlier, can be regarded as the ultimate operational performance objective that will demand constant attention. Operations managers can use several improvement strategies and techniques, and we will introduce some of these concepts in this section.

9.7.8.1 **Quality and quality management**

Chapter 8 introduced a number of approaches to raising **quality** and so delivering value. Quality is an important performance objective, and the existence of imperfection (quality gaps, defects or mistakes) is what causes the improvement (closing the quality gaps). One of the most popular of these approaches is **total quality management** (TQM). TQM is a holistic approach to quality, which tries to deliver value by looking for ways to improve all resources, processes, products, and functions. The TQM approach goes beyond checking for faults. It focuses on quality at the source, prevention of defects, and continuous improvement. A feature of this holistic approach is its wide application of tools, teams, and systems. 'Soft' components such as culture, communication, and commitment, are also naturally part of TQM. It uses international quality-management system standards, such as those based on **ISO 9000** to support quality, and it creates and supports quality improvement and control techniques (for example, statistical process control).

To manage quality, one must understand what quality is. The following are some definitions:
- Quality is fitness for the intended function.
- Quality is conformance to specification or the purchase order.
- Quality is the degree to which the client or customer is satisfied.
- Quality is a total collection of the product's dimensions (characteristics) that meet the customer's expectations.

Examples of quality dimensions regarding services are as follows:
- Reliability means that one can depend on a service as expected.
- Responsiveness is the willingness of the service provider to meet the customer's needs when these needs are expressed.
- Competence refers to the service provider's possession of skills and knowledge to perform the service.

The following characteristics relate specifically to the quality of goods:
- Performance is the way a product actually operates.
- Features are the little extras that go with a product and make it unique.
- Reliability refers to the promise that it will perform and keep on performing as promised over a specific time span.
- Conformance is the meeting of pre-set standards.
- Durability is the length of the product's life span.
- Aesthetics involves the physical qualities of the product that make it pleasant to look at.

Perceived quality is the indirect evaluation of quality, for example, the reputation of a specific brand. Excellence is going beyond the minimum requirements in an attempt to exceed customer expectations.

9.7.8.2 **Statistical process control**

Statistical process control (SPC) is one tool used by quality management. It is about checking whether the process for the manufacture of goods or delivery of services is either under control (in which case the process may continue) or outside control. If the process is outside control, it means that the variations are outside the limits of the natural process variation for one or other reason, in which case the process must be stopped, investigated, and the causes of the unnatural variation be removed. Statistical process control uses various types of **process control charts** to measure samples of process output. Many different quality-control techniques are also available, such as the fishbone diagram, the pareto diagram, and others. All of these are important tools for operations improvement.

9.7.8.3 **Maintenance and replacement**

Resources include human resources. The science of maintenance is connected to operations improvement because it aims at sustaining the operational system. Several improvements are needed just to keep the system working. Machinery and other pieces of equipment are subject to a good deal of wear because their moving parts are in constant use. The consequences of faulty equipment can be:

- threats to safety
- lower-quality products
- dissatisfied customers or clients
- reduced production capacity
- increased production costs (covering the idle time of machine operators, the cost of the repair team and the new components, and the hiring of back-up machinery).

There are several maintenance strategies:

- run-to-breakdown maintenance (fixing equipment when it breaks)
- condition-based maintenance (fixing equipment when it looks likely to break)
- preventive maintenance (servicing equipment to avoid breakage).

Preventive maintenance requires employees to prevent failures where possible. It also involves training maintenance teams, and predicting the possible times of equipment failure through good record-keeping of previous failures.

9.7.8.4 **Safety, health and environmental management**

Operations improvement also includes the environment around the operational system. Running a safe working environment is part of the responsibility of operations management. Risks in the workplace must be managed by safety managers and safety engineers. Although it has many technical issues, managing safe operations has a strong humanistic aspect since many operations solutions lie in employee motivation and well-being. One popular philosophy is behaviour-based safety. Unfortunately many entrepreneurs, when starting up a business, are more concerned with getting the business going than worrying about health and safety. This can be damaging in many ways. Today the role of operations management increasingly includes safety, health, and environment (SHE) management. Strict regulations and safety measures about the quality of working life (QWL) will continue to appear. A few QWL decisions can make a big difference in the operations environment.

9.8 **Project planning and control**

It is important to note some of the workings of **project management**. Project management is a different and active type of management, and projects are produced by means of a unique and different type of operations system. A **project** is a temporary attempt to create a unique product. Project management is needed when the scope of a project is complex. A project's complexity increases as the number of activities, resources, and people involved increase.

A **project manager** should have:
- a background in, and experience of, related projects
- an understanding of project management as a profession (which is very different to ordinary general management)
- strategic expertise of the overall project and its environment
- proven project-managerial ability based on a track record and leadership skills.

9.8.1 Project planning and Gantt charts

Project planning is a complex activity that follows project definition. Several planning tools can be used, such as **Gantt charts**. These are time charts, and they are the most commonly used scheduling technique for small projects. They are simple to construct and easy to understand. A Gantt chart gives a drawing of the progress made on a project. The work packages and work tasks are on the left-hand side of the chart, and the work weeks are at the top or bottom.

TABLE 9.5 Gantt chart for the delivery of JAZZ-MAX construction cranes

ACTIVITY	ACTIVITY NUMBER	WEEK NUMBER								
		1	2	3	4	5	6	7	8	9
Fabricate steel structure	A	███	███	███	███					
Buy power units	B			███	███	███				
Get components on BOM list	C			███	███					
Assemble	D						███	███		
Train the operator	E					███	███			
Test with operator	F								███	
Deliver	G									███

9.8.2 Network analysis

Network diagramming is another popular planning tool used for more complex projects. Several software packages are available to simplify its use. Work packages or project activities (A) with their respective durations (D) (the time they take) are put in a particular order and in terms of what comes just before or just after them. The longest route from the first to the last activity of the project is the **critical path**. The duration of activities on this path must not increase, because this will extend the project duration. The activities not on the critical path may be delayed (only if necessary) because they do have slack time available. In order to determine the amount of slack available per activity, the project manager must calculate the earliest start (ES) times, the earliest finishing times (EF), the latest start (LS) times and the latest finishing (LF) times for those activities not on the critical path. Total slack (TS) and free slack (FS) can then be determined. The nodes represent the activity (work package), and the lines indicate relationships before and after.

The following is an example of a network (using the activity-on-node method) of the Impala Hearing Conservation Project executed by Noise Clipper (Pty) Ltd. Note that A, C, F, H, I and J form the critical path, and the duration of the project is 25 weeks (see Figure 9.1).

FIGURE 9.1 Critical-path-method (CPM) network diagram of a small project

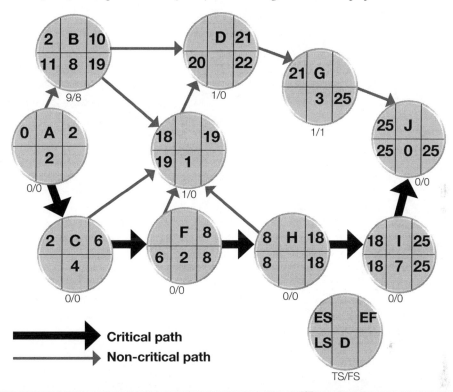

Critical path
Non-critical path

CASE STUDY: The lean paradigm at L'Oréal

The lean paradigm has been seen as a major factor contributing to business success by trimming fat from all operations, with a stable marketplace and relatively small product variety. 'Lean operations' represent a state of an operation where all waste has been eliminated, the operation is faster, more flexible/dependable and produces higher quality products and services. This is why the lean or JIT approach is also described by other terms such as continuous flow manufacture, high value-added manufacture, stockless production and short-cycle time manufacturing.

L'Oréal cosmetics is now the world's largest toiletries and cosmetics group, with a presence in over 140 different countries. In the UK the 45 000 square metre purpose-built facility in mid-Wales produces 1 300 product lines in a spotlessly clean environment which is akin to a pharmaceutical plant in terms of hygiene, safety and quality. The plant has 55 production lines and 45 different production processes, and the manufacturing system employed is of a flexibility that allows them to run each of the 1 300 production lines every two months. That means over 150 different lines each week. But the plant was not always as flexible as this. It has been forced to enhance its flexibility by the requirement to ship over 80 million items each year. The sheer logistics involved in purchasing, storing and distributing the volume and variety of goods has led to its current focus on introducing JIT principles into the manufacturing process.

To help achieve its drive for flexibility and for just-in-time production, L'Oréal organised the site into three production centres, each autonomous and focused within technical families of productions. Their processes and production lines are then further focused within product sub-divisions. Responsible for all the activities from pre-weighing to dispatch within this area is the Production Centre Manager and this role encompasses staff development, training and motivation. Within the focused production centres, improvement groups have been working on improving shop-floor flexibility, quality and efficiency. One of the projects reduced the set-up times on the line which produces hair colourants from 2.5 hours to only 8 minutes. These new change-over times mean that the company can now justify even smaller batches and it gives them the flexibility to meet market needs just-in-time. Prior to the change in set-up time, batch size was 30 000 units; now batches as small as 2 000 to 3 000 units can be produced cost effectively.

QUESTIONS

1. Briefly describe the lean paradigm and indentify the operations principles applied at L'Oréal related to JIT.
2. Why is flexibility important for any operation?
3. What were the benefits of flexibility for L'Oréal?

SUMMARY

Operations-management strategies are based on a business's strategies. Any business needs an operations system to add value by means of some type of transformation process. Operations designs (and layout) are based around the products being made, in an attempt to achieve the business's objectives. Operations management focuses on planning and control, so that value-added products are produced according to customer specifications and according to a pre-determined schedule. To do this, it is important to balance capacity against demand by monitoring, and respond to both the demand for products or services and the need for resources or inventory items. While many operations managers work in continuous operations systems, others, such as project managers, work on temporary projects.

GLOSSARY

aggregate demand: medium- to long-term demand expressed in collective terms

aggregate planning: the anticipation of aggregate demand

agility: the ability to move (respond) quickly and easily

backward scheduling: scheduling that involves subtracting lead time from an order's due date to determine when the order must be started into production

batches: a unit of output (from one kind of job) measured by volume

batch operations systems: a type of operation producing batches measured by volume

bottleneck: a typical problem (constraint) situation for operations managers when demand exceeds capacity at a given point, work station or service facility

break-even analysis: a way of determining the volume at which total revenues are equal to total cost, or when the cost to make a component equals the total cost to buy it

business strategies: strategies that reflect the organisation's large-scale, future-orientated plans to optimise the achievement of the business's objectives

capacity: the greatest workload that can be handled by a unit

capacity planning: planning for the production resources needed over a certain time period

capital cost: interest or opportunity cost

carrying cost: the cost elements to hold an inventory item in a state of idleness

continuous operations systems: systems that are similar to repetitive operations systems, producing large quantities measured by volume

critical path: the activity sequence of a project that will consume the most time

demand management: the management of all demands for goods and services, to ensure that the master production schedule goes as planned

demand time: the total length of time the customer must wait

dispatching: issuing (authorising) a shop order so that an operation can take place

economic order quantity (EOQ): the order quantity ordered in each order cycle that minimises total inventory costs (carrying costs plus ordering costs)

expediting: actions aimed at getting work (orders) done more quickly

fixed-capacity planning: capacity planning for a long-term period

forecasting: determining the demand for a product in the light of future events

Gantt charts: widely used scheduling charts where horizontal rows represent tasks and resources that are scheduled for the duration of a project

holding cost: an element of inventory carrying cost that is associated with all types of stockroom costs

inventory: a complete list of stock items, raw material, sub–assembly, work–in–progress or final product in the plant

inventory management: the planning and controlling of all types of inventory

ISO 9000: a set of quality-management system standards that provide guidance on how-to-do quality assurance, by implementing quality-management systems based on these standards

job design: the function to design and group similar tasks to form a job for an individual

just–in–time (JIT) approach: a philosophy of managing operations to have little process idle time so as to eliminate waste and idle inventories between work stations (associated with the concept of the lean organisation)

lead time: how long customers have to wait to receive products

loading: allocating amounts of work to particular work centres

lots: units of output (from one kind of job) measured by number of units

make–to–order: when output will not be stored because an item is made in response to a specific order (such as in the case of custom–made products)

make–to–stock: when output is stored as finished goods for a stable market demand

master production schedule (MPS): a document representing a detailed master schedule for the medium term or a broad plan matching capacity with demand that leads to a more detailed statement of what a manufacturer plans to produce over the medium term

material requirements planning (MRP): a computerised system that uses the master production schedule to determine how many component items or materials to order, and when

materials management: a set of activities for acquiring, handling, storing, and controlling materials

monitoring: a controlling activity where it is ensured that the planned activities are happening according to schedule

network diagramming: a scheduling tool used in project management to determine the critical path(s), total duration, and slack

operation: a process in which inputs are transformed into outputs or any major task or job that needs a new set–up

operations designs: plans for how to produce goods or services

operations management: the management of the transformation processes in a business by which goods are manufactured and/or services are provided

operations-management policy: a set of guidelines for executing and controlling prescribed actions to achieve continuity, consistency, and integration

operations strategies: the total patterns of decisions and actions that formulate the roles, objectives and activities of each part of the operation, so that these contribute to and support the organisation's business strategies

preventive maintenance: actions taken to prevent equipment failure

process: when interrelated elements (such as materials, machines, and methods) work together to transform certain parts of these elements into outputs

process control chart: one of several types of charts used in statistical process control to measure samples of process output

process management: a focus on core value-adding processes to improve flow, eliminate lead times, and address process constraints

product designs: plans for goods or services

production time: the entire throughput time

productivity: a measure of how well inputs are being used (output income + input expenses)

project: a unique large-scale undertaking with a clear commencement date and a clear completion date

project management: an established profession, discipline, and philosophy to promote the successful management of projects

project manager: the person responsible for the project team, the project, and the entire systems development cycle

project operations systems: a type of operations system designed for projects

pull system: a system in which the user signals for work from the maker or supplier

push system: a system where work is pushed out with little regard for rate of use

quality: a level of excellence, fitness for purpose, or a standard that causes great satisfaction for the customer or client

re-order point (ROP): the on-hand inventory level (including safety stock) that will trigger a replenishing order

routing: establishing the place at which, or the piece of equipment on which, an operation will be performed

safety stock: additional inventory that is kept in case a stock-out situation arises

scheduling: the determination of the quantity of jobs and when they are to be completed

sequencing: deciding on the order in which the work will be performed

shop order: an internal authorisation to produce a specific lot or batch

statistical process control: a statistical quality management tool used for plotting samples on flow charts

Theory of Constraints (TOC): an approach to operations where work is scheduled to maximise the flow rate through bottlenecks

timing: deciding when a particular operation will take place

total quality management (TQM): deliberate actions to ensure holistic quality throughout the organisation

Trade-off Theory: the theory that states that operations managers must choose to trade-off one performance objective against another

undercapacity scheduling: scheduling output at less than full capacity to allow for a focus on maintenance and quality

variable-capacity planning: capacity planning done for a short- or medium-term period

work centres: any type of place in the production layout organised and arranged to do specific related work activities

work-in-progress (WIP): partly completed work either in a state of idleness (waiting without working) between processes or being processed

MULTIPLE-CHOICE QUESTIONS

1. Operations management is regarded as the core function of any organisation. Which one alternative of the following is incorrect?
   a) Operations management is a 'make or break' activity because in most businesses it represents the bulk of its assets and resources.
   b) The service industries also produce something, whether it is tangible or not. Even not-for-profit organisations use resources to produce something and the process of adding value is an operations function.
   c) Operations decisions are the same in commercial and not-for-profit organisations but a new agenda arises due to a changing business environment and modern business pressures. Operations management will continue to remain crucial, besides all the new challenges.
   d) Operations will continue to significantly affect profitability. It will remain to be the vehicle to achieve strategic performance objectives and it will continue to attempt to satisfy a wide range of stakeholders.
   e) The banking industry may be an exception because the operations function is insignificantly small in comparison to the financial management function.

2. Which one of the following alternatives is incorrect?
   Process throughput time can be reduced by:
   a) re-engineering and obtaining new equipment
   b) increasing effective disruptions

c) performing activities in parallel
d) changing the sequence of activities
e) reducing interruptions

3. Performance objectives are those distinct competencies driving business strategy. Which one alternative is incorrect?
   a) They can also be referred to as 'strategic performance objectives'. Examples of these are quality and cost.
   b) Other examples of performance objectives are speediness, reliability, consistency, responsiveness and flexibility.
   c) It is difficult to achieve flexibility in a high volume mass producing operations system.
   d) Most businesses try to achieve more than one of these at the same time, but a trade-off is usually the reality.
   e) Once a performance objective is selected and defined, a performance agreement (legal document) is signed by the operations manager to be used during the annual performance appraisal.

4. The elements of fixed capacity planning are:
   a) labour hours, materials and safety stock
   b) machine hours and inventory
   c) outsourcing and adjusting order quantities
   d) a suitable location, machinery and the layout of the productive unit
   e) sub–contracting, inventory and safety stock

5. Which one of the following alternatives is not an element of total production time (lead time elements)?
   a) Just–in–time (JIT)
   b) Setup time and transportation time
   c) Inspection time and waiting time
   d) Queue time
   e) Processing time

REFERENCES AND END-NOTES

1. DAVIS, M.M. & HEINEKE, J. 2005. *Operations management: Integrating manufacturing and services.* 5th ed. New York: McGraw-Hill Irwin.
2. SLACK, N., CHAMBERS, S. & JOHNSTON, R. 2010. pp. 7, 10–11. *Operations management.* 6th ed. Upper Saddle River: Prentice Hall.
3. PEARCE, J.A. & ROBINSON, R.B. JR. 1985. pp. 7–8. *Strategic management: Strategy formulation and implementation.* 2nd ed. Homewood: Irwin.
4. SLACK, N., CHAMBERS, S. & JOHNSTON, R. 2004. pp. 331–346. *Operations management.* 4th ed. Upper Saddle River: Prentice Hall.
5. CAPE TOWN'S MTN SCIENCENTRE.
6. SCHONBERGER, R.J. & KNOD, E.M. 2001. p. 238. *Operations management: Meeting customers demands.* 7th ed. New York: McGraw-Hill Irwin. Used with permission from the McGraw-Hill Companies.
7. CENTRE FOR BUSINESS MANAGEMENT, UNISA. 2007. *POM study guide.* Pretoria: Centre for Business Management, Unisa.
8. SLACK, N., CHAMBERS, S. & JOHNSTON, R. 2004. pp. 331–346. *Operations management.* 4th ed. Upper Saddle River: Prentice Hall.
9. NICHOLAS, J.M. & STEYN, H. 2008. *Project management for business, engineering and technology: Principles and practice.* 3rd ed. Oxford: Butterworth Heinemann.
10. Adapted from PYCRAFT, M, SINGH, H, PHIHLELA, K, SLACK, N, CHAMBERS, S, HARLAND, C, HARRISON, A, & JOHNSTON, R. 1997. pp. 540. *Operations management.* Southern Africa Edition. Johannesburg: Pitman.

ANSWERS TO MULTIPLE-CHOICE QUESTIONS

1. Answer = e)
2. Answer = b)
3. Answer = e)
4. Answer = d)
5. Answer = a)

10

Logistics management

Danie Nel

PURPOSE OF THIS CHAPTER

This chapter explains the management of logistics (the flow of materials), from purchasing materials, goods, and services from suppliers, to delivering products to customers. The chapter explores how to manage all the aspects of logistics while minimising costs or improving customer service. It also explains integrated logistics, reverse logistics, and global logistics.

LEARNING OUTCOMES

This chapter should enable you to:
- define 'logistics' and 'logistics management'
- explain the objectives of logistics management
- discuss purchasing, order-processing, information management, and inventory management
- compare methods of transportation
- describe warehousing, materials-handling, and packaging
- describe the concept of integrated logistics
- describe the concept of reverse logistics
- explain global logistics, and give some advantages and disadvantages of using global logistics.

10.1 Introduction

For a transformation process to begin, organisations have to buy goods and services from suppliers. After the transformation process is complete, the goods and services have to be moved to customers. All of this involves logistics management.

Logistics can be broken down into purchasing, order processing, inventory management, transportation, warehousing, materials-handling, and packaging. Logistics is a complex process that can be divided into integrated logistics, reverse logistics, and global logistics.

10.2 Defining logistics management[1]

Logistics is concerned with getting materials, goods and services to where they are needed at the exact time that they are needed. Therefore logistics includes all the work needed to move inventory items through the **supply chain** of a good or service from its starting place to where it is taken up. Logistics is a process that creates value by timing and placing inventory.

Logistics is the flow of all goods that come into the organisation as well as the flow of all goods going out towards customers. Logistics covers the whole organisation, from managing the raw materials through to delivering the final product.

FIGURE 10.1 The scope (extent) of logistics

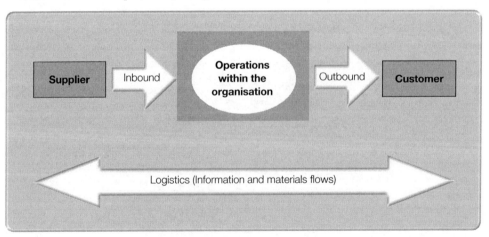

SOURCES: Adapted from Christopher, M. 2005. *Logistics and supply chain management: Creating value-adding networks.* Harlow: Prentice Hall. p. 15; & Waters, D. 2009. *Supply chain management: An introduction to supply chain management.* New York: Palgrave Macmillan. p. 6.

Logistics management has to do with the planning, implementation, and control of the forward and reverse (backward) flow of products between the starting point and the place where they are taken away. Logistics must therefore be seen as a vital link between customers and suppliers.

10.3 The objectives of logistics management

Logistics management is an important activity in any organisation, to improve its profit and its competitive (competing against others to win) performance. The objectives of logistics are:[2]
- to minimise total logistics costs
- to optimise customer service.

These two objectives are contradictory, which means that a trade-off (a deal where both parties lose something) must be made between them. An organisation cannot both reduce costs and improve service, because it will usually cost organisations money to make customer service perfect. For example, if customers want goods to be delivered sooner, then faster ways of transport will be needed, which cost more. Another example is that organisations may keep a wide variety of products to fulfil more customer needs, thus increasing their customer-service levels. But then more inventory has to be bought and stored, which again costs more.

10.3.1 Minimising total logistics costs

Logistics costs include all the costs of moving goods and services from their starting point to their end point. These costs come from information flows, transportation, and the storage of goods. Costs from information-flow come from the processing of the order and other administration costs. Transportation costs come from moving the goods and services between organisations, and the price depends on the method of transport used, the type of product, and the size of the load being moved. Lastly, storing the goods creates inventory-related costs. Organisations can aim to decrease costs in each of these areas by simplifying their information flows, using cheaper means of transport, or using more efficient ways of storage.

Because logistics costs are high, they form a significant percentage of any organisation's cost of goods sold.

10.3.2 Increasing customer service

Today organisations are moving towards improving customer service. **Customer service** has become part and parcel of every organisation. It includes everything in the process of bringing goods and services to the buyer, thus affecting the level of satisfaction that the customer enjoys. Factors that play a role in customer service from a logistical point of view include the order lead time, dependability, and convenience.

The time it takes from an order being placed by a customer to the delivery of the order to the customer, is called the **order lead time**. Order lead time plays an important part in customer service. Quicker deliveries are increasing customers' expectations and the service provided to them.

Dependability means how unchanging and accurate the supplier is. If goods are delivered late, this will cost the organisation money because of stockouts and possible production standstills. On the other hand, if goods are delivered too soon after an order is placed, it may mean that an organisation cannot store the goods because it does not have the space. Therefore, customers want suppliers to be accurate and dependable with their orders.

Convenience means that services fit customers' needs. For example, it would be convenient if customers want a certain product, and they can get it. This would result in increased levels of customer service.

10.3. **Trade-offs between minimising costs and optimising service**

It is clear that each organisation will have to decide what its logistics objectives are, because usually, reducing costs and increasing customer service cannot be done at the same time. Organisations should know what their customers want, because this is what the business is based on. Costs and the level of customer service are directly related, and costs will definitely rise when an organisation decides to increase the level of service it gives its customers. As already mentioned, the costs of buying and storing inventories will increase if inventory levels are increased to satisfy more customer needs. More expensive forms of transport may have to be used to move the goods more quickly from one point to another to reduce order lead times, and thus customer waiting times. These are just a few examples of increased logistics costs that improve customer service. These and other trade-offs must be carefully thought about before deciding how much will be spent on total logistics costs, and what level of customer service is wanted.

FIGURE 10.2 The relationship between total logistics costs and levels of customer service

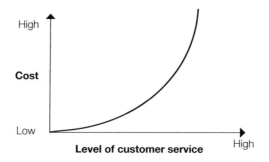

SOURCE: Adapted from Christopher, M. 2005. *Logistics and supply chain management: Creating value-adding networks.* Harlow: Prentice Hall. p. 67.

However, in some cases there need not be a trade-off between costs and service. Sometimes costs can be reduced without affecting the level of customer service. And often customer service can be improved without increasing costs. For example, it can be improved at no extra cost by simply not making unnecessary mistakes, or by ensuring deliveries on time.

Spar's logistics function – aiming to reduce costs and increase customer service[3]

Spar's logistics function has set overall objectives to get goods to customers more efficiently and cost-effectively than Spar's competitors. It has also identified several key focus areas which include providing exceptional customer service and running an optimal transport network. 'On-time' deliveries are very important to Spar, and continuous improvement in this area is a top priority.

10.4 Activities of logistics

Although there are many different activities in logistics, they can be put into six main categories. These are: purchasing (buying), order-processing, inventory management, transportation, warehousing, and materials-handling. The relationships among these activities can be quite complex, and can have significant effects on each other.

10.4.1 Purchasing management

Purchasing involves:[4]
- obtaining materials, goods, or services
- arranging how these get from suppliers to the organisation that needs them.

Every organisation, whether it is a manufacturer, wholesaler or retailer, buys materials, goods, and services to support its operations. Correct purchasing helps the other logistics processes and manufacturing processes to work effectively.

Purchasing management is a matter of identifying a need, selecting suppliers, deciding the form in which the material is to be bought, timing purchases, fixing prices, and controlling the quality. Purchasing management is really a matter of buying goods and services of the right quality and quantity, from the right supplier, at the right price and time.

The most important part of purchasing management is finding the right supplier.[5] Suppliers are generally chosen according to prices, the quality they provide, and the service they provide in the form of being reliable and capable. A sound financial position, a good location, and a stable labour force are also important factors that a supplier must have. Organisations must decide how important each of these factors is, and think about how far suppliers will go to provide them. If price is an important factor, an organisation may emphasise this as an essential quality for a supplier to have in order to be chosen.

For certain strategic or critical goods and services, organisations will want to develop their relationships with reliable suppliers, and eventually form business partnerships with them. This will ensure a continuous supply of the right products, and will ensure that both buyer and supplier together work towards continuously improving the quality of the products or reducing their total costs. This will ensure that they stay competitive (winning) in the marketplace.

Purchasing managers[6] will also try to minimise articles in inventory. A balance has to be found between holding levels of stock that are too high (which will result in high carrying costs) or too low (which may lead to out-of-stock problems). For this reason, purchasing managers will usually fix on an 'economic order quantity'[7] (EOQ) to ensure that they keep the costs of the inventory down.

In some cases, organisations do not order the EOQ, but order goods from suppliers so that they reach the buyer at the exact stage that they are wanted. This is called **just-in-time** (JIT)[8] **purchasing.** The JIT concept is that the right materials or products should arrive in the right quantities just when they are needed. JIT ordering systems have many advantages, such as lower inventory and safety-stock levels, which result in lower levels of capital being tied up in stocks. Close relations are essential between buyers and suppliers who use the JIT purchasing system.

Purchasing managers must know what the organisation's customers want. If customers want high-quality goods and services, they will be prepared to pay more for them. Purchasing managers must then purchase the right quality. If customers want low prices, they will be prepared to buy cheaper goods and services of a lower quality. Once again, purchasing managers must balance the right quality with the right price to satisfy customers' needs.

10.4.2 Order-processing

In the past, getting accurate information to achieve better logistical performance was not so important. Today processing orders is very important. **Order-processing**[9] starts with placing an order, and includes all the activities connected with the ordering process until the customer receives the product. The shorter the process, the shorter the order lead time. Many orders are given electronically, which improves the speed and accuracy of the order lead time.

Customers usually send information about what they want by means of orders, and the logistics of an organisation can only be as good as its order-processing ability. Order-processing has three basic tasks:[10]

- order entry
- order handling
- order delivery.

Order entry is when orders are placed by customers. Orders can be placed in person, by salespeople, mail, telephone, or computer (or electronic on-line) systems.

Order-handling has several steps. The order must be sent to warehouses, where someone checks if the product is available. This stage can be as simple as giving an order to a person in the same building, or as complex as sending the message to distributors around the world. The order is also transmitted to the credit department where the customer's credit rating will be checked, as well as prices and terms. If the credit rating of the customer is approved, the warehouse staff will prepare the order for the customer, and the documentation stage can begin.

Order delivery begins once the order has been prepared. The method of transport is arranged, which will depend on the service required by customers, as well as the prices they are willing to pay. (The more urgent the order, the more the customer will be willing to pay to get it.) Then an invoice is sent to the customer, giving information about the order. Inventory levels are often checked to let the salespeople know immediately whether the goods are in stock.

Efficient information systems are necessary to help with order-processing. They connect, collect, process and store basic data, and distribute information. Information systems play a major role in co-ordinating activities such as allocating resources, managing inventory levels, scheduling, and order-tracking. This process has been automated (done by machines) in most organisations, which makes it cheaper and faster. The order lead time is also reduced, which improves customer service and brings in more repeat business and more sales.

10.4.3 Inventory management

Inventory is the stock of items used in production, supporting activities, and customer service. Therefore, **inventory management**[11] involves decisions around what to stock in an organisation, and how much money to invest in inventory. Organisations must manage their inventory levels carefully because inventory is a large and costly investment (money put in, in the hope of it increasing).

There are many types of inventory.[12] When we are talking about it in the supply chain, we mean raw materials, work-in-progress, and finished goods. When we are talking about its purpose, we mean cycle stock, in-transit stock or safety stock.

Raw materials are materials ready for use in production. **Work-in-progress** inventory includes all the materials currently being worked on, and **finished goods** inventory is completed products ready for shipment or delivery. **Cycle stock** refers to materials or products that are received in bulk from a supplier and replenished (replaced) once they have been used up. Cycle stock is the result of the organisation's replenishment process, and must meet the demands of the customer. Cycle stock can thus be divided into raw-materials inventories (materials that are ready to enter the transformation process), work-in-progress inventories (materials busy undergoing a transformation in form) and finished-goods inventories (goods that are ready for consumption (use) by customers).

In-transit stock is made up of inventory items that are moving from one place to another.

FIGURE 10.3 Types of inventory

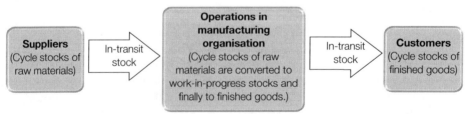

Sources: Adapted from Waters, D. 2009. *Supply chain management: an introduction to supply chain management.* New York: Palgrave Macmillan, p. 341 & Talyor, D.A. 2004. *Supply chains: a manager's guide.* Boston: Addison-Wesley. p. 24. Used with permission from Palgrave Macmillan.

Safety stock (buffer stock) is held in addition to cycle stock if one is not sure of demand or lead time.

The aim of inventory management is to reduce inventory costs while making sure that the correct levels of customer service are achieved. Minimising inventory costs while keeping good inventory levels to satisfy customers has to do with two major issues.[13] These issues are:

- the re-order point (when to order inventory)
- order quantities (how much inventory to order).

The **re-order point** (ROP) shows an organisation when to order inventory. The re-order point is reached when an organisation's inventory levels show the need to place a new order. The order lead time, safety-stock levels, and the 'usage rate' play an important part in choosing the re-order point. The usage rate is the rate at which inventory is being used or sold during a specific period.

To determine the re-order point, organisations need to know their order lead times, usage rates, and safety stocks. Once these are known, the re-order point can be calculated. This is done in the following way:

> **re-order point = (order lead time × usage rate) + safety stock**

Example of a re-order point

Let us look at an example. If the order lead time is 5 days, the usage rate is 500 units per day, and the safety stock is 1 000 units, the re-order point of a certain stock item will be:

> **re-order point = (order lead time × usage rate) + safety stock**
> **= (5 × 500) + 1 000**
> **= 3 500 units**

If the inventory levels of the stock item are at 3 500 units, the organisation will re-order inventory. If the supplier is reliable, the order will reach the organisation in 5 days (average order lead time). In this period, the organisation will have used or sold 500 units a day (usage rate), which amounts to 2 500 units, leaving the organisation with an inventory level of 1 000 units for the stock item (safety stock). If the supplier is one day late in delivering the order, the organisation will have used 500 units of its safety stock, leaving them with an inventory level of 500 units.

Once the re-order point has been determined, one must know how much inventory to order. Organisations will try to order the quantity of goods and services where the total logistics costs will be at a minimum. This quantity is called the **economic order quantity**[14] (EOQ). The EOQ is the quantity of goods where the inventory carrying costs (costs of keeping and maintaining the inventory in stock) plus the order-processing costs (for filling out the purchasing orders to get the goods) equals a minimum amount.

FIGURE 10.4   The economic order quantity

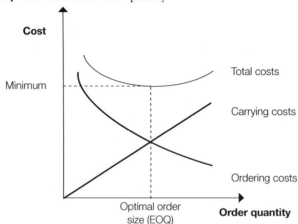

SOURCES: Adapted from Waters, D. 2009. *Supply chain management: an introduction to supply chain management.* New York: Palgrave Macmillan, p. 347 & Swink, M.; Melnyk, S.A.; Cooper, M.B. & Hartley, J.L. 2011. *Managing operations across the supply chain.* New York: McGraw-Hill Irwin. p. 423.

Organisations can improve their inventory management by using various techniques, such as forecasting techniques and the ABC analysis.

The **ABC analysis**[15] is done by management to find out how important each item is for the organisation. In organisations it often happens that a few items are costing a large percentage of the capital that is invested in inventory. It can happen that 70% of the capital invested in inventory is only 20% of the quantity (or types) of items the organisation holds. This means that a small percentage of items are extremely valuable and important to the organisation. According to the ABC analysis, organisations class their inventory into three categories. Category A inventory items are the most important and represent 20% of the total number of items, but represent around 70% of the capital invested in inventory. Category B inventory items represent 30% of the total number of items and about 20% of the capital invested in inventory. Category C represents the remaining 50% of the total number of items and about 10% of the capital invested in inventory. These percentages may vary from one organisation to the next, but all organisations should realise that their Category A inventory items are very important (and maybe even critical) to them.

FIGURE 10.5 The ABC inventory analysis

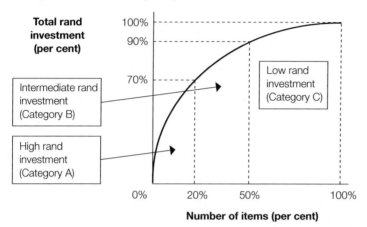

SOURCE: Adapted from Leenders, M.R., Johnson, P.F., Flynn, A.E. and Fearon, H.E. 2006. *Purchasing and supply management*. Boston: McGraw-Hill Irwin. p. 157. Used with permission from the McGraw-Hill Companies.

10.4.4 Transportation

Transportation is necessary to move goods between organisations to the customers who eventually buy those goods. Transportation physically moves and places inventory.

Transportation modes (ways)

There are five basic modes[16] of transport, which are rail, road, air, water, and pipeline. The different modes have a direct effect on customer service.

   Rail transport is used to transport huge bulky loads, so that materials-handling costs are reduced. Things like grain, coal, oil, minerals, chemicals, sand, agricultural and forestry products, steel and iron, are transported by rail. Huge containers are used for bulk movement. However, transport by rail depends on the current condition of the railways.

   Road transport is suitable for shorter trips, and handles parcel, postal, and courier services as well as trucking. Many product categories are transported by road, such as perishable products, clothing, paper goods, computers, books, fresh fruit, vegetables, and livestock. Many organisations, such as supermarkets, have their own fleets of trucks that deliver goods to their outlets. Road transport is very flexible, and has the advantage that goods can be delivered directly to customers. This mode of transport is often used together with other modes of transport. On the downside, road transport is often subject to size and weight limits, and the price of road transport is fairly high.

Air transport is the fastest of all transport modes, but it is also the most expensive. On the positive side, inventory levels can be reduced, as organisations know that goods will be delivered in a short time span. Air transport is ideal for transporting valuable goods that are fairly light and not too bulky. There are also likely to be fewer damages than with road transport. Goods that are suitable to be transported by air include jewellery, electronic parts, and perishable products such as flowers or sea foods.

There is very little **water transport** in South Africa and it is limited to international trade. It is suitable for transporting large, bulky, and non-perishable goods, but it is a very slow mode of transport. Many markets cannot be reached by water transport unless other modes of transport, such as rail or road transport, join them. Products suitable for water transport are coal, sand, grain, oil, petroleum, chemicals, and iron ore.

Pipeline transportation is low in cost, requires little energy, and is not affected by weather conditions. It is very efficient and cost-effective. The disadvantages are that transportation takes place only in one direction, and only to where the pipelines are located. It is not suitable for many kinds of goods. Goods transported in this way include crude petroleum or oil, refined petroleum products, processed coal, natural gas, and water.

Organisations can also use a combination of the various modes of transport to make use of their different strong points. This is called **intermodal transport** or multi-modal transport. For example, goods may be transported by trucks to nearby railway lines, from where they will be transported to the docks before being shipped away to foreign countries. The aim of intermodal transport is to gain the advantages of different modes of transport without the obvious disadvantages. For example, the flexibility of road transport can be combined with the low-cost advantage of rail transport in moving bulk (big, heavy objects). Intermodal transport will develop a great deal in the near future.

Factors to consider when choosing transportation modes

To select the right modes of transport, organisations have to consider various factors[17] such as cost, speed, availability, capability, frequency, and dependability. Organisations have to know what their logistics objectives are when they make these decisions.

The costs of a mode of transport are the total costs for moving a product from one place to another. These costs include loading and unloading costs as well as goods-in-transit costs. Costs must be weighed up against the expected benefits that will be received. The costs of air transport are the highest, while the lowest costs vary, being rail transport in South Africa but water transport in the USA.

Speed will also play a part when choosing a mode of transportation. **Speed** in this context means the total time taken to transport goods from the time the carrier is notified to when the customer receives the goods. Sometimes it is essential that goods are delivered quickly, as is the case with perishable goods or repair parts, while in other cases it is not important.

The availability of transportation is also an important factor to consider. **Availability** means the number of different locations that can be reached by the mode of transport. It is clear that road transport is the most available mode of transport, as trucks and vans can reach almost any destination where there is a road. Rail, air, pipeline and water transport are limited to where railroads, airports, pipelines, and docks are (see Table 10.1 below).

TABLE 10.1 Strengths and weaknesses of transportation modes

Transportation mode	Strengths	Weaknesses
Rail	Highly cost-effective for bulky items. Can be most effective when linked to an intermodal system.	Can deliver to limited locations, although less limited than water. Better reliability or speed of delivery than water.
Road	Flexibility to deliver where and when needed. Often the best balance among cost, flexibility, and reliability or speed of delivery.	Neither the fastest nor the cheapest option.
Air	Quickest mode of delivery. Flexible, especially when linked to the road mode.	Often the most expensive mode on a per-rand basis.
Water	Very cost-effective for bulky items. Most effective when linked to a intermodal system.	Can deliver to limited locations. Relatively poor delivery reliability and speed.
Pipeline	Low variable cost. Lead time reliability and dependability are high.	High fixed cost. Low availability and capability of service.

Sources: Adapted from Bozarth, C.C. & Handfield, R.B. 2006. *Introduction to operations and supply chain management.* Upper Saddle River: Pearson Prentice Hall. p. 342; & Webster, S. 2008. *Principles and tools for supply chain management* Boston: McGraw–Hill Irwin. p.247.

The **capability** of a transport type refers to its ability to handle different types and sizes of goods, such as load size. Ships can handle a wide variety of goods, while pipeline transportation is very limited. Air and road transport are limited owing to size and weight restraints.

Frequency refers to how often the mode of transport can be used. Road transport has a high frequency (can be used often). When supermarkets use their own trucks on a daily basis, they can keep lower inventory levels as inventory is checked and replenished regularly.

The **dependability** of transportation means the ability to deliver goods safely and on time. Pipelines are the most reliable, while trucks are the least reliable.

10.4.5 Warehousing

Inventory is sometimes stored in warehouses before it is sold to customers. Therefore, warehousing is a necessary activity of logistics. **Warehousing**[18] refers to any operation that stores, repackages, stages, sorts, or centralises goods or materials. Organisations must decide how many warehouses they need, and where these warehouses will be located. These decisions will be made depending on the organisation's logistics objectives.

Warehousing can be used to reduce transportation costs, improve operational flexibility, shorten order lead times, and lower inventory costs. For example, organisations can increase customer service by having many warehouses, but it costs money to operate each warehouse.

In warehouses, goods are received and sorted. The goods are then sent to the suitable areas in the warehouse to wait until they are taken out to fill customers' orders. When customers' orders are dispatched, they are packaged suitably and directed to a mode of transport. The necessary transportation and accounting documents are then prepared.

10.4.6 Materials-handling and packaging

Materials-handling and packaging are important because of the impact they can have on transportation, warehousing, and logistics information systems. **Materials-handling**[19] involves the equipment and the procedures that move goods inside a facility (building), between a facility and a transport mode, and between different transport modes. All the activities involved in materials-handling must take place in a co-ordinated manner to increase customer service and reduce costs. These activities include the packaging, loading, moving, and labelling of goods.

When we are talking about logistics, **packaging**[20] refers to the way goods and materials are packed in order to enable the flow of goods to customers. Goods must be packaged correctly to ensure minimum breakages or damage. The characteristics of the goods will determine how the goods will be moved, and then the mode of transport that is chosen will affect the packaging requirements. When organisations handle materials, they aim to:

- Ensure that materials are handled at the lowest possible cost.
- Use warehouse capacity fully.
- Minimise the handling of goods as handling increases costs and sometimes damages the goods.
- Ensure the safety of employees.
- Provide a quality service to customers or departments.

The faster goods are loaded or unloaded at an organisation's loading dock, the better for that organisation's productivity. Materials-handling equipment is usually mechanical equipment that is used to move goods over fairly short distances, usually as part of the loading or unloading process. The equipment required for materials-handling can be divided into equipment that moves around freely on the ground (such as trolleys, tractors, trailers, forklifts, and conveyor belts) and equipment that moves overhead (such as mobile cranes, overhead single rails, and lifts).

Barloworld – provider of warehousing and materials-handling equipment[21]

Barloworld is a good example of an organisation that provides warehousing and materials-handling equipment. They are the world's largest independent lift-truck dealer. They offer their customers a full range of lift trucks and related warehousing and materials-handling equipment.

10.5 Integrated logistics

The relationships amongst logistics activities can be complex, and the activities can have important effects on each other. It is therefore necessary that the logistics activities are integrated (combined). Teamwork is essential to achieve the objectives of **integrated logistics**,[22] namely of increasing customer service and decreasing logistics costs. This teamwork should occur:

- within the organisation
- between the organisation and its suppliers
- between the organisation and its customers who deliver the goods and services to the final customer.

Within the organisation all the functions have to work together to improve its overall and logistical performance. Various functions in the organisation have to work together to produce a product. Many of these functions are directly invol ed with logistical activities, and in many cases they try to improve their own performance, sometimes at the expense of other functions, or even the organisation. Decisions in one functional area will have an impact on all the others. For example, the purchasing manager may want lower inventory levels, as this reduces inventory carrying costs, while the marketing manager may want higher inventory levels, because having more products available to customers will increase customer service. Organisations must find ways to work together to optimise the logistical performance of the whole organisation and strike a balance directed towards the organisation's objectives.

FIGURE 10.6 The interrelated nature of logistical activities

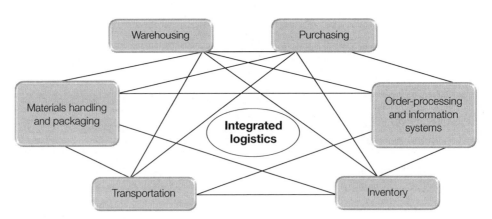

SOURCE: Adapted from Bowersox, D.J., Closs, D.J. & Cooper, M.B. 2010. *Supply chain logistics management.* Boston: McGraw-Hill. p. 27. Used with permission from the McGraw-Hill Companies.

Organisations have to work together with their suppliers and their customers to increase the logistical performance of the entire supply chain.[23] During the last couple of years, organisations have started to manage their operations across organisational boundaries. There has been a major shift from a single-organisation focus to a supply-chain focus, in which suppliers and customers work together to reach logistics objectives across organisational boundaries by either minimising costs or increasing customer-service levels.

To achieve this, organisations have recently started establishing partnerships with other organisations to work together to identify process improvements that reduce costs or increase value across the supply chain. Organisations are co-ordinating their logistics strategies, and strong partnerships are being built between organisations and some of their important customers and suppliers.

When this 'integrated' logistics works effectively in the supply chain, the order lead time is reduced, because all the organisations involved know exactly what the customers want. Therefore, when customers make a demand, the necessary logistical activities are put in motion to provide the necessary goods and services to customers in a co-ordinated manner. This improves customer service, and allows organisations to manage their supply chain based on customer responses. This can only be achieved when all the members in the supply chain work together in an integrated way. If this does not happen, organisations have to manufacture goods based on sales forecasts, because the precise demands of the customer are not known. These goods are then stored until they are required, which increases inventory carrying costs and also the risk of product going out-of-date.

10.6 **Reverse logistics**

Even when goods have been delivered to customers, there may be problems with the delivered goods. These goods then have to be sent back to the suppliers. Some items may be returned to suppliers for re-use. These include pallets, delivery boxes, cable reels, and containers. Some materials may not be re-used, but are brought back for recycling, such as glass, metals, paper, plastics, and oils. Other materials, such as dangerous or hazardous chemicals, cannot be used again, but are brought back to the supplier for safe disposal. Organisations use reverse logistics to manage these flows of materials back towards suppliers.

Reverse logistics[24] is the process of planning, implementing and controlling the efficient, cost-effective flow of raw materials, work-in-progess inventory, finished goods, and related information, from the point of consumption (leaving) back to the point of origin (starting) for the purpose of recapturing value or carrying out proper disposal. Reverse logistics therefore works in the opposite direction to the primary logistics flow. It involves reducing waste as well as managing the collection, transport, disposal, and recycling of waste, to the benefit of the organisation.

An increasing emphasis is being placed on reverse logistics because of people's increasing awareness of their environmental responsibilities. Another push for reverse logistics is the possible returns that can be obtained from the re-use of products or parts, or the recycling of materials.

Recycling at Woolworths[25]

Woolworths is extremely aware of the impact of its business on the environment. Therefore staff members work hard towards not damaging it and using as few resources as they can. For this reason they use reverse logistics (in this case recycling) very effectively. For example, they recycle their clothes hangers by collecting all unwanted plastic hangers from their stores. They then sort and clean them, and sell them back to clothing suppliers at a discount. In the same way they recycle plastic, and many of the Woolworths' supermarket baskets and trolleys are now made from recycled plastic. Furthermore, the sleeves on ready-made meals, dips, and other food products are made from cardboard, which has 80% recycled-paper content. Finally, to try and minimise the waste from their packaging, they try and use completely recyclable material such as paper and glass.

10.7 **Global logistics**

One of the most important recent events is the expanding of international business. Today, nearly all major organisations have a strong and growing presence in business outside their own country. International or **global logistics**[26] takes place when supply chains and their logistics activities cross national frontiers. An organisation can buy goods and services from a supplier in one country, use logistics to move these goods and services, and then sell them in another country. Improved communication through information flows, transport, financial arrangements, trading agreements and so on, means that organisations search the world to find the best place for their operations. Then global logistics move the related materials through long and complex supply chains across countries' borders.

There are various factors that encourage international trade (and thus global logistics). These factors include a growing demand, in new international markets, for foreign products, and a demand for higher quality. However, there are also problems directly associated with global logistics because it is so complex. These problems include customs barriers and other trade barriers, such as different political and legal systems in the various countries, changing economic conditions, differing availability of technology and support systems, different cultures, and increased geographical distances between organisations. These may result in increased order lead times. Organisations must weigh the advantages and disadvantages of global logistics against each other.

CASE STUDY: Using distribution centres to improve customer service[27]

Massmart and Pick n Pay have changed the way in which retailers and suppliers do business. They have invested in their supply chains and in improved service to their stores, by moving from direct store delivery to central distribution. With direct store deliveries, all shipments come directly from the supplier to the retail (selling to the public) outlet, while 'central distribution' means that inventories are 'pooled' together at a central location, to make distribution easier. These distribution centres have become important links in their supply chains because they aim to expand their business further into Africa. To improve their service, they have installed state-of-the-art retail software solutions. Within 48 hours of suppliers delivering goods to the distribution centres, the goods will be delivered to the retail stores. A distribution centre enables the centralisation of goods. Transportation costs can therefore be managed more efficiently.

QUESTIONS

1. Can you list all the logistics activities found in this case study?
2. Give examples from the case of how customer service can be improved.

SUMMARY

Logistics management concerns the planning, implementation, and control of the forward and reverse flow of products between the point of production and the place where this product is taken away. Organisations have to know what their logistics objectives are, because the primary logistics objectives are to either minimise costs or to increase customer value. These objectives are contradictory, and a trade-off has to be made between them. Different logistics activities include purchasing, order-processing, inventory management, transportation, warehousing, materials-handling and packaging. Reverse logistics is becoming more important as people become more environmentally aware. Global logistics is becoming more important as globalisation occurs.

GLOSSARY

ABC analysis: the analysis that categorises inventory into three classes to illustrate what items the organisation should prioritise

air transport: the mode of transport that uses aeroplanes or helicopters

availability: the number of different locations that a mode of transport can reach

capability: the ability of a mode of transport to handle a range of loads

convenience: the fit between a service and customers' needs

customer service: the factors that affect the process of making goods and services available to the buyer, thus influencing the level of satisfaction that the customer enjoys

cycle stock: materials or products that are received in bulk from a supplier and replenished again once they have been used up

dependability: the degree of consistency and accuracy shown by a supplier/the ability of transportation to deliver goods safely and on time

economic order quantity (EOQ): the quantity of goods where the sum of the inventory carrying costs and the order-processing costs are at a minimum

finished goods: completed products ready for shipment or delivery to end customers.

frequency: how often a mode of transport can be used

global logistics: when supply chains and their logistics activities cross national boundaries

integrated logistics: the state when all the organisational functions, as well as suppliers and customers, work together towards achieving the logistical objectives of the organisation

intermodal transport: when a combination of the various modes of transport are used to exploit the strengths of multiple transportation modes

in-transit stock: inventory items that are en route from one location to another

inventory management: the management of what to stock in an organisation and how much to invest in inventory

just-in-time (JIT) purchasing: purchasing where the ideal is that the right materials or products arrive in the right quantities just when they are required

logistics: the process of getting the materials, goods and services in a supply chain where they are needed at the precise time that they are needed

logistics costs: the costs incurred when goods and services are moved from their point of origin to the point of consumption

logistics management: the planning, implementation and control of the forward and reverse flow of products between the point of production and the place where consumption of this product occurs

materials-handling: the systems (both equipment and procedures) needed to move goods within a facility, between a facility and a transportation mode, and between different transportation modes

order delivery: the arrangement of the mode of transport to deliver the order when it has been prepared

order entry: when orders are placed by customers

order-handling: the preparation of a customer's order for delivery once the order has been entered

order lead time: the amount of time it takes from when a customer places an order until that customer receives the order

order-processing: the system that starts with the placement of an order and includes all the activities associated with the ordering process until the customer receives the product

packaging: the way goods and materials are packed in order to facilitate the flow of goods to customers

pipeline transportation: the mode of transportation that uses a pipeline infrastructure

purchasing: obtaining materials, goods or services and arranging how these will get from the suppliers to the organisation that needs them

purchasing management: the activities required to manage supplier relationships that result from purchasing

rail transport: the mode of transport that uses trains and railway lines

raw materials: materials ready for use in production.

re-order point: the inventory level at which an organisation must place a new order because inventory levels are low

reverse logistics: the process of planning, implementing and controlling the efficient, cost-effective flow of raw materials, work-in-progress inventory, finished goods and related information from the point of consumption to the point of origin for the purpose of recapturing value or effecting proper disposal

road transport: the mode of transport that uses road vehicles and roads

safety stock: the inventory items held in excess of cycle stock because of uncertainty in demand or lead time

speed: the total time necessary to transport goods from the time the carrier is notified to when the customer receives the goods

supply chain: where at least three organisations are linked together through all the flows of information, goods, services and finances between the original supplier and the end customer

transportation: the movement of goods between organisations to the customer who eventually buys them

usage rate: the rate at which inventory is being used or sold during a specific period

warehousing: any operation that stores, repackages, stages, sorts or centralises goods or materials

water transport: the mode of transport that uses boats and ships

work-in-progress inventory: all the materials currently being worked on to produce finished goods

MULTIPLE-CHOICE QUESTIONS

1. _____ includes the flow of all inbound goods into the organisation as well as the flow of all outbound goods towards customers.
   a) Supply chain management
   b) Logistics
   c) Operations management
   d) Transportation

2. Which one of the following is not an objective of logistics management?
   a) Organisations aim to minimise total logistics costs.
   b) Organisations aim to increase customer service.
   c) Organisations aim to reduce lead times within acceptable parameters of cost and service.
   d) Organisations aim to increase inventory levels.

3. _____ involves decisions around what to stock in an organisation and how much money to invest in different types of stocks.
   a) Purchasing management
   b) Order processing
   c) Inventory management
   d) Warehousing

4. What is the re-order point if an organisation has a usage rate of 100 units per day, safety stock of 200 units and an order lead time of 7 days?
   a) 300 units
   b) 900 units
   c) 1 500 units
   d) 2 100 units

5. This mode of transport is highly cost effective for bulky items but can only be delivered to limited locations. In fact, it is the most limited mode of transport with regards to location.

a) Rail
b) Road
c) Air
d) Water

REFERENCES AND END-NOTES

1. CHRISTOPHER, M. 2005. *Logistics and supply chain management: Creating value-adding networks.* Harlow: Prentice Hall. p. 4.; Waters, D. 2009. *Supply chain management: An introduction to supply chain management.* New York: Palgrave Macmillan, pp. 4–6; Jonsson, P. 2008. *Logistics and supply chain management.* London: McGraw- Hill. pp. 3-4.

2. LANGLEY, C.J.; COYLE, J.J.; GIBSON, B.J.; NOVACK, R.A. & BARDI, E.J. 2009. *Managing supply chains: A logistics approach.* Canada: South-Western. p. 42; WATERS, D. 2009. *Supply chain management: An introduction to supply chain management.* New York: Palgrave Macmillan. p. 17; CHRISTOPHER, M. 2005. *Logistics and supply chain management: Creating value-adding networks.* Harlow: Prentice Hall. pp. 48–50, 66–68; JONSSON, P. 2008. *Logistics and supply chain management.* London: McGraw-Hill. pp. 9-11; NEL, J.D. 2005. *Logistics management.* In: STRYDOM, J.W. (Ed.) *Distribution management.* Claremont: New Africa. pp. 67–172.

3. SPAR. [Online]. Available: http://www.spar.co.za/Uploads/e90d646f-d88c-43ac-9cdc-87de0d7ea945/Logistics.pdf [22 October 2007].

4. LYSONS, K. & FARRINGTON, B. 2006. *Purchasing and supply chain management.* Essex: Pearson. pp. 5, 367–368 ; LANGLEY, C.J.; COYLE, J.J.; GIBSON, B.J.; NOVACK, R.A. & BARDI, E.J. 2009. *Managing supply chains: A logistics approach.* Canada: South-Western. p. 42; WATERS, D. 2009. *Supply chain management: An introduction to supply chain management.* New York: Palgrave Macmillan, pp. 18–19; FAWCETT, S.E., ELLRAM, L.M. & OGDEN, J.A. 2007. *Supply chain management: From vision to implementation.* Upper Saddle River: Pearson Prentice Hall. pp. 138-139.

5. BURT, D.N., PETCAVAGE, S.D. & PINKERTON, R.L. 2010. *Supply management.* Boston: McGraw-Hill Irwin. pp. 240-253.

6. LYSONS, K. & FARRINGTON, B. 2006. *Purchasing and supply chain management.* Essex: Pearson. pp. 5, 367–368.

7. BOWERSOX, D.J., CLOSS, D.J. & COOPER, M.B. 2010. *Supply chain logistics management.* Boston: McGraw-Hill. pp. 160-164.

8. BOZARTH, C.C. & HANDFIELD, R.B. 2006. *Introduction to operations and supply chain management.* Upper Saddle River: Pearson, Prentice Hall. pp. 425, 491.

9. NEL, J.D. 2005. *Logistics management.* In: STRYDOM, J.W. (Ed.) *Distribution management.* Claremont: New Africa. p. 176.; BOWERSOX, D.J., CLOSS, D.J. & COOPER, M.B. 2010. *Supply chain logistics management.* Boston: McGraw-Hill. pp. 106-107; FAWCETT, S.E. ELLRAM, L.M. & OGDEN, J.A. 2007. *Supply chain management: From vision to implementation.* Upper Saddle River: Pearson Prentice Hall. p. 154; LANGLEY, C.J., COYLE, J.J., GIBSON, B.J., NOVACK, R.A. & BARDI, E.J. 2009. *Managing supply chains: A logistics approach.* Canada: South-Western. pp. 189-191.

10. STOCK, J.R. & LAMBERT, D.M. 2001. *Strategic logistics management.* New York: McGraw-Hill. pp. 148–150; NEL, J.D. 2005. *Logistics management.* In: STRYDOM, J.W. (Ed.) *Distribution management.* Claremont: New Africa, p. 177.

11. BOZARTH, C.C. & HANDFIELD, R.B. 2006. *Introduction to operations and supply chain management.* Upper Saddle River: Pearson Prentice Hall. p. 412.; HUGO, W.M.J., BADENHORST-WEISS. J.A. & VAN ROOYEN, D.C. 2006. *Purchasing and supply management.* Pretoria: Van Schaik. pp. 169–170.

12. BOZARTH, C.C. & HANDFIELD, R.B. 2006. *Introduction to operations and supply chain management.* Upper Saddle River: Pearson Prentice Hall. pp. 414–415; TALYOR, D.A. 2004. *Supply chains: A manager's guide.* Boston: Addison-Wesley. p.22.

13. BOWERSOX, D.J., CLOSS, D.J. & COOPER, M.B. 2010. *Supply chain logistics management.* Boston: McGraw-Hill. pp. 160-164; NEL, J.D. 2005. *Logistics management.* In: STRYDOM, J.W. (Ed.) *Distribution management.* Claremont: New Africa, pp. 184–186.

14. WATERS, D. 2009. *Supply chain management: An introduction to supply chain management.* New York: Palgrave Macmillan, p. 345; BOWERSOX, D.J., CLOSS, D.J. & COOPER, M.B. 2010. *Supply chain logistics management.* Boston: McGraw-Hill. p. 164.

15. LEENDERS, M.R., JOHNSON, P.F., FLYNN, A.E. & FEARON, H.E. 2006. *Purchasing and supply management.* Boston: McGraw-Hill Irwin, pp. 156–157; NEL, J.D. 2005. *Logistics management.* In: STRYDOM, J.W. (Ed.) *Distribution management.* Claremont: New Africa. p. 191.

16. WEBSTER, S. 2008. *Principles and tools for supply chain management.* Boston: McGraw-Hill Irwin, pp. 247–250; JACOBS, F.R. & CHASE, R.B. 2008. *Operations and supply management: The core.* Boston: McGraw-Hill. pp. 204–206; LANGLEY, C.J., COYLE, J.J., GIBSON, B.J., NOVACK, R.A. & BARDI, E.J. 2009. *Managing supply chains: A logistics approach.* Canada: South-Western. pp. 278–288; FAWCETT, S.E., ELLRAM, L.M. & OGDEN, J.A. 2007. *Supply chain management: From vision to implementation.* Upper Saddle River: Pearson Prentice Hall. pp. 156-158; NEL, J.D. 2005. *Logistics management.* In: STRYDOM, J.W. (Ed.) Distribution management. Claremont: New Africa. pp. 179–182.

17. BOWERSOX, D.J., CLOSS, D.J. & COOPER, M.B. 2010. *Supply chain logistics management.* Boston: McGraw-Hill. pp. 209–210; SWINK, M., MELNYK, S.A., COOPER, M.B. & HARTLEY, J.L. 2011. *Managing operations across the supply chain.* New York: McGraw-Hill Irwin. pp. 318–319; Nel, J.D. 2005. *Logistics management.* In: STRYDOM, J.W. (Ed.) *Distribution management.* Claremont: New Africa. pp. 183–184.

18. BOZARTH, C.C. & HANDFIELD, R.B. 2006. *Introduction to operations and supply chain management.* Upper Saddle River: Pearson Prentice Hall. pp. 344–346.

19. BOZARTH, C.C. & HANDFIELD, R.B. 2006. *Introduction to operations and supply chain management.* Upper Saddle River: Pearson Prentice Hall. p. 349; BOWERSOX, D.J., CLOSS, D.J. & COOPER, M.B. 2010. *Supply chain logistics management.* Boston: McGraw-Hill. p. 276.

20. BOZARTH, C.C. & HANDFIELD, R.B. 2006. *Introduction to operations and supply chain management.* Upper Saddle River: Pearson Prentice Hall. p. 349; BOWERSOX, D.J., CLOSS, D.J. & COOPER, M.B. 2010. *Supply chain logistics management.* Boston: McGraw-Hill. pp. 272–276.

21. BARLOWORLD. 2007. [Online]. Available: http://www.barloworld.co.za/content/group_companies/industrial.asp [22 October 2007].

22. STOCK, J.R. & LAMBERT, D.M. 2001. *Strategic logistics management.* New York: McGraw-Hill, pp. 37–48; Waters, D. 2009. *Supply chain management: An introduction to supply chain management.* New York: Palgrave Macmillan, pp. 134-142; BOWERSOX, D.J., CLOSS, D.J. & COOPER, M.B. 2007. *Supply chain logistics management.* Boston: McGraw-Hill. pp. 7–10, 260; NEL, J.D. 2005. *Logistics management.* In: STRYDOM, J.W. (Ed.) *Distribution management.* Claremont: New Africa, pp. 200–203.

23. RUSHTON, A., CROUCHER, P. & BAKER, P. 2006. *The handbook of logistics and distribution management.* London: Kogan Page. pp. 257–260; BOWERSOX, D.J., CLOSS, D.J. & COOPER, M.B. 2007. *Supply chain logistics management.* Boston: McGraw-Hill. pp. 257–260.

24. WATERS, D. 2009. *Supply chain management: An introduction to supply chain management.* New York: Palgrave Macmillan, p. 20; KUSSING, U. & PIENAAR, W.J. 2009. *Product returns and reverse logistics management.* In: PIENAAR, W.J. & VOGT, J.J. (Eds.) *Business logistics management: A supply chain perspective.* Cape Town: Oxford University Press. p. 421-422.

25. WOOLWORTHS. 2006. [Online]. Available: http://www.woolworths.co.za/Caissa.asp?Page=ITB4_RHCon [22 October 2007].

26. LYSONS, K. &FARRINGTON, B. 2006. *Purchasing and supply chain management.* Essex: Pearson. pp. 515–520; WATERS, D. 2009. *Supply chain management: An introduction to supply chain management.* New York: Palgrave Macmillan, pp. 164–167.

27. PLANTING, S. 2010. *Logistical improvement.* In: FINANCIAL MAIL [Online]. 4 August 2010. Available: http://www.fm.co.za/Article.aspx?id=117062 [4 November 2010].

ANSWERS TO MULTIPLE-CHOICE QUESTIONS

1. Answer = b)
2. Answer = d)
3. Answer = c)
4. Answer = b)
5. Answer = d)

CHAPTER

Financial management

Marolee Beaumont Smith

PURPOSE OF THIS CHAPTER

This chapter looks at financial management and its core principles. First, financial analysis and cost behaviour are examined, then the sources and types of long-term and short-term financing are described. Lastly the chapter describes a cash budget and the effective management of credit and inventories.

LEARNING OUTCOMES

This chapter should enable you to:

* define the function, tasks, and core principles of financial management
* analyse and interpret the financial statements of a business
* find the break-even point
* define and discuss break-even analysis
* compare and contrast the sources and types of available financing
* prepare a cash budget
* manage credit and inventories.

11.1 Introduction

Financial management is the part of a business that is concerned with planning and managing funds in order to achieve the business's objectives. This department must get the necessary money to run the business, and must use it in the best way in the short term and the long term.

II.2 **The functions of financial management**[1]

The financial management department has three main functions:
- analysing the financial position of the business
- managing the assets of the business
- managing the liabilities of the business.

Accurate financial analysis and efficient management of the assets and liabilities of the business will ensure that it has reasonable liquidity and profitability to function.

II.2.1 Analysing the financial position of a business

Analysing the financial position of a business means finding out how healthy it is, by measuring and checking its liquidity and profitability.

Liquidity is the ability of the business to pay its short-term financial debts continuously and on time. Many profitable businesses go bankrupt because of a liquidity crisis. A business is having a liquidity crisis if it cannot pay its debts and liabilities such as wages, taxes, and salaries because of a lack of cash (liquid) resources.

Profit is the difference between income and costs. The business's profitability is its ability to make more income than the total costs, by using its assets productively. So profitability means the amount of success of a business operation.

II.2.2 Managing the assets of a business

A business needs to invest in assets that will add value. Assets can be divided into fixed assets and current assets. **Fixed assets** are resources owned by the business with a life-span of more than 12 months (for example, land, buildings, equipment, vehicles, and furniture). **Current assets** are cash and resources owned by the business that can be turned into cash within 12 months (for example, inventory and trade receivables).

In managing the assets, financial managers must ensure that the business is not over-capitalised (having too much investment) by duplication (for instance, unnecessary amounts of certain kinds of equipment or needlessly large quantities of raw materials inventories). There must be a good balance between the fixed assets (long-term assets) and current assets (short-term assets) in the business.

II.2.3 Managing the liabilities (what is to be paid) of a business

When managing the liabilities of a business, the financial manager must decide on how best to arrange the assets. This means considering the most useful mix of short- and long-term financing, as well as the individual sources of short-term and long-term funds to be used. It is important that the business can always reach sources of long-term and short-term funds at the most favourable interest rates and repayment conditions.

Long-term funds are owners' equity and long-term liabilities. **Owners' equity** (net worth or capital) is the money invested in a business by its owners for buying assets. Examples of long-term liabilities, on the other hand, are mortgages, long-term bank loans, leases, and any other needs to pay money which must be paid to a creditor after more than one year.

Short-term funds, also called **current liabilities**, are amounts owing to creditors that are due within one year. Examples of current liabilities are trade payables (to be paid), bank overdrafts, and factoring.

11.3 **The core principles of financial management**

Sound financial management decisions are based on the following three core principles:
- the cost-benefit principle
- the risk–return principle
- the time-value-of-money principle.

11.3.1 The cost-benefit principle

In any decision that is made, the benefits should be greater than the costs. So sound financial decision-making means that we analyse the total costs and total benefits of any financial decision we take. We use the cost-benefit principle to be clear about our objectives, to work out the costs and benefits of different choices, to determine standards to measure choices, and then to decide on the best course of action to take. (The break-even analysis in Section 11.6 is an illustration of this principle.)

11.3.2 The risk-return principle

Risk is danger or exposure to loss or injury. Judging risk is part of any decision-making process. We must calculate the chance that the outcome of the decision will not be what we wanted and expected. This risk may result in a financial loss or waste of resources.

The **risk–return principle** is a trade-off between risk and return. The higher the risk that a business takes, the higher the return it wants for taking that risk. In the same way as with the cost–benefit principle, the return should always be greater than the risk taken, in order to make the decision sensible.

II.3.3 The time-value-of-money principle

The **time-value-of-money principle** means that money has value over time. A business can increase the value of an amount of money by investing it over time, to earn interest. If that business instead invests the money in, for example, motor vehicles or equipment, there will be no interest earned on these investments. So why would the business do this? From the cost–benefit perspective, the business would do this if it could earn a greater return on the investment in vehicles or equipment than if it was earning interest. From the risk–return perspective, the business would do this if the return exceeded the risk taken.

Calculating when to invest in a business

Question

If a person invests R1 million in a business, that person will not be able to earn interest on that amount, which he or she would get if the money was invested in, for example, a fixed deposit at 10% per annum – with less risk involved. So what return would justify investing R1 million in the business?

Answer

The person would need to expect to earn more than 10% on the investment in the business, as it is more risky investing in the business than in a fixed deposit. (This is based on the concept of **opportunity cost**.)

II.4 Analysing financial statements

Financial statements give a written summary of the financial activities of a business. They give the business's performance, and show its strengths and weaknesses. The two primary financial statements are the balance sheet and the income statement.

II.4.I The balance sheet

The **balance sheet** is a listing, at a specific moment in time, of all the assets and liabilities of the business, and how these net assets (total assets less total liabilities) were financed (for example, by owners' equity and profits).

At any given time, a business's assets equal the total contributions by the owners and creditors. (The owners' contributions are called owners' equity, and the creditors' loans are called **liabilities**.)

assets = owners' equity + liabilities

One side of this accounting equation represents the value of the firm's resources, and the other side simply gives the source of the funds used to get these resources. The two sides of the equation will always be equal, no matter how many transactions (business deals) are entered into, or how many sources of funds a business uses.

The accounting equation, also known as the 'balance-sheet equation', is a simple balance sheet. Its basic parts can be selected from even the most complex balance sheets, and will still apply.

Using the accounting equation

Question

What are the missing numbers below?

TABLE 11.1

Assets	–	Liabilities	=	Equity
R12 000		R 7 000		R_ _ _ _
R18 000		R_ _ _ _		R 8 000
R_ _ _ _		R 9 250		R 8 500

Answer

Assets	–	Liabilities	=	Equity
R12 000		R 7 000		R 5 000
R18 000		R10 000		R 8 000
R17 750		R 9 250		R 8 500

An example of a balance sheet

The following table is a balance sheet for Techsa as at 31 December 2010.

TABLE II.2 Balance sheet of Techsa at 31/12/2010

ASSETS	R000s	R000s
Fixed assets		348
Plant and equipment	532	
less accumulated depreciation	184	
Current assets		1 239
Inventory	751	
Trade receivables	412	
Cash on hand	24	
Prepaid expenses	52	
TOTAL ASSETS		**1 587**
EQUITY AND LIABILITIES		
Owners'equity		694
Equity	475	
Accumulated profits	219	
Long-term loan		416
Current liabilities		477
Trade payables	184	
Bank overdraft	171	
Arrear expenses	122	
TOTAL EQUITY AND LIABILITIES		**1 587**

It is clear that total assets (fixed and current assets) equal total funding of these assets which are the owners' equity, long-term liabilities, and short-term liabilities.

II.4.2 The income statement

The **income statement** is a financial summary of the profitability of a business over a period of time. To see whether the business is operating at a profit or a loss, the sales revenue (income) earned is matched with the expenses paid to get that revenue.

TABLE 11.3 Income statement of Techsa for the year ended 31/12/2010

	000s	000s
Sales		3 950
Cost of sales		**3 370**
Purchases	3 250	
Plus: opening inventory	1 780	
Less: closing inventory	(1 660)	
Gross profit		580
Operating expenses:		470
Selling expenses	310	
Administration expenses	130	
Depreciation	30	
Profit before interest and tax		110
Interest paid		61
Profit before tax		49
Tax (29%)		14
Profit after tax		**35**

The left-hand columns in the income statement give the break-down of the items making up the main totals in the right-hand column. For example, cost of sales is purchases plus opening inventory minus closing inventory.

11.5 **Ratio analysis**[2]

Financial ratios are valuable tools in financial analysis. A **financial ratio** is a comparison between two variables (values) from the financial statements. To be useful, the ratio must express a relationship that is meaningful. In other words, there should be a clear, direct, and understandable relationship between the two variables. For example, sales and the cost of goods sold would show such a relationship, while there is unlikely to be a relationship between selling costs and the amount invested in fixed assets.

Financial ratios are grouped in the broad categories of business performance and they can be used to examine:

- liquidity ratios:
  - current ratio
  - quick ratio
- asset management ratios:
  - inventory turnover
  - average collection period
  - total asset turnover
- debt-management ratios:
  - debt ratio
  - gearing ratio
  - interest coverage ratio
- profitability ratios:
  - gross profit margin
  - profit margin
  - return on total assets
  - return on equity.

11.5.1 Liquidity ratios

Liquidity is the ability of the business to honour (pay) its short-term financial commitments continuously and on time. A shortage of liquidity means that there is not enough ready cash available to settle financial obligations on their due dates. Chronic illiquidity (opposite of liquidity) can lead to liquidation (selling off the business to pay its debts). The two best-known **liquidity ratios** are the current ratio and the quick ratio.

11.5.1.1 **The current ratio**

The **current ratio** shows the relationship between the value of a business's current assets and the amount of its current liabilities. The calculation of the current ratio for Techsa for year-end 2010 is shown below, using the figures from Table 11.2.

$$\text{current ratio} = \frac{\text{current assets}}{\text{current liabilities}}$$

$$= \frac{1\ 239}{477} = 2{,}60{:}1$$

This means that the business has 2,60 times as many current assets as current liabilities. The higher the current ratio, the greater the likelihood that Techsa will be able to pay its bills. A current ratio of 2:1 is normally recommended.

11.5.1.2 **The quick ratio**

As it normally takes longer to change inventories into cash, it is useful to measure the ability of the business to pay off short-term obligations without relying on the sale of inventories. The **quick ratio**, or acid-test ratio, is calculated by deducting inventories from current assets and dividing the remainder by current liabilities. The quick ratio for Techsa is:

$$\text{quick ratio} = \frac{\text{current assets} - \text{inventory}}{\text{current liabilities}}$$

$$= \frac{1\ 239 - 751}{477} = 1,02:1$$

This shows that Techsa has R1,02 worth of current assets excluding inventory, for each rand of current liabilities. A quick ratio of at least 1:1 is the norm. Although the quick ratio is always less than the current ratio, a quick ratio that is too low relative to the current ratio may indicate that inventories are higher than they should be.

11.5.2 Asset management ratios

Asset management ratios are designed to measure how effectively the assets of the business are being used to create sales. For example, if firm Techsa and firm Competitor have the same level of sales, but Competitor has less money invested in inventories, Competitor is regarded as more efficient than Techsa in managing inventory investment. The asset management ratios discussed below are inventory turnover, average collection period, and total asset turnover.

11.5.2.2 **Inventory turnover**

The **inventory turnover** measures how well inventory is being managed. The higher the turnover ratio the better, because the more times inventory can be turned over in an operating cycle, the greater the profit. The inventory turnover ratio for Techsa is:

$$\text{inventory turnover} = \frac{\text{cost of sales}}{\text{inventory}}$$

$$= \frac{3\ 370}{751} = 4,49 \text{ times}$$

An excessively high inventory turnover could lead to stock shortages, which could stop the production line or mean the loss of a potential sale.

11.5.2.3 **Average collection period**

The **average collection period** indicates, on average, how many days it takes for Techsa to collect a credit sale.

$$\text{average collection period} = \frac{\text{trade receivables}}{\text{average sales per day}}$$

$$= \frac{412}{3950/365} = 38,1 \text{ days}$$

In 2010 it took Techsa 38,1 days to collect on their credit sales. If the average collection period is too high, trade receivables are excessively slow in being converted to cash, and liquidity could be seriously damaged.

If Techsa's credit terms (see Section 11.9.1.2) call for payment within 30 days, their average collection period is more than this, indicating that trade receivables are not, on average, keeping to the credit policy. Late payers should be identified by using an aging analysis (see Section 11.9.1.3). However, Techsa should also be careful of applying the credit policy too strictly, as this could have the effect of reducing sales.

11.5.2.4 **Total asset turnover**

The **total asset turnover** shows how efficiently the business is using its assets to create sales. It is calculated as follows:

$$\text{total asset turnover} = \frac{\text{sales}}{\text{total assets}}$$

$$= \frac{3\ 950}{1\ 587} = 2,5 \text{ times}$$

As a rule, the higher the total asset turnover, the better the assets have been used, and the more financially efficient the business operations are.

11.5.3 Debt management ratios

Solvency is the ability of a business to meet all of its debt obligations (both long- and short-term) at any time. A business must be able to assure the people who lend capital to it, that its total assets cover its total liabilities. Failure to do so will make it very difficult to attract initial and additional loan capital from external sources.

Financial leverage means the use of debt financing in the business. The more financial leverage the business has, the higher the financial risk. 'Financial risk' is the risk of not being able to meet the interest-payment obligations on debt finance. However, additional risk promises additional return: if you can earn more on the borrowed funds than you pay in interest, the result is that the return on owners' capital is magnified. Therefore there are two aspects to financial leverage: firstly, a change in financial risk and, secondly, some consequences for the owners' returns. The debt management ratios (solvency ratios) try to assess the first aspect: the impact of financial leverage on risk. These debt management ratios include the debt ratio, the gearing ratio, and the interest coverage ratio.

11.5.3.1 **The debt ratio**

The **debt ratio** measures the total amount of debt (long-term and short-term) that the business uses to finance its assets. The debt ratio for Techsa can be calculated as follows:

$$\text{debt ratio} = \frac{\text{total debt}}{\text{total assets}}$$

$$= \frac{893}{1\ 597} = 56,2\%$$

This indicates that more than 50% of its assets are funded by debt. A lower ratio is better, and a maximum debt ratio of 50% is normally recommended.

The financial risk of Techsa is tied to the fixed-interest obligations of its debt funds. This means that interest charges and profits need to be examined before a complete assessment can be made of its financial risk.

II.5.3.2 **The gearing ratio**

The **gearing ratio** is measured as follows:

$$\text{gearing ratio} = \frac{\text{owners' equity}}{\text{total debt}}$$

$$= \frac{694}{893} = 0,77:1$$

This indicates that for every R1 of debt, the business has 77c of owners' funds. The larger the ratio, the better, and a minimum gearing ratio of 1:1 is normally advised.

II.5.3.3 **The interest coverage ratio**

The interest coverage ratio measures the number of times a business can pay its interest commitments from its profit before interest and taxes. Failure to meet the interest expense could lead to legal action, and eventually insolvency (bankruptcy). The interest coverage ratio for Techsa is:

$$\text{interest coverage ratio} = \frac{\text{PBIT}}{\text{Interest}}$$

$$= \frac{110}{61} = 1,8 \text{ times}$$

Techsa's ratio reflects a high interest charge in relation to profitability. A value of between 3 and 5 is recommended.

II.5.4 Profitability ratios

Profitability ratios show the combined effect of liquidity and asset and debt management on operating results. They show how effectively the available capital has been used in the activities of the business. High ratios are always preferred. Mark-up percentages vary a great deal, depending on the type of business, and acceptable profitability margins depend on the industry in which the business is operating. Profitability can be expressed in terms of the sales of the enterprise (gross profit margin, or profit margin) and in terms of profitability of capital employed (return on total assets, or return on equity).

While debt management ratios are concerned with changes in financial risk, these profitability ratios are concerned with the implications of changes in financial risk for owners' returns.

11.5.4.1 **The gross profit margin**

The **gross profit margin** measures how profitable sales have been. It indicates the amount of funds available to pay the firm's expenses other than its cost of sales. Techsa's gross profit margin is:

$$\text{gross profit margin} = \frac{\text{gross profit}}{\text{sales}}$$

$$= \frac{580}{3\ 950} = 14{,}7\%$$

A comparison of Techsa's ratio with that of similar businesses should expose Techsa's relative strengths and weaknesses.

11.5.4.2 **The profit margin**

The **profit margin** is net profits after all expenses to sales. It is directly affected by the gross profit margin and the operating expenses, including interest paid. The profit margin is defined as follows:

$$\text{profit margin} = \frac{\text{profit after tax and interest}}{\text{sales}}$$

$$= \frac{35}{3\ 950} = 0{,}9\%$$

To strengthen Techsa's profit margin, management would have to increase revenue or decrease expenses.

11.5.4.3 **The return on total assets**

The **return on total assets** (ROA) measures the profitability of the business as a whole in relation to its total assets used. The ratio is calculated by dividing profits after tax by total assets.

$$\text{return on total assets} = \frac{\text{profit after tax}}{\text{total assets}}$$

$$= \frac{35}{1\ 587} = 2{,}21\%$$

A low ratio in comparison with industry averages indicates a use of business assets that is not efficient.

II.5.4.4 **The return on equity**

The **return on equity** (ROE) measures the profitability of own capital, and is influenced largely by how much borrowed capital the business uses. A guideline to finding the profitability of own capital is to compare the return on equity to the return on alternative investments. Techsa's ROE is calculated as follows:

$$\text{return on equity} = \frac{\text{profit after tax}}{\text{owners' equity}}$$

$$= \frac{35}{694} = 5\%$$

If the ROE is less than the rate of return on an alternative risk-free investment, it would not be worthwhile for the owners to continue investing their capital in the business.

II.5.5 Applying ratio analysis

Financial ratio analysis shows the relative strengths and weaknesses of a business. To do this, you must get a benchmark (standard), which is normally based on either previous performance or on how other businesses in the same industry perform (or both). The ratio procedure is as follows: calculate a ratio, compare it with last year's ratios to see if there is a trend, and then compare it with those of other firms in the same industry, to judge the strengths and weaknesses of your business.

> **CRITICAL THINKING**
>
> Financial ratio analysis is often divided into four areas.[3] Separate each of these areas of analysis from the others. Which area is of the greatest concern to creditors?

II.6 **Break-even analysis**

Break-even analysis examines the interrelationship between costs, volume, and profit at different levels of sales activity. For this reason it is also known as cost-volume-profit analysis. Break-even analysis answers questions such as: 'At what volume of sales are all my costs covered?' or 'How do I know what volume of sales will create a satisfactory profit figure?'.

11.6.1 Fixed and variable costs

With break–even analysis it is assumed that all costs can be split into fixed or variable costs.

A **fixed cost** is a cost that is not affected by increases or decreases in the volume of output. Fixed costs relate to the passage of time; as time increases, so will fixed costs.

FIGURE 11.1 Fixed costs, which do not change with an increase in the level of business activity

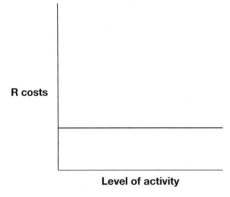

A **variable cost** tends to vary directly with the volume of output or sales. The variable cost per unit is the same amount for each unit produced. Variable costs include direct material costs, direct labour costs, sales commission paid in relation to the volume of sales and bonus payments for productivity paid to employees.

FIGURE 11.2 Variable costs, which change with the level of business activity

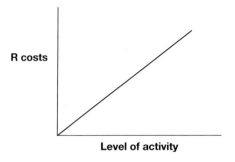

Understanding cost graphs

Questions

1. What type of costs could be represented by the graph shown below?
2. Give an example of a cost that could be illustrated in this way.

FIGURE II.3

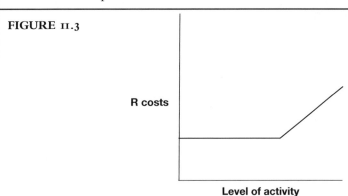

Answers

1. The above graph illustrates semi-variable costs where there is a fixed-cost element and a variable-cost element.
2. This type of cost is an expense where the fixed-cost element is part of the cost that needs to be paid, whatever the level of activity achieved by the business. The variable component of the cost is payable depending on the level of activity of the business. One example of this is the telephone bill that you receive from Telkom each month – there is the payment for the line and rental of the number (which is the fixed-cost component) and then there is the part where you pay for the number of times and minutes that you use the telephone (the variable-cost component).

I.6.2 The break-even point

The break-even point is the level of activity where a business is making neither a profit nor a loss. Break-even analysis can be used to determine what the break-even point is. The three critical elements of break-even analysis are selling price per unit, the costs (fixed and variable), and the level of activity of the business (volume of sales). A change in any one of these three critical elements will result in a change to the total profit of the business.

The break-even point is reached when total costs equal total income (when there is no profit or loss).

The break-even point can be calculated using the formula below:

$$N = \frac{F}{SP - V}$$

where:
N = **number of units where no profit or loss is made**
F = **total fixed cost**
SP = **selling price per unit**
V = **variable cost per unit**

FIGURE 11.4 The break-even point

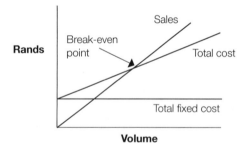

The area between total fixed cost and total cost is the variable cost. No profit is made at the break-even point. The business will make a profit on sales above the break-even point, and will suffer a loss if sales are below the break-even point.

Using break-even analysis

Sellular CC has the following data for the month of March:
- Selling price per unit (R 200)
- Variable cost per unit (R 50)
- Total fixed cost (R 300 000)
- Expected sales (units) (5 000).

Questions
1. What is the break-even volume?
2. What is the break-even value?
3. What is the profit on sales of 5 000 units?

Answers
1. Break-even volume

$$N = \frac{F}{SP - V} = \textbf{2 000 units}$$

2. Break-even value

BE point (value) = 2 000 units × R50 = R100 000

3. Profit on sales of 5 000 units

Profit = R sales − (F + V) = (5 000 × R200) − (300 000 + 5 000 × R50)
= R1 000 000 − (300 000 + 250 000) = R450 000 profit

II.6.3 Some limitations of break-even analysis

Break-even analysis is a very useful tool for a financial manager, but it has limitations, namely:
- It is often not easy to classify all costs as either fixed or variable. For example, is making a telephone call to order a product a fixed or a variable cost?
- The elements making up the variable–unit cost and total fixed costs are not constant. Instead, they are always changing.
- Break-even analysis does not consider qualitative factors such as customer ideas, competitors, or the availability of cash.

Any change in the three critical elements of break-even analysis (selling price per unit, fixed and variable costs, and the volume of sales) will result in a change in profits. These elements need to be continuously measured, calculated, and managed, to ensure that the objectives of the business are being achieved.

11.7 **Financing capital requirements**

Every business, regardless of size, requires finance for short-term commitments (such as rent, wages, and telephone bills) or medium- to long-term commitments (such as vehicles, machinery, and buildings). The rule here is that the period of the funding should match the life-span of the asset that it is financing. For example, the following would be appropriate (suitable):

- a short-term bank overdraft to finance current assets
- medium- to long-term lease financing to finance vehicles
- a long-term loan to finance building additions.

Short-term and long-term financing come in various types, with particular characteristics.

11.7.1 Short-term financing

Short-term financing is normally used to meet seasonal or temporary financing needs of less than one year, and may be in the form of trade credit from suppliers, bank credit, or factoring of trade receivables.

11.7.1.1 **Trade credit**

Trade credit is an arrangement that allows the business to pay the supplier of a product only after 30, 60 or 90 days. Trade credit is granted on an informal basis, with no obvious cost, unless a discount is made a part of the credit terms. The following example illustrates the cost of trade credit in terms of a previous discount.

There is a definite cost of trade credit when discounts are available but are not taken. However, trade credit is a useful and important source of finance, and should be used wisely. The trade credit that a firm receives will influence the amount of trade credit that the business will be able to give its own customers.

An example of trade credit

Question

A business orders R50 000 of goods from Builders Wholesalers, whose credit terms are 2/10 net 30. What is the cost of forfeiting the cash discount?

Answer

The term '2/10 net 30' means that if the business pays in full within 10 days of purchase, it will receive a 3% cash discount. In other words, it will pay R48 5000 instead of R50 000. If it fails to pay within 10 days, it will have to pay the full R50 000 by the end of 30 days. The net effect is that the business is paying 3% for the use of R50 000 for 20 days. Translated into annual interest, the cost of not taking the cash discount is calculated as follows:

$$\frac{(0,03 \times 365 \text{ days})}{20 \text{ days}} = 54,75\% \text{ p.a.}$$

II.7.I.2 Bank credit

Bank credit in the form of a bank overdraft is not linked to a particular transaction, but is valid for a certain maximum amount. The overdraft is normally unsecured (not backed by the borrower's capital), but security can be demanded in the form of inventory, trade receivables, and even fixed assets.

Overdrafts may be regarded as a relatively cheap form of finance, with the interest rate charged depending on how good the applicant's credit rating is. The cost of a bank overdraft will be the prime lending rate plus additional percentage points according to the business's risk profile. For example, if the business is a new client with no credit history, the bank may charge it the prime overdraft rate plus 3%. Interest would be paid only on the debit balance, and not on the total permitted overdraft. Unused overdraft facilities represent a useful ready supply of funds which can be called upon before the business has to look for further capital.

When applying for bank finance, it is useful to try and anticipate the firm's financial needs for at least the next 6 to 12 months, rather than only specifying the funds currently needed. (See Section 11.8 on a cash budget.)

11.7.1.3 **Factoring of trade receivables**

A business can sell off its trade receivables to a financing institution as they arise, and the institution then takes over the risk of non-payment and is responsible for debt collections. This process is called 'factoring'. The factor's commission normally amounts to 0,5 to 1,5% of the value of the invoice, making it an expensive source of financing.

However, factoring has a number of advantages. Firstly, cash is received for outstanding trade receivables immediately after the sale has been made, improving the cash flow of the business. Secondly, the credit and collection function, and all the expenses associated with this function, are assumed by the factor. This means the factoring firm has access to a specialised collection service, and collection expenses are limited to a fixed percentage of credit sales. Finally, factors provide important information concerning product prices, market conditions, and finance – areas which many firms are unable to research because of a lack of funds and skills. Therefore factoring allows smaller businesses to take advantage of the full-scale professional credit management normally associated only with larger concerns.

11.7.2 Long-term financing

Long-term financing is capital that you need over a long period, in other words for a period of more than a year. It is seen as long-term funds that are invested into capital projects, and assets that are needed for the long-term survival of the business. Long-term funds consist of owners' equity and long-term liabilities (debt funding). Sources of long-term funding are long-term loans, equity funding, and leases.

The long-term financing decision involves choosing the type and combination of finance available at the lowest possible cost (interest rate or opportunity cost) to the business. In deciding between raising funds through debt or through equity, the basic risk–return principle applies. As the risk of not being able to meet fixed–interest commitments is increased by the use of higher proportions of debt, so an increase in return to shareholders is expected.

Therefore choosing a long–term financing source is a trade-off between the owners' preference for return, risk, and control. As new ordinary shares are issued (equity funding), the existing shareholders must share future income and control, but the total risk of the firm, in terms of variability of earnings to ordinary shareholders, and the likelihood of insolvency, is reduced. As new debt is raised, the current shareholders receive the 'residual' income from investments, namely the profit remaining after the payment of fixed financial charges. Shareholders also keep their existing control, but the risk of not being able to meet fixed financial costs is increased.

The financial power of the business will influence the debt-versus-equity decision. If the business has a stable earning pattern, the owners may be prepared to take a bigger risk. On the other hand, if the business's trade is unstable, it would not be wise to take high financial risk. An economic downturn resulting in a lower profit before interest and taxes, or an upswing in interest rates, could lead to financial distress.

11.7.2.1 **Equity funding**

Equity funding (also known as 'shareholders' funds' or 'owners' interest') is the main source of long-term finance, particularly for smaller businesses. In the case of a company, this is the share capital and retained earnings, and is referred to as the **equity.**

Shareholders have a proportional interest in the dividends declared by the directors from the residual profits, after paying interest and taxation. Shareholders also have a proportional interest in the net assets of the business in the case of liquidation. Shareholders expect a higher return (dividends plus capital growth) than that of fixed-interest securities (bank loans) because the investor is taking more risk in holding the equity investment.

Part of the ordinary shareholders' equity consists of the profits that could be distributed but which have been retained (kept) in the firm. If they are distributed as dividends, replacement equity funds will eventually have to be raised. If profits are retained, they represent an immediate source of finance. The decision to retain earnings rather than pay a dividend is determined by the dividend policy of the firm.

11.7.2.2 **Long-term bank loans**

Bank loans are the chief source of long-term borrowed funds, particularly for smaller businesses. In relying on the bank as a source of funds, a long-term relationship means being able to reach capital, often to fund long-term asset-based financing. An example of this is a mortgage loan, where the security for the bank is the real estate (house or land) owned by the business.

In assessing a prospective borrower, the bank manager will evaluate the solvency, liquidity and profitability of the deal to be financed, chiefly looking at the degree of risk involved in the loan request. To make this decision, the bank manager will need information about the owner/manager of the firm, the financial position of the firm which needs the loan, and also a cash budget (see Section 11.8).

11.7.2.3 **Financial leases**

A **financial lease** is a contract agreement between a lessee (asset user) and lessor (asset owner). This agreement cannot be ended or cancelled by giving notice. The lessee must make specific payments over the term of the lease. Financial leases are normally used to finance vehicles and equipment, and they give the lessee the chance to own the asset at the end of the lease. As the entire lease payment is tax-deductible (can be taken off income tax), it is an attractive form of financing from a tax point of view.

> **CRITICAL THINKING**
> What paramount issues should management be considering when deciding on an appropriate type of financing?

11.8 **The cash budget**

A **cash budget** is a statement of estimated future cash receipts and payments, showing the forecast cash balance of the business at certain intervals. A properly prepared cash budget will show how cash flows in and out of the business, as well as the business's future ability to pay debts and expenses. For example, preliminary budget estimates may show that payments to suppliers are lumped together, and that, with more careful planning, these can be spread more evenly through the year. This could result in less bank credit being used, and lower interest costs. Banks are more likely to grant a business loan under favourable terms if the loan request is supported by a methodical cash budget. Once a cash budget has been carefully mapped out, a financial manager will be able to compare it to the actual cash inflows and outflows of the business.

Preparing and evaluating a cash budget

Janet Dube, the financial controller for Corolla Company, has prepared the following sales and purchases estimates for the period February–June.

TABLE 11.4

Month	Sales R	Purchases R
February (actual)	3 000 000	3 500 000
March (actual)	4 500 000	2 000 000
April (forecast)	1 000 000	500 000
May (forecast)	1 500 000	750 000
June (forecast)	2 000 000	1 000 000

- Dube notes that in the past, Corolla has collected 60% of sales for cash, and 40% of its sales one month later.
- Interest income of R 50 000 on an investment will be received in June.
- Corolla pays cash for 40% of its purchases and pays for 60% of its purchases the following month.

- Lease payments of R200 000 must be made each month.
- A loan repayment of R150 000 is due in April and June.
- Fixed assets costing R600 000 will be purchased in June.
- Corolla has a beginning cash balance in April of R50 000.

Questions

1. What is the cash budget for the months of April, May and June?
2. Evaluate Corolla's cash budget.

Answers

1.

TABLE II.5

Cash Budget for Corolla

Month	February	March	April	May	June
Sales	R3 000 000	R4 500 000	R1 000 000	R1 500 000	2 000 000
Cash sales (60%)	1 800 000	2 700 000	600 000	900 000	1 200 000
1 month coll (40%)		1 200 000	1 800 000	400 000	600 000
Interest rec					50 000
Tot Cash Receipts		3 900 000	2 400 000	1 300 000	1 850 000
Purchases	3 500 000	2 000 000	500 000	750 000	1 000 000
Cash purch (40%)	1 400 000	800 000	200 000	300 000	400 000
1 month purch (60%)		2 100 000	1 200 000	300 000	450 000
Salaries and wages		450 000	675 000	150 000	225 000
Sales commission		60 000	90 000	20 000	30 000
Lease payments		200 000	200 000	200 000	200 000
Loan repayment			150 000		150 000
Fixed assets purchased					600 000
Total Disbursements		3 610 000	2 515 000	970 000	2 055 000
Net cash flow		290 000	(115 000)	330 000	(205 000)
Add beginning cash			50 000	(65 000)	265 000
Ending cash balance			(65 000)	265 000	60 000

2. Corolla's cash budget helps management to forecast future cash requirements and make necessary arrangements beforehand. In Corolla's case, an arrangement must be made to get a bank overdraft to fund the anticipated cash deficit (shortage) of R65 000 at the end of April.

A monthly cash budget helps to show estimated cash balances at the end of each month, which may show up likely short-term cash shortfalls, or reveal if large sums of excess cash are lying idle and could be invested to earn a return in the short term.

11.8.1 Preparing a cash budget

CRITICAL THINKING
What options are available to a business if it thinks it has too much cash? How about too little?

There are three separate parts to the cash budget, namely estimated cash receipts, estimated cash payments, and the balance. Cash receipts are income items such as cash sales, payments from trade receivables, and others. Cash payments include cash purchases, payments to creditors, rent, wages and salaries, tax paid, interest paid, lease payments, loan repayments and assets purchased for cash. Depreciation (decrease in value over time) is not included in the cash budget because it is only a book write-off. The difference between the monthly cash receipts and cash payments is the cash flow for the month. This is added to the beginning cash balance to calculate the ending cash balance for the month.

11.9 Managing trade receivables and inventories[4]

Both trade receivables and inventories represent large investments in current assets, and should be carefully managed.

11.9.1 Managing trade receivables

A **trade receivable** is a bill for a customer who owes money to an organisation for the goods and services he or she has received. Managing trade receivables starts with the decision to give credit to customers. Credit is given in order to attract and maintain customers, because credit sales increase total revenue. The trade receivables that come from extending credit form a solid investment in current assets, and need to be managed effectively. Here the greater the size of the trade receivable and the longer the collection period, the higher the investment needed, and the greater the cost. The objective of credit management is therefore to collect trade receivables as quickly as possible without losing customers from high-pressure collecting methods. Reaching this goal involves three critical aspects, namely credit policy, credit terms, and collection policy.

II.9.I.I **Credit policy**

The **credit policy** spells out conditions that will determine which customers should get credit and how much. Basically, customers are evaluated according to their credit-worthiness in terms of the 'four Cs of credit':
- character – the customer's record of meeting obligations in the past
- capacity – the customer's ability to pay
- capital – the customer's financial resources
- conditions – current economic or business conditions.

The creditworthiness of customers can be judged by looking at sources like financial statements, the customer's bank, and credit agencies. Credit agencies provide credit ratings and credit assessments on individuals and businesses.

II.9.1.2 **Credit terms**

Credit terms are the conditions of sale that are given to credit customers. These terms include the length of time given to customers to pay, and cash discounts offered for prompt payment. Here management should consider the following:
- What are the usual terms of trade in the industry (for example, 30 days from the date of invoice)?
- What is the cost to the business of offering cash discounts for prompt payment? (Will these discounts reduce the profit made on selling the goods in the first place?)
- Are the terms of trade clear on the invoice?

Credit terms can be indicated as, for example, '2/10 net 30 days'. This means the cus-tomer will receive a 2% discount if the account is paid within 10 days of the beginning of the credit period. If not, the account must be settled within 30 days. Cash discounts are offered to encourage quicker payment.

II.9.1.3 **Collection policy**

The **collection policy** refers to the collection methods used to collect trade receivables once they become due. Slow payments lengthen the average collection period and therefore increase the investment tied up in trade receivables. Credit can be checked using the average collection period, and by aging trade receivables. Credit collection can be improved by using popular collection techniques.

The average collection period is calculated using the following equation.

$$\text{average collection period} = \frac{\text{debtors}}{\text{credit sales}} \div 365$$

By carefully watching the average collection period (see Section 11.5.2.3), we can see whether credit terms are being kept. For example, if the credit terms are net 30, the average collection period should be about 30 days (less receipt processing and collection time). If the actual collection period is a lot more than 30 days, or is increasing over time, the business needs to urgently review its credit operations.

'Aging trade receivables' means breaking down the receivables on a month-by-month basis, in order to show the balances that have been outstanding for specific periods of time. An example of a trade-receivables aging schedule is shown in Table 11.6.

TABLE 11.6

Period debt is outstanding	Amount (R)	% of value
Less than 1 month	200 000	46
1 to 2 months	80 000	19
2 to 3 months	100 000	23
3 months to 1 year	30 000	7
Over one year	20 000	5
TOTAL	430 000	100

If the policy of the firm is net 60 days, then R150 000 (debt over 60 days or two months) of the above is overdue. This represents 35% of trade receivables by value, and should be collected without delay.

It is critical to ensure that credit terms are being kept, by continuous monitoring and the following-up of slow-paying trade receivables.

A number of credit-collection techniques ranging from letters to legal action may be used. As an account becomes more overdue, the collection technique is intensified:

- Letters may be sent out after a number of days to remind customers to pay.
- If the letters are unsuccessful, a telephone call to the customer to ask for immediate payment follows.

> **CRITICAL THINKING**
>
> What are the benefits of an effective trade-receivables collection policy?
> - Benefits of effective trade receivables collections include
>   » Increased investment income from bigger cash flow
>   » Lower cost of collection function
>   » Lower bad-debt expense

- A salesperson or collection person can be sent to deal with the customer in order to collect payment.
- An attorney or collection agency can be used if the previous attempts fail. Legal action is a costly and lengthy process and could result in the customer's liquidation and therefore under-recovery of the debt.

11.9.2 Managing inventories

The inventory stock of the business includes raw materials, work-in-progress, finished goods, trading stock, and so on. The overall objective of inventory management is to minimise the investment in inventories (to meet the profit objective) without interrupting the production line, which could result in a loss of sales (endangering the operating objective).

11.9.2.1 The optimum level of inventory holdings

The basic guideline on inventory holdings is that the level of inventory should be as low as possible without reducing customer service. The critical factors that determine inventory holding levels are:

- ordering costs (The administrative costs of placing orders with suppliers.)
- storage costs (The cost of inventory storage and warehousing.)
- holding costs (The interest costs of short-term borrowings that are used to fund inventories.)
- delivery lead times (This refers to the suppliers' delivery times, and they must be calculated into the ordering process to avoid out-of-stock situations.)
- the level of demand (As indicated in the sales or production forecast, this must be co-ordinated with the purchase of inventory.)

Because inventory holdings represent a big investment in current assets, the different departments, which have different priorities (things that come first), need to adopt a co-ordinated approach. The following points are indicators of good practice regarding inventory control:

- Use a good inventory-reporting system. (Using a modern inventory-reporting system will provide accurate and timely management information on inventory movements. The minimum level of information required for any business is produced by the annual stock-take, although in practice much more detailed and timely information is needed.)
- Identify slow-moving items. (The inventory reporting system must highlight the slow-moving inventory items so that steps can be taken to dispose of these items before they become obsolete.)

PRINCIPLES OF **BUSINESS MANAGEMENT**

- Review the sales forecast for accuracy. (The sales forecast is an essential input into the planning process, particularly in the retailing and manufacturing sectors, where inventory holdings and staffing levels are usually set to match the budgeted level of sales. Comparison of budgeted and actual sales is, therefore, critical.)
- Identify the level of out-of-stocks. (Where out-of-stocks have happened, the underlying cause must be identified in order to avoid a repetition of this problem.)

Using financial ratios in inventory control

Question

Which of the ratios discussed in Section 11.5 would be of particular use in inventory control?

Answer

Inventory turnover (which is defined as cost of sales divided by inventory) would be useful to measure how efficiently the asset is being managed.

CASE STUDY: Financial ratio analysis of Polokwane Printing Company

Here are the income statement and industry averages of the key ratios of the Polokwane Printing Company. The income statement and balance sheet are shown in Table 11.9.

1. To complete the table below, calculate the ratios for Polokwane Printing for 2010.

TABLE 11.7

Key ratios	Polokwane	Industry Average
Current ratio	_____	2,0 X
Average collection period	_____	35 days
Inventory turnover	_____	7,8 X
Profit margin	_____	3,2%
Return on total assets	_____	6,5%
Return on equity	_____	15,0%
Debt ratio	_____	60,0%

2. Briefly describe Polokwane's strengths and weaknesses in relation to the industry averages.

TABLE 11.8

INCOME STATEMENT OF POLOKWANE PRINTING FOR THE YEAR ENDED 31 DECEMBER 2010	
Sales*	803 100
Less Cost of sales	(676 500)
Operating profit	126 600
Less General administrative and selling expenses	(45 500)
Depreciation	(15 100)
Profit before interest and taxes	66 000
Less Interest	(12 800)
Profit before taxes	53 200
Less Taxes (32%)	(17 000)
Profit for the year	R36 200

* Assume all sales are on credit

TABLE 11.9

BALANCE SHEET OF POLOKWANE PRINTING AS AT 31 DECEMBER 2010		
ASSETS	R	R
Total non-current assets		152 500
Current assets		
Cash	38 700	
Inventory	135 500	
Trade and other receivables	97 400	
Total current assets		271 600
Total assets		424 100
LIABILITIES AND OWNERS' EQUITY		
Total shareholders' equity	150 500	
Long-term debt	85 000	235 500
Current liabilities		
Trade and other payables	115 000	
Other current liabilities	73 600	
Total current liabilities		188 600
Total equity and liabilities		424 100

SUMMARY

The financial management department must have the necessary funds to run the organisation. It can do this through arranging loans or using owners' equity.

The financial management department must also ensure the best use of these funds over the short and long term. It does so based on the cost-benefit principle, the risk-return principle, and the time-value-for-money principle. The financial management tasks are interrelated, and should always be carried out in harmony with the other functions of the business.

GLOSSARY

accounting equation (balance-sheet equation): a business's assets are equal to owners' equity plus liabilities

asset management ratios: ratios that measure how effectively the assets of the business are being used to generate sales (for example, inventory turnover, average collection period, total asset turnover)

average collection period: trade receivables divided by average sales per day

balance sheet: a listing, at a specific moment in time, of all the assets and liabilities of a business and how these net assets are financed

bank credit: credit extended by the bank

bank overdraft: bank credit extended on a monthly basis with an agreed upon ceiling and interest rate

break-even analysis (cost-volume-profit analysis): an analysis of the interrelationship of costs, volume and profit at different levels of sales activity, which indicates the level of sales at which all costs are covered

break-even point: the level of activity where neither a profit nor a loss is made

cash budget: a statement of estimated future cash receipts and payments

collection policy: the collection principles to be adhered to in the extension of credit and collection of trade receivables

cost-benefit principle: the principle that states that the cost incurred must result in a benefit at least equal to the cost

credit policy: criteria that spell out which customers should receive credit and how much

credit terms: the terms of sale that are extended to credit customers

current assets: assets owned by the business that will be turned into sales or cash within 12 months

current liabilities (short-term funds): obligations owing to creditors that are due within one year

current ratio: current assets divided by current liabilities

debt management ratios (solvency ratios): ratios that can be used to assess the impact of financial leverage on risk (such as the debt ratio, the gearing ratio and the interest coverage ratio)

debt ratio: total debt divided by total assets

equity: the owner(s) funds invested in the business; in the case of a company, the share capital and retained earnings

equity funding: shareholders' funds or owners' interest

factoring: selling off trade receivables to a factor who assumes the risk of non-payment, and is responsible for debt collections

financial lease: a contractual agreement between a lessee (asset user) and lessor (asset owner)

financial leverage: the use of debt financing

financial management: the functional area of an organisation that is concerned with planning and managing the organisation's funds in order to achieve its objectives

financial ratio: a comparison between two variables (values) from the financial statements

financial ratio analysis: the use of ratios to determine benchmarks, and the use of these benchmarks to determine the relative strengths and weaknesses of a business

financial risk: the risk of not being able to meet the interest payments on debt

financial statements: the documents that provide a written summary of the financial activities of the business

fixed assets: assets owned and required by the business that have a life span of more than 12 months

fixed cost: a cost that does not vary according to increases or decreases in the volume of output

gearing ratio: owners' equity divided by total debt

gross profit margin: gross profit divided by sales

income statement: a financial summary of the profitability of a business over a period of time

interest coverage ratio: (profit before interest and tax) divided by interest expense

inventory turnover: cost of sales divided by inventory

liabilities: loans from creditors that must be paid back

liquidity: the ability of the business to honour its short-term financial commitments as they become due

liquidity ratios: ratios, such as the current ratio and the quick ratio, which measure the liquidity of the business

long-term financing: financing with a duration of more than a year

long-term funds: sources of funds with a maturity value of longer than a year

opportunity cost: when choosing one option, the next best alternative forgone

owners' equity: funds invested by owners for use by the business in acquiring assets

profitability: the business's ability to generate income that will be more than the total costs by using its assets for productive purposes

profitability ratios: ratios that show the combined effect of liquidity, asset and debt management on operating results

profit margin: (profit after interest and tax) divided by sales

quick ratio (acid–test ratio): (current assets minus inventory) divided by current liabilities

return on equity: profit after tax divided by owners' equity

return on total assets: profit after tax divided by total assets

risk–return principle: the principle that states that the higher the risk that a business takes, the higher the return that business will require in order to take that risk

short-term financing: temporary financing to meet the needs of less than one year

short-term funds (current liabilities): obligations owing to creditors that are due within one year

solvency: the ability of a business to meet all of its debt obligations at any time

time–value–of–money principle: the principle that states that money has a value over time

total asset turnover: sales divided by total assets

trade credit: an arrangement that allows the business to pay the supplier of the product only after 30, 60 or 90 days

trade receivable: a customer to which credit has been extended

variable cost: a cost that varies directly with the volume of output

MULTIPLE-CHOICE QUESTIONS

1. Examples of the fixed assets of the business are:
   a) owners equity, mortgages and leases
   b) furniture and equipment
   c) trade payables, bank overdraft and factoring
   d) inventory and trade receivables

2. The time-value-of-money principle:
   a) means that money has a value over time
   b) diagnoses strengths and weaknesses in the business performance
   c) states that the higher the risk that a business takes, the less the return required
      in order to take that risk
   d) calculates the costs and benefits of different alternatives

The following information on Utopia CC relates to questions 3 to 5 below: Utopia produces a single product, which sells for R40 per unit. Variable costs to manufacture and sell are R24 per unit. Fixed costs are budgeted at a total of R90 000 per period.

3. The break–even volume in units is:
   a) 240
   b) 2 250
   c) 3 750
   d) 5 625

4. The break–even point in rands is:
   a) R24 000
   b) R90 000
   c) R225 000
   d) none of the above

5. The profit to be expected from sales of R500 000 is:
   a) R12 500
   b) R45 000
   c) R110 000
   d) R500 000

REFERENCES AND END-NOTES

1. BLOCK, S.B. & HIRT, G.A. 2011. *Foundations of financial management.* 14th ed. New York: McGraw-Hill.
2. CORREIA, C., FLYNN, D., ULIANA, E. & WORMALD, M. 2007. *Financial management.* 6th ed. Cape Town: Juta.
3. GITMAN, L.J. 2009. *Principles of managerial finance.* 12th ed. Boston: Pearson.
4. SMITH, M.B. 2007. *Basic business finance.* New ed. Claremont: New Africa Books.

ANSWERS TO MULTIPLE-CHOICE QUESTIONS

1. Answer = b) p. 203

2. Answer = a) p. 205

3. Answer = d)

$$N = \frac{90000}{40 - 24} = 5\ 625 \text{ units}$$

4. Answer = c)
   BE Point (value) = 5 625 units × R40 = R225 000

5. Answer = c)
   R500 000 ÷ 40 = 12 500 units

   Profit = R sales - (F + V) = R500 000 - (R90 000 + {12 500 × R24})
      = R500 000 - (90 000 + 300 000)
      = R110 000

Human-resources management

Maggie Holtzhausen

PURPOSE OF THIS CHAPTER

This chapter discusses the function of human-resources management, specifically the strategic planning, staffing, assessment, development, and maintenance of human resources. It also defines and discusses the importance of a strategic approach to the management of human resources in the context of today's business challenges.

LEARNING OUTCOMES

This chapter should enable you to:
- define 'human-resources management' and 'strategic human-resources management'
- discuss the importance of human-resources management in the context of managing the organisation as an integrated whole
- explain the role of the human-resources manager
- identify and explain the functions of human-resources management by discussing the strategic planning, staffing, assessment, development and maintenance of human resources
- discuss the current trends in human-resources management.

12.1 Introduction

Human-resources management involves planning, organising, leading, motivating and controlling a business's human resources, which are often viewed as a business's greatest asset. Therefore when human–resources management (HRM) is done well, it makes a valuable contribution to a successful organisation.

HRM is the function in the workplace that deals with all the practices and policies related to the management of people in an organisation.[1] McKenna and Beech take it one step further by emphasising the role of HRM in organisational success: 'HRM seeks to maximise organisational performance through the adoption of best practice in the management of people'.[2] HRM therefore relates to all the dimensions of people in their employment relationships, as well as all the actions arising from these relationships, with the idea of ensuring overall business success. Hall and Gooddale define HRM as 'the process through which an optimal fit is achieved among the employee, job, organisation, and environment, so that employees reach their desired level of satisfaction and performance and the organisation meets its goals'.[3]

However, organisations are constantly changing, and so is the world of work. One such global development is the increase in different forms of employment, such as temporary workers and labour brokers. Swanepoel *et al.* therefore make a valid point when stating that HRM should be regarded as 'that part of the management of organisations that is concerned with all aspects that relate to, and interplay with, the work and the people who do the work of and in organisations'.[4]

HRM should also be described in the context of strategic business management, in other words, linking the HR function with the strategic long-term, top-level manage-ment decisions of the organisation. Because a business's strategic decisions affect its employees in a big way, the human-resources manager needs to be part of the strategic management process.

What has been decided on a strategic level must then be implemented (put into practice). HRM should be organised in an integrated way with the other organisational functions, such as finance and marketing. HRM activities deal with many different 'people issues' related to the implementation of the business strategy.

The South African HRM function is faced with many challenges, such as **affirma-tive action** and skills shortages. These issues affect many of the functions of HRM. For instance, when staffing the organisation, the HRM department has to ensure that there are no discriminatory policies, and that employment-equity legislation is used correctly. Skills shortages will affect the pool of possible applicants during the selection process. Health and safety, and the general well-being of employees must be kept in mind. The impact of global HRM trends must be considered. Ethical behaviour in organisations should be encouraged. All of these issues should be considered in HRM management.

12.2 **The role of human-resources management**

The HRM department must ensure that the organisation's human resources are managed as effectively and efficiently as possible. However, the responsibility of performing various human-resources functions lies not only with the HRM department, but rather with all managers in the organisation – all managers manage their employees – and should (with or without the help of an HRM department) do it as best as possible!

The modern trend in HRM is towards meeting two goals in an integrated way:[5]

- increasing organisational effectiveness
- satisfying each employee's needs.

Neither set of goals should be achieved at the expense of the other. The human-resources strategies should tie in with the organisation's whole strategy regarding its people and general effectiveness.

What is the role of the HRM function in this process? According to Grobler *et al.,* a human-resources approach is necessary, using the following values.[6]

- Employees are investments that will, if effectively managed and developed, give the organisation long-term rewards in the form of productivity.
- Policies, programmes and practices in the organisation should suit both the economic and emotional requirements of the employees.
- At the same time they should also meet the needs and goals of the organisation.
- The work environment should encourage employees to use and develop their skills to the maximum extent.

It is necessary to determine who will be responsible for which HRM-related activities. In big organisations, the HRM staff will design HRM policies and procedures, then the operating staff will implement them.[7] Differently put, the human-resources (HR) manager uses the human resources of the organisation, through line management, for the good of the organisation.[8] Therefore HRM fulfils a co-ordination function.

A smaller organisation may not have the luxury of a whole HRM department. Line managers may then have to fulfil many HRM activities in addition to their normal duties. Whenever possible, though, a successful organisation will combine the knowledge and skills of line managers with the specific expertise of the HR manager in order to make the most of its people. Ideally, line management and HR management will work side by side. Whatever the size of the organisation and who manages which HRM functions, the critical HRM processes must be in place.[9]

The primary responsibility of the HR manager can be summarised as ensuring the best use of the human resources of the organisation. To do this, he or she will be: partly a strategist (making sure that the HR strategy and policies are in line with the bigger organisational strategy and policies, as well as forming new policies, practices and pro-cedures as the need arises); partly an adviser (advising line management on HR-related issues, policies and practices); partly a manager (through planning, organising, leading, and controlling the HR tasks and functions of recruitment, selection, performance management and so forth); partly a trainer and developer (ensuring that staff is optimally trained and developed); and partly a counsellor (listening to and advising employees and management regarding staff issues such as low morale, discipline, grievances and so forth).

This list can even be expanded. However, the most important aspect to take from this is that it is no easy task to ensure that the human resources of an organisation ('its greatest asset') are well taken care of.

HR managers need sound interpersonal skills, including good problem-solving and motivational skills. They need administrative skills and specific types of knowledge (for example, how to do performance appraisals and rewards systems). They also need busi-ness skills such as strategic planning, change management, analytical and conceptual skills, and general management skills.

FIGURE 12.1 The skills needed by an HR manager

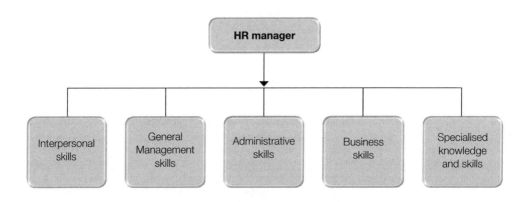

12.3 **The human-resources management process**

The HRM function covers a variety of processes and functions, which can be divided into four major activities, namely HRM planning, staffing, training and development, and maintenance. All these activities should be contributing all the time to human resources, as well as overall organisational success.

12.3.1 Strategic human-resources planning

Byars and Rue summarise the value of HRM planning by saying that the long-term success of any organisation depends on having the right people in the right jobs at the right time.[10] In a strategic approach to HRM, this planning must be in line with the overall business planning. In other words, **strategic human–resource planning** is the process of planning an organisation's HR needs by finding, developing, and keeping a qualified workforce.[11] This can provide quite a challenge, especially in South Africa with its shortage of highly skilled workers, and an oversupply of unskilled or semi-skilled labour.

According to Grobler *et al.,* HRM objectives and plans are essential in strategic HRM planning.[12] HRM objectives state what is to be achieved, while HRM plans are blueprints for action – stating what will happen, when, how, and by whom.

This process of strategic HRM planning (see Figure 12.2 below) has four phases, namely:
- a **situational analysis**: identifying internal and external HRM issues such as staff turnover (internal) and developments in the labour market (external)
- an **analysis of HR demand** (determining the future total manpower require-ments of the organisation)
- an **analysis of HR supply** (an evaluation of the future supply of labour)
- the **development of an HRM strategy** (using the information supplied by the previous stages to develop the HRM strategy, and design action plans).

FIGURE 12.2 Four phases of strategic HRM planning

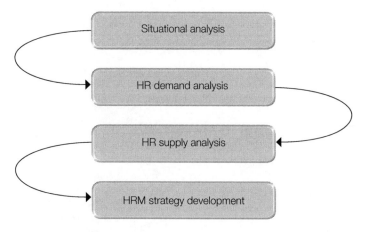

Strategic HRM planning should be undertaken by top management, in line with the organisation's strategy. Once the HR strategy has been determined, two steps remain:
• job analysis
• HR forecasting.

12.3.1.1 **Job analysis**

A **job analysis** determines the content of a job, as well as the behaviours and qualities that it will need. To do this, questions will be asked such as: 'What activities is the employee responsible for?', 'What tasks are to be done?', 'What decisions are to be made?' and 'What skills will the employee need to do the job properly?'. In summary, a job analysis identifies the tasks, skills, abilities and responsibilities that an employee needs in order to do the job.

There are many ways of doing this:[13]
• observation (where the job analyst will watch what the employee does and record the information)
• interviews (where the employee is asked to describe the job)
• questionnaires (where the employee fills in the information on a form).

Once this information is gathered, two end-products result, namely job descriptions and job specifications.[14] A **job description** gives the content of the job, the environment it takes place in, and the conditions under which it is done. It therefore provides information on what the job involves.

A **job specification**, on the other hand, describes the personal skills and characteristics an employee needs to get the job done.

FIGURE 12.3 A job analysis gives two end-products

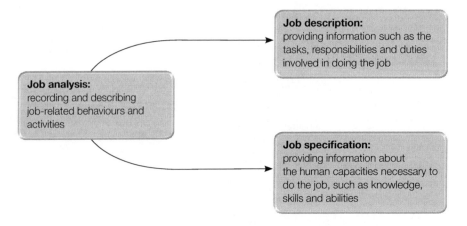

Job description:
providing information such as the tasks, responsibilities and duties involved in doing the job

Job analysis:
recording and describing job-related behaviours and activities

Job specification:
providing information about the human capacities necessary to do the job, such as knowledge, skills and abilities

A job analysis can be used for the following:[15]

- HR forecasting (Information about different jobs.)
- recruitment (Recruitment advertisements can be developed, and applicants given information about the job for which they are applying.)
- interviewing and selection (To match the best job applicant to the job, the interviewer needs concise, accurate information about the job.)
- induction (New employees can gather more information about what is expected of them in their new jobs.)
- training and development (Relevant training can be planned, and suitable employees can be chosen for this training.)
- job evaluation and salary decisions (Jobs can be more easily compared and evaluated to determine their worth.)
- organisational restructuring (Owing to changes in the environment, the organisation may need to make changes in the jobs.)
- performance management (An employee can be judged against clear criteria during performance appraisals.)
- job redesign (Rapidly changing organisations need to fit in with external challenges, and may need to redesign jobs to keep up with their competition.)
- organisational restructuring (Duplicated responsibilities can be removed if accurate information is available.)
- labour relations (Chances of communication gaps about job responsibilities and roles are minimised.)

12.3.1.2 **Human-resources forecasting**

Human-resources forecasting (workforce planning) involves developing and implementing plans so that the right employees fill the right type and number of jobs, allowing the organisation to achieve its goals and objectives. The organisation's strategic business plan is the starting point for this process,[16] but, because the organisation's needs are always changing, HR forecasting is an ongoing process.

The purpose of HR forecasting is to balance the supply and demand of the organisation's human resources.[17] Information regarding the supply and demand of the workforce is gathered, analysed, and used to make the forecast. The demand is affected by the business objectives, while the supply is affected by the programmes that provide the human resources.

When analysing the information, the HRM department must consider the following issues:
- The business might need to grow or shrink in response to the state of the economy.
- Technological changes might cause job descriptions to change.
- A skills shortage or a skills glut in certain areas might make it difficult to find the right people for the right job.

HR managers must keep up with these developments.

A human-resources plan is then developed (considering the results of the forecast) to provide guidelines for the organisation's short- to long-term HR requirements. Once the plan is implemented, it should constantly be monitored and evaluated.

12.3.2 Staffing the organisation

The objective of **staffing** is to find suitably qualified workers to fill particular jobs. This is done through recruitment, selection, and induction.

12.3.2.1 Recruitment

Recruitment refers to all the HRM actions that can be used to get several qualified job applicants to apply for a job so that the best one can be chosen. The recruitment process is ongoing and will start anew each time new staff are needed.

There are two basic sources of applicants that can be used to attract the required pool of candidates, namely internal or external recruitment sources. Most organisations will use both of these methods in their recruitment drives (if no suitable candidate is found inside the organisation, outside sources will be used). Organisations must keep current legislation in mind during these processes.

Internal recruitment takes place when an organisation tries to fill vacant positions from inside the organisation. There are various advantages and disadvantages to this policy.[18] Advantages include the following:
- Employees may see a future for themselves in the organisation, which would have a positive effect on morale.
- Judging applicants becomes much easier as the organisation already has information on the possible candidates' performance, abilities and potential.
- This form of recruitment is cost-effective and fast.
- Staff will mostly need to be appointed only at entry level.
- A chain effect of promotion is achieved in the organisation.

Disadvantages of internal recruitment are:
- The business may stop being creative because new ideas are not coming into the organisation.
- Staff appointed at lower levels do not necessarily have the potential to be promoted to higher positions.
- A lot of personal competition may be created amongst colleagues, which may be an obstacle to co-operation.
- A morale problem may occur among the employees who were not promoted.
- A strong management-development programme may become necessary (which may be costly and time-consuming).

There is a range of internal recruitment sources and techniques. These include the following:[19]
- A record system, that lists employees in the organisation with their specific skills, may be kept for easy reference.
- Available positions can be posted on notice boards, in-house information bulletins, Intranets, and so on.
- Supervisors may recommend staff members or nominate them for certain positions.

When an organisation tries to fill available positions from the outside, this is called **external recruitment**. As with the internal methods of recruitment, external recruitment has various advantages and disadvantages.[20] The advantages of external recruitment include the following:
- An active effort is made to find the best person for the job.
- The pool of possible candidates is bigger, which allows for a larger selection of candidates.
- New ideas, new contacts and fresh approaches to problem-solving are usually brought into the organisation with this approach.

Some disadvantages of external recruitment are:
- It takes longer and is more expensive than inside recruitment.
- The success of the candidate can only be determined once he or she has been employed by the organisation.
- Adjustment problems will be bigger with candidates from the outside.
- The morale of existing employees may be negatively influenced. Some employees may leave the organisation because they do not want to stay indefinitely without a promotion. At the very least it may destroy their incentive to strive for promotions.

There is a range of external recruitment sources and techniques. These include the following:[21]

- Employment agencies will, on the instruction of the organisation, recruit a number of possible applicants, from whom the organisation can choose to do its own selecting, or it may ask the agency to help in the selection process.
- 'Walk-ins' are applicants who apply directly to the organisation in the hope that a position may be vacant. This will happen more often in well-known, highly successful companies.
- Referrals take place mostly when employees, by word-of-mouth, refer candidates from outside the organisation for specific positions.
- Professional bodies, like engineering institutes, may look after the interests of their members by advertising positions in their publications.
- 'Head-hunting' (looking for special people) occurs when top professional people are approached by 'head-hunters'(people who are skilled in persuasion) to fill vacancies. These people are approached personally and offered a position at an organisation.
- Educational institutions are often visited to recruit potential applicants for entry-level positions. This form of recruitment is mostly undertaken for positions requiring scarce skills.
- The Internet, television or radio can also be used in recruitment. The Internet is becoming a very important source of recruitment, and is easily accessible to most people 24 hours a day.

Most organisations will use either internal or external recruitment approaches. For example, if the organisation wants to employ a new cleaner and there are no possible candidates among the current employees, a process of word-of-mouth recruitment, posting an advertisement on the notice board of the business, and/or personal referrals will most probably be enough to get a pool of candidates to choose from. This is so because this is a lower-skilled job, and with the high unemployment rate and huge number of lower-skilled people looking for jobs in South Africa, filling a position like this is fairly easy. A cleaner will probably not have access to the Internet, and it would also not be cost-effective for the organisation to spend too much money on filling a lower-level position. But the process would be very different if a business was looking for a Chief Executive Officer to run a huge multi-national organisation.

Once a suitable pool of possible candidates exists to choose from, the selection process can start.

12.3.2.2 **Selection**

Selection is the process in which the person who best suits a particular position is chosen from a group of applicants. Swanepoel *et al.* emphasise that consideration should be given to individual differences, the requirements of the job, and the organisation's external and internal environment.[22]

The organisation should know about current legislation, ensuring that the selection process is fair and shows no kind of discrimination, unless affirmative-action principles apply. The HRM department would normally perform the selection process, although the level of position to be filled will determine whether anybody else becomes part of the process, and at what stage that will happen. A manager may, for example, choose to sit in on the interviews of applicants who have applied for a job in his or her division.

This selection process is improved by using pre-determined selection standards of judgement.[23] Selection begins with a job description and a job specification. This ensures that the organisation knows exactly what is wanted from the ideal candidate. The selection process has various phases, as explained in the diagram (Figure 12.4)[24] on the next page. Applicants can be rejected or accepted after each phase.

Step 1: *Obtaining CVs and/or application blanks*
The process starts when applications from candidates (gathered through the recruitment process) are evaluated. CVs (curriculum vitaes – a short written account of one's life and abilities) may be asked for, and interviewees may be asked to fill in application blanks that have been developed by the organisation. An application blank standardises all the information of the various candidates, and also ensures that the interviewer has all the necessary information. The main advantage of this step is that a short-list can be compiled, which saves a lot of time in interviewing less suitable candidates.

Step 2: *Screening and short-listing applications*
Candidates who meet the requirements as set out in the job descriptions and job specifications are short-listed. Relevant labour legislation such as the Employment Equity Act must be considered.

Step 3: *Contacting short-listed candidates and arranging for interviews and pre-employment tests (when necessary)*
Not all jobs will require pre-employment tests. The type of job will determine whether it is necessary or not. For instance, it makes a lot of sense to test a typist's abilities through a typing test. Applicants for senior positions will often undergo a range of pre-employment tests. These tests must tie in with to the job, be fair and valid, and not biased against any specific group.

FIGURE 12.4 The selection process

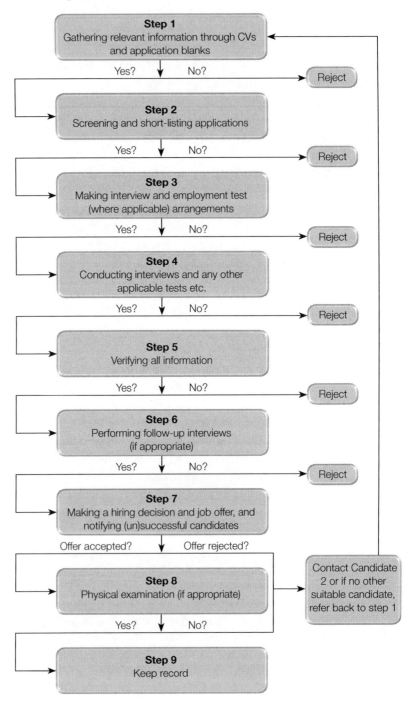

Unless the recruitment advertisement specifies that unsuccessful candidates will not be contacted, all unsuccessful applicants should be notified.

Step 4: *Conducting interviews and, where applicable, employment tests, simulations, and so on*

The next step is the interviewing of short-listed candidates. This is usually done by the HRM department, although the relevant line manager may choose to sit in on the interview. In smaller companies without their own HRM department, the line manager will conduct the interviews.

It is important that interviews are conducted in a professional, efficient, way, without any form of discrimination. Only questions relevant to the requirements of the job may be asked. It is advisable that a structured process be followed, and that the interview setting be prepared beforehand. This will ensure that the right type of interview for the specific job is held. Interviewers can ask themselves questions such as: 'Is a panel interview necessary?', 'Who will take part in the panel?', and 'Who will lead such a panel interview?'. Other employment tests, simulations and so on can also be conducted if applicable to the specific position.

Step 5: *Checking background information and references*

Selected candidates' employment history, qualifications and references are checked. This may turn out to be a cost-effective and time-saving process as it cuts out unsuitable candidates. Although various methods exist for doing this, telephonic reference checks are the most widely used method.

Step 6: *Doing follow-up interviews (if necessary)*

In some cases, a selected number of applicants may be asked for a further round of in-depth interviews. The purpose of this interview is usually to discuss the requirements of the job. The supervisor of the specific job will probably be part of this interview. It enables both the supervisor and the job applicant to determine his or her interest in the job.

Applicants for lower-skilled jobs will generally not be asked for a second interview.

Step 7: *Making a final hiring decision and fair job offer, and notifying successful and unsuccessful candidates*

Once a final hiring decision has been made, the best candidate is offered the job. If the candidate accepts, placement is made, and induction can start as soon as he or she starts work. If the offer is rejected by the first candidate, another applicant can be asked, unless no other suitable candidate was identified in the recruitment process, which will result in the whole recruitment process being repeated. Unsuccessful candidates should be notified as well, unless the advertisement stated otherwise.

Step 8: Organising a physical examination (if appropriate)

A job offer is often made conditional to the passing of a medical examination. However, the HR manager must consider the Employment Equity Act No 55 of 1998 s 7(1) & (2),[25] which says that medical testing of an employee is only allowed if legislation permits or requires the testing, or if it is justifiable in the light of medical facts, employment conditions, social policy, the fair distribution of employment benefits, or the requirements of the job. This may be especially important when good health is a requirement of the job – miners who have to go underground, or pilots who need good eyesight are two examples. Testing for employees' HIV/Aids status is prohibited (not allowed) unless it is found justifiable by the Labour Court.

Step 9: Keeping complete records for legal purposes

Companies should keep records of the recruitment and selection processes because of various labour laws. It may at some point be necessary to prove that no discrimination took place.

12.3.2.3 **Induction**

Once the selection process has been completed and a suitable candidate has accepted the job offer, arrangements can be made to welcome the new employee, and to orientate the employee into the organisation. This orientation process is called **induction**. The first impression left on the employee counts a lot towards the way he or she will see the company. It is therefore very important for the new employment relationship to start off in the right way.

All organisations should have an induction programme. The goal of such a programme is to gradually orientate the employee to his or her new work environment. The programme should include information on the employee's job and the organisation, as well as on his or her fellow workers. Often an information folder on various job aspects (such as leave arrangements, or the grievance and disciplinary procedures of the company) is put together and given to the new employee to look at. The objectives of the induction programme are therefore two-fold – to make the new employee feel more at ease, and to introduce him or her to everyone and everything that may be necessary to start work.

12.3.3 Developing and assessing the organisation's human resources

Developing and assessing employees' skills are important tasks of the HRM section in any organisation. Much has been written about the **learning organisation**, which means an organisation that has a background of constant development of its employees. For example, managers are encouraged to develop coaching and mentoring skills. Encouraging this habit ensures that the organisation keeps up with changes, and that its workforce is as productive, efficient and effective as possible. At the same time, employees need to be continuously assessed on how they do their jobs. This is necessary not only for the employee's own development, but also for the organisation, which can, through this process, determine and manage the training and development programme that it offers.

12.3.3.1 **Training and development**

It is not only the responsibility of HRM to staff the organisation, but also to develop all employees to their best abilities, ensuring a productive and effective workforce. This involves training and development. **Training** means improving the employees' skills and knowledge to do a specific job, and **development** has a more long-term focus on preparing employees for future work responsibilities. The training and development that take place in organisations are also influenced by South African labour legislation. The South African government passed two Acts to deal with the serious skills shortages in the country: the Skills Development Act No 97 of 1998 (amended as the Skills Development Amendment Act 37 of 2008) and the Skills Development Levies Act No 9 of 1999.[26] Both these Acts have a direct influence on training and development conducted at the organisational level.

A structured training and development process should be followed in the organisation. To ensure such a structured approach, close co-operation between the HRM department and line managers on the subject of training and development is needed.

The training and development process usually involves identifying needs, setting goals, designing and administering a programme, and evaluating this programme.[27] In some organisations (although this is still relatively new) one more step is included, namely that of assessment.[28]

FIGURE 12.5 The training and development process

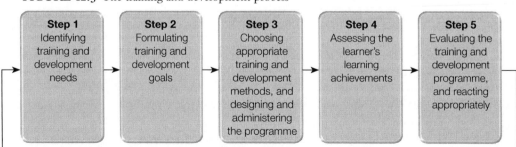

Step 1	Step 2	Step 3	Step 4	Step 5
Identifying training and development needs	Formulating training and development goals	Choosing appropriate training and development methods, and designing and administering the programme	Assessing the learner's learning achievements	Evaluating the training and development programme, and reacting appropriately

Step 1: Identifying training and development needs

To determine the organisation's and individual employees' needs, different techniques can be used (such as questionnaires, attitude surveys and observations). On an organisational level it is necessary to determine the current and future needs according to the organisation's strategic planning. The process is therefore also referred to as **strategic training and development**. On an individual level, the employee's regular performance appraisal information may show specific needs and performance gaps that can be treated through a training and development programme.

Step 2: Formulating training and development goals

Training and development goals are formulated on the basis of the needs that are identified. This ensures that training and development do not occur without a plan, but rather in a focused and structured fashion. These goals are also used later in the evaluation of the training and development programme.

Step 3: Choosing appropriate training and development methods, and designing and administering the programme

A variety of training and development methods exist. These are sometimes divided into **on-the-job training** and **off-the-job training**, but usually they are used together in a single training and development programme.

'On-the-job training' refers to training and development schemes at the workplace, and these are normally conducted by the supervisor. For example, in job rotation, employees are moved systematically from one workstation to the next in order to learn how to perform a whole range of duties. The Skills Development Act 97 of 1998 has also introduced learnerships, where learners are employed by the company with the sole purpose of providing on-the-job training, in this way combining the knowledge and work experience parts of learning. The workplace therefore becomes an active learning environment, and opportunities are also provided for new entrants to the labour market to gain experience. The Skills Development Amendment Act 37 of 2008 also brought back apprenticeships. An apprenticeship is a type of learnership that results in an occupational award that is registered by the Department of Labour as a trade.[29]

Off-the-job training involves formal training away from the workplace, such as formal study programmes presented by a training institution.

Step 4: Assessing (judging) the learner's achievements

Assessment is a strategic process used by a qualified and registered assessor, in which evidence is collected to find out the learner's knowledge, abilities, actions, performance, values, and attitude. This helps assessors to make informed decisions about a learner's ability. As it is such a new process in organisations, the support of management is very important, especially because it can be a costly and time-consuming activity. Apart from giving information about gaps in training and development, it also motivates a learner, improves training intervention programmes, and helps in accurate programme design.[30]

Step 5: Evaluating the training and development programme, and reacting appropriately

The training and development programme should be judged against what it set out to do, to see if it has achieved these goals. This can be done through evaluations of the courses attended, as well as by seeing whether a trainee's work performance has improved after training.

Performance management, which is discussed in the next section, is closely related to training and development, because it is only through proper performance management that an organisation can identify the training and development needs of its staff.

12.3.3.2 **Performance management**

Performance management is a formal and methodical ongoing process of shared checking by the manager and the employee, by means of which the employee's job-related strengths and weaknesses are identified, measured against set objectives, and followed by a development plan to assist the employee in improving his knowledge and skills. It therefore has parts of both past performance and future objectives.[31] This process begins with breaking down the overall objectives of the organisation into clear objectives for each individual employee.[32] The whole process can therefore be called **strategic performance management**.

Performance management is useful in evaluating (for example, for staffing purposes) and in developing (for example, for identifying the training and development needs of employees).[33]

There are three types of performance criteria that can be used in a **performance appraisal**:[34]

- trait-based criteria, which focus on the personal characteristics of an employee (for example, loyalty to the organisation and co-workers)
- behaviour-based criteria, which focus on specific behaviours that lead to job success (for example, the ability to work well with co-workers)
- outcomes-based criteria, which focus on what was achieved or produced.

Many techniques are available for making appraisals (official judgements). Even though the line manager will be conducting the appraisals, it remains the responsibility of the HRM function to use a suitable way of judging (as determined by the objectives of the appraisal), to provide training on the process where necessary, and to ensure that performance management is used constructively. The reason for the appraisal often determines the method chosen.

Management should realise that the method and the way that the appraisal is conducted will have an important effect on the way that the employee sees the process. Poorly handled performance appraisals may lead to a loss of morale and productivity, and may even have legal consequences.

Constructive, relevant, concise and specific feedback to employees is especially important to prevent these problems.[35] Good performance should be rewarded. At the same time, employees who perform poorly should receive counselling if needed, and should be helped with training programmes and so on. The main point is that the process should be managed in a positive way, so that it is not thought of as a tool for future punishment.

How easy is HRM?

According to Tom Boardman:[36]

... the single most difficult thing to do is select the right people, and then to make sure that they are motivated, committed, and passionate about what they are doing.

People are the most complex element we have in business ... So when people talk about HR as being a soft issue, they don't understand – it's the hardest thing to handle.

12.4 Maintaining the organisation's human resources

Maintaining the organisation's human resources involves compensation. **Compensation** is defined as 'the extrinsic and intrinsic rewards provided by the organisation for an employee's fulfilment of his or her job requirements aimed at achieving organisational objectives'. Extrinsic rewards are financial rewards (for example, salaries, fringe benefits and incentive schemes) as well as non-financial rewards (for example, status rewards such as office furniture, and social rewards such as praise). Intrinsic rewards are opportunities for personal growth and more interesting work.

FIGURE 12.6 Some compensation examples

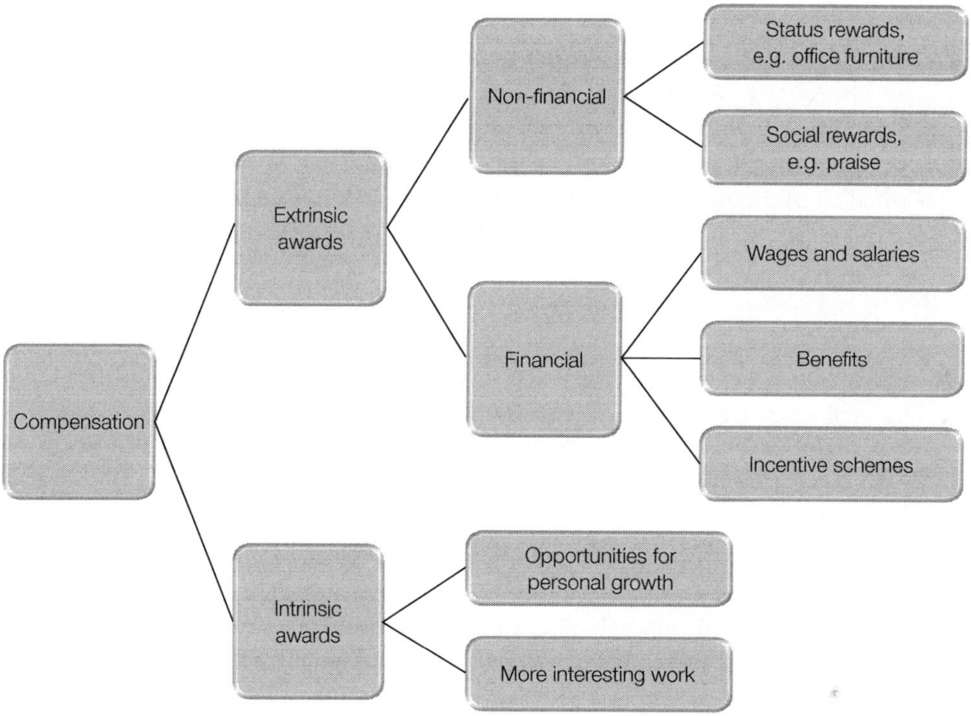

Compensation management can be defined as the management of extrinsic rewards and intrinsic rewards. The HRM function should use both extrinsic and intrinsic rewards to compensate employees.

Some of the possible compensation objectives are:[37]
- to attract good applicants (This is achieved by doing regular wage surveys to determine the relevant going-rate in the labour market.)
- to retain good employees (Wage surveys help this objective, and so do job-evaluation systems that employees see as fair.)
- to motivate employees (Employees are rewarded for good performance, based on fair and equitable job evaluations.)
- to comply with current legislation (Government legislation determines such things as minimum wage levels in certain sectors. To reach this objective, records of compensation must be held.)

The way the compensation system is designed has a direct influence on getting and maintaining good qualified employees.[38] These systems also have a strong influence on employees' motivation to strive towards reaching the organisation's objectives.

12.5 **Important trends in human–resources management**

The Society for Human Resource Management (SHRM) has reviewed some key trends in HRM. In their research they confirmed that some broader trends influence HRM directly. The following themes were found likely to have an impact on HRM:[39]

- The effect of the international depression on business strategy and employees;
- The influence of social networking, especially as it relates to recruiting;
- The ongoing significance of work or life-balance as employees deal with multiple caring responsibilities and, in some cases, multiple paid jobs;
- The need for measurement of results and the development and consistency of key HR measures;
- The increasing need for organisations to demonstrate a commitment to ethics, sustainability and social responsibility;
- Safety issues, particularly workplace aggression and the possible impact of a global disease epidemic;
- The significance of globalisation and integrating markets;
- Continued emphasis on performance management;
- The ongoing need for skilled employees and concerns about the capability of education systems to produce the needed skilled workers of the future;
- Demographic change and its impact on diversity and labour availability;
- The implications of government legislation.

Grobler *et al.* list a couple of challenges facing HR managers in the future. According to them, HRM will need to create and assist new procedures and processes to help the organisation to identify:[40]

- Future talent needs;
- The required make-up of the organisations' human resources;
- Ways to encourage optimal internal talent development;
- External knowledge and skills requirements;
- Ways of engaging and energising the organisation's demographic profile.

CASE STUDY: Oyster Bay Lodge

Background information

Oyster Bay Lodge is a privately owned lodge and coastal reserve about 2 km away from a small village named Oyster Bay in the Eastern Cape. Its closest city is Port Elizabeth. The lodge's owner and CEO, Mr Hans Verstrate bought the property 10 years ago – at the time only a small and dilapidated farmhouse was on the premises. Nowadays, the lodge has expanded to a main building (with fully equipped kitchen, a restaurant seating 40 diners, a bar and lounge area, as well as a pool and outside area), 11 rooms sleeping 28 people a night and a boma for entertainment purposes. In addition, a gate-house was built to serve as offices, a reception area and a small house for the management couple. Furthermore, staff-quarters were built where 12 staff members can overnight when they work late shifts. Staff does not stay there on a permanent basis. The lodge serves breakfast, lunch and dinner in the restaurant, although the rooms also have some self-catering facilities. It also offers entertainment in the form of dune safaris, picnics, walking trails and horse-back riding.

In order to offer all of the above, the lodge has a total staff compliment of five permanently appointed personnel, and seven workers on contract basis. Of these, three people are appointed on management level: the Operational Management Couple (2) and the Food and Beverage Manager (1). Some workers have to be appointed on a contract basis as the tourism industry is seasonal – during peak season (November–April) the lodge needs more staff to cope with the increase in bed-nights sold as well as day visitors. June–August are quiet months, and less personnel are needed.

On the company's HR practices, Mr Verstrate commented: 'It is about creating a highly motivated workforce that can work together in intimate surroundings. We are located out in the countryside. The closest small town is 20 km away. Staff often have to overnight in the staff village. They have to work together as a team, as customer satisfaction depends on all facilities and services being offered at a high standard – whether it is the cleanliness of rooms, a tasty meal, friendly service, or a well-directed walking trail. Even a dirty waste basket in a room may cause a visitor not to come to the lodge again. It has to be a well-oiled machine.'

The company believes that its key assets are people and that it is important to bring its employees in line with other similar world-class tourism destinations. In spite of its rapid expansion over the last five years, Oyster Bay Lodge is still a small company. Decision-making on strategic aspects remains with the CEO, but the day-to-day running of the business is left to the Operational Management couple and Food and Beverage Manager who are knowledgeable about particular processes. Mr Verstrate advocates a mentorship approach – the managers (including him) play the role of mentors and use their experience to guide their team members.

HR practices

Most of the HR practices advocate simplicity and the image of a small company is maintained. Verstrate stressed that: 'Attracting the best personnel and creating a milieu where employees operate at their highest potential are very important. This is quite a challenge as the tourism industry is seasonal, necessitating varying numbers of staff throughout the year. We are also some distance from bigger cities offering a bigger source of staff to choose from. Many of our staff members only have very basic education. We are a small business, and even though we pay a lot of attention to training and competency building, we do not have sophisticated appraisal systems, nor do we reward performance for general staff through variable pay – although tips are divided fairly amongst all staff through a centrally collected tip box. Management staff has an additional bonus paid out monthly based on certain performance criteria like Staff cost and Food and Beverage cost. There is no appointed HR manager, these duties form part of the responsibility of the Operational Management couple.'

Recruitment and Selection

Oyster Bay Lodge takes care to identify the right candidates. On the qualities they look for in a candidate, Verstrate said: 'We focus on recruiting candidates with an outgoing personality who understand that they are "on stage" when they are on duty. We also place significant importance on working with daily checklists. Other qualities we look for are the ability to learn fast, teamwork and leadership potential, communication and innovative skills, along with a practical and structured approach to problem solving. Our staff has to be able to function under high pressure, often working long hours.' Management staff are recruited and selected by the CEO through using specific recruitment Internet sources for the tourism sector (see for instance www.lodgestaff.co.za or www.hoteljobs. co.za), and by conducting interviews and reference checking. Other employees are recruited by the Operational Management couple, mostly through word-of-mouth from staff, and walk-ins. Staff is always appointed on a probation period first.

Training

Training at Oyster Bay Lodge is an ongoing, but informal process. New recruits are trained on all processes through a hands-on approach (on-the-job training). Students are appointed to do their learnerships at the lodge, thus enabling Verstrate to identify possible future leaders for the company. However, no formal training programmes are conducted for experienced recruits. Verstrate believes in the power of experience, and uses a mentoring approach to indicate areas to the management staff where they may increase service delivery, productivity and general management skills. The lodge takes into account individual performance, organisational priorities and feedback from the clients.

The challenges

The culture at Oyster Bay Lodge is very much that of a small family-business where all employees work together. No formal HR practices are in place. Staff do not have job descriptions, and no performance appraisal system is in place. Although it is run as a very professional and successful small business, the personnel are managed in an informal manner without the guidance of any formal processes and procedures.

(SOURCE: Based on an interview with Mr Verstrate, owner and CEO of the lodge. Also refer to www.oysterbaylodge.co.za)

QUESTIONS

1. Discuss the HR practices of a small business such as Oyster Bay Lodge. Take into consideration the lodge's unique culture and setting.
2. Discuss the recruitment and selection practices of the lodge. Would you change anything about these, and if so how and why?
3. Discuss the training practices of the lodge. Do you feel that the full potential of staff is developed through the approach that is followed? Substantiate your answer.
4. What are some of the challenges faced by Oyster Bay Lodge on the HR front? In your answer consider issues both broader issues (e.g. performance management), and more specific issues such as handling staff numbers in a seasonal business, arranging shifts, meetings, rest periods and so forth in a business that runs seven days a week with working hours from 07h00–22h00, to name but a few. For instance, according to labour law, the employer needs to pay 1,5 (150%) wages on a Sunday – would you employ less people on a Sunday by closing certain departments whilst still ensuring guest satisfaction?

SUMMARY

The main function of human-resources management is to assist line managers in obtaining the objectives set by the organisation. The process of managing human resources includes strategic planning, staffing the organisation, and assessing, developing, and maintaining the organisation's human resources. All of the processes have to be evaluated all the time to ensure optimum achievement of the goals set by HR, and also, by the organisation. A well-run HRM function can make a big contribution to an organisation's success.

GLOSSARY

affirmative action: policies that aim to correct imbalances that have arisen through unfair discrimination

analysis of HR demand: the second phase of strategic HR planning, where the total manpower requirements of the organisation are determined

analysis of HR supply: the third phase of strategic HR planning, where the future supply of labour is evaluated

assessment: a strategic process facilitated by a qualified and registered assessor through which evidence is collected to ascertain the learner's knowledge, abilities, actions, performance, values and attitude.

apprenticeship: A type of learnership that culminates in an occupational award that is registered by the Department of Labour as a trade.

compensation: the extrinsic and intrinsic rewards provided by the organisation for an employee's fulfilment of his or her job requirements aimed at achieving organisational objectives

compensation management: the management of extrinsic rewards and intrinsic rewards

development: preparing employees for future work responsibilities

development of an HRM strategy: the fourth phase of strategic HR planning, where the HR strategy is developed and action plans are designed

external recruitment: when an organisation tries to fill available positions from the outside

human-resources forecasting: developing and implementing plans so that the right employees fill the right type and number of jobs, thus allowing the organisation to achieve it goals and objectives

human-resources management: planning, organising, leading, motivating and controlling a business's human resources

induction: orientating the employee to his or her new work environment

internal recruitment: when an organisation tries to fill vacant positions from inside the organisation

job analysis: an analysis of a job that determines the content of the job and the behaviours and attributes that will be necessary to master the content

job description: information on what a job entails (the nature of the job content, the environment it takes place in, and the conditions under which it is done)

job specification: a description of the personal skills and characteristics an employee needs to get the job done

learning organisation: an organisation that has a culture of constant development of its employees

learnerships: Learners are employed by a company with the sole purpose of providing on-the-job training, thereby combining the knowledge and work experience components of learning

off-the-job training: formal training away from the workplace, such as formal study programmes presented by a training institution

on-the-job training: training and development schemes at the workplace, which are normally conducted by the supervisor

performance appraisal: a method by which the job performance of an employee is evaluated

performance management: a formal and methodical on-going process of joint review between the manager and the employee, by means of which the employee's job-related strengths and weaknesses are identified, measured against set objectives, and followed by a development plan to assist the employee in furthering his job-related knowledge and skills.

recruitment: the HRM actions that can be used to draw a sufficient number of available and qualified job applicants to apply for a job so that the most appropriate one can be selected

selection: the process where the individual that best suits a particular position is chosen from a group of applicants

situational analysis: the first phase of strategic HRM planning, where internal and external HRM issues are identified

staffing: finding suitably qualified workers to fill particular jobs and ensuring this process occurs (through recruitment, selection and induction)

strategic human-resources management: a general approach to the strategic management of human resources in line with the goals and objectives of the organisation on the future direction it wants to take

strategic human-resources planning: the process of planning an organisation's HR needs through using the organisation's goals and strategies to forecast these needs in terms of finding, developing and keeping a qualified workforce

strategic performance management: a formal and methodical process by means of which the employee's job-related strengths and weaknesses are identified, measured and developed in line with clear objectives set for each individual employee according to the overall strategic objectives of the organisation

strategic training and development: an approach to training and development in an organisation that ensures that this function of HR management is done in line with the organisational goals and strategies

training: enhancing employees' skills and knowledge to do a specific task or job

MULTIPLE-CHOICE QUESTIONS

1. Because of the increase in atypical work, a definition of HRM that would also include this aspect would be:
   a) HRM entails all the practices and policies related to the management of people in an organisation.
   b) HRM seeks to maximise organisational performance through the adoption of best practice in the management of people.
   c) HRM relates to all the dimensions of people in their employment relationships, as well as all the dynamics arising from these relationships, with the perspective of ensuring overall business success.
   d) HRM is concerned with all aspects that relate to, and interplay with, the work and the people who do the work of and in organisations.

2. When strategically managing the HRM function in a South African organisation, the HR manager faces many challenges, including
   a) affirmative action and skills shortages
   b) health and safety, and the general well-being of employees
   c) global HRM trends
   d) ethical behaviour in organisations
      A) a and b
      B) a, b and d
      C) a, c and d
      D) all of the above

3. Human-resources strategies should be representative of the overall organisational strategy regarding its people and general effectiveness. Which of the following values provide(s) the foundation for such an approach?
   a) Employees are investments that will, if effectively managed and developed, provide the organisation with long-term rewards in the form of productivity.

b) Policies, programmes and practices within the organisation should suit both the economic and emotional requirements of the employees.

c) Policies, programmes and practices within the organisation should meet the needs and goals of the organisation.

d) The work environment should encourage employees to utilise and develop their skills to the maximum extent.

   A) a, b, c and d

   B) a, b and d

   C) b, c and d

   D) b and d

4. To enable the HR manager to fulfil his or her primary responsibility of ensuring the optimisation of the human resources of the organisation, he or she needs to be:

a) strategist only

b) part manager and part trainer and developer

c) part strategist, manager, trainer and developer and adviser

d) part counsellor and part adviser

5. The training and development process in an organisation optimally involves:

a) identifying needs, formulating goals, and designing and administering a training and development programme

b) identifying needs, designing and administering a training and development programme, and evaluating the programme

c) formulating goals, designing and administering a training and development programme, and evaluating the programme

d) identifying needs, formulating goals, designing and administering a programme, and evaluating and assessing the learner's learning achievement

REFERENCES AND END-NOTES

1. DESSLER, G. 2009. *A framework for Human Resource Management.* 5th ed. New Jersey: Pearson Prentice Hall. p. 2.

2. McKENNA, E. & BEECH, N. 2008. *Human Resource Management: A Concise Analysis.* 2nd ed. Pearson Prentice Hall UK. p. 1

3. HALL, D.T. & GOODDALE, J.G. 1986. *Human resources management: Strategy, design and implementation.* Glenview: Scott Foresman. p. 6.

4. SWANEPOEL, B.J. (Ed.), ERASMUS, B.J. & SCHENK, H. 2008. *South African human resource management: Theory and practice.* 34th ed. Lansdowne: Juta & Co. p. 4.

5. GROBLER, P., WARNICH, S., CARRELL, M.R., ELBERT, N.F., & HATFIELD, R.D. 2011. *Human resource management in South Africa.* 4th ed. Hatfield: Thomson. p. 8.

6. Ibid.

7. GROBLER, P., WARNICH, S., CARRELL, M.R., ELBERT, N.F. & HATFIELD, R.D. 2011. *Human resource management in South Africa.* 4th ed. Hatfield: Thomson. pp. 10–20.

8. AMOS, T., RISTOW, A., RISTOW, L. & PEARSE, N.J. 2008. *Human resource management.* 3rd ed. Lansdowne: Juta & Co. p. 10.

9. AMOS, T., RISTOW, A., RISTOW, L. & PEARSE, N.J. 2008. *Human resource management.* 3rd ed. Lansdowne: Juta & Co. p. 13.

10. BYARS, L.L. & RUE, L.W. 2000. *Human resource management.* 6th ed. New York: McGraw-Hill. p. 126.

11. DU TOIT, G.S., ERASMUS, B.J. & STRYDOM, J.W. (Ed.). 2010. *Introduction to business management.* 8th ed. Cape Town: Oxford University Press. p. 294.

12. GROBLER, P., WARNICH, S., CARRELL, M.R., ELBERT, N.F. & HATFIELD, R.D. 2011. *Human resource management in South Africa.* 4th ed. Hatfield: Thomson. pp. 116–120.

13. DU TOIT, G.S., ERASMUS, B.J. & STRYDOM, J.W. (Ed.). 2010. *Introduction to business management.* 8th ed. Cape Town: Oxford University Press. p. 294.

14. SWANEPOEL, B.J., ERASMUS, B.J. & SCHENK, H. 2008. *South African human resource management: Theory and practice.* 4th ed. Lansdowne: Juta & Co. p. 229.

15. SWANEPOEL, B.J., ERASMUS, B.J. & SCHENK, H. 2008. *South African human resource management: Theory and practice.* 4th ed. Lansdowne: Juta & Co. pp. 230–231; Grobler, P., Warnich, S., Carrell, M.R., Elbert, N.F. & Hatfield, R.D. 2011. *Human resource management in South Africa.* 4th ed. Hatfield: Thomson. pp. 165.

16. SWANEPOEL, B.J., ERASMUS, B.J. & SCHENK, H. 2008. *South African human resource management: Theory and practice.* 4th ed. Lansdowne: Juta & Co. p. 243.

17. DU TOIT, G.S., ERASMUS, B.J. & STRYDOM, J.W. (Ed.). 2010. *Introduction to business management.* 8th ed. Cape Town: Oxford University Press. p. 295.

18. GROBLER, P., WARNICH, S., CARRELL, M.R., ELBERT, N.F. & HATFIELD, R.D. 2011. *Human resource management in South Africa.* 4th ed. Hatfield: Thomson. pp. 184-195.; DU TOIT, G.S., ERASMUS, B.J. & STRYDOM, J.W. (Ed.). 2010. *Introduction to business management.* 8th ed. Cape Town: Oxford University Press. p. 297.

19. SWANEPOEL, B.J., ERASMUS, B.J. & SCHENK, H. 2008. *South African human resource management: Theory and practice.* 4th ed. Lansdowne: Juta & Co. p. 264.

20. GROBLER, P., WARNICH, S., CARRELL, M.R., ELBERT, N.F. & HATFIELD, R.D. 2011. *Human resource management in South Africa.* 4th ed. Hatfield: Thomson. pp. 184-195.; DU TOIT, G.S., ERASMUS, B.J. & STRYDOM, J.W. (Ed.). 2010. *Introduction to business management.* 8th ed. Cape Town: Oxford University Press. pp. 297-298.

21. SWANEPOEL, B.J., ERASMUS, B.J. & SCHENK, H. 2008. *South African human resource management: Theory and practice.* 4th ed. Lansdowne: Juta & Co. pp. 264–265.; DU TOIT, G.S., ERASMUS, B.J. & STRYDOM, J.W. (Ed.). 2010. *Introduction to business management.* 8th ed. Cape Town: Oxford University Press. pp. 298-299.

22. SWANEPOEL, B.J., ERASMUS, B.J. & SCHENK, H. 2008. *South African human resource management: Theory and practice.* 4th ed. Lansdowne: Juta & Co. p. 279.

23. AMOS, T., RISTOW, A., RISTOW, L. & PEARSE, N.J. 2008. *Human resource management.* 3rd ed. Lansdowne: Juta & Co. p. 121.

24. GROBLER, P., WARNICH, S., CARRELL, M.R., ELBERT, N.F. & HATFIELD, R.D. 2011. *Human resource management in South Africa.* 4th ed. Hatfield: Thomson. pp. 200-215.; AMOS, T., RISTOW, A., RISTOW, L. & PEARSE, N.J. 2008. *Human resource management.* 3rd ed. Lansdowne: Juta & Co. p. 123-126; DU TOIT, G.S., ERASMUS, B.J. & STRYDOM, J.W. (Ed.). 2010. *Introduction to business management.* 8th ed. Cape Town: Oxford University Press. pp. 299–303; SWANEPOEL, B.J., ERASMUS, B.J., & SCHENK, H. 2008. *South African human resource management: Theory and practice.* 4th ed. Lansdowne: Juta & Co. pp. 282–294.

25. The Employment Equity Act No 55 of 1998. Government Printer. *(*Also see www.labour.gov.za for various pieces of labour legislation.)

26. The Skills Development Act No 97 of 1998. Government Printer.; The Skills Development Levies Act No 9 of 1999. Government Printer.

27. AMOS, T., RISTOW, A., RISTOW, L. & PEARSE, N.J. 2008. *Human resource management.* 3rd ed. Lansdowne: Juta & Co. pp. 325-332.

28. COETZEE, M. (Ed.), BOTHA, J., KILEY, J. & TRUMAN, K. 2007. *Practising education, training and development in South African organisations.* Lansdowne: Juta. pp. 214-215.

29. The Skills Development Amendment Act 37 of 2008.

30. COETZEE, M. (Ed.), BOTHA, J., KILEY, J. & TRUMAN, K. 2007. *Practising education, training and development in South African organisations.* Lansdowne: Juta. pp. 214-215.

31. SWANEPOEL, B.J., ERASMUS, B.J. & SCHENK, H. 2008. *South African human resource management: Theory and practice.* 4th ed. Lansdowne: Juta & Co. p. 372.

32. AMOS, T., RISTOW, A., RISTOW, L. & PEARSE, N.J. 2008. *Human resource management.* 3rd ed. Lansdowne: Juta & Co. p. 286.

33. GROBLER, P., WARNICH, S., CARRELL, M.R., ELBERT, N.F. & HATFIELD, R.D. 2011. *Human resource management in South Africa.* 4th ed. Hatfield: Thomson. pp. 297-298.

34. GROBLER, P., WARNICH, S., CARRELL, M.R., ELBERT, N.F. & HATFIELD, R.D. 2011. *Human resource management in South Africa.* 4th ed. Hatfield: Thomson. p. 297.

35. DU TOIT, G.S., ERASMUS, B.J. & STRYDOM, J.W. (Ed.) 2010. *Introduction to business management.* 8th ed. Cape Town: Oxford University Press. p. 309.

36. BOARDMAN, T. (2007) *HR Future.* Nedbank. p. 22.

37. GROBLER, P., WARNICH, S., CARRELL, M.R., ELBERT, N.F. & HATFIELD, R.D. 2011. *Human resource management in South Africa.* 4th ed. Hatfield: Thomson. p. 28.

38. SWANEPOEL, B.J., ERASMUS, B.J., VAN WYK, M. & SCHENK, H. 2003. *South African human resource management: Theory and practice.* 3rd ed. Lansdowne: Juta & Co. p. 513.

39. SOCIETY FOR HUMAN RESOURCE MANAGEMENT. 2010. *Future Insights.* Alexandria: Society for Human Resource Management. p. 3.

40. ICFAI CENTRE OF MANAGEMENT RESEARCH. [Online]. Available: http://www.icmrindia.org/ casestudies [2 May 2008].

ANSWERS TO MULTIPLE-CHOICE QUESTIONS

1. Answer = d)   The reference to people who do the work of and in organisations also make reference to atypical forms of work such as part-time workers, temporary contractors and so forth.

2. Answer = D)   All of these issues should be considered by this function.

3. Answer = A)   All four values provide the foundation for an approach where human-resources strategies are representative of the overall organisational strategy regarding its people and general effectiveness.

4. Answer = c)   To enable the HR manager to fulfil his or her primary responsibility of ensuring the optimisation of the human resources of the organisation, he or she needs elements of all four those roles.

5. Answer = d)   In new developments assessment of the learner's learning achievement also take place.

Marketing management

Sharon Rudansky-Kloppers, Johan Strydom

LEARNING OUTCOMES

This chapter should enable you to:
- define the term 'marketing'
- demonstrate an understanding of the marketing process
- demonstrate an understanding of the market offering by highlighting its four variables
- describe the evolution of marketing thought by highlighting the management thinking during each era
- analyse the behaviour patterns of consumers by identifying the determinants of consumer behaviour and the consumer's decision-making process
- demonstrate an understanding of marketing research by explaining the steps in the marketing-research process
- demonstrate an understanding of how the consumer market can be segmented by emphasising the components of market segmentation, target-market selection, and product positioning
- understand how consumer products can be classified
- demonstrate an understanding of the importance of branding
- explain the phases in the product-development process
- differentiate between the different distribution channels that can be used to distribute the product
- explain the concepts of channel leadership, market coverage, and physical distribution
- understand the process of determining the price for a good or service
- differentiate between the various adaptations that can be made to the final price
- distinguish between the four elements of marketing communication.

13.1 **Introduction**

The main objective of a business is to maximise profitability in the long term. It is generally recognised that marketing is central to this objective, because of its role in defining customer needs and wants, and directing the resources of the business to meet these needs and wants.

The rapid change in the business environment over the past decade has heightened an awareness of the importance of marketing, because businesses have had to face increasing competition, economic fluctuations, political changes, and the need to become more aware of the environment. Successful marketers are those who can best satisfy consumer needs in the context of the changing environment where threats must be coped with and all opportunities grasped, in order to survive.

An example of such a business is Edgars, which is continually doing research to determine the clothing needs of the different market sections that it targets. Edgars then adapts its marketing strategy according to these needs by designing clothes for the different segments, charging prices which these segments are prepared to pay, selling these clothes in stores which are easily accessible to customers, and advertising these clothes in media that are purchased by these customers, as well as in the *Edgars Magazine*. This whole process of marketing is discussed in the rest of this chapter.

13.2 **The nature of marketing**

Marketing is everywhere. It is something we experience every day of our lives. You switch on the television and an advertisement for Omo washing powder appears on the screen; you stroll down a supermarket aisle and you are handed a coupon for All Gold tomato sauce, and at the end of the next aisle you try a sample of a new brand of Vienna sausages. At home, you answer a telephone call asking you to take part in a survey about the television programmes you watch, and then you complete an order form to subscribe to *Garden and Home* magazine.

All these situations involve marketing. Many people mistakenly think of marketing only as selling and advertising, and no wonder, because every day they are bombarded with the above types of messages. Therefore many people are surprised to hear that selling is only one of several marketing functions. This does not mean that advertising and selling are unimportant, but rather that they are part of a larger set of tools that are used together, to affect the marketplace. Today's businesses face increasingly stiff competition, and the rewards will go to those who can best identify customer wants, and deliver the greatest value to their customers. The essence of marketing is the development of exchanges in which businesses and customers voluntarily engage in transactions that are designed to benefit both of them. For example, customers receive benefits from purchasing Crosse & Blackwell Mayonnaise and Ricoffy, while Nestlé, the company that sells these products, receives benefits by getting money for them.

FIGURE 13.1 The marketing process

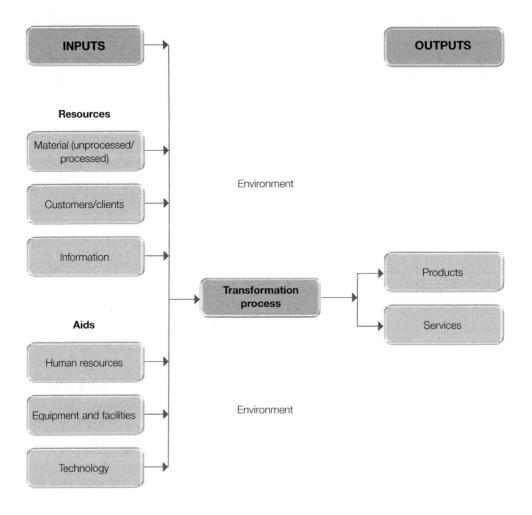

SOURCE: Du Toit, G.S., Erasmus, BJ & Strydom, J.W. 2010. *Introduction to business management.* (8th ed.) Cape Town: Oxford University Press. p. 254.

Marketing consists of management tasks and decisions aimed at successfully meeting opportunities and threats in a dynamic (lively) environment, by effectively developing and transferring a need–satisfying market offering to consumers in a way that achieves the objectives of the business, the consumer and society.[1]

Toyota's market offering according to the four decisions it made regarding its variables

The product decision

Toyota has many different vehicles (products) that cater for the needs of the different market segments. For instance, the Yaris is aimed at the lower-income groups (in the car–buying market), while the Corolla and Auris are directed at the middle-income groups. The Lexus, on the other hand, is aimed at the higher-income segments of the market.

The distribution decision

Toyota's vehicles are available at dealers countrywide, which makes it possible for customers to buy these vehicles at places that are convenient to them. (Distribution will be discussed in Section 13.8)

The marketing-communication decision

Toyota makes use of various methods to persuade the markets to buy its products, such as advertising in *Car* and *You*, as well as on radio and television, employing knowledgeable sales people in their dealerships, and using competitions where consumers can win a motor car. (Marketing communication will be discussed in Section 13.10.)

The pricing decision

Different prices have been set for the different vehicles.[2] The selling price of the Yaris, for instance, starts at R126 900, while that of the Corolla and Auris respectively start at R179 500 and R182 000. The selling price of the Lexus starts at R395 800. (Pricing will be discussed in Section 13.9.)

13.3 **Marketing thinking through the years**

Over the years, marketing has evolved through various eras (periods) of management thinking. These are the production era, the sales era, and the marketing era.

13.3.1 The production era

The production era lasted from the time of the Industrial Revolution in the 18th and 19th centuries, until the 1920s. In this era, management believed that the products would sell themselves. The needs of consumers and the marketing function were thus not a focus, and businesses concentrated mainly on production. A good example of consumer needs being ignored was Henry Ford's mass production of the Model T Ford. Ford stated that consumers could buy 'any colour of the Model T as long as it was black.'

13.3.2 The sales era

The sales era lasted from the mid–1920s to the early 1950s. During this era, organisations concentrated on selling as much as possible. Consumer needs were again ignored, and, because marketers tried to persuade consumers to buy, in any and every way, many dishonest sales practices and false claims existed.

> **CRITICAL THINKING**
> Do you think the marketing principles followed in the sales era would be effective today?

13.3.3 The marketing era

During the marketing era, which is still the situation today, organisations have realised that although production and the sales message are both important for selling a product, these are not the only ingredients for success. They know that they also have to consider aspects like the quality of the products, the packaging, the selection of distribution channels, and the promotion methods used to persuade consumers to buy the products.

Because of continual changes in the marketing environment, and the need for the survival and growth of businesses, organisations realised that they also needed to focus attention on strategic long-term issues and environmental awareness. They became aware of the fact that they had to identify environmental changes such as technological innovations, changes in consumer preferences, and economic and political influences. During this era, marketing management experienced a mindshift towards an ethical code (a set of moral principles) called the **marketing concept**. This marketing concept,

as indicated in Figure 13.2, is based on the four principles of profit orientation –
consumer orientation, social responsibility, and organisational integration.

13.3.3.1 **Profit orientation**

The marketing concept views customer orientation as a means to get profit. By providing market offerings that satisfy customer needs, a business will achieve its own objectives too. These objectives can be expressed in many ways, for example by achieving a
rate of return of 25% on investment, or increasing market share from 10% to 12%. The
overall objective of **profit orientation** can be seen as trying to survive and grow.

13.3.3.2 **Consumer orientation**

Consumer orientation sees the customer as king or queen, and tries to satisfy the customer's needs within the boundaries of making a profit. Such businesses provide good
customer service, including after-sales service. They also do research to find out how
satisfied customers are with their goods and services, and take steps to improve customers' satisfaction.

   Consumer-orientated businesses emphasise **relationship marketing**, where the
importance of maintaining long-term relationships with customers and other role-
players in the environment is stressed. An insurance sales person or an estate agent, who
keeps in touch with a client after a transaction has taken place, increases her or his
chances of doing business with the client again, at a later stage.

13.3.3.3 **Social responsibility**

The principle of **social responsibility** implies that businesses have a responsibility
towards society and that they should make a contribution to the community. Many
businesses sponsor campaigns that contribute towards the well-being of society, for
instance anti-pollution, 'Don't drink and drive', and 'Save the seals' campaigns. Other
businesses sponsor sporting competitions such as soccer and rugby matches. This not
only promotes goodwill in the society, it also gives them an opportunity to advertise
their goods and services.

   In order to demonstrate social responsibility, businesses should also be law-abiding.
For example, they should not take or offer bribes, should not exploit (make use of)
customers, and should not harm the environment with smoke or other waste
materials.

   Information on Toyota's social-responsibility programme appears in the next box.

Toyota's social contribution[3]

Seeking to contribute toward a prosperous society and its sustainable development, Toyota has been engaged in various social contribution activities worldwide with the goal of becoming 'a good corporate citizen'. The Corporate Citizenship Division was established in January 2006 to reinforce social contribution activities and integrate corporate social contribution functions that had been performed by multiple divisions. Toyota focuses on environmental issues, traffic safety, and education on a global basis. In Japan, in addition to these areas, Toyota works to actively promote corporate social contribution activities, using its technology and expertise in response to societal needs in areas such as the arts and culture, and achieving a harmonious society.

Some of Toyota's activities are listed below:

Environment

As part of its global warming prevention activities, Toyota conducts reforestation programmes and environmental educational activities, as well as reforestation experiments.

Traffic safety

In addition to making safe vehicles, Toyota conducts traffic safety programmes for all people who use or are affected by road transport.

Education

Toyota conducts programmes designed to encourage interest in science and technology, and supports the implementation of educational programmes on a global scale, that will develop future leaders.

Arts and culture

Toyota conducts activities to support the arts and culture with an emphasis on nurturing culture, expanding horizons, and promoting regional culture.

Harmonious society

Regional contributions

Toyota conducts activities to promote philanthropy (helping people in need), welfare and self-reliance on a local basis, to maintain greater communication with local communities and harmony in regional society.

> **Volunteer activities**
>
> Toyota provides relief in the event of natural disasters, assists welfare organisations, supports various activities conducted near its business sites throughout Japan, and supports volunteer activities by employees.
>
> **Activities of the Toyota Foundation**
>
> The Toyota Foundation is a private, non-profit, grant-making organisation dedicated to creating a more people-orientated society and greater individual happiness. It was established by Toyota Motor Corporation in 1974 to mark the 40th anniversary of the start of automobile production. The Foundation looks at events from a global point of view, as it works to support activities for the benefit of society. Its support aims to identify current problems in the following areas: 1) human and natural environments; 2) social welfare; and 3) education and culture. Grants are provided for research and projects that fit in with these interests.

13.3.3.4 Organisational integration

Organisational integration means that all functions, departments, and employees in the business should work together to satisfy the needs of the customers, and maximise profitability.

Organisational integration is particularly important when it comes to co-operation between departments. Imagine the chaos if Daimler Chrysler's marketing department promised a customer that she or he would receive the ordered vehicles by a certain date, but the production department did not bother to manufacture those vehicles on time. Internal conflict, poor service, and even loss of sales, could be the result.

Pick n Pay's application of the marketing concept

Pick n Pay holds to all four principles of the marketing concept.[4] For example, it follows the consumer-orientation principle because it is portrayed as the home-maker's friend. Their price checks show that Pick n Pay offers customers exceptional value, and they project an image of offering a better shopping experience at no extra cost. Regular surveys are also conducted to determine customers' satisfaction with the goods and services offered.

Pick n Pay also supports the profit orientation. This is clear from the increase in turnover for the Pick n Pay Group for the year ended 28 February 2010 by

9.8% to R54,7 billion. Pick n Pay and Boxer grew by 11.5% and Franklins by 1.4% in Australian dollars.

The principle of organisational integration is also followed, since all the different departments work together to achieve objectives and to satisfy customer needs. For instance, Pick n Pay's marketing section will not advertise a discount on Skip washing powder without first checking if the purchasing department has bought an adequate quantity of Skip.

Pick n Pay shows its responsibility towards society by sponsoring various educational and charitable events. It sponsors the Comrades Marathon, the Knysna Oyster Festival, and the Argus Pick n Pay Cycle Tour.

13.4 **Consumer behaviour**

Because a business should satisfy its consumers, its marketers need to know what the business's customers need and want. They also need to know how their customers make their decisions about buying and using products.

A housewife who does grocery shopping, for instance, is continually influenced by her own needs and preferences, as well as those of her family and friends, and also by the advertisements she has seen. When she does her shopping, she is a consumer who is satisfying certain needs. Marketers need information about her needs and preferences, why she has those needs and preferences, and how she makes her decisions. When this information is known, marketers can try to adapt their marketing strategies in order to satisfy these needs and preferences.

13.4.1 Determinants of consumer behaviour

Marketers must investigate the factors that influence consumer behaviour. There are two sets of factors that do this, namely individual factors and group factors.

13.4.1.1 **Individual factors**

There are six **individual factors** that influence customer behaviour, namely motivation, attitudes, perceptions, learning ability, personality, and lifestyle.

Motivation
The consumer has specific needs that will motivate her or his purchasing behaviour. For instance, if a young lady wants to feel beautiful and be loved by her boyfriend, she may buy Estée Lauder cosmetics.

Attitudes

A consumer may have a positive, neutral, or negative attitude towards a product, depending on her or his experience with the product or the organisation. Whatever the attitude, it is usually firmly held. For instance, if a consumer has had a bad experience with a particular business, the resulting negative attitude will make her or him ignore any advertisement of the business.

Perceptions

How a consumer reacts to something depends on her or his perception of the situation. This refers to the way the customer sees, hears, smells, touches and tastes stimuli in the environment, and **interprets their meaning**. For example, if a young girl sees an advertisement for Estée Lauder's Pleasures perfume her interpretation may be that the perfume's smell demonstrates femininity, leading her to buy the perfume.

Learning ability

Learned behaviour results from experience. It refers to the consumer's ability to grasp and remember the marketing message. For example, a househusband may learn through experience that Omo washing powder makes clothes clean and fresh. This experience could then influence him to buy Omo washing powder.

Personality

Every person's specific personality influences her or his consumer behaviour. There are many different personality types, for instance, introverted, extroverted, aggressive or competitive people. An introvert, for instance, is less likely to buy flashy clothing than an extrovert is, who will not be shy to draw attention to her or himself.

Lifestyle

This refers to the consistent patterns that people follow in their lives. It includes aspects such as the social behaviour, leisure activities and interests that will influence the consumer's response to the market offering. A person might, for instance, like to party during weekends, play tennis regularly, buy DIY magazines and travel overseas frequently. This will affect that customer's purchases.

13.4.1.2 **Group factors**

There are five **group factors** that influence customer behaviour, namely family, reference groups, opinion leaders, cultural groups, and social class.

Family

Many buying decisions are made in the **family**, and family members play different roles during the buying process. For instance, there is usually an initiator who starts the process, an influencer, a decider, a buyer, and a user. These roles and the persons portraying these roles vary according to the specific products bought. Children, for example, are known to be the initiators and influencers when buying products such as cereals and toys. With more women working these days, the traditional roles (where women were the main buyers of products such as groceries) have also changed, since women have less time available now for these purchases. Many men today are also involved in buying food for the home.

Reference groups

Reference groups are groups that positively or negatively influence our attitudes or behaviour. Reference groups act as a guide for 'correct' behaviour. For example, teenagers typically use their friends as a reference group for deciding what clothes are attractive. There are many different types of reference groups, such as membership groups (for example, a church or a work group), aspirational groups (for example, a golf club to which the person would like to belong) and negative groups (for example, a bikers' club to which a person may not want to belong). Marketers often use these groups in their advertisements, to appeal to specific target markets.

Opinion leaders

Opinion leaders are reference people to whom others look in forming opinions and taking consumer decisions. Advertisements that show a well-known actress who uses Lux soap will influence consumers who admire her to buy Lux soap.

Cultural groups

The **cultural groups** to which consumers belong also influence their purchasing patterns.[5] 'Culture' is a complex system of values, norms(habits) and symbols, which have developed in society over time, and in which all the members of a society share. These values, norms, and symbols are transmitted from parents to children through the generations, to ensure survival and to facilitate adaptating to circumstances. Each cultural group comprises several subcultures, each with its own norms, values, and symbols. Advertisements should not portray unacceptable behaviour that might be insulting to certain cultural groups.

Social class

A **social class** is a group of people who have the same social rank. Factors that are often used to rank people into lower, middle, or higher social classes include occupation, education, income, and possessions. The social class to which a person belongs will influence her or his buying behaviour. A consumer from the higher social classes will, for instance, be more likely to consider buying an expensive 4×4 vehicle than someone from the lower social classes.

13.4.2 The consumer's decision-making process

The consumer's decision-making process consists of five phases through which the consumer progresses systematically. During all stages of this process, marketers try to convince consumers to buy their products. These five stages are explained below.

13.4.2.1 **Awareness of an unsatisfied need or problem**

The process by which consumers buy goods and services begins with the recognition of an unsatisfied need. For example, a woman's car might break down for the third time in one month. This could indicate to her the need for a new car. Marketers often make use of advertisements to make consumers aware of unsatisfied needs.

13.4.2.2 **Gathering information on how best to solve the problem**

When the consumer is aware that she or he needs something, she or he collects information to help with the buying decision. For example, the woman shopping for a new car can turn to information that she already has, recalling her earlier experiences with different motor vehicles or those of friends and family. She then collects information regarding motor vehicles that she can afford, for example the Toyota Yaris and Ford Focus. In order to collect this information she consults friends, motor-car dealers such as McCarthy Toyota, car magazines such as *Car* and *Wiel*, and advertisements that appear in newspapers, magazines and on television. (Marketers should, of course, see to it that all the required information is available.)

13.4.2.3 **Evaluating all possible solutions**

During this phase the consumer compares and evaluates the information regarding the different available products. For example, the woman shopping for a new car would compare makes and models in terms of price, colour, engine size, and features (such as air bags and central locking). (Marketers should see to it that product utility and the advantages of the cars are emphasised in advertisements.)

13.4.2.4 **Deciding on a course of action**

In this phase the consumer must decide whether to buy or not. If the consumer decides to buy, she or he also makes a decision on what to buy. For example, the woman shopping for a new car would choose which make and model to buy, and which dealer to buy it from. She might decide to buy the Toyota Yaris from Motorcity because they have offered the best price. During this phase, aspects such as friendly and efficient sales staff, advertisements that encourage consumers to 'Buy now!', point-of-purchase promotions, and credit facilities, will encourage consumers to actually buy the product.

13.4.2.5 **Post-purchase (after purchase) evaluation**

During this phase the consumer evaluates her or his decision and uses this evaluation for future decision-making. For example, the woman might be satisfied with her choice of vehicle or she could be dissatisfied because it might have serious defects. If she is dissatisfied, she might decide never to buy this make of vehicle again. Alternatively, the consumer might just doubt whether she has made the correct decision. This feeling of doubt or uncertainty is known as 'cognitive dissonance'. Marketers often direct advertisements at people who have purchased their products to reassure them that they have made the correct decision. Customer satisfaction with a product is very important, because if a customer is satisfied with her or his purchase, this could result in her buying the same brand again, and therefore becoming brand loyal.

13.5 **Marketing research**

All marketing decisions are based on information obtained from the environment. Information about internal strengths and weaknesses and external opportunities and threats are thus collected by marketing departments on a continual basis. It does, however, happen that problems occur about which very little information is available. In such cases, marketing management makes use of a systematic marketing-research process in order to investigate specific problems. **Marketing research** can be defined as 'the systematic gathering, analysis and interpretation of information on all types of marketing problems by using recognised scientific methods to collect information to facilitate marketing management's decision-making'.[6]

13.5.1 The marketing-research process

The marketing-research process consists of five steps.

FIGURE 13.4 Steps in the marketing-research process

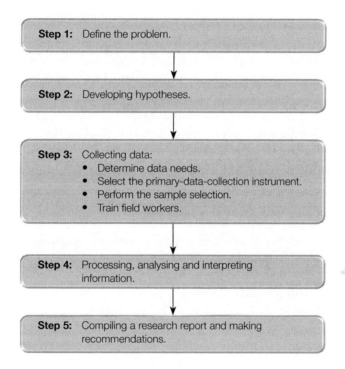

Step 1: Define the problem.

Step 2: Developing hypotheses.

Step 3: Collecting data:
- Determine data needs.
- Select the primary-data-collection instrument.
- Perform the sample selection.
- Train field workers.

Step 4: Processing, analysing and interpreting information.

Step 5: Compiling a research report and making recommendations.

13.5.1.1 **Step 1: Defining the problem**

In the first step, the problem to be investigated should be clearly defined, and specific objectives for the marketing research should be set. Marketing management in a computer company might, for instance, realise that sales of their products have declined by 50% during the last six months.

13.5.1.2 **Step 2: Developing hypotheses**

Hypotheses or possible causes and explanations for the problem should be developed in the second step. Possible causes of the decline in the above-mentioned computer sales could, for instance, be poor advertising, a change in consumer preferences, or the introduction of a technologically advanced computer by a competitor.

13.5.1.3 **Step 3: Collecting data**

This step consists of four different activities, namely: the determination of data needs, the selection of the primary-data-collection instrument, sample selection, and the training of field workers.

The determination of data needs
The first activity is the determination of the data needs. Two types of data are available to marketing researchers, namely secondary and primary data. **Secondary data** involves information that already exists and has been collected by other people. This type of data can be collected from internal or external sources. Company records are usually the most important internal secondary source, while libraries and trade journals are external sources. The Internet is also often used to collect secondary data. In the example of the decline in computer sales, researchers could make use of secondary data such as trade magazines, newspapers, sales records, advertising records, or records of customer complaints.

If the cause of the research problem cannot be found in the secondary data, primary data must be collected. **Primary data** is information that is collected through original research for a specific purpose. This data can also be found internally, for example from the business's employees, or externally, for example from customers or competitors.

The selection of the primary-data-collection instrument
If primary data needs to be collected, there are three different ways to do it. These are called primary-data-collection instruments, and are observations (recording of behaviour); experimentation (usually conducted in a laboratory or field setting); and surveys. The most common instrument is the survey, which means gathering information from respondents by mail, telephone, or in person. A well-designed questionnaire must be used for a survey. The objectives and hypotheses decided on in steps 1 and 2 should influence the type of questions included in the questionnaire. Aspects such as the choice of words and the sequence of the questions should be carefully planned. In the above example, if the cause of the decline in computer sales could not be found in the secondary data, the company could collect primary data by contacting customers by telephone in order to find out why they have stopped buying the company's computers.

Sample selection
The third activity is sample selection. In this activity, the researchers have to select the respondents who will be interviewed. It is, however, important that a 'representative sample' should be chosen, meaning a selection which is characteristic of the total number, and every person in the market has an equal chance of being selected. For instance,

the computer company could give the researcher a list of all its customers, and the researcher could then randomly (using chance) draw as many customers as the size of the sample requires. Only these customers should then be interviewed.

The training of field workers

The fourth and last activity is the training of field workers. The field workers who interview respondents should be thoroughly trained in order to get reliable results. They should, for instance, be trained not to make mistakes when asking questions or recording responses, not to prompt respondents (help them to give answers), and not to fill in questionnaires themselves.

13.5.1.4 Step 4: Processing, analysing and interpreting information

This step is the conversion of raw data into findings that are used as a base for conclusions and recommendations. Statistical methods are normally used to do the processing and interpretation of the results. When the researcher has interpreted all the data, the initial hypotheses must be proved or disproved, and final conclusions should be drawn.[7] In the example of the decline in computer sales, conclusions should be drawn regarding the actual reasons for the decline in sales. For example, the conclusion could be that the advertisement for the company's computers was ineffective and was directed at an incorrect target market.

13.5.1.5 Step 5: Compiling a research report and making recommendations

The last step involves writing a report of the research findings and presenting these findings in tables, figures, and graphs. Based on the research findings, certain recommendations or practical suggestions now have to be made in order to solve the problem. For example, where the decline of computer sales is concerned, a recommendation regarding the design of a new advertising campaign could be made. Marketing management can then decide whether to accept the recommendation or not.

13.6 Market segmentation, target marketing, and product positioning

Market segmentation, target marketing, and product positioning are three steps that organisations take to satisfy the needs of consumers.

13.6.1 Market segmentation

Market segmentation is the process in which the total 'heterogeneous' market is divided into smaller, relatively 'homogeneous' groups of consumers with relatively similar characteristics and needs.

Why is market segmentation important? Simply because it is very seldom that one product can satisfy the needs of everyone in the consumer market. People have different needs, different tastes, different interests, and so on, which is what the word 'heterogeneous' means. The purpose of market segmentation is to identify consumers within the total consumer market who have similar needs, tastes, interests, and so on – in other words, to identify a homogeneous group. Even in such a group, the consumers will not all be the same – that is why we refer to a 'relatively' homogeneous group.

There are three approaches to market segmentation, namely the market–aggregation approach, the single-segment approach, and the multi-segment approach.

13.6.1.1 **The market–aggregation approach**

The **market–aggregation approach** (total–market approach) to market segmentation is to treat all consumers as relatively homogeneous, which means that segmentation is not actually occurring. There are not many products that will satisfy the needs of everyone in the consumer market, but basic products such as sugar and salt can be marketed according to this approach. However, such products are definitely in the minority.

FIGURE 13.5 The market-aggregation approach

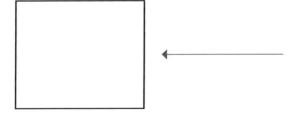

13.6.1.2 **The single-segment approach**

In the **single-segment approach**, the marketer identifies one single group and directs the product offering only to that particular segment. Some game lodges in South Africa direct their product exclusively at overseas tourists to the point where their rates are quoted in US dollars. Obviously local tourists can also stay at these lodges, but the marketing message is not really aimed at them.

FIGURE 13.6 The single–segment approach

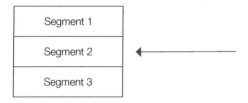

Another example of a company that uses the single segment approach is Fisher-Price. Although they market over 400 products, they focus on toys for children of six years and under. The *Daily Sun* also directs its newspaper at only one target market, namely urban adults throughout South Africa who are English-literate, reasonably educated, and extremely patriotic.

13.6.1.3 **The multi–segment approach**

In the **multi–segment approach**, the same product is aimed at different market segments. The marketing of a small car may be directed at young people (one market segment) and may therefore be advertised as 'sporty' and 'trendy'. It may also be directed at house-wives (another market segment) as 'the ideal economical second car'. The same product is therefore directed at more than one market segment, with a different marketing message to each segment.

> **CRITICAL THINKING**
>
> Which type of market segmentation approach does 1Time Airlines make use of?

FIGURE 13.7 The multi-segment approach

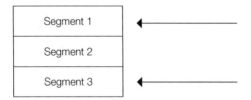

13.6.1.4 **Using variables to describe the market structure**

There is no single way to segment the market. Marketers must use different segmentation variables to describe the market structure. When developing a segmentation strategy, the important step is to select the correct basis on which to segment the market. These bases or criteria are demographic, geographic, psychographic, and behavioural.

TABLE 13.1 Bases for market segmentation

Bases	Variables
Demographic	Age, gender, income, education, race, occupation, family size, religion
Geographic	Region, province, city, town, climate
Psychographic	Lifestyle, personality, social class
Behavioural	Product-usage rate, brand-loyalty status, price sensitivity, product benefits looked for

Demographic criteria are used to divide the market into groups based on variables such as age, gender, income, education, and race. For example, products such as clothing, perfumes, and toiletries are marketed differently to men and women. In order to perform market segmentation, a company that sells upmarket, luxury furniture, should exclude the lower-income groups and focus only on the higher-income groups.

Geographic criteria are used to divide the market according to geographic locations such as provinces, cities, and towns. The company that sells upmarket furniture could target consumers in upmarket areas of the different provinces. For example, in Gauteng they could target Pretoria consumers in Waterkloof, Johannesburg consumers in Sandton, and in Cape Town they could target consumers in Camps Bay.

While demographic and geographic segmentation are relatively simple to understand, they do not directly address the needs and wants that lead people to make purchases. In an attempt to more specifically identify the consumers who would be interested in particular products, marketers have developed **psychographic segmentation** that helps them to understand the lifestyle, personality, and social-class characteristics of the target market. The furniture company mentioned above could select consumers in the suburbs mentioned above.

Marketers also segment consumer markets in terms of various purchase behaviours such as product-usage rate, brand-loyalty status, price sensitivity, and product benefits. These variables are known as **behavioural criteria.** The above furniture company could aim at consumers who want the benefit of prestige (social admiration) when they buy upmarket furniture.

13.6.2 Target marketing

Once the market has been divided into smaller homogeneous segments according to the segmentation criteria, the marketer has to engage in the next step, namely **target**

marketing. Marketing management must choose one or more segments that they want to serve. The objectives and resources of the business have to be carefully considered before a target market can be selected.

13.6.3 Product positioning

Once one or more target markets have been selected, **product positioning** has to take place. A product's positioning is the place the product occupies in the minds of customers in relation to competitors' products. Marketers must choose a positioning strategy that will create a certain image of their product in the minds of consumers that will differentiate it from those of rival companies. For instance, kulula.com has positioned itself as a low-fare airline compared to many of the other airlines in South Africa. Their well-known slogan 'Now anyone can fly' clearly reflects this image. The product decision and the effect of product decision-making using branding is discussed in more detail below. We are now ready to look at the four elements of the marketing mix, namely the product; distribution; pricing; and marketing communications decision. The last element also includes public relations management.

13.7 **The product decision**[8]

13.7.1 Definition of a product

A **product** can be described as anything of a tangible or intangible nature that is offered to consumers to satisfy a need or a want. These need-satisfying aspects are found in ordinary **consumer products** such as a loaf of bread or a carton of milk, services such as those provided by a medical doctor or a travel agent, personalities such as a soccer player or a television star, places such as Cape Town, non-profit organisations such as the Treatment Action Campaign, and ideas such as 'Casual Day'. For the purposes of this book, we focus more on consumer products. Product decisions, however, do apply to the other types of 'products', as illustrated in the previous sentences.

13.7.2 The product concept

The product concept usually consists of the following five key ingredients:
- the **core product**, which refers to the technical and physical qualities of the product (For example, a sports utility vehicle (SUV) has four fitted tyres and a spare tyre, an engine of 2.4 litres, and seating capacity for 5 adults.)
- the **formal product**, which adds specific features to the core product and

includes styling, quality, and a brand (For example, a Toyota RAV4 or a Mitsubishi Pajero has a specific identity.)

*   the **need-satisfying product**, which comprises further need-satisfying benefits, such as guarantees, installation, repair services, and free delivery (For example, the RAV4 has a 3-year or 75 000 km warranty, and a motor plan for its first 5 years.)
*   the **product image**, which gives the product symbolic value by means of the type of marketing message, price, and choice of distribution outlet (For example, Lexus cars are sold only at exclusive dealerships and at a price 30% higher than the Avensis.)
*   the **total product**, which consists of all the above-mentioned components (as in the case of the Lexus, where the manufacturer claims that this is the best car in the world.)

Consumer products differ in their particular features, their manufacturing and marketing methods, and the purposes for which they are used. For product planning, it is therefore necessary to classify products in more or less homogeneous categories, but according to their unique qualities.

13.7.3 Classification of consumer products

Consumer products are intended for immediate use by consumers. A distinction can be drawn between **intangible** (cannot be touched) **consumer products** and **tangible consumer products**. Intangible consumer products are services such as legal advice, medical consultations, and hairdressing services. Tangible consumer products can be further classified as durable or non-durable. **Durable consumer products**, such as microwaves, cars, and furniture, can be used by the consumer over a longer period, whereas **non-durable consumer products**, such as fruit, bread, and milk, have a relatively short life-span.

Consumer products can also be classified on the basis of consumer buying habits, into convenience products, shopping products, speciality products, and unsought products.

13.7.3.1 **Convenience products**

Convenience products are usually non-durable products such as chocolates, soap, milk, bread, and beer, which are used on a daily basis by the consumer. Convenience products are reasonably homogeneous. The products must be advertised to be sold, the markup is usually low, and the product must be available in as many outlets as possible.

13.7.3.2 **Shopping products**

Shopping products are durable products, which means that most consumers will compare the suit-ability, quality, price, and style of the products before choosing to buy one. The consumer seldom has enough information and knowledge to visit just one store to buy the product, so she or he will 'shop around' to get information about the products. Examples of shopping products are furniture, used cars, clothing, and jewellery.

> **CRITICAL THINKING**
>
> Can the same product be a convenience, shopping, and speciality product?

13.7.3.3 **Speciality products**

Speciality products are products with unique characteristics for which consumers will make a special purchasing effort. A purchaser will often insist on a specific brand. Examples of such products are cars (for example, a BMW X5 SUV), flat-screen television sets (such as those made by LG) and digital cameras (such as those made by Canon).

13.7.3.4 **Unsought products**

Unsought products are those that the customer does not think about, such as life insurance and fire extinguishers. This type of product requires heavy advertising and personal selling.

13.7.4 Brand decisions

One of the most important decisions that the marketer has to make based on the nature of the product is the choice of brand. All consumer products have brands to distinguish them from competing products.

The **brand** can be defined as a mark that is unique to the product manufactured and marketed by the organisation, which is used to distinguish it from similar competing products. The branding of a product includes the brand name and a specially designed **trademark**. The **brand name** is a word, a letter, or a group of words (for example, BMW). Consumers use this name when they intend to buy the product. The concept of a brand name is therefore a much narrower concept than that of a brand (in this case the whirling propeller which typifies the BMW trademark).

Some brands consist only of a brand name written in distinctive lettering. Pick n Pay is a good example (you will remember that Pick n Pay was previously spelled with an apostrophe ('n) which was changed a few years ago). In other cases a trademark may be so familiar that the brand name is almost unnecessary (for example, the three-pointed star of Mercedes Benz). The distinctive names and trademarks are often used in reminder advertising.

In today's highly competitive markets, it is impossible to market consumer products successfully without brand identification. Even branded products that traditionally did not have brand names, such as milk (Dairy Maid) and bread (Uncle Salie's) are now reaping the benefits of brand identification.

Organisations use branding to build brand loyalty in their customer base.

FIGURE 13.8 Some leading brands

13.7.4.1 **Brand loyalty**

Brand loyalty is what consumers show when they buy certain brands on a regular basis. It is the result of various factors, such as good product quality, proven usefulness to the consumer, and effective marketing communication. There are three stages of brand loyalty through which the consumer gradually moves, namely:

- brand recognition, which is consumers recognising the brand and knowing what it stands for
- brand preference, which is consumers preferring the brand to other competing brands
- brand insistence, which is the consumer insisting on the specific brand and refusing to accept a substitute.

When an organisation first launches a new product, the first stage it must achieve is brand recognition. However, marketers naturally aim at achieving the third stage, because this gives the product special value in the eyes of consumers. When this stage is achieved, the consumer will shop around until she or he finds the branded product, making it difficult for a competitor to compete in the market. But communicating the product and the brand will still be necessary to bring it to the attention of consumers.

Manufacturer, dealer, or generic brands

Manufacturers usually give their own brands to the products they market. For instance, the label 'Levi's jeans' is an example of a **manufacturer brand**. Large retailers (or dealers) also often buy unmarked products from manufacturers and give these products their own brands. An example of dealer brands is when Edgars does this with different ranges for different market segments, using the label 'Elements' for a range of clothes for small children, 'Free2BU' for clothes for teens and young adults, and 'Merien Hall' for clothes for stately elder adults. Then there are the **generic brands**, the so-called 'no-name' brands.

A manufacturer must decide whether to market her or his products with their own brand or else market unbranded products directly to dealers. Sometimes large manufacturers have excess manufacturing capacity that they use to produce generic products for dealers. In such cases, there should be clearly distinguishable target markets at which the market offering can be directed – otherwise cannibalism occurs (when sales of a new product eats into the sales of a product of the same line; this weakens the brand), aggravating the competitive situation.

Individual and family brands

Marketers must also decide whether they are going to choose an **individual brand** for each product item (for example, Millers Light, Carling Black Label, and Hansa Pilsener Beer from South African Breweries) or whether they are going to use a **family brand** (for example, Kellogg's Rice Crispies, Kellogg's All Bran, and Kellogg's Corn Flakes) for the whole range of products. Both decisions have advantages as well as disadvantages.

If a family brand is chosen, the costs of introducing a new product in the range into the market are lower. Spending on marketing communication usually decreases, because consumers already know the name of the products in the range. The new product can 'piggy-back' on the popularity of the other products. But the opposite is also true: if one product in such a range performs poorly, the reputation of the others with the same name is damaged.

Individual brands are expensive to market, because separate marketing communication has to be made for each individual product. But this gives a chance to make an original and strong marketing effort aimed at specific target markets. For example, Toyota did this with the re-launch of the Lexus car, which has a different brand name and trademark from the normal Toyota cars.

13.7.4.2 **Packaging decisions**

Packaging can be described as the group of activities concerned with the design, manufacturing and filling of a container or wrapper around the product, so that it can be effectively protected, stored, transported, identified, and marketed. The main aim of packaging is to ensure that the product can be handled without being damaged. Packaging should also improve the sales of the product. The consumer should be able to recognise the packaging of a specific product separately from competing products. The packaging therefore consists of a label with the characteristic brand and other important information. Bright colours and striking designs are used on packaging to attract consumers' attention.

13.7.5 Product strategies

Some difficult decisions need to be made regarding an organisation's long-term strategy for its range of products. Some of the issues that must be considered are product differentiation, product obsolescence, the product portfolio, new product development, and the product life cycle.

13.7.5.1 **Product differentiation**

Product differentiation is the way in which a business distinguishes its product from similar competing products, so that consumers see it as being different. Physical and psychological differentiation can take place when the design of the packaging or the size of the container is changed. Other ways to differentiate are branding the product, changing the price (for example, charging a premium price), changing the way it is being promoted, or using a unique distribution channel to sell the product. One of the best examples of differentiation is found in the car market when a new model is added to the range to make it different from competitors' products. By introducing a new model, the manufacturer creates excitement and desires in the customer, who sees the new product as completely different from the rest. This is why a new model car usually sells extremely well in its first year of sales, but after this, sales start to decline.

13.7.5.2 **Product obsolescence**

A product may be deliberately made technically and/or psychologically out of date in order to push the consumer to buy a new version of the product. This is called **product obsolescence**. At the technical level, products can be designed to have a specific life-span, such as a disposable cigarette lighter, which will be disposed of once the gas and flint have run out. 'Psychological obsolescence' refers to the introduction of a new model or style resulting in the consumer rejecting the still functional older version of the product. New car models and new clothing fashions are well-known examples of planned psychological obsolescence.

13.7.5.3 **The product portfolio**

Marketers also have to decide on the composition of the product offering. A business seldom manufactures and markets only one specific product item. The **product port-folio** usually consists of a range of products that is continually changing. When existing businesses are bought by other businesses, of course the products marketed by those businesses are bought too, which might mean a repositioning of some of the products. New products are also developed in response to profitable opportunities occurring in the market.

13.7.5.4 **The development of new products**

Product decisions also relate to the development of new products. A product starts its life as an idea, invented by someone. The idea for a new product may be unique and original, and is then called an 'innovation'. The product may also be a modification in that it is an improvement on, or a modification of, an existing product. The risk of failure and financial loss is usually greater with the marketing of an innovative product, but it is also a chance to get higher profits. For example, when high–definition television sets were introduced, the price that was at first charged for this innovative product was R10 000 more than a similar-sized old-technology TV.

A factor that must always be considered in the development of new products is the threat of product cannibalisation. An organisation usually has a range of products, and the introduction of a new product may cannibalise on the sales of older products that are further in their product life cycle.[9]

The process of new product development is planned and carried out, and the new product idea goes through various phases until it is eventually introduced into the market.

TABLE 13.3 Phases in the development of new products

Phase 1	Development of the product idea
Phase 2	Screening of product ideas according to the criteria for likely success, such as financial criteria regarding sales projections and profitability analyses
Phase 3	Removal of product ideas that do not appear to be viable
Phase 4	Development of the physical product by the manufacturing division, during which time a prototype (single original one) is manufactured
Phase 5	Development of the marketing strategy, which entails the following: • positioning of the product in the market • branding of the product • packaging design • development of the marketing-communication message • determining the price to be charged • selection of the distribution channel and specific outlets to be used
Phase 6	Marketing in a small segment of the market, for example in Gauteng only, to test the market's reaction
Phase 7	Commercialisation of the product (introduction into the market as a whole)

Before each of these phases there is intensive research, and several factors can lead to the end of a new product idea. However, the continuous creating of product ideas remains essential for the survival and progress of the business involved.

13.7.6 The product life cycle

In general, products have a life cycle similar to that of a person. Four phases are identified in the **product life cycle**, namely the introduction, growth, maturity, and decline phases.

During each phase of the life cycle, different marketing decisions need to be taken. For instance, in the **introductory phase**, the brand name must be established, marketing communication is aimed at informing the customer about the availability of the product, and the product is usually available at only a few outlets. The **growth phase** brings changes as more customers know about the product, and

> **CRITICAL THINKING**
>
> There is a link between the new product development process and the product life cycle. See if you can find the link between these two concepts.

the marketing communication is now aimed at informing and reminding the consumer, the price is usually under competitive pressure, and more retailers are stocking the product. During the **maturity phase**, the focus is more on selling to the existing customer-base, reminding the customers about the product, and surviving the price competition. During the **decline phase**, products that do not meet requirements or are no longer profitable can be withdrawn. The decision to withdraw a product or range from the market is a very difficult one. This action may be seen as being negative for the image of a business, and may cause employee problems (workers could be laid off because there are no more jobs available). The marketing department usually does everything in its power to avoid having to withdraw a product.

FIGURE 13.9 The product life cycle

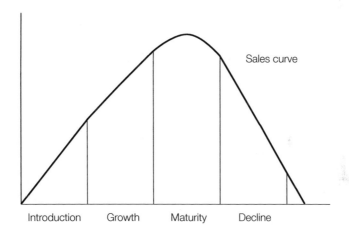

13.8 **Distribution decisions**

Distribution focuses on the transfer process of taking the product to the consumer, and this is where the distribution decision comes into play. Transfers take place by using distribution channels, which consist of **intermediaries** or 'middlemen' (**wholesalers and retailers**), who transfer products from the manufacturer to the consumer. It is the job of the marketer to link up the manufacturer with various middlemen, so that the product is made available to the consumer in the right place and at the right time.

Distribution therefore means selecting the type of distribution channel, the specific middlemen to employ, and the performing of logistical activities such as transport-scheduling and stock-keeping.

13.8.1 Selecting the distribution channel

The first decision to be made in respect of distribution strategy is the selection of the channel and the middlemen. There are five different distribution channels, as shown in Figure 13.10 and discussed below.

FIGURE 13.10 The different types of distribution channels

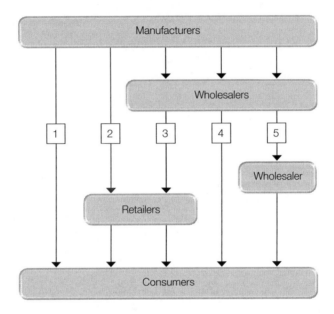

The first channel is called the **direct distribution channel**. There is no middleman involved, but the activities necessary to transfer products between the manufacturer and the customer still need to be performed. For example, the producer (farmer) who sells vegetables at a farmstall directly to the customer, still needs to do packaging and storing. Another example is where manufacturers of products such as batteries sell directly to other businesses such as car manufacturers, who use these products in their manufacturing processes to deliver another product, namely a car. The car battery that is sold in this way is called an 'industrial product'.

The second channel is an **indirect distribution channel**, where manufacturers sell to large retail businesses that then sell to consumers. The Shoprite Group, which consists of, among others, OK Bazaars, Checkers and Shoprite, buys directly from manufacturers to sell to its customers.

The third channel is the traditional indirect distribution channel, where manufacturers sell to wholesalers, who sell to retailers, who then sell to consumers. This is still regarded as the most effective route by a large number of manufacturers. An example is where manufacturers supply stock to wholesalers (such as Makro or Metro), who supply stock to the informal retailing sector, who sell to consumers. An example of a business in the informal retailing sector is a spaza shop in a township.

The fourth channel is another indirect distribution channel. This is where wholesalers, such as Makro, Metro and TradeCentre, may sell directly to the final consumer.

The fifth channel is an indirect distribution channel with two wholesalers. In this case, the first wholesaler is usually a speciality wholesaler, who gets a specific product from numerous manufacturers and then sells it to the second wholesaler, who sells it to a retailer who sells it to the consumer. An example is where the first wholesaler is located in a foreign country. The wholesaler buys products from the manufacturers in that country and delivers them to a wholesaler in South Africa for sale to the retailers, who then sell them to the final consumers.

13.8.2 Factors that play a role in the determination of a distribution channel

Various factors play a role in determining the best distribution channel. These factors include the type of product, the type of market, and the existing distribution infrastructure.

13.8.2.1 **The type of product**

The type of product will influence how it is distributed. If the product is perishable (will not last beyond a short time) and the target market is local, then direct distribution is the ideal method. A roadside farmstall where a farmer sells fresh fruit and vegetables is an example of where a direct distribution channel (producer to consumer) works better. If the product has to be handled and transported in bulk, and the market is widespread, the manufacturer has to depend on the specialised knowledge and facilities of middlemen (such as the wholesaler and retailer) to make her or his product(s) available to consumers. One of the indirect channels would be the best choice in such a case.

13.8.2.2 **The type of market**

The type of market will influence how products are distributed in it. For example, if the market requires specialist after-sales service, then a shorter, direct channel could be the answer.

13.8.2.3 **The existing distribution channels**

The existing distribution infrastructure also plays a role in determining what distribution channel is chosen. For example, if the existing channel cannot be used because it is too small, then a new distribution channel must be developed.

13.8.3 Channel leadership

The business that controls or dominates a channel is known as the **channel captain.** Traditionally, it was the manufacturer of consumer products who made distribution-channel decisions, and therefore chose which retail outlets would market the business's products the best. Today it is frequently the large retailing organisations such as Shoprite or Spar that make the decisions, and therefore dominate the channel.

Intermediaries may be persuaded to push a product by actively encouraging sales of products in a store. This is called a **push strategy**. A product may also be 'pulled' through the channel by means of consumer demand (where the middleman has to stock the product, because the consumer demands it). This is called a **pull strategy**. See Figure 13.11 below:

FIGURE 13.11 Push and pull strategies in the distribution channel

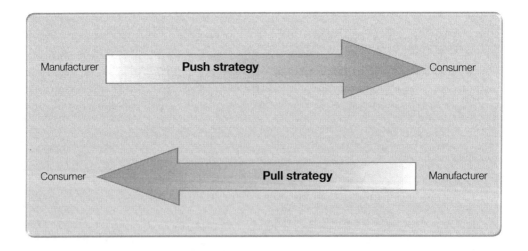

Two personal computer manufacturers and their distribution channels

Both Dell and Acer are global computer manufacturers who sell their range of computers in South Africa as well as in various other countries in the world.

Acer South Africa started in 1996 and is focusing on the small- and medium-business sector as its target market. Its distribution system is a channel-leveraged model, which means setting up a traditional distribution channel in which it is working closely with its partners, distributors, dealers, and resellers. Acer's distribution partners are Tarsus Technologies, which is the distribution partner for the full range of notebook, desktop, and server products in South Africa. There is also Aziz, which is a focused IT infrastructure distributor for in-campus computing, which sells servers, desktops, mobiles, printers, networking, storage, memory, peripherals, components, and consumables. Jet Distribution is a specialist distributor selling Acer's whole product range throughout Africa, but excluding South Africa. Acer is following a traditional push distribution strategy.[10]

Michael Dell started his Dell company in 1984 using a direct-to-consumer sales model. This involved selling computer systems directly to customers, using advertisements, the Internet, and the telephone network.

Dell has a negative cash-conversion model where customers pay upfront for the ordered computer before Dell has to pay for the material to build the computer. In 1990 Dell tried using the traditional distribution channels such as wholesalers and retailers, but without success. They thereafter re-focused on the direct-to-consumer sales model. By 1999 Dell was the largest seller of personal computers in the USA. The distribution model used by Dell is typically a pull strategy, where the customer requests an item from the manufacturer, who then develops a customised personal computer for the customer.

13.8.4 Market coverage

Market coverage means the manner in which the product is distributed throughout the market. Ideally, the manufacturer would like to have the product on all the shelves of all the shops that could possibly sell the product. This is, however, not always possible for various reasons such as finances and special agreements between suppliers and retailers. The number of intermediaries in the channel is directly linked to the type of market coverage being aimed at.

Three types of market coverage can be identified, namely intensive, exclusive, and selective market coverage. This is depicted in Figure 13.12 and discussed thereafter.

FIGURE 13.12 Market-coverage options

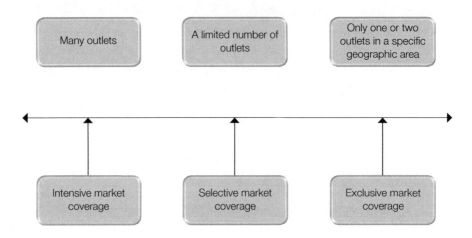

Intensive market coverage occurs when as many suitable and available middlemen as possible are used. This is especially relevant to convenience-product manufacturers, such as Coca-Cola, whose products are distributed through all available distribution options, namely cafés, liquor stores, restaurants, supermarkets, wholesalers, hypermarkets, spaza shops, and petrol stations.

Selective market coverage refers to the selection of a limited number of capable intermediaries who will distribute the product efficiently. Sporting goods such as running shoes and clothing are distributed in this manner.

Exclusive market coverage takes place when a manufacturer limits the number of middlemen handling its product to only a few intermediaries, who get exclusive rights to sell the product in a specific geographic area. This type of market coverage is found particularly in shopping and speciality products such as fast-food franchises and car dealerships.

13.8.5 Logistics (also called physical distribution)

A further aspect of distribution decision-making relates to the logistical activities that have to take place to make a product available to the final consumer at the right time. These logistical activities include:
- transportation (for example, by road or air)
- storage (for example, in warehouses, or in containers in the case of fuel)
- inventory holding (for example, how many items to keep in stock)

- receipt and despatch (for example, how to process the products)
- packaging (for example, whether to pack the items on pallets)
- administration (for example, what to document)
- ordering (for example, how to order stock).

The purpose of the logistical function is to maintain a satisfactory service level to clients at the lowest possible distribution costs. The optimal service level is the level above which an increase in costs of logistical activities will not result in a corresponding increase in sales.

Logistics is becoming increasingly important because when it is done efficiently, it can result in large cost savings for a business (see for instance the case study at the end of this chapter). In addition, it can ensure that the product is in the right place at the right time for the convenience of consumers.

The three main components of logistics are:
- selecting warehouses
- selecting the most suitable mode of transport
- selecting optimal inventory-holding levels.

A compromise between cost and service levels must be reached in all three components.

The most effective performance of logistical activities ensures:
- the reliable delivery of orders on time
- adequate available inventory so that shortages do not occur
- careful handling of stocks to prevent damage and shrinkage as far as possible.

Close connection between the marketing manager and the supply chain/purchasing manager is therefore required, and the marketing manager must be involved in the planning and decision-making of the logistical process.

13.9 **Price decisions**

13.9.1 Price defined

Price is the value paid by the consumers (usually in the form of money) to obtain something of value, namely a product. The value of a good or service is determined by its benefit to the consumer, and the sacrifice required in terms of money and effort to get the product.

13.9.2 The price-determination process

The **price-determination process** consists of four steps.

FIGURE 13.13 The process of price determination

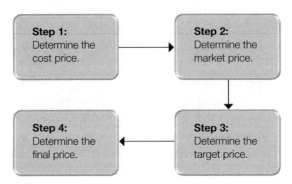

The first step in determining the price of a product is to find out the **cost price** of the product. The unit cost of manufacturing and marketing the product is determined by the management accountants of the organisation. The price of the product should not be lower than the cost price, because this would mean financial loss, which could ruin the organisation.

The **market price** is the price the consumer is currently prepared to pay, or the current market price at which competing products are sold. The market price is determined by means of market research, which surveys customers' general perceptions regarding the price and value of a product, and the pricing strategy being followed by competitors. If the cost price is lower than the market price, there is room to change; if the cost price is much higher than the market price, it means a cost–reduction adjustment has to be made on the product, or the marketer will have to make a special attempt to convince consumers that the particular product is worth a higher price.

The **target price** is the price that must be realised to obtain the target rate of return, taking into consideration the cost structure, the business's needs for capital, and the potential sales volume of the product. One way of calculating the target price is the **cost-plus method**. This is done by adding the profit margin to the total cost of the product. The accepted rate of return determines how large the profit margin will be.

The **final price** is the price at which the product is offered to consumers. This price is determined by finding the middle ground between the market price and the target price. For example, if the market price for an item is R10, and the target price is R7, then the final price may be set at different levels between R7 and R10. The final selling price can still be further adjusted, as discussed next.

13.9.3 Adaptations of the final price

Various adjustments can still be made to the price that the consumer will be charged.

A **skimming price** is a high price charged for a new unique product. This may result in a high profit margin, although the organisation will have to recover research and development costs before a profit can be made. There are consumers who would be prepared to pay the high price, because

CRITICAL THINKING

There is a link between distribution and the pricing decision in the marketing mix. If you were to select an intensive distribution option, what would the price of the product be? Very low or very high?

such new inventions usually have prestige value. If the price was set too low, consumers could perhaps doubt the new product's usefulness. As the product gains popularity, the high starting price can gradually be reduced. The more units manufactured and sold, the lower the costs will be, which means that the price can drop. Competitors will also notice if a business is making high profits, and will then enter the market with competing products. This will mean that the organisation cannot maintain a skimming price for a long time.

The organisation may decide against using a skimming price, and rather decide on a **market-penetration price**. Here the initial price of a new product is lower, and the organisation hopes to penetrate the market rapidly, discouraging competitors in the process. Competitors may decide that the small profit margin is not worth the effort of competing in this specific market.

If there is keen competition and similar products are competing against one another, an organisation has to maintain the **market price**. If the organisation sets the price of its product higher than that of its competitors, consumers will tend to avoid this product. If the price is lower than that of competing products, consumers may think there is something wrong with the product. The organisation can escape the limitations of the market price only if its product is successfully differentiated and is therefore regarded as unique.

Leader pricing concerns special offers, which are widely used by retailers. A very small profit is made on leader-price products. These products are sold at less than the current market price for a limited period only. The retailer uses this method to attract consumers into the shop. These purchasers then buy the low-priced 'specials', as well as many other products with a higher profit margin. Manufacturers do not usually like leader pricing. Even though they can sell more products, the profit margin is inadequate, and later, when competitors' products are selected as leader-price items, sales figures drop.

Odd prices are the final prices of products that have odd numbers. Prices that are even, for example, R2, R4 and R10, are avoided, and products are rather marked

R1,99, R3,79 and R9,95. It is thought that consumers are more likely to accept odd prices, and that an odd price looks smaller (cheaper) than an even price.

Bait prices are advertised prices that are particularly low, but when purchasers come to buy the item, they are encouraged to buy a far more expensive item (the bait-and-switch approach). The retailer does not really intend to sell the bait-price item – most of the time it is not really in stock, or only one is available at the low price. This type of pricing is unethical (morally wrong), and is usually avoided by middlemen.

13.10 **Marketing-communication decisions**

13.10.1 Marketing communication defined

Marketing communication is the process of informing, persuading, and reminding the consumer about the availability of an organisation's product. There are four elements in marketing communication that can be used in a specific combination to communicate with consumers. These four elements are:
- advertising
- personal selling
- sales promotion
- public relations, publicity, and sponsorships.

Figure 13.14 shows the four elements of marketing communication. All four elements have to work together to convey the marketing message to the target audience. This message is called the 'specific marketing mix' that is being used by the organisation.

FIGURE 13.14 The elements of marketing communication

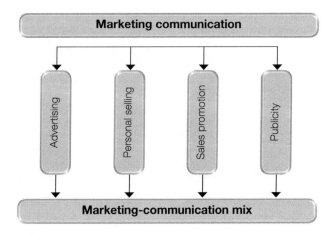

A marketing-communication budget allocates funds to each of the four marketing-communication elements to make consumers aware of the organisation's range of products, to persuade consumers to buy these products, or to remind them to buy the products again.

13.10.2 Advertising

Advertising can be defined as controlled and paid non-personal marketing-communication activities about a good or service aimed at a specific target market.

Advertising takes place on television, in the movies, on the radio, or in magazines and newspapers. A single placement of such an advertisement is very expensive – consequently marketing managers need to pay careful attention to the choice of the media used and the marketing-communication message. It is important that the message reaches the target market, and that this audience will notice the message, understand it, accept it, and react to it by repeatedly buying the same product.

Outdoor advertising on billboards, posters, bus stops and public-transport vehicles reaches consumers at a time when they are out of their homes and busy with other activities. This is also the best way to reach a target market that does not read regularly or does not have access to television and the movies.

13.10.2.1 **The advertising message**

An advertisement in the print media usually consists of three main components, namely the heading, the illustration, and the copy. The heading is supposed to attract the consumer's attention and to deliver the main appeal of the product, as well as the most important reason why it should be bought. The most important message is often repeated at the bottom of the copy. The headline and sub-headline are printed in big bold letters to attract attention.

The illustration may be a drawing or a photograph, in black-and-white or in colour. The illustration stimulates interest and invites the reader to read the copy, which contains information about the product and the needs it can satisfy. The message may use sensible reasons (for example, the safety features of a car) or emotional reasons (for example, claiming that a deodorant will make a woman irresistible). The product itself, the package and the label also appear in the illustration. All the parts of the illustration are chosen to transmit a symbolic message. It is important to have all three parts, headline, illustration, and copy, working together and not telling conflicting stories.

The message of the past is not always correct in the modern world

Some of the advertising messages of the past are not effective in modern society. For instance the message used since 1928 by Cadbury referring to 'a glass and a half of milk in every half pound of Cadbury chocolate' was found to be misleading by the UK Trading Standards Institute, and it came under pressure from European Union legislators. However, the new permitted message does not sound right – 'The equivalent of 426 ml of fresh milk in every 227 g of chocolate'. Currently the old message is still used in South Africa, for how long, no-one knows.

Source: Mokgata, Z. 2010.Advertsing: poetry and precision. FM 8 October, vol 208, no 4. p,24

In radio advertisements, only words and sounds are used to transmit the advertising message. Music is often used to reinforce the message or to create a specific mood. Jingles and slogans are especially effective in teaching the brand name to potential consumers.

Television advertisements are effective because the spoken and written word can be used to spell out the message clearly. Pictorial material, music, jingles and other sounds can be used to reinforce the message.

Buddy the dog – another memorable campaign for Toyota

Toyota has been through some trouble lately with worldwide product recalls, something that is especially worrying for a global vehicle manufacturer that has built a global success story based on a foundation of quality and reliability in its range of products.

Since the early 1960s when Toyota started its marketing campaign in South Africa, it has built a reputation on trust and sharing the 'ordinary South African' lifestyle. With the new campaign that introduced Buddy the Brindle Boxer as spokesperson for Toyota, this was taken into consideration, and Buddy, the dog with the human mouth, is seen to be honest, loyal and warm-hearted – all the things that Toyota believe are the core essentials of its brand in South Africa.

Various advertisements have been shown since Buddy trotted onto centre stage for Toyota. This dog has in two years become the icon that is remembered by millions of South Africans. It is an icon in that it has transcended the race, gender, and age barriers in South Africa – something that is only reached by a handful of marketing communications campaigns. It has also developed an emotional association with South Africans. Buddy first came on the scene in September 2009, debuting with the launch of the refined Toyota Corolla. Buddy tries to behave with the sophistication of the Corolla but fails because of his down-to-earth nature. The message that filters through this TV campaign is that beyond the sophistication of the Corolla, there still remains the same reliable, solid and fun-loving vehicle as before.

Buddy – the spokesperson for Toyota

The Buddy campaign was developed with Draftfcb Johannesburg, and is used to launch new products of Toyota. One such memorable example is the TV advertisement of the refined Toyota Auris X range. Buddy and a friend, a Chihuahua, look appreciatively at the car as Buddy praises the features of the car. Buddy growls the sound of the Auris Sport X's engine in a deep and rumbling voice…the Chihuahua tries to repeat the noise of the engine but makes a hash of it. Buddy demonstrates again … but with no success. A frustrated Buddy then says to the audience under his breath, that the Chihuahua is 'hopeless'.

SOURCE: Toyota's new star to steal consumers' hearts. 2010. Marketingweb. [Online]. Available: http://www.marketingmix.co.za/pebble.asp?relid=9888 [October 2010].

13.10.3 Personal selling

Personal selling can be defined as the verbal presentation of a good, service or idea to one or more potential purchasers in order to conclude a transaction. Sales representatives inform buyers about a business's products and persuade them, through face-to-face communication, to buy the business's products on a regular basis.

Sales representatives of manufacturers visit other businesses and dealers, passing the marketing message directly to them. In the same way, wholesalers' sales representatives can be used to visit retailers to try to sell the variety of products handled by the wholesaler. In door-to-door selling, personal selling between a retailer's sales representatives and final consumers also takes place. Examples of this are door-to-door sales representatives selling insurance policies and water filtration devices.

13.10.4 Sales promotions

Sales promotions are additional marketing-communication methods that are not classified as advertising, personal selling or publicity, but which add to these other three elements in trying to influence consumer behaviour.

Examples of sales-promotion methods are diaries, calendars, and T-shirts displaying the brand name and a short sales message. Competitions, demonstrations, and the handing out of samples (like a sachet of a new perfume in a *Cosmopolitan* magazine) are also examples of sales promotions. Sales promotions often have short-term objectives only, for example, to introduce a new product to the market.

Sales promotions often reinforce the message of the other marketing-communication elements. For example, if a consumer has seen a supermarket demonstration of the preparation of a new frozen product (a sales promotion), she or he will perhaps understand the associated television advertisement better (advertising), and find it easier to accept the message, especially if she or he has also read an article in the housekeeping column of the newspaper in which the columnist explains the new product (publicity).

13.11 Public-relations management[11]

The public-relations-management function inside a business is separate from the marketing function. The aim of public-relations (PR) management is to build good relations with the different stakeholders of the organisation (this includes internally with employees and shareholders, as well as externally with government, suppliers, and competitors). Public-relations management is a formal and systemic effort to portray the organisation in a favourable light and to counteract unfavourable publicity. See Table 13.3.

One of the main instruments that the PR function has is publicity, for example news items appearing in the mass media[12] about the organisation, its products, or its people. (See for example the activities mentioned in Table 13.4.) One of the methods by which to get favourable publicity is sponsorships. A sponsorship can be described as an investment of cash or kind in an activity, in return for access to the exploitable commercial potential that is expected from this activity.[13] An example of a sponsorship is that of MTN (the South African cellular-telephone company) which sponsored the 2010 Soccer World Cup in South Africa. MTN spent millions of rands in sponsoring this event.

While the marketing function concentrates on the direct customer or potential customer, the PR function has a wide range of audiences that it is targeting.

Although the organisation should always try to obtain positive publicity, negative publicity may occur. Examples include the angry customer who opened a bag of poisonous snakes in an Absa branch because of a dispute with the bank manager, or the poison scare and attempt to extort money from Pick n Pay a few years ago. The immediate effects of these types of events are quite negative for the organisation. These organisations managed these events in an open and proactive manner and tried to correct the situations as soon as possible. For example, Sean Summers, the previous CEO of Pick n Pay, was the figurehead in a Pick n Pay publicity campaign to reassure stakeholders after this negative event. Later research found that Pick n Pay actually benefited because of the way it handled this event.

TABLE 13.3 Example of public-relations activities

Open-house policy and fairs	Plant tours offered to ordinary people create a feeling of transparency and goodwill. Guided tours are done by organisations such as Amalgamated Beverage Industries (ABI), Toyota, BMW and South African Breweries (SAB).
Exhibitions and shows	Exhibitions at shows such as the Rand Easter Show raise the exposure of organisations and their ranges of goods or services.
Lobbying	Lobbyists are used by certain organisations, such as alcohol and tobacco organisations, to try and influence the decisions made by stakeholders, such as governmental institutions.
Organised social activities	An organisation's yearly Golf Day is an example of an organised social activity that is used to project a favourable image of the organisation. It also provides an opportunity for networking with the organisations' external stakeholders.

TABLE 13.4 Ways of an organisation getting favourable publicity

Press news releases	Newsworthy information is given to the press for publication.
Special events	Journalists can be invited to a special event with the expectation that this will bring favourable publicity.
Sponsorships	Sponsorships can achieve good publicity for the organisation.

CASE STUDY: Pick n Pay moving forward[14]

Raymond Ackerman was the founder of the Pick n Pay group in South Africa in 1967. The group concentrates on food, clothing, and general merchandise, and is divided into three divisions, each with its own management board. These divisions are the Pick n Pay Retail Division, the Group Enterprises Division, and Franklins Australia, which is to be sold off so that Pick n Pay can concentrate on its domestic retailing operations. The South African retailing operations consist of Hypermarkets, Supermarkets, Clothing Stores, the Pick n Pay franchise operations, liquor stores, pharmacies in the Hypermarkets, and Score supermarkets that are at present being converted into family stores.

The strategy of Pick n Pay regarding its target market was spelled out in its Financial Report for 2010. It focuses on the following areas:

- Defend and grow in its market share in the top LSM groupings. (Living Standard Measure is a method used to segment the market into different categories based on different criteria such as income and access to different assets.) This is seen as the core market for Pick n Pay, and they profess to meet and exceed the needs and demands of this group of consumers. To do this, Pick n Pay focus on getting in-store delivery right, focusing on value for money, and getting their fresh products right.
- Getting market share in the lower LSM groupings (LSM 4–7) which is traditionally in the black township areas. The feel and product range in the townships should be similar to other areas in South Africa.
- Focusing on getting the message across through marketing communication that the Pick n Pay product prices are low. Pick n Pay also has a solid reputation with the upwardly mobile black middle class.
- Investing to improve the supply chain operations of Pick n Pay. The objective is to distribute the majority of the merchandise from a central warehouse to its retail stores in South Africa. This will improve the on-shelf

availability and in-store space utilisation, and achieve cost efficiencies that will eventually provide even lower prices. Specifically for 2010, the aim was to reduce the supply chain costs through further improvements at Longmeadow, the first of the new central distribution centres, and to roll out the concept of central distribution to the rest of South Africa. The central distribution outlet in Longmeadow increased volumes by 57% and reduced the cost per case by 15%. Five more distribution centres are envisaged.

There has been a lot of investigation on the success that Pick n Pay's biggest competitor (Shoprite) had with central distribution. Pick n Pay was the leader in direct distribution where the manufacturer delivered directly to the stores. This was, however, in the time when retail stores carried fewer items on their shelves. The net effect of this was that every store had to have a massive loading and storage area, in some instances up to 40% of the total area, which was not a productive selling area.

There is also a lot of discussion about the franchising route that Pick n Pay is actively growing. It is an excellent vehicle to bring black entrepreneurs on board, and helps with equity, but it is not the route followed by its major competitors, Shoprite and Woolworths.[15] Only the future will tell if the franchising route that Pick n Pay is following will be the correct option.

QUESTIONS

1. Is Pick n Pay following a marketing orientation? Please explain your answer.
2. Would the consumer decision-making process be the same for the different LSM groupings?
3. Which of the four marketing-mix instruments is getting the most attention in the proposed new marketing objectives of Pick n Pay?
4. Would you say that the distribution decision of keeping stores open 24 hours a day will be to the benefit of the four large retailing groups in South Africa?
5. There is a growing trend to buy more convenience products at retailers such as Spar and Woolworths. How would this trend influence the competitive situation at other fast-food retailers such as Steers and Wimpy?
6. Can low prices alone change the fortunes of a retailing company such as Pick n Pay? Explain.

SUMMARY

Today's marketing era makes a major effort to match products to customers' needs. Marketers also try to understand the consumers' decision-making process and the determinants of consumer behaviour.

Marketing involves making decisions regarding four variables: products, distribution, marketing communication, and pricing. Marketing can be segmented into target marketing and product positioning. According to the marketing concept, contemporary businesses must have a profit orientation, a consumer orientation, social responsibility, and organisational integration in order to be successful. In the last part of the chapter it was pointed out that the four elements of the marketing mix must be made to work together to fit in with the needs of the consumer. Marketing-mix decisions involve price, distribution, and marketing communication. Distribution decisions consist of decisions regarding the various distribution channels and market coverage. Price decisions entail deciding on a price that will create a demand for products. The marketing-communication decision consists of deciding how to inform and persuade consumers to buy a specific brand on a continuous basis.

GLOSSARY

advertising: controlled and paid non-personal marketing-communication activities about the product aimed at a specific target market

bait prices: low advertised prices of particular products that are hardly stocked, so that consumers who come to buy them can be encouraged to purchase a more expensive substitute product

behavioural criteria: criteria used to divide the market according to factors such as price sensitivity, product benefits sought and brand-loyalty status

brand: a mark that is unique to the product manufactured and marketed by the organisation, and which is used to distinguish it from similar competing products

brand loyalty: loyalty that consumers show for certain brands by buying them on a regular basis

brand name: a word, a letter or a group of words used to identify a product

channel captain: the distributor or organisation that controls or dominates the channel

cognitive dissonance: the feeling of uncertainty when a consumer doubts whether he or she has made the correct decision

consumer's decision-making process: five phases through which the consumer progresses systematically when deciding whether or not to buy a product, namely: awareness of an unsatisfied need, gathering information on possible solutions, evaluating the solutions, deciding on a course of action and post-purchase evaluation

consumer orientation: one of the principles of the marketing concept that implies that the needs of customers should be placed first

consumer products: products intended for immediate use by consumers

convenience products: products of a non-durable nature that are used on a daily basis

copy: the message that is delivered to the customer

core product: the technical and physical qualities directly related to the product

cost–plus method: a way of calculating the target price by adding the profit margin to the total cost of the product

cost price: the unit cost of manufacturing and marketing a product

cultural groups: groups that consist of people with similar values and norms

dealer brands: brand names given to products when these are purchased by large dealers or retailers (for example Edgars's Free2BU range)

decline phase: the fourth phase of a product's life cycle, when products that do not meet requirements or are no longer profitable can be withdrawn

demographic criteria: criteria used to divide the market according to factors such as gender, income, age and education

direct distribution channel: a channel of distribution that goes directly from the manufacturer to the consumer

distribution: the channels and strategies that ensure availability of the product at the right time and place for the targeted customers to buy it

durable consumer products: products that have a long life expectancy (such as cars)

exclusive market coverage: a situation where only one distributor is allowed the right to sell a product (for example, a Porsche car dealership in Gauteng)

family: related people in a household who affect each other's buying decisions

family brand: a brand given to a whole range of products

final price: the price at which the product is offered to consumers

formal product: the specific features that are added to the core product

generic brands: where a retailer puts a very basic label on a product (not the retailer's brand nor the manufacturer's)

geographic criteria: criteria used to divide the market according to geographic locations such as provinces, cities and towns

group factors: the family, reference groups, opinion leaders, cultural groups and social class that influence consumer's buying behaviour

growth phase: the second stage in a product's life cycle, when marketing communication is now aimed at informing and reminding the consumer about the product, the price is usually under competitive pressure, and more retailers are stocking the product

heading: the copy in a large font that attracts customers' attention and encourages them to read further

illustration: the picture used in an advertisement

indirect distribution channel: a channel of distribution where manufacturers use an intermediary to distribute their products further to the consumer

individual brand: when every product has an own-brand identity, such as Yaris, Conquest or Camry

individual factors: the motives, attitudes, perceptions, learning ability, personality and lifestyle of consumers that influence their buying behaviour

intangible consumer products: services such as legal advice, medical consultations and hairdressing services

intensive market coverage: the representation or availability of the product in the market

intermediaries (middlemen): the people that help to sell the product by moving it along in the distribution channel

introductory phase: the first stage in a product's life cycle when the brand name must be established, marketing communication is aimed at informing the customer about the availability of the product, and the product is usually available at only a few outlets

leader pricing: a pricing strategy where products are sold at a lower than market price for a limited period only (as 'specials') and where a small profit is made

manufacturer brand: a brand given to products by the manufacturer

market-aggregation approach (total-market approach): an approach where the market is not divided into segments for targeting

market coverage: the manner in which a product is distributed throughout the market

marketing communication: the process of informing, persuading and reminding the consumer about the availability of an organisation's product

marketing concept: an ethical code or philosophy followed by marketing management in all their marketing tasks and activities

marketing research: the process of defining a marketing problem or opportunity, and collecting and analysing data in order to solve the problem

market-penetration price: a product's low initial price, as the organisation hopes to penetrate the market rapidly, discouraging competitors in the process

market price: the price the consumer is currently prepared to pay, or the current market price at which competing products are sold

market segmentation: the process of dividing the market into smaller, homogeneous market segments consisting of people with more or less similar needs, to allow for the design of a market offering that will more precisely meet the needs of individuals in selected segment(s)

maturity phase: the third phase in a product's life cycle, when the focus is on selling to the existing customer-base, reminding the customer about the product, and surviving the price competition

multi–segment approach: the market segmentation approach where the same product is aimed at different market segments

need–satisfying product: a product that fulfils the needs of the customer

non–durable consumer products: products that are consumed within a short time span (for example, milk)

odd prices: final prices of products that have odd numbers to make them seem cheaper (for example, R1,99)

opinion leaders: reference people to whom others look in forming opinions and taking consumer decisions

organisational integration: when every function, department and employee in the business works together to satisfy the needs of the customers and maximise profitability

packaging: the group of activities concerned with the design, manufacturing and filling of a container or wrapper with the product so that it can be effectively stored, transported, identified and marketed

personal selling: the verbal presentation of a good, service or idea to one or more potential purchasers in order to conclude a transaction

price: the amount of money that the business wants from the consumer in exchange for a product or the value forfeited by the consumers (money) to obtain something of value, namely a product

price-determination process: the process used to determine the price of a product, which includes looking at the cost price and the market price and then setting the price for the product

primary data: information that is collected through original research for a specific purpose

product: anything of a tangible or intangible nature that is offered to the consumer to satisfy a need or a want or the good or service that a business provides to consumers in exchange for money

product differentiation: the way in which a business distinguishes its product from similar competitive products, so that consumers of this type of product perceive it as being different

product image: the product's symbolic value given by the type of marketing message, the price and the choice of distribution outlet

product life cycle: the phases a product goes through during its life, namely the introduction, growth, maturity and decline phases

product obsolescence: when a product is deliberately made technically and/or psychologically obsolete in order to push the consumer to buy a new version of the product

product portfolio: an organisation's range of products

product positioning: the process of creating in target consumers' minds a specific image of a product relative to that of competing products

profit orientation: the first principle of the marketing concept, which aims at maximising profits in the long term

promotion: the communication messages that a business sends to its targeted customers in order to persuade them to buy its products

psychographic segmentation: the division of the market into segments according to lifestyle, personality and social class

publicity: news items appearing in the mass media about the organisation, its products or its people

public-relations management: a management function that aims to have good relations with different stakeholders of the organisation

pull strategy: where intermediaries are persuaded to stock a product owing to consumer demand

push strategy: where intermediaries are persuaded to actively encourage consumers to buy products in a store

reference groups: groups that positively or negatively influence people's attitudes or behaviour

relationship marketing: a perspective on marketing where the importance of maintaining long-term relationships with customers and other role-players in the environment is stressed

retailers: intermediaries who distribute products from manufacturers and/or wholesalers to consumers at the right place and at the right time

sales promotions: those additional marketing-communication methods that are not classified as advertising, personal selling or publicity, but which complement these other three elements in trying to influence consumer behaviour

secondary data: information that already exists and that has previously been collected by other people

selective market coverage: a market-coverage strategy where only a few intermediaries are selected to help sell a product

shopping products: products of a durable nature where the consumer will want to compare the suitability, quality, price and style of competing products before selecting one

single-segment approach: the market segmentation approach where the marketer identifies one single group and directs the product offering only to that particular segment

skimming price: a product's initial high price, which will be gradually lowered over time

social class: levels of social standing allocated to people according to their occupations, education and income

social responsibility: the perspective that businesses have a responsibility towards society and that they should make a contribution to the community

speciality products: products with unique characteristics for which consumers will make a special purchasing effort

sponsorship: an investment of cash or kind in an activity, in return for access to the exploitable commercial potential which is expected from this activity

tangible consumer products: products that can be seen and tasted

target marketing: where marketers select one or more market segments that they want to serve or target

target price: the price that must be realised to obtain the target rate of return, taking into consideration the cost structure, the business's capital needs, and the potential sales volume of the product

total product: all the components of the product, namely technical and physical qualities, added features and the symbolic value related to the product

trademark: a name or symbol that identifies a product, the use of which is legally restricted to its owner

unsought products: products that customers do not usually think about and which therefore require heavy advertising and personal selling

wholesalers: intermediaries who distribute products from manufacturers to other intermediaries and/or directly to consumers at the right place and at the right time

MULTIPLE-CHOICE QUESTIONS

1. The third stage of brand loyalty is known as:
   a) brand recognition
   b) brand preference
   c) brand insistence
   d) brand unawareness

2. After buying a new Nikon camera, Sarah suddenly wonders whether she has made the right decision and whether she should rather have bought a Canon camera. This feeling of doubt or uncertainty is known as:
   a) dissatisfaction
   b) cognitive satisfaction
   c) the bottom line
   d) cognitive dissonance

3. Distribution channels bring the supplier and the customer together by providing the product at the point of selling where it is needed. Clover is distributing milk right through South Africa. What type of market coverage does Clover try to reach?
   a) Exclusive market coverage
   b) Selective market coverage
   c) Intensive market coverage
   d) Mass coverage

4. Apple Computer is introducing new software to compete with Microsoft's market leader, Windows. Apple believes that, if it can undercut Microsoft's price, customers should respond by using more Apple software and hardware. This is called:
   a) penetration pricing
   b) price skimming pricing
   c) leader pricing
   d) predatory pricing

5. Which type of market segmentation approach does Mango Airlines use?
   a) market aggregation approach
   b) single segment approach
   c) triple segment approach
   d) multi segment approach

REFERENCES AND END-NOTES

1. Du Toit, G.S., Erasmus, B.J. & Strydom, J.W. 2010. *Introduction to business management.* 8th ed. Cape Town: Oxford University Press. p. 365.
2. *Pretoria News* (Motoring section). 23 September 2010. p. 22.
3. Toyota. 2010. Social Contribution. [Online]. Available: http://www.toyota.co.jp/en/social_contribution/index.html [23 September 2010].
4. Pick n Pay. 2010. Pick n Pay Stores Ltd year-end results – April. [Online]. Available: http://www.picknpay.co.za/picknpay/content/en/news?oid=13692&sn=Detail&pid=10563 [23 September 2010].
5. Du Toit, G.S., Erasmus, B.J. & Strydom, J.W. 2010. *Introduction to business management.* 8th ed. Cape Town: Oxford University Press. p. 377.
6. Du Toit, G.S., Erasmus, B.J. & Strydom, J.W. 2010. *Introduction to business management.* 8th ed. Cape Town: Oxford University Press. p. 369.
7. Du Toit, G.S., Erasmus, B.J. & Strydom, J.W. 2010. *Introduction to business management.* 8th ed. Cape Town: Oxford University Press. p.371.
8. Du Toit, G.S., Erasmus, B.J. & Strydom, J.W. 2010. *Introduction to business management.* 8th ed. Cape Town: Oxford University Press, pp. 385–411.
9. Srinivasan, S.R., Ramakrishan, S. & Grasman, S.E. 2005. Importing cannibalisation models into demand forecasting. *Marketing Intelligence & Planning.* 23(5). pp. 470–485.
10. [Online]. Available: http://www.acer.co.za/acer/home.do?LanguageISOCtxParam=en&ctx2.c2att1=23&CountryISOCtxParam=ZA&ctx1.att21k=1&CRC=3486119666 [7 February 2011].
11. Strydom, J.W. 2007. *Basics of business communication.* Johannesburg: Red Pepper. pp. 142–144.
12. Gasper, J.E., Beerman, K., Kolari, J.W., Hise, R.T., Murphy Smith, H. & Arreola-Risa, A. 2006. *Introduction to business.* Boston: Houghton Mifflin. p. 355.
13. Kitchen, P.J. 2004. *Marketing communications: Principles and practice.* London: Thompson. p. 362.
14. *Pick n Pay Annual Report.* 2010. [Online]. Available: http://financialresults.co.za/mainsite/annual-reports/141-pick-n-pay-annual-report- [14 October 2010]; & *Business Day, 2010 THE BOTTOM LINE COLUMN: Kagiso digs into distribution at Pick n Pay.* [Online]. Available: http://www.businessday.co.za/Articles/Content.aspx?id=119998 [15 October 2010].
15. Based on Marsland, L. 2007. 'Fresh look for iconic Pick n Pay brand'. [Online]. Available: www.bizcommunity.com/Article/196/11/19612.html [7 February 2011]; & Robbins, T. 2007. 'Pick n Pay poaches three head managers'. [Online]. Available: http://www.fastmoving.co.za/news-archive/retailer-news/pick-n-pay-poaches-three-head-managers [7 February 2011].

ANSWERS TO MULTIPLE-CHOICE QUESTIONS

1. Answer = c) The third stage is known as brand insistence. See par 13.7.4.1. Brand unawareness is not a stage in the brand loyalty process.
2. Answer = d)
3. Answer = c) The correct answer is intensive market coverage as milk is a convenience product that should be available at all outlets throughout SA. See par 13.8.4.
4. Answer = a) The correct answer is penetration pricing. See par 13.9.3.
5. Answer = b)

PART FOUR

Entrepreneur-ship and the business plan

Entrepreneurship is essential when starting a new business, but it is also a necessary tool to produce innovation in an existing business. Chapter 14 examines the role of entrepreneurship throughout the life of a business.

Chapter 15 discusses the business plan, as well as feasibility and viability studies. A business plan is used when starting a new business or when radical change occurs to an existing business. A business plan provides direction and allows entrepreneurs to approach banks for funding.

Entrepreneurship

Cecile Nieuwenhuizen

PURPOSE OF THIS CHAPTER

This chapter explains the concept of entrepreneurship and the contribution of entrepreneurs to the economy of a country. It identifies typical entrepreneurial skills, and describes the different types of businesses in which entrepreneurs are typically involved. These include the informal sector, and small, micro-, medium, and large businesses. The role of entrepreneurs in existing franchises and corporations is also discussed.

LEARNING OUTCOMES

This chapter should enable you to:
- understand the definition of an 'entrepreneur', and what being an entrepreneur entails
- identify the contribution of entrepreneurs to the economy of a country
- discuss the difference between entrepreneurship, leadership, and management
- describe the different types of businesses in which entrepreneurs can be involved.

14.1 Introduction

Entrepreneurs are among the most important contributors to economic development in a country. They are unique individuals who identify creative business opportunities, take the risk of establishing a business, and have the talent and skills to manage and grow a business – in the process, creating wealth and employment. Entrepreneurs directly influence the level of economic growth in a country. Job creation is highly correlated with the level of business start-up activity, and there is a positive, statistically significant association between national economic growth and entrepreneurship.[1]

Entrepreneurial businesses create or innovate by doing something new or different to create wealth for the entrepreneur. **High-potential entrepreneurs** are those that intend to grow their businesses. They are responsible for growth and job creation in the economy, and can be found in their own enterprises as part of a team owning an enterprise, or as corporate entrepreneurs and 'intrapreneurs' in large companies and in the public sector. However, their own business is the most natural place for an entrepreneur to be, and that is mostly in **small, micro-** and **medium enterprises** (SMMEs), or in large businesses that they have grown from SMMEs. These are the opportunity entrepreneurs (as identified by the **Global Entrepreneurship Monitor** report of 2009) as opposed to necessity entrepreneurs, who start a business because they have no other choice. Businesses are established by entrepreneurs who identify an opportunity in the market. Their intentions are to establish and grow a business, not merely to start any business out of necessity and a lack of employment. Opportunity businesses are entrepreneurial with the intention to grow, increase profitability, and create employment for others. They are invaluable to the economy of any country, and therefore it is encouraging to note that in 2008, 79% of entrepreneurs in South Africa were opportunity-driven, and only 21% necessity entrepreneurs.[2]

Not everyone who starts a new business is an entrepreneur. Some may be enterprising (in the sense of being active and smart) in starting a micro-business, but do not achieve anything new or different, merely survive and find only limited customers, do not grow or cannot obtain finance. Although these businesses often bring in an income to their owners, and perhaps one or two employees, they are merely **survivalist businesses**, often born from the need for an income but with limited or no future opportunities. They are ordinary businesses based on ordinary business ideas. Entrepreneurial businesses, on the other hand, are created by entrepreneurs who usually have higher levels of education, earn higher incomes from their businesses, apply technology, have multiple business sites, and are export-orientated.

SMMEs form 97.5% of all businesses in South Africa. They employ 55% of all the formal private-sector employees. However, more than 90% of SMMEs employ less than 20 people, with the average business in South Africa employing 13 people. In South Africa the overall entrepreneurial activity is 7.2%, indicating the percentage of economically active adults who are entrepreneurs. Excluding Russia, South Africa is the lowest in the group of middle-to-low-income economies in the world, or 35th of 54 countries (2009:59).[3]

Statistics about SMMEs exclude businesses that were started by entrepreneurs but have grown into large, successful businesses, often public companies. SMMEs that are merely surviving or are not actually entrepreneurial are included in the statistics. Thus

SMME statistics do not in actual fact reflect entrepreneurial statistics, but they do give a valuable indication of the level of entrepreneurial activity in a country.

CASE STUDY: Dimension 5 Business Services Group (Pty) Ltd[4]

After 20 years' experience in various businesses, primarily the volatile construction industry, Mr Nel decided to start a new business. Owing to the needs that he experienced in his own businesses, Mr Nel knew what the needs of small and medium enterprises (SMEs) were. SMEs require professional services but due to the size of these businesses it is usually not viable to appoint full-time employees to provide it. Professional services include the accounting, auditing, payrolls, tax, law, labour, management and marketing functions. In addition, services to assist in business's turnaround and change management are also often required. Turnaround involves assisting entrepreneurs or managers of businesses to become profitable where they have previously lost money and to increase profitability where potential profits are higher than actual profits. Change management involves the need of a business to adapt to changing circumstances to ensure the continued and even increased profitability of a business.

Mr Nel established Dimension 5 Business Services Group (D5BSG) in 2004 with a founding team of five highly professional, dedicated people. Mr Nel identified the founding team from a network of family, friends and business contacts. Each member of the founding team is responsible for a different area of specialisation including financial services; financial management; human-resource management; general management and specialist business management. D5BSG not only provides advice but also implements systems and procedures to increase the profitability of a client's business/es. In 2004 the business consisted of a total of seven people: the founding team of five and two employees.

Mr Nel started the business with personal investments, loans and where available with contributions from some of the founding members. All available funds and access to loans were used to ensure sufficient money to start the business. In addition, the founding members committed themselves to the business on a full-time basis. At first they had to be satisfied with salaries that were lower than they earned in their previous positions. However, according to their calculations it would be necessary for a few months only.

In 2010, after five years D5BSG is growing at 40% per year and profits increase on a monthly basis. There are now five founder members and 30 employees involved in the business. The owners as well as employees enjoy their work and the business grows through the expansion of client businesses as well as personal references from their clients to new businesses. Mr Nel attributes the success of the business to continuous close contact with clients – and because clients experience positive results and increased profits in their businesses.

When the business was established in 2004 it had six clients, a number which grew to 98 clients in 2010. This growth was also due to the identification of additional needs of SMEs and the related extension of services to attend to these needs by D5BSG. Additional services added include doing payrolls, contracting employees and managing labour related problems such as strikes, disciplinary hearings and labour cases.

The clients of D5BSG have annual turnovers that range between R10 million and R80 million and the majority are growth businesses. The client businesses include property developers, storage companies, car-rental firms, retirement villages, and a variety of manufacturing companies that amongst them produce rubber products, pasta, biscuits and plastic containers.

While the client businesses are varied, all the same basic business principles apply in achieving success. Most are found and managed by entrepreneurs who realise that they cannot do everything themselves and see the value in assistance from specialists. The services of D5BSG are brought in as most clients know that they would not be able to afford any of these services on a full-time basis. Through their service and close involvement D5BSG becomes an essential part of the client businesses.

14.2 **The economic impetus of entrepreneurial business**

The combination of all businesses – namely small, micro- and medium enterprises (SMMEs) and large national and international businesses – determines the state of the economy. The aim in South Africa is to reach 6% growth in the economy in the next few years, to sustain and improve the economic development of the country. The contribution of entrepreneurs will be relied on for a large part of that prospective 6% growth.

Employment is closely linked to the state of the economy. When there is no growth in the economy, there are fewer jobs. The approximate unemployment rate is 25.6%.[5] Established firms are important for employment creation and sustainability, but SMMEs form the most important growth sector in the world's leading economies, such as the

United States of America, Japan, and the United Kingdom. While many business start-ups fail, entrepreneurship is still regarded as the best business opportunity that exists. Often SMMEs are formed when established firms lay off staff and give out non-core (secondary) work to be done by outsiders, such as SMMEs. For example, three employees of a large mining group that unbundled a few years ago bought two mines that would have been closed down. They had experience in the field, developed a plan, took some risks, started off with a loan, took over the operations, restructured, and made some crucial changes. Their enterprise, Edelweiss Mines, has been extremely profitable and is growing. It is in the process of buying additional mines and providing employment for many people.

According to the GEM report,[6] the age group 25-34 years was responsible for 26% and the age group 35-44 years for 28% of the Total Early-Stage Entrepreneurial Activity in South Africa. This shows that young adults in South Africa are very interested in entrepreneurship as a career opportunity. Even the age group 45-54-year-old entrepreneurs increased from 13% in 2006 to 21% in 2009, which is a positive indication. The interest of young adults in entrepreneurship is important because they are regarded as ideal for becoming involved in their own businesses because they are technologically advanced, more exposed to business, inclined to be innovative, independent, and prepared to face challenges.[7]

14.3 Who is an entrepreneur?

An **entrepreneur** identifies business opportunities, and is prepared to take a calculated risk in order to take advantage of worthwhile business opportunities in the quest for making a profit. An entrepreneur is able to find the resources to establish and grow a business. An entrepreneur has a real need to build something and feel that what was built is due to her or his efforts.

Important skills of successful entrepreneurs which contribute to the establishment of a successful business are ingenuity, leadership, and calculated risk-taking.

14.3.1 Ingenuity

Ingenuity includes knowledge, skills, understanding of a business environment, and creativity. **Creativity** can involve the adjustment or refinement of existing procedures or products, and recognising opportunities and solutions to problems. Basically, ingenuity involves new ideas.

Any application of new ideas is based on innovation. But, although entrepreneurs understand the importance of innovation, they often see the risk and the high investment that the development of innovative goods or services requires, as being smaller than the chance to make a profit. This explains why owners of small businesses often creatively adapt innovations of competitors, by, for example, product adjustments, marketing, and client service.

For example, Mr Nel had sufficient knowledge and experience of the needs of Small and Medium Enterprises (SMEs) as well as good business skills, to diversify in a new business. His creativity ensured that he identified a need in the market, namely the provision of much needed services to SMEs. Mr Nel and the team also expanded the services provided by D5BSG according to the needs of SMEs that they identified over time. They continually applied creativity to adapt the business to the changing needs of SMEs. However, while creativity is crucial, it can be applied only if the entrepreneur has business-specific knowledge and skills as well as knowledge of the industry in which the business operates.

14.3.2 Leadership

Sound human relations and a positive attitude are the basis of **leadership**. A good leader is positive, well-adjusted, realistic, self-confident, group-orientated, and a team-builder, who seeks solutions, motivates people, gives individuals responsibility, and gives credit for achievements. Being comfortable with people and having good personal interactions, confronting problems, being open to differences in opinion, trusting people, and giving recognition where it is due, are all forms of behaviour linked to good leadership. Leadership has strong similarities to entrepreneurship.

Successful entrepreneurs realise the importance of business relationships. They have good relations with clients, see human relations as an important source for the enterprise, and regard long-term goodwill as more important than short-term benefits. They are believable and reliable, and they develop networks and display important types of interpersonal behaviour such as motivation, persuasion, team-building, and conflict management. Successful entrepreneurs ensure employee performance by finding various ways to judge and reward good performance, and making ownership available to those involved in the business. Entrepreneurs maintain good personal relations by, for example, using their personality to develop business contracts and influence people to help achieve their goals. They are able to persuade people to buy a good or service, or to provide financing.

For example, Mr Nel's leadership ensured that through his networks he managed to involve professional and experienced partners in the establishment phase of his businesses. His networks included family, friends as well as business connections from various backgrounds and, through his natural leadership, they became, and remained, involved in the business. Their motivation ensured the continued success of D5BSG. Clearly Mr

Nel is a team–builder, as indicated by the five founders he managed to get together and keep together in the business. His ability to convince people to become involved in his business indicates his good interpersonal relations, which is a basis of successful leadership.

14.3.3 Calculated risk-taking

Successful entrepreneurs do not take chances, but sometimes they feel it is necessary to take **calculated risks**. They first determine what the risk entails by evaluating it themselves, for example, by doing market research or feasibility (is it achievable?) and viability (is it practical?) studies, and with the help of experts. The use of experts ensures objectivity and careful evaluation. Entrepreneurs calculate the probable results before they make decisions. Successful entrepreneurs avoid opportunities where it is likely that they will fail, regardless of the possible reward.

Entrepreneurs manage the risk in their business by accepting control and being involved in the basic aspects of the business. They control their business by getting access to information. They reduce their chance of financial loss by involving investors. In order to limit the risk of competition, they try to shorten the period between the birth of an idea and the time that the product enters the market.

The successful entrepreneur has thorough knowledge, skills, and understanding of finance, the market needs, competitors, client service, quality, leadership, human relations, planning, and other management functions. But successful entrepreneurs also know when their own knowledge, expertise and skills are limited, and then they make use of both internal experts (by appointing permanent employees) and external experts (such as consultants), and they outsource (send out) some of the functions in the business. They also develop their own skills and knowledge in the areas where they realise it is important to do this.

Mr Nel and the founding team were willing to take the risk and dedicate themselves to the business by contributing all their available funds to the business. They also committed themselves full time to the business and were willing to work for a brief period at a reduced salary.

14.4 **The entrepreneurial process**

Entrepreneurs are responsible for the establishment of a business. To make this possible, an entrepreneurial process is followed. The **entrepreneurial process** involves the identification and evaluation of a business idea, the development of a business plan for a viable business idea (ensuring that the required resources are available for the business), and the establishment and growth of the business.

In the initial (formative) phase, a business is usually spontaneous and free-spirited, with informal communication and centralised decision-making. The second (growth) phase is characterised by the efficient operation of tasks, formal communication during scheduled meetings, and policies and procedures.[8]

14.5 Temporary entrepreneurs versus growth-orientated entrepreneurs

While some entrepreneurs always try to grow their business, others become non-entrepreneurial once they have established a business. Gray, for instance, determined that not many small firms are seriously interested in growth. Their primary motives are to be self-governing and independent, not necessarily to grow their businesses.[9]

According to Thomson and Gray, the complications of growing and being innovative, as well as the personal motivations of many SMME owner-managers, are real external and internal psychological barriers to sustained entrepreneurial behaviour in most SMMEs.[10] In line with Schumpeter's comment that most firms settle for a non-entrepreneurial steadiness,[11] Gray confirms that most small businesses do not want to grow.[12]

However, growth-orientated entrepreneurs, who not only establish businesses but also grow their businesses, are the ones who boost the economy of a country. Their success is determined by their ability to not only establish businesses but also to adapt their managerial and leadership styles to changes that happen in the growth phases of the business. Growth-orientated business owners are also more inclined to introduce constant or major changes in their businesses.

Mr Nel is a typical growth-oriented entrepreneur. He constantly seeks new business opportunities and has continued to expand the services provided to SMEs and insures a steady increase in clients businesses.

14.6 Entrepreneurship, management and leadership in entrepreneurial businesses

Mayo and Nohria suggest that there are three basic types of leadership, namely entrepreneurs creating new businesses, managers growing and optimising them, and leaders transforming them at critical points.[13] When classifying business executives, these authors considered how entrepreneurs approach their businesses at the beginning of their time as founder or chief executive officer (CEO), namely as creating something new, as maximising potential from a defined business opportunity, or as transforming a business.

They determined that the entrepreneur with a vision often understands and fulfils the potential of a specific development, but is not necessarily able to take the established business into the future in a sustainable way. Examples show that start-up entrepreneurs may be too conceited, heavy-handed, or tyrannical to become great. When growth maximisation is required, a manager may be the best choice, and in times of crisis or decline, a leader may be needed.

A positive and significant relationship between the characteristics of an entrepreneur and the characteristics of a transformational leader in an SMME have been identified. Entrepreneurs and transformational leaders have a dynamic style of leadership, creating dramatic changes in organisations, developing visions for the future, and ensuring commitment and support from others in reaching those visions.[14] Eight common characteristics between leaders and entrepreneurs have been identified, namely that they are visionary, risk-takers, achievement-oriented, able to motivate others, creative, flexible, patient, and persistent.[15]

Schein has identified different career anchors indicating the core of various careers. According to Schein, 'If you have an entrepreneurial career anchor, your primary concern is to create something new, involving the motivation to overcome obstacles, the willingness to run risks, and the desire for personal prominence in whatever is accomplished. A strong need to build something and to feel that what was built is due to your efforts, is a primary motivation for you. You do not want to work for others unless you have the freedom to build your own organisation in your own way.'[16] The managerial career anchor indicates a primary concern to integrate the efforts of others, to be fully accountable for total results, and to tie different functions in a business together.[17] A person with a managerial career anchor prefers a generalist position, managing various business functions. This career anchor implies advancement, climbing up the corporate ladder, high levels of responsibility, contribution to the welfare of the business, leadership opportunities, and a high income. Competencies essential for successful general management are analytical competence, interpersonal and inter-group competence, and emotional competence.[18]

14.7 **Types of entrepreneurial business**

Entrepreneurial businesses can be informal, micro-, very small, small, medium or large. Each of these types of business has specific characteristics according to its different needs and features.

There are also different forms that suit specific businesses. Business forms include sole proprietorships, partnerships, close corporations, companies, and public companies. According to the Department of Trade and Industry, in the formal sector there are about 880 000 close corporations, 300 000 private companies and 6 000 public companies.[19]

14.7.1 The informal business sector

An informal business is defined as any business that is not registered for VAT or income tax with the Receiver of Revenue. According to World Bank estimates, the informal sector accounts for 28.4% of South Africa's GDP. In developing countries, informal activity accounts for between 30% and 80% of the workforce.[20] The businesses in the informal sector range from commercial activities to production and service activities, with the majority of them operating in the retail-trade sector. These businesses provide for the specific needs of the poor and less affluent people in society, with most goods and services being provided at more affordable rates, although in some instances, such as in the case of branded products, the products are more expensive.

The informal sector plays a critically important role in South Africa. Without the large informal sector, South Africa would be in a far worse state. There would be much more poverty and hardship if it were not for entrepreneurs who, often with no or very limited resources, successfully start and maintain their businesses in this sector. However, the role of the informal sector is debatable because owners of informal businesses do not comply with tax, labour, and other regulations. The real challenge is to ensure an enabling environment to formalise this sector to the advantage of these businesses as well as the economy.

14.7.2 The micro- and small business sectors

The great majority of businesses initiated by entrepreneurs begin as micro- or small businesses. These businesses are usually started and entrepreneurially managed by one person. They often remain small, but can grow and become larger small businesses or even medium and large businesses if the entrepreneur does not become a manager. An entrepreneur has a distinctly different mindset from that of a manager or bureaucrat, but often the entrepreneur becomes self-satisfied with a specific level of achievement in her or his business. She or he then becomes the content manager of a small business who dislikes risk, change, and innovation. The entrepreneurial business is then replaced by a managerially focused small business.

On the other hand, businesses that have been successfully established often fail because the entrepreneur is not able to adapt to the changing needs of the business, which can include a more managerial and functional approach. It often happens that ideas are good and the people behind them are competent, but they do not know how to manage a business and do not have a basic understanding of business fundamentals.

The business then fails owing to a lack of management skills and behaviour, as well as a lack of knowledge regarding the different functions of a business.

The true entrepreneur is adaptive, innovative, and willing to take risks, but as the business grows, a more managerial style may become necessary. This can happen when the business is small, but the challenge usually presents itself sharply when the business has become medium-sized.

Some entrepreneurs prefer not to become managers, even to a limited extent, and rather sell their businesses when they become too big or when they require less entrepreneurial input, in order to pursue new opportunities. These entrepreneurs are known as 'habitual entrepreneurs'. In some instances habitual entrepreneurs do not sell their businesses but appoint managers, and the established business becomes part of a portfolio of their businesses.

Examples of micro-, very small and small businesses are Wielligh with his exclusive range of jewellery shops, Chantal Dartnall of the award-winning restaurant Mosaic, Brands Tree Felling which cuts down trees, Herber Plastics which produces a range of plastic containers for the cosmetics and the pharmaceutical industries, and Cutie which manufactures specialised children's clothing.

The Small Business Act of South Africa (1995) and the National Small Business Amendment Act (2003)[21] have set out criteria according to business size in each sector of industry. Businesses are defined as **micro-businesses** if they have 5 or fewer employees and a turnover of up to R100 000 per year. **Very small businesses** employ between 6 and 20 employees, and **small businesses** employ between 21 and 50 employees. The upper limit for turnover in a small business varies from R1 million in the agricultural sector to R32 million in the wholesale-trade sector, as indicated in Table 14.1.

TABLE 14.1 Small business size according to industrial sector, employment and turnover[22]

Sector or subsector in accordance with the standard industrial classification	The total full-time equivalent of paid employees	Total turnover
Agriculture	50	R 3m
Mining and quarrying	50	R10m
Manufacturing	50	R13m
Electricity, gas and water	50	R13m
Construction	50	R 6m

Sector or subsector in accordance with the standard industrial classification	The total full-time equivalent of paid employees	Total turnover
Retail and motor trade and repair services	50	R19m
Wholesale trade, commercial agents and allied services	50	R32m
Catering, accommodation and other trade	50	R13m
Transport, storage and communications	50	R13m
Finance and business services	50	R13m
Community, social and personal services	50	R 6m

14.7.3 The medium and large business sectors

Entrepreneurial skills at the medium and large business level are very different from those at the micro- and small business level. At this level, a fine balance between entrepreneurial and managerial skills is essential. Owing to size and manageability, specialisation in areas of the medium-sized business is necessary, with different departments for functions such as finance, marketing, and human-resources management. Entrepreneurial businesses are inclined to remain flat in structure even when they become medium or large, but those which are more administrative sometimes become more of a hierarchy. The entrepreneur at this level has to be or to become better at managing different functional areas and levels, rather than a managerial and strategic level. Managing growth by way of expansion, diversification and vertical integration become more critical in medium and large businesses.

Medium businesses usually employ up to 200 people (100 in the agricultural sector), and the maximum turnover varies from R5 million in the agricultural sector to R51 million in the manufacturing sector and R64 million in the sector labelled 'wholesale trade, commercial agents and allied services'.

Large businesses employ more than 200 people (except in agricultural businesses where it is 100), and their turnovers are higher than the highest total turnover in the various sectors (as shown in Table 14.1).

Entrepreneurs in this sector are often excluded from the definition of an entrepreneur. Their contribution to the economy through employment creation is also not included in the statistics of SMMEs, and is therefore usually not seen as the involvement of entrepreneurs. But in actual fact those who have grown their businesses into large and often diversified businesses are the ultimate entrepreneurs. In this sector we find our more prominent entrepreneurs, often in public companies, such as: Richard Branson of Virgin Atlantic; Tokyo Sexwale, Chairman of Mvelephanda Resources and Batho Bonke-consortium; Mr Cyril Ramaphosa, Chairman of Johnnic Holdings, MTN and the Shanduka-group; Mr Patrice Motsepe of African Rainbow Minerals; Christo Wiese of Pepkor; and GT Ferreira of Rand Merchant Bank Holdings.

14.7.4 Franchisors and franchisees

A **franchise** is the legal right to use another firm's business model and name. The **franchisor** is an entrepreneur who owns the original business and sells this right, whereas a franchisee is the person who conducts a smaller business under the same name. She or he does not have the freedom to experiment, operate, and market their business based on their own vision of how things should be done, but must usually stick strictly to the plans of the franchisor. However, a recent study has proved that franchisees do show an entrepreneurial orientation in certain situations, such as multiple-outlet franchisees.[23] Franchisors in many sectors have recognised the benefit of multiple-unit franchisees,[24] and this is seen as an entrepreneurial continuation of the franchise trend.

Franchisors usually fall into the medium-to-large business category, as the more successful franchisors usually manage large numbers of franchises as part of their business, apart from the overall management of the franchise group. In South Africa alone there are 391 franchise systems, of which 90.5% originated and developed in South Africa. There are 37 international franchise systems in South Africa. Combined, the franchise systems are responsible for 22 825 outlets, employing 284 447 people.[25] The contribution of the franchise industry to the GDP is 11%.[26]

An example of a franchise system is Kobus Oosthuizen's Butterfield Bakery. He started his first bakery franchise in 1997. Now he is franchisor to more than 120 franchisees. These franchises have a defined market and are close to mines and other areas inadequately serviced by traditional bakeries. The turnover of these franchises is more than R300 million per annum.

Another example of a franchise is Nando's, started in the south of Johannesburg 18 years ago by Robert Brozin and Fernando Duarte as a fast-food shop selling spicy, grilled chicken meals. In 2001 there were 343 Nando's worldwide. Of the total, 184 are franchises, while 70 are owned by Nando's and 159 are international, mainly in Britain and Australia and also the Middle East. By 2008 Nando's franchises had been established on five continents and in 25 countries.

Other examples of franchises are McDonald's, Mr Video, and various estate agencies such as Seeff.

14.7.5 Corporate entrepreneurship

Corporate entrepreneurship is entrepreneurship that occurs in an existing business. It begins when a person or team develops a new business unit within an existing business through identification of a new opportunity or business idea. Corporate entrepreneurship is a method by which a corporation or large business introduces new and diversified products to an existing business. This is done through internal processes and the use of the corporation's resources. It creates an opportunity for diversification, and enables investment and profits by starting new businesses inside a business.

A corporate entrepreneur is a person in a large business or corporation who sees an opportunity, and is willing to take moderate risks to establish a new business unit and manage the resources to ensure successful implementation and profit. The corporate entrepreneur is usually creative and is also a leader who strives towards added value for the business. She or he usually has good sales and negotiation skills, and ensures collaboration through teamwork.

Corporate entrepreneurs are also valuable wealth-creators in an economy. The advantage of new businesses established in this manner is that sufficient funding or seed capital is usually available for the capital-intensive establishment phase and the growth phases.

Examples of corporate entrepreneurship are Outsurance and Discovery Medical Aid. Both these businesses originated from First National Bank (FNB), part of the Rand Merchant Bank Holdings. An opportunity for short-term insurance was identified by corporate entrepreneurs in the bank, and Outsurance was started as an independent business unit inside FNB. Discovery Medical Aid was a business opportunity identified by Mr Adrian Gore, who established Discovery Medical Aid as an independent business unit also inside FNB. These two new and diversified businesses that originated from an existing, traditional bank contribute not only to the profit of FNB, but also to the economy of South Africa.

CASE STUDY: Craig Lyons

Entrepreneur Craig Lyons is involved in various businesses. Some businesses he established and grew and other businesses were bought and developed. He is co-founder and director of Kayema Renewable Energy, an energy company that integrates solar and wind energy solutions. Energy solutions are provided to utility, domestic and commercial users throughout Africa. Kayema was recently named 'Energy Company of the Year'. Mr Lyons develops business ideas to become great businesses and also buys and develops underperforming businesses. He now has nine businesses including a Sowetan shebeen and six months ago he also acquired Mr Delivery. Since then he has obtained a liquor licence and now Mr Delivery can also deliver alcohol. He finds new business ideas and opportunities exciting.

Mr Lyons studied at Wits University and Oxford and has degrees in economics and finance and also relies on various mentors including Tokyo Sexwale for his business expertise. He is passionate about his businesses. He has had his fair share of failures but from these he learned a lot. For example, his expectations are now more realistic and he has also learned not to trust everyone and to discern when he is being used by people. Personal relationships with business partners and colleagues are important to him and he will spend time getting to know pro-spective partners well before going into business with them. As he knows how important funding is for a business he will assist businesses or entrepreneurs to access the necessary funds. He is always looking for the next outstanding business opportunity.

SOURCE: Roos, J. 2011. *Helping hand. Always looking for something outstanding.* Fin Week, 20 January 2011, p. 41.

QUESTIONS

1. Would you describe Mr Lyons as an entrepreneur? Give reasons for your answer.
2. Describe how Mr Lyons contributes to the economy of the country.
3. Identify the entrepreneurial skills that Mr Lyons has and explain why you think he has these skills.
4. Would you regard Mr Lyons as a growth-oriented entrepreneur or not? Motivate your answer by giving examples.
5. What type of businesses does Mr Lyons start or become involved in?

SUMMARY

Entrepreneurs begin and develop businesses. They play an important role, not only in the business environment, but also in the economic development of a country. Different types of entrepreneurial businesses range from the informal sector through to those that started off small and are now large corporations.

GLOSSARY

calculated risks: risks that have been carefully evaluated

corporate entrepreneurship: entrepreneurship in an existing business, where a new business unit is developed within an existing business through the identification of a new opportunity or business idea

creativity: new ideas, the adjustment or refinement of existing procedures, and the identification of opportunities and solutions to problems

entrepreneur: a person who identifies a business opportunity, evaluates the risk related to the establishment of a business, and is prepared to take the risks associated with starting the business in the quest for making a profit

entrepreneurial process: the identification and evaluation of a business idea, the development of a business plan for a viable business idea (ensuring that the required resources are available for the business) and the establishment and growth of the business

franchisee: someone who opens up a branch of a franchise system, and pays the franchisor a fee and percentage of the sales or profits

franchisor: an entrepreneur who starts a franchise system

high-potential entrepreneurs: entrepreneurs who intend to grow their businesses

informal business: any business that is not registered for VAT or income tax with the Receiver of Revenue

ingenuity: a quality of an individual or enterprise that includes success factors, namely relevant business knowledge, skills and understanding, and creativity

large businesses: businesses that usually employ up to 200 people (100 in the agricultural sector), and where the maximum turnover varies from R5 million in the agricultural sector to R51 million in the manufacturing sector and R64 million in the sector labelled 'wholesale trade, commercial agents and allied services'

leadership: a quality that a person may have that enables him or her to lead others to achieve certain goals

medium businesses: businesses that usually employ up to 200 employees, and which have a turnover ranging between R5 million to R64 million

micro-businesses: businesses that have five or fewer employees and a turnover of up to R100 000 per year

small businesses: businesses that employ between 21 and 50 employees

small, micro- and medium enterprises (SMMEs): companies whose head-count or turnover falls below certain limits

survivalist businesses: micro- or very small businesses that do not achieve any-thing new or different, do not grow, find limited customers, and merely ensure an income to survive

very small businesses: businesses that employ between 21 and 50 employees

MULTIPLE-CHOICE QUESTIONS

1. Opportunity entrepreneurs start a business because they:
   a) had no other alternative employment
   b) grow the business
   c) identified a business idea with potential to grow

2. Combine each of the following (1 or 2) with the relevant definition (a or b):
   1) Survivalist business
   2) Entrepreneurial business

   a) Business owners who might be enterprising in starting a business, but do not achieve anything new or different, do not grow, find only limited customers, cannot obtain finance, often ensure an income to their owners, and perhaps one or two employees, with limited or no future opportunities, usually involved in more basic business ideas.
   b) Business owners who have higher levels of education, earn higher incomes from their businesses, apply technology, are growth oriented, have multiple business sites and are export-oriented.

3. Important skills of successful entrepreneurs that contribute to the establishment of a successful business are:
   a) Creativity; management skills and risk-taking
   b) Ingenuity, leadership and calculated risk-taking
   c) Knowledge, understanding of a business environment, and creativity

4. The entrepreneurial process does not involve:
   a) the identification and evaluation of a business idea
   b) the development of a business plan for a viable business idea (ensuring that the required resources are available for the business)

   c) benchmarking the business plan against existing businesses

   d) the establishment and growth of the business

5. Entrepreneurial businesses can be:
   a) informal, micro–, very small, small, medium or large.
   b) informal, micro–, very small or small
   c) small or medium
   d) small, medium or large

6. The informal business sector is defined as any business that:
   a) operates in the low income section of the market
   b) operates illegally and provides illegal products and services
   c) is not registered for VAT or income tax
   d) is in the start-up phase of establishment of the business

7. Entrepreneurs can be found in the:
   a) Informal sector only
   b) Informal, micro and small business sectors only
   c) Newly established and start-up businesses
   d) Informal, micro, small– , medium– and large business sectors

REFERENCES AND END-NOTES

1. BYGRAVE, W.D., REYNOLDS, P.D. & AUTIO, E. 2004. *Global entrepreneurship monitor: 2003 executive report.* London: Babson College. p. 5.
2. HERRINGTON, M., KEW, J. & KEW, P. 2009. *Tracking Entrepreneurship in South Africa: A GEM perspective.* [Online]. Available: www.gemconsortium.org/download [1 November 2010]. p.43; & HERRINGTON, M., KEW, J. & KEW, P. 2009. *Tracking Entrepreneurship in South Africa: A GEM perspective.* [Online]. Available: www.gemconsortium.org/download [1 November 2010]. p. 58/9.
3. Ibid.
4. NIEUWENHUIZEN, C. 2008. *Principles of Business Management.* Cape Town: Oxford University Press Southern Africa. p. 317.
5. *Labour Force Survey*, March 2006.
6. HERRINGTON, M., KEW, J. & KEW, P. 2009. *Tracking Entrepreneurship in South Africa: A GEM perspective.* [Online]. Available: www.gemconsortium.org/download [1 November 2010]. p. 70.
7. *GEM report. 2006.* p. 19.
8. SWIERCZ, P.M. & LYDON, S.R. 2002. Entrepreneurial leadership in high-tech firms: A field study. *Leadership & Organization Development Journal,* 23(7):383.
9. GRAY, C. 2002. Entrepreneurship, resistance to change and growth in small firms. *Journal of Small Business and Enterprise Development,* 9(1):61–72.
10. THOMSON, A. & GRAY, C. 1999. The determinants of management development in small businesses. *Journal of Small Business and Enterprise Development,* 6(2):113-127.
11. SCHUMPETER, J. 1934. *The theory of economic development.*

12. GRAY, C. 2002. Entrepreneurship, resistance to change and growth in small firms. *Journal of Small Business and Enterprise Development,* 9(1):67.
13. MAYO, A.J. & NOHRIA, N. 2005. Zeitgeist Leadership. *Harvard Business Review,* October:48.
14. VISSER, D.J., DE CONING, T.J. & SMIT, E.v.D.M. 2005. The relationship between characteristics of the transformational leader and the entrepreneur in South African SMEs. *South African Journal of Business Management,* 36(3):51.
15. Fernald, L.W., Solomon, G.T. & Tarabishy, A. 2005. A new paradigm: Entrepreneurial Leadership. *Southern Business Review,* 30(2):2.
16. SCHEIN, E.H. 1985. *Career anchors: Discovering your real values.* San Diego: University Associates. p. 30.
17. SCHEIN, E.H. 1985. *Career anchors: Discovering your real values.* San Diego: University Associates. p. 29.
18. SCHEIN, E.H. 1985. *Career anchors: Discovering your real values.* San Diego: University Associates. p. 42.
19. Mpahlwa in: Loxton, L. 2005. Inside Parliament: New law to boost close corporations. *Star business report.* 20 June 2005.
20. KARL, K. 2000. The informal sector. *The Courier: Africa-Caribbean-Pacific-EC,* 178, December/January 1999–2000.
21. South Africa. 2003. National Small Business Amendment Act 26 of 2003. *Government Gazette,* 461(25763), 26 November 2003.
22. Ibid.
23. MARITZ, P.A. 2005. *Entrepreneurial service vision in a franchised home entertainment system.* University of Pretoria. (Unpublished DCom thesis: Business Management.)
24. JOHNSON, D.M. 2004. In the mainstream, multi-unit and multi-concept franchising. *Franchising World,* April, p. 36.
25. Franchise Advice and Information Network (FRAIN) Franchise Census. 2004.
26. Ibid.

ANSWERS TO MULTIPLE-CHOICE QUESTIONS

1. Answer = c)
2. Answer = 1a); 2b)
3. Answer = b)
4. Answer = c)
5. Answer = a)
6. Answer = c)
7. Answer = d)

The business plan

Cecile Nieuwenhuizen

PURPOSE OF THIS CHAPTER

This chapter tells you more about the entrepreneurial process. First the various sections of the entrepreneurial process are introduced. Then the chapter discusses a business opportunity, and describes a feasibility study and a viability study as methods to evaluate a business opportunity. If a viable business opportunity has been identified, a business plan is the next step in the entrepreneurial process, and this chapter describes the content of a business plan.

LEARNING OUTCOMES

This chapter should enable you to:
- understand the connection between entrepreneurship and the entrepreneurial process
- identify the stages of the entrepreneurial process
- distinguish between the feasibility and the viability of a business idea
- describe the different components and contents of a business plan.

15.1 Introduction

Entrepreneurship involves a business idea, deciding whether the idea is a feasible and viable business opportunity, developing a business plan, checking for the necessary resources, and establishing and growing a business. This is called the **entrepreneurial process**, which is driven by the entrepreneur.[1]

15.2 **Identifying an opportunity**

An 'opportunity' is a gap in the **market**. Good ideas are not necessarily good opportunities. A good opportunity is attractive, solid and timely, and is based on a product or service that creates or adds value for its buyer or end-user.

The entrepreneur must identify a **business opportunity** by considering her or his skills, expertise or abilities, and the needs and problems in the market. The business opportunity should be evaluated, by doing a feasibility study and a viability study to determine whether it would actually be right to start the business.[2]

15.3 **Performing a feasibility study**

The **feasibility study** is an examination of the potential (future posssibility) of a business idea, with the focus on the ability, skills and knowledge of the entrepreneur. When a feasibility study is carried out, the potential of the business idea is examined. The entrepreneur must also determine her or his personal ability to start, and interest in starting, the type of business suggested by the idea.

Answers to the following questions are important when determining the feasibility of a business idea:[3]

- Do you want to do what the business idea suggests?
- Is there a market for your business idea?
- Can you meet the needs of your consumers?
- Can you get the idea across to the consumers?

A person who wanted to start a tour-operating business might answer these questions as follows:

- Yes, I want to do what tour-operating suggests. This means that I must like travelling, I must be interested in the places I would be taking my clients to, and be willing to take them on guided tours.
- I would have to decide if there is a market for my business idea. I would have to see if there are enough tourists visiting the area in which I plan to start the business, and if there are enough interesting places to take them to on tours.
- I would have to think whether I would be able to meet the needs of the clients by providing the services they expect. That means I would have to think of comfortable transport, and interesting tours at a price they can pay.
- I would have to sell the idea of my tour-operating business to people who could become my clients (for example, through the reception desks at hotels and/or the tourist-information services in a small town).

15.4 **Performing a viability study**

If the business idea is found to be feasible, a viability study is done. The **viability study** is a detailed analysis of the market and the possible profitability of the business. It shows whether an idea has the potential to be converted into a business.

An entrepreneur would take the following steps when compiling a viability study:
- Establish who the consumers would be and what their needs are.
- Develop the purpose or mission statement of the business.
- Define the business goals and business objectives.
- Determine her or his own share of the total market.
- Calculate the income of the business.
- Calculate the expected net profit to determine whether the business idea is viable or not.
- Calculate the break-even point.

15.4.1 Establishing who the consumers would be and what their needs are

During this phase, the entrepreneur would do market research. **Market research** is a means of getting more information about the potential **consumers** and their needs. To do market research is often expensive when performed by specialist businesses. If an entrepreneur cannot afford to have it done by a specialist, she or he should person-ally work out the need for the product, and the profile of the clients, following these guidelines:
- List the product(s) or service(s) and the most important features (aspects).
- Find out what the most important features mean to the clients.
- Identify competitors, leaders in the industry, and experts, with the product(s).
- Find possible consumers to fill in questionnaires or to form part of focus groups.
- The results of the questionnaires and/or focus groups should be put together and analysed to determine the needs that the product(s) will meet, the final features of the product(s), and the profile of the target market.

A **focus group** is a group of people with an interest in the proposed product(s) or service(s), for whom the entrepreneur sets up a meeting to get information and to exchange ideas. For example, if the entrepreneur plans to put on the market a new product for babies, she or he will get a group of mothers together to form a focus group.

Topics and questions to be included in the questionnaire or focus group should cover:
- the strong and weak points of the product(s) or service(s)
- the characteristics of the possible clients to create a profile of the **target market** (the group of people to whom the products are aimed).

Regarding the product, the following questions could be included in a questionnaire:
- What do you regard as the outstanding feature of the product/service?
- What don't you like about the product/service?
- When will the product/service be used?
- What similar product/service are you using at the moment?
- What is the major benefit of the product/service at the moment?
- Why will you use the product/service?
- How often will you buy the product/service?
- What are you willing to pay for the product/service?
- Who/what are the major competitors of the product/service?

Regarding the consumer, the following questions could be included in the questionnaire:
- Where do you live?
- What is your age?
- What is your occupation?
- What do you earn?
- What is your level of education?
- What do you do in your leisure time?
- Who decides to buy the product/service?

When a focus group is conducted, some personal details of the participants, such as income and age, should be noted.

It is also important to read newspapers, magazines and industry-related publications and get information from knowledgeable people. Entrepreneurs can test-market their products on potential clients and experts in that field. Their inputs can be used to determine the actual need for the product(s) and to finalise these product(s).

15.4.2 Developing the purpose or mission statement of the business

In a mission statement for the business the entrepreneur will have to address:
- who the consumers of the business will be
- which needs will be satisfied
- how these needs will be satisfied by the business.

Two examples of mission statements

Transit Transportation Services
Transit Transportation Services provides the full spectrum of transportation services, covering regional and national routes, and the transportation of full truckloads for industrial customers. Specialised services include storage and warehousing facilities.

Afrique Hair and Skin
Afrique Hair and Skin provides a range of hair- and skin-care products for the unique needs of ethnic African hair and skin. Products are provided through dedicated specialists directly to African women who value personal care and image.

15.4.3 Defining the business goals and business objectives

The **business goal** is what the entrepreneur wants to achieve with the business, and it must be measurable and achievable. The primary goals of a business are to ensure profitability over a period of time, and to direct all the activities of the business towards achieving profitability.

An example of a goal for a business may be to ensure a salary of at least R15 000 per month for the owner and a 10% return on the capital that was put into the business for the first year. For example, a woman owns a small factory that manufactures plastic containers for cosmetics and the pharmaceutical industry. She has to use her capital to buy machinery, other equipment and materials. She uses R2 000 000 of her own money and borrows capital. A 10% profit will be R200 000, which she sets as a profit goal for the business for a year.

The **business objectives** support, and are in line with, the goal of her business. Objectives must have specific time and money or percentage values. It is important to set objectives that are achievable and which can be adapted when situations change.

The following are examples of objectives that are in line with her goal:

- To ensure sales of at least R100 000 per month for the first year
- From the second year, to increase sales to 15% per year for small cosmetic jars and 25% for large cosmetic jars
- To ensure 20% of the market share for cosmetic jars within three years.

15.4.4 Determining the business's share of the total market

The expected market share is the part of the target market that a business will be able to serve on the basis of its production capacity and the state of the economy. It is very important to calculate the expected market share as realistically and accurately as possible, as this determines the business's possible income.

However, it is not easy to determine the potential market share of a business. Information such as number of potential clients, details of competitors, and needs of customers, has to be gathered to ensure that the calculation is done as reliably as possible. Even then, the entrepreneur will have to rely partly on her or his own judgement.

To calculate the business's market share, the entrepreneur first has to calculate the total market potential for the business's products. After that, the entrepreneur must determine what section of the potential market is or will be served by competitors, and what section can be served by her or his business.

An example of market research

Thandi plans to open a spa in an upmarket residential area. Through her market research she has found that approximately 30% of the women living in the area where she plans to open her business have at least one appointment per month at a spa or beauty salon. She has also found that an additional 10% of the women in the area go for beauty treatments to a spa or beauty salon at least once in two months.

Thandi has identified her target market as women who go for spa and beauty-salon treatments such as salt seaweed or salt mud therapy baths and treatments, hydrotherm floating massage, Thai steam cabinets, steam and saunas, float tank, and jetted and spa baths. Facials, pedicures and manicures will also be treatments that she is planning to provide. She will also have a selection of healthy light meals and refreshments available.

There is only one existing beauty salon in the area. This salon does not offer treatments in a spa environment.

Thandi calculates that she will be able to gain 20% of the total business in the first month, as she is sure there is a need for the broad service that she is planning to provide. She plans to advertise widely. Her goal is to ensure 50% of the existing market in the area in the first 6 months. This will mean that her spa and the existing beauty salon will share the total market for spa and beauty treatments in the area. In addition, she might attract additional customers in the area, as well as customers from nearby areas, because of the extensive service she is planning to offer.

Thandi has to decide whether this will create an adequate income, or whether she should follow a different business idea.

The section of the potential market to be served by the entrepreneur's business is the business's expected market share, and is also the target market of the business.

The business's target market is the specific section of the market at which the business will aim its products. The business might add specific features and/or services to satisfy a specific section of the target market.[4]

15.4.5 Calculating the income of the business

The entrepreneur must calculate the total cost involved in producing or supplying the product(s). The total costs of a product or service are equal to the fixed costs plus the variable costs.

> **total costs = fixed costs + variable costs**

Fixed costs, also called 'overheads' or indirect costs, are costs that cannot be allocated directly to a product. Examples are rent, electricity, water, and the salaries of the owner and other employees not directly related to the manufacturing or provision of products and services.

Variable costs are costs that can be allocated directly to the product at the manufacturing or provision stage. Examples are the materials used for the manufacturing of products, and the wages of employees who are involved in the manufacturing or provision of the products.

The total cost per product made or service rendered has to be calculated, and then the selling price has to be determined. The selling price and the benefits of the product must be compared to those of competitors. A business cannot charge less for a product than the total cost of the product, and the selling price must be related to the selling price of competitors.

15.4.6 Calculating the expected net profit of the business to determine if the business idea is viable

The viability of a business is determined by its potential profitability. Profit is calculated by deducting total expenses from total income.

profit = total income – total expenses

When the income is higher than the expenses, the business idea is profitable, but when the expenses are higher than the income, it is not a viable business idea and the business will be running at a loss. The net profit is calculated by drawing up an income statement by using estimated figures. This is known as a *pro forma* income statement.

To draw up a *pro forma* income statement, the entrepreneur must determine what the monthly expenses of her or his business will be (see Table 15.1 below).

TABLE 15.1 The expected monthly expenses of Peter's Snack Factory

Rent on factory:	R3 000
Water and electricity for the factory:	R1 000
Depreciation on assets:	R1 600
Delivery costs:	R30 00
Marketing costs:	R2 000
Telephone:	R600
Stationery:	R200
Direct materials (ingredients, packaging material, etc.):	R8 000
Salary to owner:	R8 000
Administrative salaries:	R4 000
Direct wages (labour):	R12 000

The entrepreneur also has to determine the expected monthly sales. Peter expects to sell 4 000 boxes with 12 packets (48 000 units) of snacks at R15 per box per month. The expected monthly sales of Peter's Snack Factory are expected to be 4 000 × R15 = R60 000.

The following table (15.2) could therefore serve as the *pro forma* income statement for Peter's Snack Factory for the first year of operation.

TABLE 15.2 *Pro forma* income statement for the year 2012

Sales (R60 000 x 12)		R720 000
Less: Cost of sales		R288 000
Direct materials (R8 000 x 12)	R 96 000	
Direct labour (R12 000 x 12)	R144 000	
Manufacturing overheads:		
Rent on factory (R3 000 x 12)	R 36 000	
Water and electricity (R1 000 x 12)	R 12 000	
GROSS INCOME		**R432 000**
LESS: EXPENSES		R232 800
Marketing costs (R2 000 x 12)	R 24 000	
Delivery costs (R3 000 x 12)	R 36 000	
Salary of owner (R8 000 x 12)	R 96 000	
Administrative salaries (R4 000 x 12)	R 48 000	
Telephone (R600 x 12)	R 7 200	
Stationery (R200 x 12)	R 2 400	
Depreciation on equipment	R 19 200	
NET PROFIT		**R199 200**

Peter's Snack Factory will show a very favourable profit at the end of the year. His next step will be to calculate how many units of snacks (for example, boxes with packets of chips or cheesenaks) he will have to sell in order to break even.

15.4.7 Calculating the break-even point

The **break–even point** determines the number of units to be sold where no profit or loss will be made. At the break–even point, income and expenses are equal. The break–even point can be calculated in units by using the following formula:

$$\text{units} = \frac{\text{fixed costs}}{\text{price per unit} - \text{variable costs per unit}}$$

A *pro forma* income statement can be used to calculate the fixed and variable costs. Peter's *pro forma* income statement was used to supply information for the calculations that follow (Table 15.3).

TABLE 15.3 Fixed and variable costs

Variable costs	R288 000
Direct materials	R 96 000
Direct labour	R144 000
Water and electricity	R 12 000
Delivery costs	R 36 000
Fixed costs	**R232 000**
Rent on factory	R 36 000
Depreciation of equipment	R 19 200
Marketing costs	R 24 000
Salary of owner	R 96 000
Administrative salaries	R 48 000
Telephone	R 7 200
Stationery	R 2 400

$$\text{units} = \frac{\text{fixed costs}}{\text{price per unit} - \text{variable costs per unit}}$$

$$\text{units} = \frac{\text{R232 000}}{\text{R15} - \dfrac{\text{R288 000}}{\text{48 000 units}}}$$

$$= \frac{\text{R232 000}}{\text{R15} - \text{R6}}$$

$$= \frac{\text{R232 000}}{\text{R9}}$$

$$= 25\ 788 \text{ packets of chips or cheesenaks}$$

$$= \frac{25\ 788}{12} = 2\ 148 \text{ boxes with 12 packets of snacks}$$

If Peter sells less than 2 148 boxes of snacks a year, he will show a loss. He has to ensure that he will be able to sell more than 2 148 boxes of snacks if he wants to establish a successful business.

After the calculation of the break–even point, the viability study is complete, and the entrepreneur can decide whether the business idea should be transformed into a business.

15.5 Developing the business plan

A **business plan** is developed to clarify where a new business is heading or how an existing business will expand. It is a detailed explanation of how these objectives will be reached. The business plan helps the entrepreneur to focus all her or his activities in an organised manner on reaching these objectives. The primary functions of a business plan are to:

- guide management
- chart the future prospects of the business, and define goals and the strategies that will be used to accomplish them
- raise funds to start or grow the business
- inform investors about the potential of the business.

An important benefit of a business plan is risk reduction of the business. In writing and developing a business plan, the entrepreneur has to evaluate and consider all the aspects of the proposed business. This means all relevant information will be gathered and formulated.

15.5.1 The contents and framework of a business plan

A comprehensive (containing all relevent details) business plan is required for starting up or expanding a business. Variables to be considered are the size, composition, growth of the market, manufacturing technology, service complexity, and competitiveness. But all business plans are not equally complicated. The size and complexity of the proposed business will influence the amount of detail required.

The level of detail of the business plan is also affected by the recipient's needs. A simplified version may be enough for employees, but a much more detailed plan will be required by a potential investor or financial institution. A general plan can be drawn up and modified for different needs, for instance:

- to plan a new business
- to transform or expand an existing business
- to create a strategic document for a new business or an existing business
- to get a loan
- to attract shareholders or partners
- to sell the business
- to give direction for management and staff in a new or existing business
- to prepare the business for a merger (joining) with another business
- to prepare the business for the takeover of another business
- to help position the business in the market.

15.5.2 Key elements of a business plan

A business plan will consist of the following:
* a cover sheet
* a table of contents
* an executive summary
* a list of the business team
* an analysis of the macro- and market environment and the positioning of the business in the market
* the history and profile of the business
* a products and/or services plan
* a marketing plan
* a production or operational plan
* a financial plan
* a risk assessment
* a timetable for putting the plan into action
* a summary and concluding remarks
* appendices (extra bits) and references.

15.5.2.1 The cover sheet

The following information needs to be included in the cover sheet:
* the full name of the business
* the ownership status
* the full street address
* the postal address, if different from the street address
* the telephone, fax, e-mail and website information
* a contact name and title
* the date of the plan.

15.5.2.2 The table of contents

The table of contents is a list of all the main headings and sub-headings for easy reference.

15.5.2.3 The executive summary

The **executive summary** is a shortened description of the business plan in one or two pages. This is a very important section of the business plan as it will determine the interest of the reader or investor. It is usually written after the business plan, and gives the most important and relevant information for an investor. The summary will cover the opportunity (its size and profitability), growth prospects, the business team, how the business will add value and penetrate the market, and possibly the funds required and what the entrepreneur is offering in exchange.

15.5.2.4 **The business team**

The section on the **business team** gives information on the most important people who will be involved in the business:

- The entrepreneur's special experience and related abilities must be mentioned, as these support the reasons why the business is expected to be successful.
- Information on the background and achievements of the management team and technical experts must be included.
- Short CVs should be included in an appendix.
- The role of consultants, the board of directors and other advisors should also be included.
- The contribution of key personnel such as scientists and innovators should be mentioned, as they could be the primary drivers of the business's vision.
- Information about ownership should be included, such as the type of ownership, (company, close corporation, and so on), the share split between management and the entrepreneur, the share breakdown in the case of multiple investors, and the specific pay, fees, stock options, and other benefits, along with payroll size (as this affects profitability).

15.5.2.5 **The analysis of the macro- and market environments and the positioning of the business in the market**

The information regarding the macro- and market environments, and the positioning of the business in the market, should include:

- an analysis of the macro- and industry environments in which the market is located
- the new business's position in the market
- information obtained from the Internet, industry studies, statistical yearbooks, surveys, and so on
- an industry analysis with an estimate of current and projected trends in the total demand for the product, customer needs and tastes, the benefit of the business's products beyond what is offered by competitors, and the growing need for the product (if relevant)

- information on how strong the competition is (the numbers of the competition and their strengths and weaknesses), information on how the business will be positioned in the market to clarify the target market's size and growth potential, the degree of competition in the target market area, the prospects of sustainability, the specific market segment and location, and the consumer needs that the business hopes to meet.

15.5.2.6 **The history and profile of the business**

Information on the history and nature of the business should include:
- a description of the new business's mission and goals
- reasons for its creation
- critical success factors
- any development work completed so far
- products and processes
- any trademarks, copyrights or patents (licences to have the sole right to sell)
- the proposed location (as well as the required space, cost, renovations, parking space, zoning restrictions, labour availability, roads, electricity and sewage infrastructure)
- whether the building will be owned or leased
- whether the equipment will be owned or leased
- the entrepreneur's experience with this kind of business.

15.5.2.7 **The products and/or services plan**

The plan about the products and/or services that the business will be offering must:
- explain the products (products and/or services)
- include documents such as photographs, drawings or specifications that will describe the products
- give the primary and secondary uses of the products
- give the products' unique qualities and their importance
- explain their superiority to existing products in the market
- specify the payback period (the time it will take to recover the investment)
- state how near to being ready the products are
- give any limitations and flaws the products may have
- clarify potential expansion of the product line.

15.5.2.8 **The marketing plan**

The **marketing plan** explains how the products will be brought to the attention of the consumers and where they will be able to get them. The following details must be provided:

- the target market (customer groups, their needs, and the appropriate products and/or services to meet those needs)
- explicit forecasts on the size of the market, its growth rate, segments and the targeted area
- compiled estimates of monthly sales for the first year and quarterly sales for the next two, together with the anticipated market share and how it is to be realised
- the seasons when it will be wanted, and its impact on cash flow
- the business's product, pricing, distribution and promotion strategies, with explanations
- the business's competitive advantage.

15.5.2.9 **The production or operational plan**

The **production plan** (operational plan) explains how a manufacturing business will produce products, or how a service business or a trading business will operate.

A manufacturing business should include details on manufacturing and outsourcing (if relevant). If the business will manufacture its own products, details need to be given about the size of the plant and its layout, equipment, raw materials and their source, manufacturing costs, and future requirements. If the business will outsource anything, the reasons need to be given, the subcontractors and amounts should be given, and any special needs should be mentioned.

A service business should describe the nature of the processes, the equipment, the controls, the experience needed, and other similar information.

A trading business should specify the suppliers it will use, its stock–control systems, its storage, and its business-procurement and sales processes.

15.5.2.10 **The financial plan**

The **financial plan** has to prove that the business has the potential to work profitably. It also explains how much money is needed to start and operate the business, how the business will be financed, and the additional funds required.

The establishment costs must include:

- the product-development costs
- the legal costs

- the product-testing costs
- the market-research costs
- the cost of purchasing business premises (if they are not being rented)
- the cost of machinery and equipment
- the cost of installing machinery and equipment
- the cost of office equipment and modifications
- provision for operating costs (six months for factories and three months for retailers)
- provision for unforeseen expenses
- the cost of current assets such as stock.

The operating costs must include the costs of:
- people:
  - salaries and wages
  - owner compensation
  - pension-fund contributions
  - medical-fund contributions
  - Unemployment Insurance Fund (UIF) contributions
  - registration of workers
  - bonuses
  - secretarial services
  - auditor's fees
- facilities:
  - equipment
  - rental of building, machinery and equipment
  - maintenance of the building, machinery and equipment
  - depreciation on furniture, equipment, machinery and vehicles
  - water and electricity services
  - insurance
- promotion:
  - advertisements in print media such as newspapers and magazines
  - advertisements on the television or radio
  - pamphlets and free samples
  - demonstrations of products and promotion campaigns for specific products
  - outdoor advertising
  - sponsorships and competitions
- administration:
  - postage
  - telephone calls and faxes

- – stationery and printing
  - – local taxes
  - – trade licenses
  - – legal expenses and collection costs
- money:
  - – interest on loans
  - – bank charges.

All costs not included in the relevant subsections of 'People', 'Facilities', 'Promotion', 'Administration' and 'Money' can be filled in as 'Sundry costs'.

The financial plan should include a break–even analysis and budgeted financial statements. The following budgeted financial statements, known as *pro forma* financial statements, need to be drawn up for a three-year period:

- the *pro forma* cash–flow statement
- the *pro forma* income statement
- the *pro forma* balance sheet.

15.5.2.11 **The implementation timetable**

The **implementation timetable** schedules the activities and dates when each thing will be done. The implementation plan should include the following:

- an activity schedule that lists important objectives and activities together with key dates and milestones
- deadlines by which crucial activities must be completed
- if relevant, a monthly timetable of activities such as production planning, advertising campaigns and product development
- cut-off dates for critical activities such as registering the company, designing, developing and completing prototypes of new products, contracting reliable suppliers and distributors, hiring key personnel, ordering raw materials and other supplies, commencing production or key processes, delivering to distributors, and collecting amounts due.

For each activity, the entrepreneur should anticipate potential delays and cost overruns, and plan for unexpected problems.

15.5.2.12 **The summary and concluding remarks**

The summary should re-emphasise the highlights of the plan and the attractiveness of the opportunity, its viability and repayment potential, its competitive advantage, and the mutual benefits for the investor and the entrepreneur.

15.5.2.13 **The appendices and references**

The appendices and references should include supporting material such as maps, designs, photographs, contracts and other legal documents, market surveys, press coverage, detailed financial statements, tax returns, CVs and testimonials. A list of references used in the document should also be included alphabetically to support claims and arguments.

It is important to use outside sources of assistance such as attorneys, marketing specialists, engineering and production experts, accounting firms and business incubators. (A **business incubator** is a facility that is generated by government or overseas funding where budding entrepreneurs are allowed to proceed with their business ideas under the supervision of veteran managers and in facilities that are subsidised by the sponsor.) An entrepreneur might also want to refer to local municipalities and government, business partners, consultants, the Internet, business chambers, the Department of Trade and Industry, journals and books, Statistics SA and competitors.

15.6 **Determining the resources and starting the business**

The resources are the capital available for investment in the business, people who need to be employed, and physical assets such as equipment, machinery, buildings and vehicles. Intangible assets such as trademarks and patents will also require an outlay of capital.

This process starts with the entrepreneur determining her or his own resources and how much investment or how much in loans will be needed to start operating. Resources cannot be determined without a cash-flow projection, which is done at the same time as the business plan.

After the minimum capital for start-up has been acquired, the entrepreneur must use it by implementing the business plan. Initially, the business might be small, with only one or two employees besides the entrepreneur. Once the business starts to grow, the management style and key variables for success will need to be decided on.

CASE STUDY: Afrique Cosmetics executive summary

Afrique Cosmetics Range (Pty) Ltd operates in the West Rand, Roodepoort. The company specialises in ethnic hair- and face-care products. Their range consists of seven face-care products and 27 hair-care products. Afrique's face-care range consists of face wash, toner and beauty creams. The hair-care range consists of shampoo, conditioner, moisturising oils, hair food, hair masks and relaxers. The target market is black people with a middle income, falling between LSM groups 5 to 7, who care about beauty and their appearance. The product will be made available in a personal and direct-selling approach.

The direct-sales approach means that customers will receive personal attention and guidance on using the products and getting the most value for their money. At the same time business opportunities are created for sales agents.

Suppliers include Azochem Laboratories for production of the products, Lithotech for labels, Herber Plastic for the manufacturing of containers, Consupaq for the manufacturing of the tubes, Purple Hat Graphic Designers for the design and development of marketing material, and Total Outsourcing South Africa for administration and human-resources management.

The capital required will be R1 300 000 for product development, and R500 000 for running costs for the next 10 months.

QUESTIONS

1. What would be an appropriate vision and mission for Afrique Cosmetics?
2. What is the target market? Draw up a marketing plan for Afrique Cosmetics.
3. What would you include in the goods and/or services plan of Afrique Cosmetics? Discuss this with specific reference to the products of Afrique Cosmetics.
4. Various establishment costs will have to be considered in the establishment of Afrique Cosmetics. Identify at least six.
5. Develop an implementation timetable for Afrique Cosmetics.

SUMMARY

The entrepreneurial process starts with the identification of a business opportunity, and then the feasibility and the viability of this opportunity needs to be established. If the idea is feasible and viable, a business plan must be developed. This is a long process because a business plan is a detailed plan of everything that has to be considered and done when a new business is started or an existing business is expanded.

GLOSSARY

break–even point: the point at which a number of units are sold where no profit or loss is made (where income and expenses are equal)

business goal: an outcome that is measurable and attainable that an entrepreneur would like to achieve with his or her business

business incubator: a facility that is generated by government or overseas funding where budding entrepreneurs are allowed to proceed with their business ideas under the supervision of some veteran managers and within facilities that are subsidised by the sponsor

business objectives: objectives that are supportive of and in line with the goal of the business

business opportunity: an opportunity in a specific market for a business that currently serves that market or intends to enter that market

business plan: a formal statement to clarify where a business is heading, containing a set of goals, the reasons why they are potentially attainable, as well as a detailed explanation of how the goals will be reached

business team: the most important people that will be involved in the business

consumers: the final users of goods and services

entrepreneurial process: identifying a business idea, determining whether the business idea is a feasible and viable business opportunity, developing a business plan, ensuring the availability of the required resources, and establishing and growing a business

executive summary: a one- or two-paged abbreviated description of the business plan

feasibility study: a preliminary study undertaken to determine the potential of an idea that an entrepreneur would like to convert into a business

financial plan: a plan to prove that the business has the potential to be operated profitably

fixed costs: costs that are not directly related to a product, such as the overhead or indirect costs of a product (for example, rent, electricity and water)

focus group: a group of people with an interest in the potential products for whom a researcher sets up a meeting to get qualitative data and to exchange ideas

implementation timetable: a schedule of when the implementation of the activities should occur, the activities involved, the completion dates and deadlines

market: a group of people or organisations with similar characteristics that cause them to have similar product needs

marketing plan: an explanation of how the products will be brought to the attention of the consumers and where they will be made available for purchase

market research: a business activity in which the market environment is investigated (especially the customer but also competitors)

mission statement: a brief statement regarding the purpose of an organisation

production plan (operational plan): an explanation of how the products will be produced or how a business that will provide a service will operate

profit: the increase in wealth for an organisation when total income exceeds total expenses

pro forma **income statement:** an income statement that uses estimated figures to calculate the net profit of a business

target market: a specific section of the market at which a company aims its product

total cost: fixed costs plus variable costs

variable costs: costs that can be allocated directly to the product at the manufacturing or provision stage, and which vary according to the volume produced

viability study: an in-depth investigation of the potential of an idea to be converted into a business

MULTIPLE-CHOICE QUESTIONS

1. Which of the following statements are relevant when determining the feasibility of a business idea?
   a) Develop the mission or purpose statement of the business.
   b) Define the business goals and business objectives.
   c) Determine one's own share of the total market.
   d) Do you want to do what the business idea suggests?

2. Which of the following steps will an entrepreneur take when doing a viability study?
   a) Is there a market for your business idea?
   b) Can you meet the needs of your consumers?
   c) Calculate the income of the business.
   d) Can you get the idea to the consumers?

3. Identify a variable cost from the list:
   a) Salary of owner
   b) Direct labour
   c) Administrative salaries
   d) Telephone

4. Which of the following are primary functions of a business plan?
   1) Guide management
   2) Inform investors about the potential of the business
   3) Determine who the consumers of the business will be
   4) Raise funds to start or grow the business

   a) 1, 2, 4
   b) 1, 2, 3, 4
   c) 1,2,3
   d) 2, 3

5. The analysis of the macro- and market environments and the positioning of the business in the market involve the following:
   1) The role of consultants, the board of directors and other advisors should also be included.
   2) An analysis of the macro- and industry environments within which the market is located
   3) The new business's position within the market
   4) Information obtained from the Internet, industry studies, statistical yearbooks, dedicated surveys, and so on

   a) 1, 2, 3, 4
   b) 1, 3, 4
   c) 2, 3, 4
   d) 1, 2, 3

REFERENCES AND END-NOTES

1. NIEMAN, G., AND NIEUWENHUIZEN, C. (Eds.). 2009. *Entrepreneurship: A South African perspective.* 2nd ed. Pretoria: Van Schaik. p. 410.
2. DU TOIT, G.S., ERASMUS, B.J. AND STRYDOM, J.W. (Eds.). 2007. *Introduction to business management.* Cape Town: Oxford University Press.
3. STRYDOM, J., NIEUWENHUIZEN, C., ANTONITES, A., DE BEER, A., CANT, M. AND JACOBS, H. 2007. *Entrepreneurship and how to establish your own business.* Cape Town: Juta & Co. p. 68.
4. Ibid.

ANSWERS TO MULTIPLE-CHOICE QUESTIONS

1. Answer = d)
2. Answer = c)
3. Answer = b)
4. Answer = a)
5. Answer = c)

Index

NONVERBATIM